W9-BAJ-686

Also by Diarmuid Jeffreys

Aspirin: The Remarkable Story of a Wonder Drug

HELL'S CARTEL

HELL'S CARTEL

IG FARBEN AND
THE MAKING OF
HITLER'S WAR MACHINE

DIARMUID JEFFREYS

METROPOLITAN BOOKS
HENRY HOLT AND COMPANY · NEW YORK

For Laura and Joe

Metropolitan Books
Henry Holt and Company, LLC
Publishers since 1866
175 Fifth Avenue
New York, New York 10010
www.henryholt.com

Metropolitan Books® and ® are registered
trademarks of Henry Holt and Company, LLC.

Copyright © 2008 by Diarmuid Jeffreys
All rights reserved.
Distributed in Canada by H. B. Fenn and Company Ltd.

Library of Congress Cataloging-in-Publication data

Jeffreys, Diarmuid.
  Hell's cartel : IG Farben and the making of Hitler's war machine / Diarmuid Jeffreys.
      p.   cm.
  Includes bibliographical references and index.
  ISBN-13: 978-0-8050-7813-8
  ISBN-10: 0-8050-7813-4
  1. Interessengemeinschaft Farbenindustrie Aktiengesellschaft—History.
2. Nationalsozialistische Deutsche Arbeiter-Partei.   3. Industrial policy—Germany—
History—20th century.   4. Forced labor—Germany—History—20th century.
5. Holocaust, Jewish (1939–1945)   6. World War, 1939–1945—Atrocities.   I. Title.
  HD9654.9.I5J44 2008
  940.53'18134—dc22   2007050398

Henry Holt books are available for special promotions
and premiums. For details contact: Director, Special Markets.

First Edition 2008
Designed by Victoria Hartman
Printed in the United States of America
1   3   5   7   9   10   8   6   4   2

CONTENTS

HELL'S CARTEL

PROLOGUE

The courtroom was eerily familiar. Most of those in attendance had already seen the chamber in the newsreels or heard it described on the radio or read about it in the newspapers and photographic magazines. This was the place, after all, where only twelve months before, the most famous trial in history had been concluded, where twenty-one leading officials of Adolf Hitler's Third Reich had been called to account for crimes so unprecedented and dreadful that new legal definitions had to be found to describe them. Those men were now all gone, of course; gone to suicide, or to the executioner, or to long prison terms, or even, in the case of three of them, to acquittal and freedom—but their names continued to echo through the building and probably always would: Göring, Hess, Speer, Sauckel, Dönitz, Ribbentrop, Streicher, Frank, Jodl, Keitel, Rosenberg, Schacht, Kaltenbrunner . . .

Now another tribunal was getting under way at the Palace of Justice in Nuremberg, a new drama that, like its more famous precursor, promised to address many important questions and consequently, on this first day at least, was attracting almost as much attention. The court was packed. Three hundred spectators had been squeezed into the public gallery and demand for places in the press section was so fierce that reporters had to draw lots for a seat or else retire to an adjoining corridor to listen to the proceedings over a loudspeaker.

Those who remained gazed down on the full cast assembled in the wood-paneled chamber below. For much of the morning the many supporting players had been the most active: the functionaries, clerks, translators, technicians, and military police of the war crimes trial administrative staff who would be responsible for the smooth running of things in the weeks and months to come. Although it wasn't strictly necessary for them all to be in court at the same time, it had become something of a tradition to turn up at key moments in important cases and they had all found excuses to be here, bustling about with the papers and equipment that helped to justify their presence.

At the head of the room, four solemn-faced gray-haired judges sat behind a long elevated wooden desk. One was polishing his glasses on his black robe; another jotted notes on a block of yellow paper. The other two were whispering to each other, perhaps discussing the curious history of their "bench." Two years earlier, for a few riotous weeks, GIs from the U.S. Army's First Infantry Division had used it as a bar. Up above, in a space once reserved for a glowering portrait of the Führer, they had hung a picture of the movie star Lana Turner in a provocatively tight sweater. Now the only decoration was a large Stars and Stripes on a stand behind the president's chair.

In the central well of the court, the sixty lawyers of the defense team and the dozen or so men and women from the prosecution side sat around tables strewn with documents and law books. Professionally at home in this environment and not easily given to betraying nervousness or anticipation, they were making a languorous show of adjusting their headphones and squaring off their papers.

The twenty-three defendants sat behind them in a two-tiered dock raised to the eye level of the judges. A couple were writing notes, but most were looking around in bemused indignation as though they couldn't quite believe where they were. Earlier that morning they had been taken out of their cells and marched along the covered walkway that connected the jail with the court building. The subsequent two hours had passed in something of a blur. First they had been told to stand as the judges were announced and they came face-to-face with the men who would decide their fate. Then a spokesman for their counsel had tried, with great bluster but no obvious expectation of success, to get the trial postponed on the grounds that the defense had not been given sufficient time and resources to adequately prepare. When the motion was denied, a court official had passed among them with a microphone on a long pole and they were asked to answer the charges. Had they been served with a copy of the indictment in German and had they read it? If so, how did they plead? Each of them had replied "Not guilty" but only one or two had made this statement with any real show of defiance. Everyone else just wanted the real proceedings to begin.

A low, expectant murmur rippled through the public gallery as a crisply uniformed figure got to his feet at the prosecution table and walked across to a lectern in the center of the court. A clerk glanced up at a clock on the wall and made a note of the time. It was shortly before noon on August 27, 1947.

"May it please the tribunal."

As he waited for silence to fall, General Telford Taylor looked across at the men in the dock. They were all older than him, most well into middle age and conservatively dressed in suits and ties. Although they had been in custody for some months and a few had an obvious prison pallor, to his eye they still seemed to exude an air of affronted authority. In another setting they might have been taken for a group of civic dignitaries brought together for a commemorative photograph and tediously detained for a few minutes longer than was necessary. Taylor knew that what he was about to say, and how he said it, could change their lives for better or for worse. He dearly hoped it would be for worse. It had taken a considerable effort to get these men into court: exhausting months of planning and preparation, of frustrating searches for evidence and witnesses, of sifting through thousands of pages of arcane technical documents in an alien language and reading hundreds of statements about shocking crimes. The process had taken a toll on his patience and left him with little sympathy for the lords of IG Farben.

He looked back at the judges and continued.

The grave charges in this case have not been laid before the Tribunal casually or unreflectingly. The indictment accuses these men of major responsibility for visiting upon mankind the most searing and catastrophic war in modern history. It accuses them of wholesale enslavement, plunder and murder. These are terrible charges; no man should underwrite them frivolously or vengefully or without deep and humble awareness of the responsibility, which he thereby shoulders. There is no laughter in this case, neither is there any hate. . . .

The world around us bears not the slightest resemblance to the Elysian Fields. The face of this continent is hideously scarred and its voice is a bitter snarl; everywhere man's work lies in ruins and the standard of human existence is purgatorial. The first half of this century has been a black era; most of its years have been years of war or of open menace or of painful aftermath and he who seeks today to witness oppression, violence or warfare need not choose his direction too carefully nor travel very far. Shall it be said, then, that all of us, including these defendants, are but children of a poisoned span? And does the guilt for the wrack and torment of these times defy apportionment?

It is all too easy thus to settle back with a philosophic shrug or a weary sigh. Resignation and detachment may be inviting, but they are a fatal abdication. God gave us this earth to be cultivated as a garden, not to be turned into a stinking pit of rubble and refuse. If the times be out of joint, that is not accepted as a divine scourge, or the working of an inscrutable fate which men are powerless to affect. At the root of these troubles are human failings and they are only to be overcome by purifying the soul and exerting the mind and body. . . .

The crimes with which these men are charged were not committed in rage or under the stress of sudden temptation; they were not the slips or lapses of otherwise well-ordered men. One does not build a stupendous war machine in a fit of passion, nor an Auschwitz factory during a passing spasm of brutality. What these men did was done with the utmost deliberation and would, I venture to surmise, be repeated should the opportunity to recur. There will be no mistaking the ruthless purposefulness with which the defendants embarked upon their course of conduct.

As General Taylor's words rang through the court, they transfixed the spectators up in the now hushed gallery. They were an eclectic group, with a strong multinational flavor. Some were his professional peers from the Nuremberg war crimes community who had dragged themselves away from their overburdened desks and the lunch tables at the Grand Hotel to see how the new American chief prosecutor would handle this difficult brief.* Others had traveled hundreds or even thousands of miles to be there. A special train from Berlin had brought a sizable contingent from the British, French, and American military administrations, and yet more had come from London and Paris and Washington: legal observers and civil servants tasked with sending regular reports back to their political masters.† Together they greatly outnumbered the few Germans present, relatives and friends of the defendants and one or two of their former colleagues and employees who were brave enough to show their support. Otherwise, there had been no great demand for seats from the countrymen of the accused.

This apparent indifference might seem curious given the gravity of the allegations that Taylor was laying out before the court—"Planning, Preparation, Initiation and Waging of Wars of Aggression and Invasions of Other Countries," "Plunder and Spoliation," and "Slavery and Mass Murder" were just some of the headlines in the indictment. But there was little appetite in what was left of this shattered country for more soul-searching. Outside in the Nuremberg streets, throughout the whole of Germany, in fact, people were more interested in clearing away the rubble and in trying to find food and tracking down missing relatives than in what they saw as another set piece denunciation of the war crimes committed in their name. If pressed,

---

*Taylor had been appointed U.S. chief prosecutor at Nuremberg in October 1946, some months after his predecessor, Justice Robert Jackson, had returned to America on the conclusion of the famous Four-Power International Military Tribunal's case against Göring and the other Nazi leaders. Taylor had assisted Jackson at that trial but all subsequent prosecutions at Nuremberg (including the IG Farben case) were conducted under U.S. jurisdiction alone, presided over by American judges applying international laws of war. The other occupying powers—the Soviet Union, Great Britain, and France—either held their own subsequent war crimes trials in the territories they controlled or left it to the Americans.

†Though not from Moscow—the heady days when Soviet prosecutors had cooperated with their Western counterparts in this very courtroom were long gone. Indeed, as will be seen, the increasingly frosty atmosphere between the former Allies would play a significant role in the IG Farben case.

most would lay the blame for such things on Hitler and the other Nazi bigwigs or just shrug and deny any personal knowledge of atrocities. After all, twelve months earlier, here in Nuremberg, the international community had convicted Göring and the others of those crimes. Surely that had been enough? If the Americans wanted to pursue a vendetta against another group of Nazis, no one could stand in their way but, equally, no one was eager to get involved in more proceedings that brought back guilty and shameful memories or raised difficult questions about collective responsibility.

In any case, as a few bolder skeptics muttered over their rationed ersatz beer in the city's semiderelict *Keller*, why put these particular men on trial? The name of IG Farben might once have been instantly recognizable as a proud symbol of the nation's industrial virility but that, on its own, was no evidence of a crime. Nor was the status of its executives, scientists, and technicians, however exalted the prosecution might claim them to be. If they had worked hard in the nation's interest in time of war, then surely they had done no more than their patriotic counterparts in Britain and America. It was well known that some of the accused had been responsible for great advances in chemistry and medicine. To suggest that such men could have had any personal influence over the catastrophic events of the past few years or had been directly involved in the grotesque excesses of the Nazi regime was absurd. Laying such charges at the doors of the SS and Gestapo or even the Wehrmacht was one thing; it was something else entirely to point a finger at ordinary businessmen and scientists who were only doing their duty to country and company, probably under duress. Shouldn't the Americans be focusing their energies and attention on the Bolsheviks instead? The Soviet Union—that was the real menace now.

These were all wearisomely familiar objections to the prosecution team; they had been hearing much the same things from their own side for weeks and expected to hear them again from the defense in the months to come. But Taylor and his colleagues were convinced they better understood the true nature of the men in the dock. Far from being humble businessmen, the twenty-three defendants and the vast organization they controlled had been fundamental to the success of the

Nazi project. Knowingly, willingly, they had put the resources and expertise of Germany's greatest industrial enterprise at the disposal of Adolf Hitler and his lieutenants. The consequences had been catastrophic for the whole world and that responsibility could not be set aside.

As General Taylor paused to take a sip of water, a few of his colleagues looked down at the next paragraph in the text of their chief's opening statement. If there was one passage in it that went to the heart of their case, summing up the motives, intentions, and culpability of the accused *and* the necessity of bringing them to justice, this was it. The defendants, Taylor attested, had had just one purpose in mind:

> To turn the German nation into a military machine and build it into an engine of destruction so terrifyingly formidable that Germany could, by brutal threats and, if necessary, by war, impose her will and dominion on Europe, and, later, on other nations beyond the seas. In this arrogant and supremely criminal adventure, the defendants were eager and leading participants. They joined in stamping out the flame of liberty, and in subjecting the German people to the monstrous, grinding tyranny of the Third Reich, whose purpose it was to brutalize the nation and fill the people with hate. They marshalled their imperial resources and focused their formidable talents to forge the weapons and other implements of conquest that spread the German terror. They were the warp and woof of the dark mantle of death that settled over Europe.

IN THE SIX DECADES since these words echoed through the Palace of Justice, the Third Reich has been studied and examined from almost every conceivable angle, resulting in a huge body of scholarly—and not so scholarly—appraisal and analysis about this one extraordinary period in history. Yet, remarkably, there are gaps still, facets of the story of Nazi Germany that have been neglected or glossed over or distorted by the passage of time. IG Farben occupies one of these gaps. Sixty years ago, America's chief war crimes prosecutor stood before four judges and alleged that twenty-three employees of a privately owned chemical company bore a significant share of the responsibility for the suffering that Hitler and the Nazi regime visited on humanity. They were, he said, "the men who made war possible . . . the magicians who made the fantasies of *Mein Kampf* come true." Even allowing for juridical hyperbole, this was an astonishing claim that one might have expected to ring down the years. But it hasn't. Outside of a dedicated circle of specialist historians and a shrinking group of individuals with some personal reasons for remembering, few people today have more than a vague idea of what IG Farben actually was (the name is actually a short form of Interessen Gemeinschaft Farbenindustrie Aktiengesellschaft, which can be loosely translated as the Community of Interests of Dye-Making Companies) or the extent to which its executives may have been involved in the events described by the prosecution at Nuremberg. Those with an interest in the history of the Third Reich might have heard something about the concern's financial support for Hitler, or its production of synthetic fuel and rubber that allowed the Wehrmacht to move across Europe, or its use of slave labor and its association with the horrors of Auschwitz. But much else about the IG— its extraordinary origins and evolution, its enormous political and economic significance to prewar Germany, its innovative science and ruthless business practices, and, above all, the complex reasons behind its slow but inexorable descent into moral bankruptcy—has been either forgotten or ignored.

Perhaps this is not completely surprising. IG Farben is no more. A company that was once as internationally famous as Microsoft is today effectively ceased to exist at the end of 1945 (although for reasons that will become clear it didn't vanish entirely until 2003). When so much of the appraisal of Nazi Germany is focused on Hitler and his immediate subordinates, the political and military aspects of World War II, and, of course, the ghastly atrocities of the Holocaust, perhaps some things are bound to get sidelined. But this is a matter of great regret. IG Farben's story is as important and relevant today (uncannily so, some might say) as it was when General Taylor addressed the court at Nuremberg. It deserves to be remembered.

At IG Farben's prewar zenith in the 1930s, it would have seemed inconceivable that its star might wane one day or that the combine might ever be forgotten. The business was then a mighty corporate colossus, a vast, sprawling octopus of an organization with tentacles reaching to every major country. Its domination of the global chemical industry—one of the twentieth century's most significant economic, political, and scientific fields of endeavor—was profound and all-encompassing. Through a complex network of subsidiaries, holdings, and international partnerships, it controlled the production and sale of many of the world's most vital commodities. Its tens of thousands of products included pharmaceuticals, intermediate chemicals, dyestuffs, explosives, camera film, fertilizers, light metals, fuels, plastics, rayon, synthetic rubber, magnetic recording tape, paints, pesticides, lightbulbs, auto tires, safety matches, detergents and cleaning products, poison gases, and much, much more. Although it was only—*only*—the fourth-largest industrial concern in the world (after America's General Motors, U.S. Steel, and Standard Oil), it was the largest in Europe and so strategically important to Germany that a chancellor of the Weimar Republic, Gustav Stresemann, had once declared, "Without coal and IG Farben I can have no foreign policy."

But there was always more to it than just aggressive capitalism. For a time, the company's executives were some of the cleverest, most influential and innovative businessmen in the world. Its scientists had won a host of Nobel Prizes and were globally famous for their contributions to the advancement of medical science and for the many benefits their prowess had brought to society. When economic circumstances allowed, its hundreds of thousands of workers were among the best trained, best paid, and most highly skilled in Europe, with access to well-built company housing, sponsored orchestras and libraries, subsidized schools and medical facilities. The firm's factories and laboratories were the envy of chemists in every other developed nation, its philanthropic gestures as dazzling as any in the world. IG Farben, in short, was both powerful and farsighted, a proud symbol of German efficiency and success and a shining example of the country's enterprise, scientific acumen, and technological achievement.

So how did the IG fall so low? What exactly had its leading executives done to merit the accusation of direct complicity in the crimes of the most inhumane dictatorship in history, of a collaboration so close that without it, as Taylor put it, "Hitler and his Party followers would never have been able to seize and consolidate their power in Germany, and the Third Reich would never have dared to plunge into war"? A relationship that, if the Nuremberg indictment was to be believed, made IG Farben and its managers as culpable as the Führer and his coterie for the catastrophe that enveloped Europe in the middle part of the twentieth century. And were the defendants really the war criminals that the prosecution alleged; ruthless men with a self-serving mind-set shaped by years of struggle in a tough industry, driven by greed and ambition into a corrupt alliance with the Nazis? Or were they merely incautiously patriotic businessmen caught up in events beyond their control, guilty only of naiveté in believing that the risks inherent in an association with Hitler's regime would be outweighed by the eventual benefits to their enterprise and their country?

The best way to answer these questions, to fully understand the intentions and influences of those who created and ran IG Farben, and to grasp just how and why its business rose so high and then plummeted so far, is to track the combine's evolution over history—from its origins in the nineteenth century, when intense domestic and international competition forged the nascent German chemical industry's determination to achieve global dominance, through to its golden era, when its genius for synthetic chemistry made anything and everything seem possible, and then on to its fatal alliance with the Nazis, to World War II and to the trial that followed. It is an extraordinary story with many unexpected twists and turns and much to tell us about the fallibility and failings of humankind and the way a nation gave up its soul. More directly, though, it contains a clear warning about the risks inherent in any close relationship between business and state and what can go wrong when political objectives and the pursuit of profit become dangerously entwined.

1

FROM PERKIN'S PURPLE
TO DUISBERG'S DRUGS

It is curious that a story destined to end amid the drab, achromatic grays and blacks of rubble-strewn Germany should have begun with a vivid splash of color found on a scrap of silk. Nevertheless, the origins of IG Farben can be traced back to a serendipitous discovery by a young English chemistry student during Easter week of 1856. In that one moment, in a small attic room overlooking London's docks, seventy years of disparate scientific, social, and technological development coalesced in the haphazard holiday experiments of a teenager— and gave birth to a new industry.

By the middle of the nineteenth century, organic chemistry had evolved into a vibrant intellectual discipline. Once popularly derided as the eccentric pastime of crank alchemists and gentlemen amateurs, it had become an important gear in the great engines of change—war, political upheaval, and new ideas in economics, philosophy, science, and technology—that had transformed society since the onset of the industrial revolution. Over those years a new generation of professional scientists had begun using innovative techniques of systematic research to investigate the basic matter of the world around them. The genesis of modern industrial chemistry lay in that inquisitiveness, because what started as an academic interest, a straightforward desire to know what everyday substances were made of, soon blossomed into a marathon, if hit and miss, effort to reproduce those same substances artificially. Well before things came to a head in a London attic, laboratories in Europe's old universities and newer technical institutes were bubbling with experiments designed to reveal the chemical composition of materials that had hitherto seemed part of the given world. And where inquiring minds led, more entrepreneurial ones followed. To many of these pioneers the science held out the promise of dazzling rewards—a host of new discoveries with practical applications and great commercial potential.

William Henry Perkin was one of the more unlikely beneficiaries of this enthusiasm. In 1856 he was an eighteen-year-old student at the Royal College for Chemistry, which had recently opened in London in response to public unease that Britain might be falling behind its European competitors in an important new scientific field. After sailing through the institution's basic syllabus with apparent ease, Perkin came to the attention of its young German director, August Wilhelm von Hofmann. An inspirational teacher who had won his scientific spurs at the renowned chemistry faculty of the University of Giessen, Hofmann was always on the lookout for students with special aptitude for pure laboratory research. Noticing Perkin's interest, he asked him to help out on a number of his own pet projects.

One of these was an attempt to find a procedure for making quinine, the active substance in the bark of the Peruvian cinchona tree, which for over 250 years had been the most effective treatment for malarial fever—or ague, as it was then commonly called. Because cinchona bark was expensive and hard to obtain—the tree flourished only in its native South America—a synthetic version had been the target of ambitious chemists for decades. Hofmann was convinced the answer lay in coal tar, a noxious black gunk that was a by-product of gaslight, formed when coal was burned in a vacuum. Scientists had been investigating coal tar's murky properties for over a quarter of a century and had found it chock-full of interesting chemicals but were still far from completely understanding it. Nevertheless, Hofmann knew that one of its derivatives, naphtha, when crystallized, had a chemical formula curiously close to that of quinine. Although he had been unable to turn this insight into a successful synthesis himself, he was sure that some patient tinkering with similar coal tar chemicals might yield the right result. And so, as Hofmann prepared to return to his native Germany for the Easter holidays, he gave the problem to his young assistant as an interesting vacation assignment.

Perkin took the task home to the laboratory he had built on the top floor of his family's house in London's East End. It was a simple room furnished with a small table and a few shelves for his rudimentary equipment, and although there was a view of sorts from the window (in idle moments he could gaze out on the engines shunting along an adjacent railway line), there was little else in the way of distraction. He assembled his beakers, test tubes, and small collection of chemicals and set to work.

His first attempt to create quinine involved a coal tar derivative called allyl-toluidine, which, like naphtha, had a chemical makeup very similar to that of the famous medicine. Using two standard laboratory procedures, oxidization and distillation, Perkin attempted to change the formula of the allyl-toluidine to make it identical to that of quinine by adding oxygen and removing hydrogen (in the form of water). His experiment failed. Instead of reproducing the colorless medicine, he came up with a red powder instead. A little frustrated, he tried replacing the allyl-toluidine with aniline, yet another coal tar derivate (identified by a German scientist, Friedlieb Ferdinand Runge, some twenty years earlier), which he thought might oxidize or distill more easily. This attempt failed, too, but the resultant reaction left a black sludge that turned his test tubes a striking purple color when he tried to wash them in water. Intrigued, he went off and found a scrap of silk and stained it with the product of his experiments. He had no real reason to do such a thing; chemists stumbled across all sorts of strange colors when playing with coal tar chemicals and mostly just ignored them. But something about the brilliance and luster of this particular shade piqued his interest. A question popped unbidden into his mind: Could this chemical combination possibly form the basis of a new artificial dye? As the days went by and his new purple-stained cloth didn't fade and survived all his attempts to launder it clean, Perkin decided to make a larger quantity of the dyestuff and seek the opinion of a commercial dye producer. From a friend of his brother Thomas, he got the name and address of a reputable company in Perth and sent it a sample. On June 12, 1856, its owner, Robert Pullar, wrote back.

> If your discovery does not make the goods too expensive, it is decidedly one of the most valuable that has come out for a very long time. This colour is one which has been very much wanted in all classes of goods, and could not be obtained fast on silks and only at great expense on cotton yarns. I enclose you [*sic*] pattern of the best lilac we have on cotton—it is dyed only by one house in the United Kingdom, but even this is not quite fast and does not stand the test that yours does, and fades by exposure to air. On silk the colour has always been fugitive.

Pullar's excitement was understandable. Unwittingly, Perkin had chanced upon a way to make one of the dye trade's most sought-after products—a color synonymous with emperors, cardinals, and kings.* But perhaps more importantly he seemed to have found a new manufacturing process, a method of producing dyes in any quantity required, of a standardized quality and without many of the costs and risks associated with the industry. Traditionally, dyes could be produced only from animal or vegetable bases, yet even the most popular and commonly used colors, such as the Turkish red of the madder root, native to the Levant, or the saffron yellow of Cretan lilies, or the deep blue of India's indigo plant, involved extraordinarily challenging extraction procedures. Madder, for example, had to be put through twenty distinct stages of separation before it would release its precious red cargo, whereas indigo would give up its color only after several weeks of complex and tedious fermentation. Any innovation that promised to bypass such laborious work was therefore certain to be eagerly embraced.

---

*When Roman emperors began to follow Julius Caesar's habit of wearing imperial purple, they set strict limits on the supply of the murex mollusk from which it was drawn. In 1464 the Vatican put a similar embargo on the use of the kermes insect; only its crushed shell could provide the exact shade of cardinals' purple beloved by Pope Paul II.

Of course, it was one thing to stumble upon an interesting discovery; it was another thing entirely to turn it into a successful commercial enterprise. The news from Perth was thrilling and came with a clear suggestion that Perkin should consider manufacturing his new dye himself, but he was only eighteen and had no experience of any sort of business, let alone one as complicated as the dye industry. Nonetheless, he took the plunge. He patented his idea in August 1856, visited Pullar for advice and moral support, and then traveled the country giving demonstrations to fascinated scientists and potential backers. Finally, after several frustrating months trying to raise capital from skeptical bankers, he persuaded his father and brother to sink all their savings into the project. In June 1857 they found a spot for a factory at Greenford Green in Harrow and less than six months later the first aniline purple went on sale.

Even then it could have gone horribly wrong. Perkin had decided to call his discovery mauveine after the French word *mauve*, partly in the hope that its Gallic connotations would make people think of glamorous Parisian haute couture, but what if the new color was considered gaudy or unfashionable?

As luck would have it, in the summer of 1857 Empress Eugénie, the style-conscious young wife of France's Napoleon III, took a great liking to light purple because she thought it set off her eyes. Although the silk gowns she wore were actually colored with natural dyes produced in Lyons (extracted from rare lichens at great expense), she sparked a fad for the color that soon crossed the Channel. It helped that she was a close friend of Queen Victoria and gave her fashion tips from time to time. When Victoria was considering what to wear to the wedding of her daughter in January 1858, Eugénie's favorite shade naturally came to mind. A few days after the ceremony, the *Illustrated London News* celebrated her choice in suitably gushing terms: "The train and body of Her Majesty's dress was composed of rich mauve (lilac) velvet, trimmed with three rows of lace; the corsage ornamented with diamonds and the celebrated Koh-i-noor brooch; the petticoat, mauve and silver moiré antique, trimmed with a deep flounce of Honiton lace." The British public patriotically took note and gave itself over to mauve mania. Within a few weeks every grand function and ballroom in London was awash in swathes of purple silk, and every fashion-conscious young woman in the provinces was seeking to emulate the party clothes of the high society debutantes she read about in the newspapers. Dressmakers, glove makers, and umbrella manufacturers were inundated with requests for mauve goods. They passed this demand on to the dyers and as there was no one else *they* could turn to (rare lichens being all very well for French empresses but far too expensive for lesser folk), Perkin's company reaped the rewards.

News of the extraordinary success of this new dye product soon traveled back across the Channel to Europe, where the mauve fad picked up again with even greater intensity than before. Unfortunately, although Perkin held the patent to the color in England and was making much money from it, he had neglected to secure one overseas. During his trips around Britain to raise interest in the project, he had naively revealed too much information about the chemical process. When details began to appear in the scientific journals, continental dye producers pounced. In 1858, within a year of mauve's first appearance on the streets of London, several of them were conducting their own aniline experiments. Even as Perkin began receiving widespread recognition from the European scientific community for his discovery and accepted the medals and honors that were his due, it was becoming clear that the genie was out of the bottle.

IF AUGUST VON HOFMANN'S appointment to the Royal College for Chemistry in 1845 had been an implicit acknowledgment of German supremacy in the science, then his return home in 1865 was a clear indication—Perkin's achievements notwithstanding—that his country intended to retain its lead. Hofmann told his friends that he had been wooed back to a new professorial chair in Berlin by promises of vast sums of money to spend on a new laboratory but it was equally true that, disheartened by battles with some of the more conservatively minded backers of the Royal College in London (who had never ceased to irritate him with requests that his students apply their skills to stolid British concerns like mining and agriculture), he had also been yearning for a more sympathetic environment in which to work. In Germany he found it. The country was alive with political and economic energy. Most of its thirty-nine independent states had joined together in a single customs union, or *Zollverein*, in 1834, and ever since then the country had been driving toward its common destiny. It would not formally achieve that goal until 1871, but in many ways Germany was already one nation. And like other new countries it was hungry to make its mark, politically and economically. The hundred or so arcane treaties and laws that had once governed commerce between its separate states—and thereby hampered its industrial development in comparison with Britain and France—were gradually being streamlined. A new entrepreneurial spirit was taking hold and Germany was preparing to make full use of its many commercial advantages.

One of the most significant of these was its scientific acumen. German scientists were undoubtedly the best trained in Europe. For more than a generation, universities and technical colleges at Marburg, Göttingen, Heidelberg, Giessen, Berlin, Munich, Dorpat, Keil, and elsewhere had been putting science—and in particular chemistry—at the heart of their curriculum. The hundreds of graduates these institutions produced had been welcomed with great enthusiasm into a society that valued their skills and hoped that they might one day help propel Germany to its rightful place at the top table of industrialized nations. In the interim, this huge talent pool was of immense benefit to German manufacturers when it came to exploiting innovative technologies and gave rise to whole new industries and commercial opportunities.* Inevitably, the synthetic dye business was one of them.

When news of William Perkin's invention spread across Europe, it was actually the French who reacted first (a scientist called Verguin formulated a shade of fuchsine called magenta in 1859) and for most of the next decade the initiative was batted back and forth across the Channel as tinctorial science became *the* field to be in. New color had followed new color—Manchester brown, Magdala red, Perkin's green, Nicholson's blue—even August von Hofmann had gotten into

---

*Some measure of the scale of Germany's educational advantage may be grasped from the fact that in 1876, twenty years *after* Perkin's discovery, the United States had only eleven graduate students in organic chemistry.

the game during his last years in London, devising Hofmann's violet and, perhaps more importantly, analyzing the complicated molecular composition common to all aniline dyes. But it was his countrymen who would derive much of the long-term benefit of this work. Enthralled by the emerging science, young German chemists had flocked to London, Manchester, and Paris to learn its secrets. When they returned home, they fell straight into the arms of waiting entrepreneurs.

German textile manufacturers had long resented Anglo-French dominance of the production of natural dyes and the high prices they had been forced to pay. Now, with abundant cheap coal being produced in the Ruhr, the scientific wherewithal to exploit the new aniline chemistry, and the economic impetus that came from political unification, German businessmen saw how this position could be reversed. Coal tar dyestuff companies began to spring up everywhere. By 1876 there were six major synthetic dye works in Britain, five in France, and seventeen in Germany. Europe's newest nation had seized the initiative.

Most of the successful German dye businesses were set up close to the Rhine and its tributaries, rather than in proximity to the domestic textile producers (spread throughout the country) who would be their first major customers. Because dye was a low-bulk, high-value commodity, the finished product could easily be sent anywhere by rail or carriage without adding appreciably to its cost. As the manufacturers soon found, however, making even small amounts of dye took huge quantities of fresh water, acids, alkalis, salts, fuels, pyrites, and coal tar that had to be either transported to the plant or found on-site. Fortunately, Germany's longest navigable river network was ideal, both as a shipping route for these heavy raw materials and as a natural water source, and many of the new dye makers were canny enough to realize that any firm close to it would have an advantage over those in less geographically favorable locations. Thus, in 1863, Friedrich Bayer and Company began manufacture at the northern Rhine town of Barmen (and then Elberfeld), near Cologne, followed a few months later by Kalle and Company, which set up a plant in Biebrich, at the mouth of the Main (a Rhine tributary). Leopold and Cassella chose Frankfurt am Main for their firm, while Messrs

Meister, Lucius, and Bruning opted for nearby Hoechst, and later named their company after that town.

There were some exceptions, of course, the most notable being Agfa (Aktiengesellschaft für Anilinfabrikation, or Company for Aniline Production), founded by Carl Martius and Paul Mendelssohn Bartholdy at Rummelsburg, near Berlin, in 1867. Martius had studied chemistry with August von Hofmann in London and, while working with a Manchester dyestuffs manufacturer, had developed his own dye, Martius yellow. Bartholdy, whose family provided much of the money to start Agfa, was the son of the composer Felix Mendelssohn. Both partners had strong emotional ties to Berlin that overrode the economic case for locating their company elsewhere.

One of the biggest dye firms was established at the small river port of Ludwigshafen. Its founder, Friedrich Engelhorn, embodied the new industry's entrepreneurial energy more than anyone else. Born in Mannheim in July 1821, the fourth child of a local brewer, Engelhorn had little formal education. After a few brief years at grammar school, he was apprenticed to a local goldsmith and his family naturally assumed that this would eventually be his trade too. But though he set up a small workshop in Mannheim in 1846, he soon closed it again. His travels on business for his master had opened his eyes to the much wider opportunities offered by Germany's growing industrialization and he was determined to take full advantage of them. His first large-scale enterprise, established in 1848, was a company that made and sold bottled coal gas; within three years he had expanded it into a business that operated the municipal gas-lighting works. Thus he was ideally placed, when news of Perkin's discovery reached Germany, to switch his attention to the lucrative new world of coal tar dyes. In 1860, with two partners, Engelhorn began building his own aniline factory on a plot adjacent to the gas works. Five years later, as both competition and demand began to increase, he needed to expand once more and brought in additional investors and capital. By now he knew enough about the synthetic dye business to appreciate the high costs of shipping raw materials and the need for an adequate water supply. Unable to find an appropriate site at Mannheim, he decided to relocate to Ludwigshafen on the western bank of the Rhine, which, like many other settlements along the river, had woken up to the employment potential of the new industry and was offering dyestuff entrepreneurs generous subsidies and cheap land. In the process Engelhorn also arrived at the final shape of the firm that would later play a leading role in the IG Farben project. It was called Badische Anilin und Soda Fabrik—or, as it was soon to be known, BASF.

The company flourished. Within two years of its opening the Ludwigshafen plant was making more than eighty different products. Admittedly at first most of them were barely disguised imitations of dyes produced by others—like many of the German synthetic dye pioneers, Engelhorn took advantage of his country's chaotic patent laws—but fairly soon BASF was investing in its own research, hiring scientists, and taking part in an industrywide race to find methods of synthesizing the two most commercially successful natural dyes on the market, madder red and indigo blue. While the various aniline dyes that had followed the invention of mauveine in 1856 were considered superior in terms of the purity and brightness of their color tone, many of them still looked artificial compared with natural dyes. A chemical process that could accurately replicate, or even improve upon, the more genuine tones of these traditional products would be worth a fortune.

BASF struck lucky with madder red. In 1868 two Berlin research students, Carl Graebe and Carl Liebemann, having worked out a complex procedure for synthesizing the dye that used the chemical bromine as a catalyst, began hawking it around to the major manufacturers. Most turned it down because bromine was so expensive it rendered the process unviable for industrial production. But BASF's Engelhorn passed the two young scientists and their ideas on to his firm's newly appointed technical director, Heinrich Caro, who quickly came up with a better solution, substituting cheap sulphuric acid for bromine. The resulting dye, called alizarin red, was such an improvement over the expensive traditional product—with more nuances of shade and greater speed and ease of application—that it would destroy the ancient madder industry in less than a decade. Just as important, as far as BASF was concerned, alizarin red was hugely profitable. Because the company was able to patent the process in the United States,

France, and England (where, ironically, it would enter into a joint production agreement with Perkin and Sons), the discovery helped secure the company's long-term financial future.

But the success of alizarin red exposed as never before the problems with Germany's patent procedures. Although the rules were being rationalized as unification approached, different patent laws still applied in different German states and the regulations were full of exploitable loopholes. These ambiguities allowed rival firms to copy one another's best ideas and led to many protracted and essentially irresolvable arguments about the provenance and timing of successful inventions. The Hoechst firm, for example, also rejected the expensive bromine process for synthesizing madder and, unbeknownst to BASF, had been working on its own solution to the problem. Apparently Hoechst scientists had independently arrived at the idea of using sulphuric acid as a cheaper catalyst, and though there was some heated debate between the parties about exactly when and how this had happened, BASF could not prevent Hoechst from climbing on board the alizarin gravy train.

Others followed suit, most notably Friedrich Bayer and Company of Elberfeld, Germany's oldest synthetic dye business. After a typically optimistic start in the industry, the firm had seen its profitability badly hit by aggressive competition. The invention of alizarin was a shot in the arm. While Bayer was not as obviously successful as BASF or Hoechst, it was just as able to skip through loopholes in the patent laws when a good idea came along. Heinrich Caro's inspired idea of using sulphuric acid as a catalyst was well publicized and relatively easy to replicate. By hanging on to the marketing coattails of its bigger neighbors and feverishly making as much of the new dye as its small works could manage, Bayer was able to turn its fortunes around. The profits were not yet huge, but the money was sufficient to ensure the firm's survival and allow it to begin hiring its own academic researchers—something its founders, Friedrich Bayer and Johann Weskott, had belatedly realized was essential to continued success.

Of course, every German synthetic dye company faced similarly intense competitive challenges and many failed to respond. In and around Bayer's base at Elberfeld a dozen promising start-up businesses collapsed into bankruptcy within the first decade of their existence. But such pressures energized the survivors, making them unusually sensitive to consumer demand and urging them on in their search for new products and better ways to make them. This, in turn, made them stronger, leaner, and more aggressive—particularly relative to their foreign rivals. Less nimble chemical companies operating in Europe's older industrial economies (where investors had a wider and less risky range of investment opportunities) found it harder to raise capital and often struggled to keep up with the scientific ingenuity and pace of developments in Germany. Eventually the strain began to tell. By the early 1870s, companies like BASF, Hoechst, and even struggling Bayer had snatched control of the industry away from England and France and were racing away into an unassailable lead.

Almost certainly their growing confidence was influenced by the successes that Germany was enjoying in other arenas. In 1870, helped by the sophisticated new artillery of the Krupp steel and armaments business, spike-helmeted Prussian forces had demolished the army of Napoleon III at Sedan, bombarded a briefly republican Paris into submission, and forced a successful conclusion to the Franco-Prussian War. The victory gave the final impetus, if any was needed, to the establishment of the Second Reich in 1871, joining together four kingdoms, five grand duchies, seven principalities, three free cities, and the imperial domain of Alsace-Lorraine under a single emperor, the Hohenzollern Kaiser Wilhelm I, and his chancellor, Otto von Bismarck. Commerce blossomed briefly in the aftermath, creating more jobs, more demand, and more capital, and although there was a brief readjusting slump in 1873, the implications of *Ein Volk, ein Kaiser, ein Reich* were clear: a united and economically vibrant Germany was now a force to be reckoned with.

For those running the young country's newest and most innovative industry, the exhilarating sense of national pride fostered by these events undoubtedly contributed to their willingness to take risks their more cautious foreign rivals shied away from. Their audaciousness would prove crucial to the industry's development. In just over a decade, Germany's synthetic dye makers had come from nowhere to command the field. The stage was now set for their successors, men with the foresight and scientific acumen to recognize that dyestuffs were only the beginning, that out of the same set of basic chemical compounds could come other, more remarkable discoveries of a kind unimaginable to earlier generations.

FOR A MAN destined to be described one day as "the world's greatest industrialist," Friedrich Carl Duisberg came from decidedly humble origins. His father, a thrifty, conservative man, made dressmakers' ribbons on a pair of looms in the family home on Heckinghauser Strasse in Barmen, but the profits from this business were so modest that his wife, Wilhelmine, had to sell milk to supplement their income. From the moment he was born on September 29, 1861, young Carl's life was therefore framed in simple austerity. He attended the local schools, dutifully did his chores, and generally kept his head down, glumly resigned to a future that seemed set to revolve around cheap braid and dairy products. But then in his early teens he took his first science lessons at secondary school and experienced an epiphany. From that moment he knew his future lay elsewhere: he was going to be a chemist.

Duisberg Senior thought otherwise. Determined that his son should leave school at fourteen and join the family business, he insisted that expensive and nonsensical notions about science be set aside. Carl argued with him again and again but could not change his mind. Fortunately, Wilhelmine had more imagination than her husband. She knew little about chemistry or even where Carl's interest might lead (she had vague ideas about a career in pharmacy) but was bright enough to appreciate that he would have to continue with his education if he was to better himself. So she took his side and after many furious rows managed to coax her stubborn spouse into agreement.

Aware that he was on a very short leash, Carl applied himself with all the fervor and obsessive attention to detail that would mark much of his subsequent career. He took his high school diploma at the age of sixteen, rushed through a foundational chemistry course at Elberfeld technical college, and then enrolled at Göttingen University for a year. Into those twelve months he managed to pack as much study as another student would in three years and completed his thesis in record time. It was only then he found out that he was ineligible for a degree because he didn't have the requisite Latin to pass a mandatory test. In a blazing fury he transferred to a college at Jena, coming under the wing of Anton Geuther, a leading academic chemist of the day, who insisted that his hyperactive student slow down a little and take the time to learn basic laboratory technique. Although he was desperately impatient to get on, Duisberg took the delay in his stride and earned his doctorate on June 14, 1882, at the age of twenty.

For all his qualifications he was still financially dependent on his obdurate father and Carl knew he had to find employment. He began scouring the scientific journals and trade magazines for advertisements and sent application letters to every academic institute and chemically related business he could think of. But there were far more chemistry graduates coming out of German universities than there were jobs for them and all but one of his approaches failed. It was a sign of his utter frustration that when he was offered work as a clerical assistant in the Food Inspection Office in Krefeld (a more dead-end job would have been hard to find), he thought seriously of taking it. It was then his old tutor, Anton Geuther, took pity on him and said he could help out in the college laboratory in return for a bed in an attic room and a little spare cash for his meals. The idea was that he would stay until he found a proper job and keep his chemistry skills fresh, but after a few months Duisberg had had enough. He had convinced himself that his lack of military service might be putting potential employers off. After a furious row with his mentor, who believed he was wasting his time, he stormed out and signed up for a year as a volunteer with the First Bavarian Regiment. Twelve unhappy months later, in September 1883, he was back at Heckinghauser Strasse, unemployed once more. He closed his ears to his father's protestations and hurled himself into one last frenzied round of applications. And then finally—long after someone less driven would have given up—his luck turned. A local dye company asked to see him.

Friedrich Bayer and Company's success with alizarin red had carried it through more than a decade but now the dye's popularity had largely run its course, competition was even more brutal than before, and industry experts were openly speculating about the company's survival. By 1881, Friedrich Bayer and Johann Weskott had died and Carl Rumpff, Bayer's son-in-law, had picked up the reins. His first task after his father-in-law's death was to sell the firm's stock to the public to raise some much-needed capital—in the process renaming it Farbenfabriken vormals Friedrich Bayer & Co. (the Dye Company formerly known as Friedrich Bayer and Company). But Rumpff knew that the only real answer to the business's problems lay in attracting top scientific talent. There may well have been a surplus of bright chemistry graduates on the German job market but there were a fair number of indifferent ones, too, and for firms without a strong scientific tradition it was hard to spot or attract the right people. So Rumpff tried a new approach. He had the idea of sponsoring three young chemistry graduates through a postdoctoral fellowship at Strasbourg University for a year, getting them to conduct research into possible new dye combinations. At the end of that time, if they had proved themselves, they would join the company as employees and bring the results of their work with them.

As word of his intentions got around, he was inundated with letters from hopeful applicants. One of them was from a local man, a twenty-two-year-old Barmen chemist with an impressive set of academic qualifications who had recently returned from military service. He had actually applied to Bayer once before and had been turned down.* Please could he be reconsidered? Moved by the note of desperation in this appeal, Rumpff asked Duisberg to come and see him—and then offered him the fellowship.

Uncharacteristically, having worked so long and hard for the opportunity, the young chemist agonized about whether to take it. The role was only probationary, and the pay was pitiful—about 150 marks a month. And, on his return from Strasbourg (if he was lucky enough to be offered a full contract), the low salary would force him to live

---

*In May 1882 Duisberg had written to Rumpff, "Unfortunately, it is extremely difficult to be hired for a position as a works chemist if one does not already have some professional experience. Since it is my greatest desire to work in a chemical company, and more specifically in the dye industry, I would like to take the liberty of asking you for your kind support in achieving this goal." In truth, Duisberg would have been happy to get work in *any* chemical business.

with his parents again, something he'd been hoping to avoid. But after a few days' reflection he realized he had little choice. At least the fellowship would give him a start in an industry where there was much interesting chemistry to be done.

He must have balked a little more when given his first research assignment—to find a synthetic equivalent of indigo, the hugely popular natural dye that had tantalized chemists for decades. Every attempt to reproduce it artificially, at least in a form that could be produced in bulk, had failed. Some scientists even joked that it was impossible, a kind of dyers' grail that was never meant to be found. Nevertheless, perhaps reasoning that it was a test of his character, Bayer's latest recruit set about the task with a will. To no one's particular astonishment the great prize eluded him, too, but something about his determination must have impressed his new bosses. On September 29, 1884, his twenty-third birthday, Duisberg was delighted to be able to tell his father that he had been given a proper job and that his salary had been bumped up to a relatively handsome 2,100 marks a year. Shortly thereafter, he began courting Carl Rumpff's niece and for a time it must have seemed as though his life were complete.

But Duisberg soon realized that to succeed in the cutthroat world of the German synthetic dye industry a chemist needed more than just scientific acumen, a capacity for hard work, and promising connections. He had to have a good grasp of the arcane rules and patent procedures of his trade—and a ruthless business streak as well. Shortly after he began work at Elberfeld (his first laboratory was in a tiny room behind the dye department's toilets), he had an opportunity to see if he was made of the right stuff. He was asked to reproduce a popular new scarlet dye known as Congo red. Another Bayer scientist had actually found this color a year earlier but in defiance of his contract he had skipped the company, quietly patented the discovery himself, and sold the rights to a competitor. Infuriated as much by the man's disloyalty as by the lost opportunity for profits, Rumpff tasked Duisberg with finding an alternative. One of the many peculiarities in German patent law was that a company was allowed to copy a rival's product if it could come up with a different way of making it. Inventors knew this, of course, and would do everything in their power to preempt future imitators by patenting as many different permutations of their production process as they could think of. But occasionally they would miss something and competitors would pounce. As might be imagined, the courts would usually then be asked to resolve the matter and so ideally any potential imitators would try to find a manufacturing method that was as demonstrably unlike the original as possible. If they managed to do so and were able to convince the authorities of the novelty of their process, the rewards could be enormous. If not, the penalties and legal costs could be crippling.

Duisberg was fortunate. After several weeks of playing with variants of the Congo red recipe and getting absolutely nowhere, he came in one day and noticed that the muddy brown residue of one of his early experiments (contained in a test tube that he had meticulously labeled and set aside in a cupboard) had turned bright scarlet. Working back through his notes, he realized that he had found something that was both chemically identical to Congo red and arrived at in a way that was sufficiently unique to let Bayer's lawyers fight off any claim of infringement. As it happened, the original manufacturers went ahead and sued anyway, but before the matter was settled Duisberg cleverly managed to persuade them that an expensive legal battle was in no one's interest and that the two companies would be best served by getting together to share the patent and jointly monopolize the dye's production. They were, in effect, agreeing to the creation of a minicartel, the first of many such deals that Duisberg was able to pull off and a foreshadowing of much bigger things to come.

He repeated this trick with two other colors over the next three years and gradually made Bayer enough money to solve its short-term financial problems. Rumpff and his fellow directors quickly understood that they had found a chemist with a rare blend of scientific flair and business skills. In recognition of his achievements and desperate to prevent him from taking his talents elsewhere, they made him head of all the company's research and patenting programs and even hired several new employees to work under his supervision. Duisberg now had a brief to think creatively, to look around for new business prospects. It was a heady responsibility for a young man who only a few years before had been writing letters begging for a job, and he wasn't quite sure what to do with it. But his short experience in the industry, with all its crucifying competition, had already taught him one thing: the field was too crowded; it was time to get involved in something other than making dyes.

The most promising opportunities seemed to lie in pharmaceuticals. For some years, German scientists, building on the work of August von Hofmann, had been investigating the medical potential of coal tar derivatives, with chemical similarity to naturally derived medicines such as quinine. Most of these experiments had ended in failure, but in 1884 the Hoechst dye firm, owned by Eugen Lucius and Adolf Bruning, used a graduate student's research to produce an aniline-based fever-reducing tonic known as antipyrine. Although the tonic's deeply unpleasant gastric side effects soon forced its withdrawal from the market, antipyrine enjoyed a brief commercial success and inspired a number of imitators. Two years later, for example, the Biebrich dye firm of Kalle and Company started selling a similar medicine drawn from the coal tar derivative acetanilide. Before its launch, however, Kalle had to overcome a significant commercial problem. Acetanilide was widely available and impossible to patent. Every synthetic dye business in the country already used it as an intermediate in the manufacturing process. If Kalle launched acetanilide as a promising new drug, many of its competitors would, too, and the benefits of sole ownership would be lost. So the company came up with a novel solution. It coined a catchy new brand name for the product, Antifebrine, and then, ingeniously, registered the name as a protected trademark.

At the time drugs sold by licensed pharmacists (as opposed to the quack remedies peddled on the street by patent medicine salesmen) were known by their generic chemical names and were similarly described in the medical journals that doctors read to inform themselves about new treatments. Naturally, doctors used these same generic names when filling out their prescriptions and left it up to the pharmacists to decide which chemical supplier they obtained the substances from. This practice allowed pharmacists to shop around for the best deals, which helped keep drug prices affordable for the patient. But Antifebrine upset this happy state of affairs. As its manufacturers had hoped, physicians found the new brand name, which was widely advertised, easier to remember than acetanilide, the drug's generic name, and began putting it on their prescriptions instead. Because a doctor's instructions were legally sacrosanct and had to be followed to the letter, pharmacists soon found, to their considerable fury, that they were having to order Antifebrine from Kalle and Company, the sole owners of the trade name, and were prevented from substituting acetanilide from other suppliers—even though the generic drug was identical, widely available, and much cheaper. Of course, once it was clear that it had established an effective monopoly, Kalle hiked its prices and sat back to enjoy the benefits.

To Carl Duisberg, tasked by his employers with finding new areas of business, Kalle's well-publicized success acted like a goad. He sat down with his small research team and brainstormed. Surely Bayer could be equally inventive. It was then he remembered that lying around at the back of the Elberfeld plant were thirty thousand kilos of a waste chemical called paranitrophenol. This was another incidental by-product of synthetic dye manufacture, similar in composition to acetanilide, and he began to wonder if it might have some of the same antipyretic properties. He asked Oskar Hinsberg, one of the other sponsored graduates hired by Rumpff, to see if he could make anything of it. A few weeks later Hinsberg came back with remarkable results. He had produced a substance called acetophenetidine. It promised to be an even more effective fever reducer than acetanilide and, better still, it didn't seem to have as many harmful side effects.* Duisberg leapt at the opportunity. After a few simple trials on volunteers around the factory he persuaded Rumpff and the Bayer board (by now falling more and more under his spell) to market the compound as a

---

*After it had been in use for a few years doctors began to notice that acetanilide (Antifebrine), when taken in large or continuous doses, produced almost as many gastric side effects as its predecessor, antipyrine, and even turned some patients' skin an alarming blue. As it turned out, Bayer's acetophenetidine (Phenacetin) had some of the same problems, but they were much less marked. This modest advantage allowed the company to claim that the product was safer than any of its rivals.

medicine. With Kalle and Company's clever prescription trick firmly in mind, he gave the drug a catchy brand name, Phenacetin, and registered it as a trademark.

Phenacetin was a groundbreaking product, the first really big hit of the nascent pharmaceutical business and the true forerunner of the drugs made and sold by today's multibillion-dollar industry. Altruistic scientists and academics driven by curiosity had played no part in its development. It was the result of a purely industrial process, invented and marketed by a commercial manufacturer with the sole aim of making money. And it was hugely profitable. A few months after its launch in 1888, Europe and North America were swept by a major flu epidemic and fever-reducing treatments were in great demand. Phenacetin was one of the few effective therapies available and Bayer cashed in. Indeed, it struggled to meet the incoming orders. Transforming a dye-making business into a pharmaceutical manufacturer was no easy task and the first batches of the drug were brewed in hundreds of discarded beer bottles found in a shed on the company premises. But Duisberg had become a man with a mission, and he shrugged off the problems. Later that year Bayer scientists came up with another profitable drug, a sedative dubbed Sulfonal, which led in turn to a more advanced version called Trional. Each one made the company handsome profits and cemented Duisberg's reputation and position.

When Carl Rumpff died in 1890, the board gave in to the inevitable and handed effective control of the business to his protégé. Bayer was still making dyes, of course, and by now was also branching out into other chemical products such as paints and detergents, but henceforth a large part of its focus was to be on medicines. Duisberg set up a separate pharmaceutical division and spent 1.5 million marks (a huge sum for the time) on building a state-of-the-art laboratory for his growing team of researchers. Previously condemned to working in any spare space they could find at Elberfeld—corridors, bathrooms, even an old wood shed—the scientists now moved into a modern three-story block lavishly furnished with all the latest equipment, gas and water supplies, and efficient ventilation to get rid of toxic fumes. To many of the company's older chemists, who remembered the times they had been found slumped unconscious by their benches, few things could have been more symptomatic of their new chief's understanding of the demanding complexities of their trade.

In less than six years, Duisberg had transformed his company's ailing fortunes, lifting it out from its position amid the struggling also-rans of the German chemical industry and setting it on the road to the top. He celebrated this burgeoning success by marrying Carl Rumpff's niece, Joanna, and moving into a sumptuous new home in Elberfeld full of expensive furniture and objets d'art. He indulged his four children in a manner that his father had so singularly denied him, and he began to put on weight, showing the first signs of the portliness that would characterize him in later years. With his full moustache and well-cut clothes, he would have appeared to a casual observer like any other successful, complacent member of the new German bourgeoisie.

In fact, though, Duisberg put in punishingly long hours at work, plowing through an exhausting daily agenda of memoranda, reports, and meetings and demanding the same total commitment from all his subordinates. His ambition and his energy were boundless. Even as he packed more scientists into the laboratory at Elberfeld, urging them on to greater and greater achievements, he was drawing up the master plans for a massive new Bayer factory at Leverkusen, north of Cologne. He knew that the company's continued survival in one of the most competitive industries in the world could be ensured only by developing a range of compelling new products, each of which would have to be efficiently manufactured, marketed with imagination, and sold at the greatest possible profit. From now on, from the shop floor to the boardroom, no one would be allowed to forget that simple formula.

In the meantime, of course, he wasn't the only one with plans for the future. Germany's dyestuffs world was full of aggressively ambitious men and each of them was energized by the same desire to mitigate or evade its crippling competition. While some followed Bayer into pharmaceuticals, with varying degrees of success, others found different solutions to the problem; the basic coal tar science that had underpinned all the industry's early achievements was proving to be adaptable to an extraordinary range of commercial applications, from paints and printing inks to photographic materials and cleaning products. It would be a mistake, however, to assume that all this activity signified a collective rush out of the core business of manufacturing and selling dyes. Profit margins had been tightly squeezed but there was always money to be made by anyone able to come up with an attractive new shade, and, in any case, the chemicals produced in the dye-making process were the foundation of everything else. Moreover, as scientists at one of the most powerful of Bayer's future allies were even then finding out, the old color trade hadn't yet lost its capacity to surprise. They were on the verge of solving a problem that had been baffling chemists for a generation. At long last, somebody had pierced the mystery of indigo.

NATURAL INDIGO was derived from a plant, *Indigofera tinctoria*, first brought to Europe from India in the thirteenth century. Initially, it was a rare and extremely expensive color, more likely to be found on artists' palettes than in clothes. But after the Dutch and British opened up the Far East to large-scale commerce in the 1600s, it became hugely popular as a textile dye. By the early nineteenth century, the indigo trade was one of the world's richest commodity businesses— particularly for Britain, which dominated supply and pricing through thousands of small plantations in and around the Bengali territories of its Indian colony.

It was inevitable that Germany's synthetic dye industry would challenge this lucrative monopoly just as soon as scientists found a way to replicate indigo's deep blue luster. In 1880 a Berlin chemist called Adolf von Baeyer came very close (by using the chemical toluene as a base material) to producing the dye in tiny, test-tube-sized doses. He patented the idea amid much excitement, and for a while it seemed as though a breakthrough had been made. As Baeyer began looking around for a partner to develop his discovery, his close friendship with Heinrich Caro at BASF—the most technically proficient of the dye producers—gave the company an edge over its rivals. For a onetime payment of 100,000 marks and a promise of 20 percent of all future profits, Baeyer was persuaded to join the firm.

A formula that worked in a test tube proved impossible to reproduce on an industrial scale. "Little indigo," as Baeyer's substance became known, could just about be made to fix onto cotton but couldn't be used for anything else, and even for cotton it was extraordinarily expensive. More problematically, it stank. The odor the dye gave off was so unpleasant that people coming near it found themselves gagging repeatedly. After three years, Baeyer managed to decode the complete structure of natural indigo, which promised for a while to make an affordable process easier to find, but all further efforts ended in the same blind alleys. The starting chemicals were too costly and the yield was depressingly small.

With further developments held up by a power struggle on BASF's board—during which Engelhorn was replaced as head of the business by Heinrich Brunck, a professional industrial chemist—the search for indigo wasn't fully resumed until 1891. That year a fresh team of company scientists finally found a cheap way to make antranalic acid, one of synthetic indigo's most essential ingredients. The first modest production runs began in 1894 and then, after an expensive new plant was installed at Ludwigshafen, the dye went into full-scale mass production in 1897. It had taken forty-one years from William Perkin's groundbreaking discovery of mauve in 1856 to unpick the grandest of the old natural colors and to get an artificial version onto the market.

But if the effort it took to get there had been exhausting and expensive (the additional production facilities had cost in excess of 18 million marks, almost equivalent to the firm's total stock value at the time), the commercial benefits reinforced BASF's belief in the merits of investing heavily in research and development. Indigo was a license to print money, at least in the short term, and within three years was responsible for a quarter of the company's total sales. There was competition, of course, but less than might have been expected. German patent laws had recently been tightened and it was getting harder for the smaller dye manufacturers to re-create the complicated science of the industry's leaders. Hoechst, one of the few other companies with the necessary technical competence, did manage to find its own route to indigo synthesis, but the two rivals soon agreed to jointly fix production and price levels and effectively closed the door on any new entrants—an increasingly common practice. After a few years, other new blue dyes began appearing, but indigo reigned supreme well into the next century. Indeed, the only real losers were the producers of the natural version of the color. The success of synthetic indigo devastated the British-dominated organic industry; the number of plantations in India shrank by two-thirds in less than five years, creating widespread local unemployment and unrest and leading to calls for retaliatory tariffs. The resulting souring in relations between Britain and Germany, although temporary, would have long-term political and economic consequences.

None of this mattered much to BASF at the time. It was too busy celebrating its success. In 1900 the imperial German government, keen on trumpeting the achievements of the German chemical industry, asked it to take part in a collective exhibit at that year's World Exposition in Paris. Precluded from bragging openly about itself—the official catalog had no index linking individual products on display to the firms that made them—BASF nonetheless made sure, by handing out glossy promotional brochures to all and sundry, that everyone knew the company was responsible for many of the most important items. And, of course, it *did* have much to boast about. As well as being the world's single largest producer of artificial dyes (a vast crystal bowl full of its indigo was one of the show's prize exhibits), it also produced a host of heavy and intermediate chemicals—hydrochloric and sulphuric acid, caustic soda, liquid chlorine, and a great many more—almost all of which had been developed using new methods devised by its scientists.

To anyone from the smaller, struggling British, French, and American dye and chemical industries, flicking through those brochures would have been a disquieting experience. The company's vital statistics were horribly impressive. The competitors would have read, for example, that BASF's Ludwigshafen plant comprised 421 buildings spread over an area of 206 hectares, each connected to a forty-two-kilometer-long company rail network with 223 turntables and loading points; that the company employed a core workforce of 6,300, with 146 chemists, 75 engineers and technicians, and a commercial sales force of 433; and even that it annually consumed 243,000 tons of coal, 20 million cubic meters of fresh water, 12 million kilos of ice, almost 13 million cubic meters of gas (for heat and light), and another 132 million kilos of assorted raw materials. But chilling though this barrage of numbers must have been, it would have been nothing compared with the realization that it actually applied to only *one* company, that this giant business was just a small part of a much wider industrial infrastructure. Because BASF wasn't the only German chemical company with exhibits at Paris; Hoechst was there, too, as were Bayer, Cassella, Agfa (the Berlin dyestuffs business established by Carl Martius), and a half dozen others, each of which had access to impressive resources and could boast of its scientific and manufacturing achievements. Indeed, one of those companies had just launched a product that would eventually be found in almost every household in the world.

THE FULL STORY behind the development of aspirin has been told at great length elsewhere, from its origins in the herbal treatments used by the ancient Egyptians through to the rediscovery of willow bark's therapeutic potential as a fever reducer in the 1760s. Suffice to say, by the early nineteenth century, when scientists were beginning to tinker with the chemical composition of organic materials, it had become known that the leaves and bark of certain plants and trees, including willow, meadowsweet, and poplar, contain an active ingredient called salicin. The substance has many remarkable properties, one of the most notable of which is its suppressing effect on human temperature, and several chemists understandably became interested in trying to isolate it for use as a remedy. This they managed to do and gradually learned how to refine salicin to a synthetic equivalent, salicylic acid, which, when crystallized, could be more easily dispensed to patients.

Unfortunately, salicylic acid has a corrosive effect on the lining of the stomach and is exceedingly disagreeable to take (as indeed is salicin). Although by the late nineteenth century its effectiveness as a treatment for rheumatic fever in particular had been proven by physicians, it had never really taken off as a commercial medicine because no one had been able to diminish its causticity. The one chemist who came close, Charles Gerhardt at Strasbourg in 1854, had tried extracting the hydrogen element of salicylic acid (responsible for the irritation to the stomach) and replacing it with a milder acetyl group, but the process was tricky and he managed only to obtain a crude and impure version of the final substance. Nonetheless, Gerhardt was the first person to chemically synthesize a recognizable form of acetylsalicylic acid. When we swallow an aspirin today that's what we are taking—a compound called acetylsalicylic acid, or ASA. Sadly, Gerhardt found the whole procedure so complicated he decided to shelve it. In the decade or so following, various other chemists had a go at refining his process but with limited success. As a result, the medicine began to languish as just another of the stable of antipyretic substances that hadn't quite made the grade.

Interestingly, few of these antecedents featured in Bayer's official version of how the drug finally came to market. According to a long-promulgated company legend, ASA's creation was a strictly in-house affair. The father of Felix Hoffmann, one of Bayer's scientists, suffered badly from rheumatism and had been taking salicylic acid to relieve the pain. As it affected his stomach, he asked his son to find a way to make it easier to take. Young Hoffmann set about his task, trying various formulas, until in a stroke of genius he reportedly came up with the original idea of combining salicylic acid with an acetyl group. The combination proved effective and so aspirin was invented.

The real story is more complicated. The idea for taking a new look at salicylic acid actually came from Arthur Eichengrün—Hoffmann's superior in the pharmaceutical department who was setting his team of young researchers a range of targets in accordance with instructions issued by Carl Duisberg to all Bayer scientists on their first day at the company. Their task, Duisberg explained was to

> find new ways of presenting familiar, especially patented pharmaceuticals by making use of the whole range of chemical, pharmaceutical, physiological, and medical literature and also discover new,

technically utilizable physiological properties in new or familiar substances, so that the dye works are in a position to include the specialties of competing firms in their manufacture and bring to the market and introduce new pharmaceutical preparations.

Almost certainly Eichengrün told Hoffmann to go to the library and read up on the medical literature—and there he would have found Charles Gerhardt's account of his 1854 experiments.*

Hoffmann got to work and before long—on August 10, 1897, to be exact—he entered the successful formula into his journal, noting that he had found a way of making ASA that neutralized the chemical element of salicylic acid responsible for its stomach-turning acidity. This was essentially what Gerhardt had done forty years earlier but Hoffmann's procedure was simpler and more effective.

So far so good, but now the new substance had to be handed over to the company's pharmacology unit for testing. Arthur Eichengrün was present several weeks later at ASA's first evaluation and to his delight it performed very effectively. Obviously, Eichengrün felt, it should go on to the next stage, clinical trials. But Heinrich Dreser, the unit's cautious chief pharmacologist, had other ideas. Salicylic acid enfeebled the heart, he announced (some doctors believed this was so because the high doses given to rheumatic patients sometimes made the heart race), and acetylsalicylic acid would be just the same. He refused to give the drug a seal of approval.

Eichengrün was furious but Dreser was immovable and, in any case, all his attention was taken up with another Hoffmann "discovery," made at almost the same time. This was a substance called diacetylmorphine (an opium derivative), and Dreser believed it had stronger commercial potential, both as a remedy for coughing fits and as a drinkable health tonic.† Indeed, the volunteers in the Bayer factory

---

*There is some evidence to suggest that Arthur Eichengrün's role in the development of aspirin was written out of Bayer's corporate history in the mid-1930s because he was Jewish. The company has always denied this claim but Eichengrün, who was incarcerated in the Theresienstadt concentration camp by the Nazis in 1943, was convinced it was true.

†Like ASA, diacetylmorphine had been found before. In 1874, an English chemist, C. R. Alder Wright, formulated the substance while conducting experiments with opium derivatives at St. Mary's Hospital, London. Presumably Hoffmann found an account of Wright's work during a trawl through old medical literature.

who tried it loved the substance so much that Dreser gave it a name to reflect the heroic way it made them feel. Thus heroin was created and Bayer and Hoffmann earned the curious distinction of "discovering" in the same fortnight one of the most useful substances known to medicine and one of the most deadly. Unfortunately, getting heroin ready for manufacture was a lengthy process that left no one much energy for Hoffmann's other formulation. So Eichengrün was forced to act on his own initiative.

He secretly arranged for some doctors in Berlin to conduct trials and within weeks they were returning glowing assessments. Not only was ASA free of the unpleasant side effects associated with salicylic acid, it also appeared to have another remarkable property—it was a general-purpose analgesic. Eichengrün immediately circulated these reports among the laboratory staff. Hopeful, Carl Duisberg ordered another full set of trials. Yet again the responses were enthusiastic and this time Dreser had to concede. In accordance with standard company practice, ASA was baptized with a typically memorable brand name and then it went into production.

Aspirin was launched quietly with only a few hundred samples sent out to doctors across Germany in 1899. But it quickly took off. Patients declared there had never been anything like it for relieving their aches and pains. Word spread and soon Bayer had an extraordinary best seller on its hands.

BY THE DAWN of the new century, innovative developments such as these had given the leading German dyestuff producers an unshakable grip on the global chemical industry's key technologies and largest markets, an ascendancy they would strain every sinew to maintain until their power reached its zenith in the IG Farben era. For now, of course, competition between them continued as fiercely as ever, and there was little diminution in their appetite for encroaching on one another's specialist fields whenever they could. Hoechst, for example, mirrored Bayer's growing success with pharmaceuticals when it invented Novocain, the local anesthetic, in 1900, and both companies continued to challenge BASF's lead in synthetic dyes.

Other German dye firms—Agfa, Kalle, Cassella, and Weiler-ter-Meer, to name but a few—also remained strong contenders and in some novel areas of business were forging far ahead: in 1898, for example, Agfa began manufacturing photographic X-ray plates for use in the new medical science of radiology. But, collectively, these firms' dominance over their international rivals—even the biggest of them— was very clear. The French and British chemical industries, having started so boldly in the middle years of the nineteenth century, were in a woeful condition fifty years later. Uncompetitive, inefficient, bereft of initiative, and badly managed, they had all but given up the ghost.

Belatedly, there was some recognition that this sorry state of affairs had gone on long enough. In 1906, in an article to mark the jubilee of William Perkin's discovery of mauve, the *Daily Telegraph* noted caustically, "We have forfeited our heritage, and upon the foundation of an Englishman's work the superstructure of the commanding scientific industry in the Fatherland has been erected." And at long last in the political sphere moves were afoot to amend British patent laws, which had hitherto failed to ensure that foreign companies worked their protected processes on British soil.* It would still be some years, however, before anyone would truly comprehend the strategic consequences of Germany's triumph.

In the meanwhile, the Rhineland chemical chiefs enjoyed their preeminence, mischievously rubbing salt into their foreign rivals' wounds (particularly those of the British) whenever the opportunity occurred. In 1900, for example, Heinrich Brunck, the boss of BASF, outraged public opinion in London by suggesting that all Indian indigo producers should switch to growing food instead. And Carl Duisberg, never shy about being forthright, noted that Britain could hardly complain about German success in one industry when it had for so long enjoyed a lead in many others. After all, it wasn't Germany's fault that the British had failed to display the right degrees of

---

*As a consequence, German chemical firms regularly obtained British patents for their inventions but then only manufactured the goods at plants in Germany, for export to the United Kingdom. This way, they managed to prevent knowledge about innovative production methods from slipping into the hands of potential British competitors.

Teutonic forbearance and hard work necessary to allow its chemical industry to thrive. "It requires," he said, "a singular ability to wait and abide things coming, combined with endless patience and trouble. . . . We Germans possess in a special degree this quality of working and waiting at the same time and of taking pleasure in scientific results without technical success."

The fruits of this patience were beginning to flood the world's markets. Over the next few years a cornucopia of remarkable new products would follow dyes and pharmaceuticals out of Germany's chemical factories: soaps, detergents, photographic materials, printing inks, fertilizers, paints, glazes, explosives, chemical processes for iron and steel production (which were also beginning to outstrip those of Britain and were already well beyond France), and much, much more. To the consternation of its competitors, Germany was becoming an economic and industrial powerhouse. When allied to the growing political and military ambitions of its young imperial dynasty and the Junker class that supported it, this was cause for deep concern.

2

THE GOLDEN YEARS

In 1947, when the IG Farben defendants at Nuremberg were mulling over the long sequence of events that had brought them to the Palace of Justice, the first decade of the twentieth century would have stood out as a golden age for their industry, a period of comparative calm when everything still seemed gloriously possible. It is true that the international atmosphere was turning sour and that bellicose voices were echoing across Europe. But Germany's industrial chemists had good reasons for optimism. Business was buoyant and an expanding array of innovative products had propelled their firms to a dominant position. Until foreign competitors were able to mount an effective challenge, BASF, Bayer, Hoechst, and the rest had the field to themselves.

They used the time to develop more extraordinary new technologies, including one discovery that would have a significant effect on the lives of millions. Innovation in those years was not restricted, however, to new science or new products. The industry's rapid international expansion, its relentless domestic competitiveness, and the sheer novelty of many of its manufacturing processes had often thrown up complex problems. But these very crises also sometimes opened up unexpected avenues to further growth and consolidation. By learning how to identify and take advantage of such opportunities, those running Germany's chemical businesses had become strategically sophisticated in their thinking and better able to measure risk against likely reward. Their more mature outlook allowed them, for the first time, to recognize fully the merits of working in concert rather than in isolation.

AS THE NEW CENTURY broke, no company was more golden than Bayer. Most of its medicines were selling well and aspirin, one of its most recent inventions, was a worldwide success.* Although the product's launch had been a modest affair, soon thousands of physicians were clamoring to try it. A rash of confirming scientific articles appeared—an astounding 160 of them were published in its first three years—and with each fervent endorsement aspirin's reputation grew. Its advocates realized it was much more than just a simple, if effective, antifever treatment. It was a powerful remedy for a range of other conditions, too—headache, toothache, neuralgia, migraine, the common cold, influenza, "alcoholic indisposition," tonsillitis, and arthritis, to name just a few. Prescription sales began to soar.

But protecting and exploiting this success wasn't as straightforward as it might have seemed. One of the company's first acts had been to apply for worldwide patents on the discovery, yet to Carl Duisberg's great consternation the claim was rejected in Germany and across much of Europe, the authorities judging that Charles Gerhardt and other scientists from the 1850s onward had devised the medicine's chemical formula before Bayer's Felix Hoffmann. In the world's two largest potential markets, Britain and the United States, patent officials adopted a less stringent attitude and gave Bayer lucrative exclusive rights over the drug's production and sale—albeit only until 1916

---

*Bayer's other top brands—Phenacetin, Sulfonal, Trional, and heroin—were also proving popular with consumers.

and 1917, respectively.* Elsewhere it could only rely on its trademark of the aspirin brand name. Of course, Duisberg knew that, properly exploited, a brand name could be an even greater asset than a patent; as he had learned from the company's earlier success with Phenacetin, if a manufacturer could fix the name of a product in the mind of consumers, they would return to it again and again, no matter how effective or inexpensive a rival's identical but differently branded offering might be. But it would be harder to pull off the same trick with aspirin because the international medical community, increasingly concerned about the indiscriminate sale of harmful quack remedies, had begun to frown on any attempt to advertise prescription medicines.

Even as the company's marketing specialists were working out how to get around this problem, Carl Duisberg was wrestling with another. Bayer's American business was conducted through a subsidiary, the Farbenfabriken of Elberfeld Company, which had been established in New York to handle sales of its dyestuffs and other chemicals. Historically these sales had made a healthy contribution to Bayer profits, but the recent move into pharmaceuticals had been more difficult. Although Bayer had won a U.S. patent on Phenacetin, high import tariffs had made the product an attractive target for smugglers who bought it cheaply in Europe and dumped it on the American black market. Bayer had fought back through the courts with injunctions and infringement claims but the loss of revenue had still been considerable. The situation was only likely to worsen in 1906 when the Phenacetin patent expired and legitimate American competitors would be able to sell the drug cheaply as well.

Determined to prevent the same fate for aspirin and other products, Duisberg set sail for America in 1903 to explore a possible solution. If Bayer drugs could be manufactured in the United States rather than Germany they would be tariff-free, bringing down the price to consumers and depriving bootleggers and mainstream rivals of their competitive advantage. Duisberg didn't much like the loss of control this would entail—as an arch centralist he found the idea of

---

*For the duration of a patent license in the United States and Britain, usually between fifteen and twenty years, the holder had a legal monopoly on the product.

a semiautonomous U.S. operation alarming, and he was worried that it would cause him "a lot of anger and tedious work"—but he couldn't see that he had much choice.

He found the answer at Rensselaer in upstate New York, where Bayer owned a stake in a small manufacturing firm, the Hudson River Aniline and Color Works. It was an untidy little dyestuffs business but the site had great potential. The area had good communications links and—a useful bonus—a large pool of immigrant German labor in nearby Albany. If Bayer acquired the rest of the company and then invested heavily in a new plant and facilities for pharmaceutical production (he estimated the total cost at around $200,000), it would have an American home for its drug production and a base for any further expansion. Swallowing his misgivings, Duisberg concluded the deal.*

Before returning to Germany, Bayer's boss embarked on a grand fact-finding tour of American industry. For the most part he wasn't impressed. The plants and factories were old-fashioned and ill-equipped, their managers uncouth, badly educated, and lacking in ambition. More troubling, for someone who had rigid ideas about the correct relationship with labor, was that the workers appeared to be obsessed with gaining union rights. On May 13, 1903, a few days after he returned to New York to prepare for his journey home, he was invited to share his wisdom at a lecture to the city's Chemical Society. The organizers presumably expected a few platitudinous remarks about the importance of science; what they got instead was a tirade. In his usual forthright manner, Duisberg told the audience that labor was strangling the nation's economic growth and that, as a result, Americans were "not able to perform the exact and exhausting work necessary to make the principles of chemical science fruitful for industry." To anyone who knew Duisberg well such views were consistent with his long-held belief that Teutonic patience was indispensable to chemical innovation; indeed, he was to make much the same complaint about the British a few years later. But

---

*The subsequent construction work took some years to complete, but the finished factory ranked as one of the most modern and technically impressive in the United States. Though smaller than Leverkusen, Bayer's extraordinary new plant near Cologne, which was also then nearing completion, Bayer Rensselaer was built to many of the same exacting standards and high technological specifications and, inevitably, attracted covetous eyes from within the nascent American chemical industry.

his New York listeners were outraged. He was heckled from the floor and booed off the stage at the end of his speech. When he finally caught the boat home the following week, the city's newspapers announced that they were glad to see the back of him.

On the whole, though, Duisberg counted the visit a great success. He had secured his company's immediate future in America and laid the groundwork for further expansion. He had also—despite his outburst in New York—been deeply impressed by at least one aspect of American business: the power of the big American industrial trusts, notably John D. Rockefeller's Standard Oil. The very scale of these cartels, the way they managed to mitigate damaging competition by coordinating their efforts on pricing and supply (despite the 1890 Sherman Antitrust Act, which was supposed to outlaw such things), was an inspiration to a man whose career had been forged in the crucible of German industrial rivalry. He spent the voyage home deep in thought.

Six months later, these musings came together in a fifty-eight-page memorandum he sent to Gustav von Bruning, the head of Hoechst; Heinrich Brunck at BASF; and Franz Oppenheim, the leading director at Agfa, the Berlin-based photochemicals business. His great vision, he explained, was an immediate American-style amalgamation of the sales, purchasing, and research departments of their companies, with the possibility that other, smaller firms might later be invited to join them in an industrywide coalition. He made it clear that the proposal was on a scale far beyond any of the ad hoc, project-specific partnerships the firms had occasionally entered into in the past. Each would retain its corporate autonomy, but by working in harness they would be able to limit the competition that was always threatening to undermine their profitability.

Duisberg was convinced his fellow moguls would find his scheme irresistible. Several of their more successful patents were getting close to expiration and the wellspring of technological innovation in their core dye businesses—still a major source of income for each firm—seemed to be running a little dry. By pooling their research resources they would be able to put more effort into finding new product lines, while a joint sales operation could control supplies to the marketplace and fix prices to the companies' mutual benefit.

He was delighted when von Bruning, Brunck, and Oppenheim agreed to discuss his proposals at a private meeting in Berlin's Kaiserhof Hotel in February 1904, and he briefly allowed himself to hope that his grand plan might be bearing fruit. But while Brunck and Oppenheim greeted his ideas with cautious interest, it became apparent during the session that von Bruning was implacably opposed. Duisberg was deeply puzzled. He couldn't understand the Hoechst director's refusal to consider something so clearly advantageous to all.

In September of that year, he opened his morning newspaper and the mystery was solved. Hoechst had been in secret negotiations with Leopold Cassella and Company, the Frankfurt-based dye business. The outcome of their talks was nowhere near a full merger, but the two companies had agreed to swap stock and consult each other at all levels of business. The arrangement was called an *Interessen Gemeinschaft*, or community of interests, with the directors of both firms sitting on each other's boards and making decisions for their joint advantage. Two other smaller firms, Kalle and Company and Griesheim Elektron (a dyestuffs business with important interests outside organic chemistry), were scheduled to join them later.

Fearful of being on the receiving end of this new combine's strength in the marketplace and infuriated by the way he had been outsmarted, Duisberg immediately reopened negotiations with BASF and Agfa. The result was the Dreibund, or Triple Association, established in late November 1904. Similar in composition to its rivals' confederation, the association was a relatively loose arrangement that left its constituent companies independent while they cooperated on many aspects of their business.* As such it was still a considerable way from Duisberg's grander vision of an industrywide amalgamation, but at least it ironed out some of the problems of competition

---

*Henceforth the firms would cooperate in various ways, such as consulting one another on big investment decisions, abandoning some product lines in favor of the most efficient manufacturer in the group, and establishing joint sales operations in selected foreign markets. The companies still had their differences. For example, both Bayer and Agfa objected to BASF's attitude on bribery, or the giving of "discretionary payments" to potential customers, which was commonplace in the industry. BASF wanted the practice scrapped, especially in the United States, where it was rife, but the other firms resisted, insisting that an immediate ban on such kickbacks would damage sales and endanger the interests of their stockholders.

that had bedeviled the industry for so long. A more substantial merger would have to wait for more propitious times.

In May of the following year, as though to underline Duisberg's point about the merits of German chemical businesses working in harmony rather than against one another, Bayer came up against exactly the kind of problem that a full industry coalition might have avoided. Its lawyers discovered that another German company, Chemische Fabrik von Heyden, had been selling its own version of acetylsalicylic acid in England. When Bayer went to court in London to assert its intellectual property rights and sue for damages, the judge, a Justice Joyce, affirmed what European authorities had claimed earlier—that Bayer's 1898 application for a UK aspirin patent had been written in such vague terms that it was impossible to determine whether the drug was really a new invention or merely an enhancement of work done by Charles Gerhardt and others. Clearly irritated by this document, which he found "erroneous and misleading, . . . by accident, error or design so framed as to obscure the subject as much as possible," Joyce concluded that

> it would be a strange and marvellous thing, and to my mind much to be regretted, if after all that had been done and published with regard to acetylsalicylic acid before the date of this patent, an ingenious person, by merely putting forward a different, if you like a better mode of purification . . . could successfully claim as his invention and obtain a valid patent for the production of acetylsalicylic acid as a new body or compound. In my opinion, it was not a new body or compound and I hold the patent in question in this case to be invalid.

The ruling meant that anyone, in theory, could now make and sell acetylsalicylic acid in the British Empire—a nightmare for Carl Duisberg since aspirin was his company's most successful export product.* Judge Joyce's words were also symptomatic of a growing international

---

*UK pharmaceutical companies did not have the expertise necessary to begin manufacturing acetylsalicylic acid straightaway, but by 1908 British brands such as Xara and Helicon began to appear on the market. However, these products could not yet be called aspirin because the name remained a Bayer trademark in the UK until 1914. As it happened, the quality of the drugs was poor and most consumers stuck with the Bayer product for some years to come.

unease at the hold that the German chemical companies had on the secrets of their trade. Used to denying their domestic competitors the slightest advantage, German businesses had gotten into the habit of writing their patents in an obscure way in order to make it as hard as possible for rivals to copy their products. They were comfortable enough with this custom themselves and had become well versed in finding ways around it when necessary, but their foreign competitors took great exception to the practice. Whether he had intended it as such or not, Joyce's decision was therefore hailed as the start of a fight back, the first round in a David and Goliath battle.

In 1907 British industrialists' frustration with German patent habits became coterminous with official government policy. After much lobbying and pressure in Parliament, the minister of trade, David Lloyd George, announced that the patent laws were to be changed. Henceforth, goods that were granted a patent in the UK had to be made in the UK, allowing British manufacturers the opportunity to gain an insight into how they were made and thereby to develop new skills and technologies. If the patent was not worked in Britain, the license could be withdrawn. Lloyd George's justification for this decision was clearly influenced by Joyce's ruling.

> Big foreign syndicates have one very effective way of destroying British industry. They first of all apply for patents on a very considerable scale. They suggest every possible combination, for instance, in chemicals, which human ingenuity can possibly think of. These combinations the syndicates have not tried themselves. They are not in operation, say, in Germany or elsewhere, but the syndicates put them in their patents in obscure and vague terms so as to cover any possible invention that may be discovered afterwards in this country.

His announcement was greeted with glee by the small British chemical industry, and it resulted in the transfer of some German manufacturing capacity to the UK. In 1907 Hoechst and BASF, which had maintained their lucrative agreement on the production of indigo despite their participation in rival confederations back home, jointly established the Mersey Chemical Works at Ellesmere Port, near Liverpool, to make the dye for the UK market. In reality, this move was little more than a token nod toward British sensibilities because the Germans allowed the factory to produce only a very small proportion of the country's needs (by 1913 the UK was still importing four times as much synthetic indigo from Germany as it was making locally), and of course all the profits still flowed back to the Rhineland. Nonetheless, the gesture emboldened the companies to cheekily send a barrel of the dye to the British government, marked with the words *Made in England.*

Although Lloyd George's declaration applied only to manufacturing, it reflected a broader malaise in international relations and the general suspicion with which German interests were now being viewed by the rest of Europe. The continent was beginning to polarize. In Germany, where Kaiser Wilhelm II seemed to have abandoned the restraint and diplomatic ingenuity of the Bismarck years in favor of a more erratic belligerence, public opinion increasingly held that the country was being denied its rightful place at the economic and political top table. In Britain and France, the two major powers whose security was most obviously threatened by German muscle flexing, an unhealthy chauvinism was developing, inflamed by the yellow press, which published lurid warnings about German militarism and its expansionist ambitions. At a time when books like Erskine Childers's best-selling *The Riddle of the Sands* (1906) and William Le Queux's *Spies of the Kaiser* (1909) were alarming British readers with tales of German plots, conspiracies, and invasion threats, German preeminence in the chemical sciences assumed a significance beyond the merely commercial.* Any future conflict would clearly be an industrialized conflict. The nation that commanded the resources, technology, and know-how to equip and support a war machine would surely have an advantage.

In the meantime, business was business and Bayer wasn't the only German chemical company with momentous matters on its hands. One of its partners in the new Dreibund was in the process of making

---

*The British weren't alone in being influenced by the fanciful imaginings of popular novelists; Germany had its best-selling doommongers, too, for example, Karl Eisenhart's novel *The Reckoning with England* (1900).

a scientific breakthrough of comparable magnitude to that of William Perkin half a century earlier. The discovery of a method to "fix" nitrogen would have wide-ranging implications for peace and war. It would also be crucial to the development of IG Farben.

THE EVENTS THAT led to this breakthrough began one evening in June 1898, when members of the British Association for the Advancement of Science gathered in Bristol to hear a lecture. There were few signs that the occasion would be especially memorable; it was just another of the regular get-togethers that academics and researchers seem to enjoy so much, an opportunity to hear a distinguished colleague expounding on his current work or airing his views on a topical scientific theme. Nonetheless, it promised to be interesting. The speaker was one of the country's most eminent chemists, the recently knighted Sir William Crookes. Known for his breadth of interests, ranging from pure and applied science to the more esoteric study of psychical research, Crookes had won fame some years before for his discovery of thallium, a new metallic element. Since then much of his attention had been focused on two arcane fields of inquiry: how highly rarefied gases react to electricity and the composition of "rare earths"— elements so chemically similar to one another that special methods had to be devised for their separation. These were important matters, to be sure, and his research would one day have a significant bearing on the understanding of radioactive materials like uranium, but there must have been some that evening who were glad that he had chosen a more comprehensible subject for his talk. His topic was nitrogen—or rather the lack of it.

Nitrogen is as essential to plant and animal life as the air that we breathe. Indeed, 78 percent of the air we breathe *is* nitrogen. It is also vital to the successful cultivation of crops. Thousands of years ago farmers began habitually planting legumes (peas and beans) among cereal and rice crops because they had learned that somehow legumes replenished overworked soil. What they didn't know was that certain bacteria, including some that lived on these plants, could absorb, or "fix," nitrogen out of the air. It was this that helped fertilize their harvest. Manure and animal bones are also rich in fixed nitrogen and when spread on a field have a similarly beneficial effect. But the yield from all these sources is relatively small. Although it was more than sufficient until well beyond the medieval era, as the centuries advanced—and the world's population grew and more land was cultivated to grow cereals—fresh sources of nitrogen had to be found. By the nineteenth century, when the burgeoning human population had increased demand for grain to unprecedented levels, the hunt had become so competitive that English gangs were traveling to the Continent to exhume cadavers that could be ground up for essential nutrients.

England "is robbing all other countries of their fertility," wrote one prominent German chemist, Justus von Liebig. "She has turned up the battlefields of Leipzig and Waterloo and of Crimea. Already from the catacombs of Sicily she has carried away the skeletons of generations. . . . [She] removes from the shores of other countries the manurial equivalent of three and half million of men. Like a vampire she hangs from the neck of Europe."

Of course, this lust for fertilizer wasn't restricted to England. In China, human waste was regularly recycled in rice paddies, even though there were undeniable health risks associated with the practice. In nineteenth-century Paris, a million metric tons of horse dung were collected annually for the market gardens around the French capital. In America, an ever-lengthening railroad network hauled hundreds of thousands of bleached buffalo bones back to processing factories in the East.

Other parts of the world were more blessed. In the early 1850s a few barren islands off the coast of Peru were found to be hundreds of feet deep in guano, the nitrogen-rich droppings of countless generations of seabirds. The discovery sparked an extraordinary export trade that saw 20 million tons of the substance excavated and shipped off to the grain-hungry nations of the industrialized world. By 1870 this supply was all but exhausted and even an American government appeal to U.S. adventurers and merchant seamen—asking them to take possession (as a national resource) of any guano-rich islands they discovered—failed to yield more. Attention switched to Chile, the world's last significant source of nitrates. Its deserts were rich in deposits of fossilized saltpeter (sodium nitrate), which had accumulated over millions of years. But even as the extraction of these deposits got under way and ships battled round the Horn to take the saltpeter back to Europe, anxiety persisted about what would happen when it, too, ran out.

It was this fear that most preoccupied Sir William Crookes when he stood up to deliver his speech in June 1898. He had thought long and hard about what he had to say and in the process had come to a startling yet inescapable conclusion. Sooner or later (about twenty years was his estimate) demand for organic nitrogen would outstrip supply. And this, as he explained to his increasingly uneasy listeners, would result in only one outcome: unless new sources could be found, the world—or at least the industrialized Western world—would face starvation. Nitrogen, he went on, was "vital to the progress of civilised humanity and unless we can class it among the certainties to come, the great Caucasian race will cease to be foremost in the world and will be squeezed out of existence by the races to whom wheaten bread is not the staff of life."

For all his apocalyptic gloom, Crookes was a scientist, a rational man who believed that a solution could and would be found. The answer, he was convinced, lay in the discipline to which he had devoted much of his life. "It is the chemist who must come to the rescue," he said. "It is through the laboratory that starvation may ultimately be turned to plenty." After all, no one should forget that nature *had* provided humankind with abundant supplies of nitrogen; it was everywhere, in the very air that everyone breathed. The only problem was how to tap it.

Even as his distinguished audience stumbled out into the night, greatly disturbed by what they had heard, Crookes's remarks were finding their way to the newspapers and from there to the wider world. Such a dire prediction, from an internationally respected chemist, had considerable impact on the world's scientific community. Researchers had been worrying away at the nitrogen problem for many years—and many had tried and failed to find a solution. But now Crookes had thrown down the gauntlet in terms that couldn't be ignored. There had to be some way of getting nitrogen from the air. The time had come for science to meet that challenge.

It was easier said than done. As every chemist knows, atmospheric nitrogen (N_2) is relatively inert. Its two atoms are so strongly bound that few biochemical reactions can break it. Lightning can occasionally crack it open, making an irregular contribution to Earth's biological cycle through rainfall, but for the most part nitrogen is chemically inaccessible. Nineteenth-century scientists had been able to establish its composition but not to find a method of "fixing" it. They understood that any successful synthesis would probably have to involve the application of extraordinary pressures or perhaps the reproduction of the incredible electrical forces found in a great storm, but at the time of Crookes's speech no one had yet been able to find a way of achieving either.

By 1903, however, it seemed that some progress was being made. In Norway that year, Kristian Birkeland and Samuel Eyde designed arc furnaces that formed nitric acid by passing an electric arc through the air—in effect, replicating the natural process of lightning's action on atmospheric nitrogen, albeit on a much smaller scale. They established a company to develop the process industrially and attracted investment from around Europe, including a modest injection of cash from BASF, which was becoming interested in finding a commercial solution to the nitrates problem. But the power required for Birkeland and Eyde's process was enormous; it could be made to work only at a site where electricity was abundant and extremely cheap, and even then the yields of nitrogen were very small. Although Norsk Hydro picked up the idea and built experimental plants at Notodden and Rjuken, by early 1908 it was apparent to most other investors, including BASF, that this route to synthetic nitrogen was not economically viable.

It would fall to a German scientist, Fritz Haber, to discover what has rightly been hailed as one of the most significant inventions of the twentieth century. Born in Breslau in 1868, Haber was destined for chemistry. His father, a Jewish businessman, had made a small fortune trading in synthetic dyestuffs and had set his heart on his son's doing the same, but he believed that a solid understanding of the natural sciences would lay the groundwork for a successful career in the field.

Thus Fritz had a typically excellent German education. He studied chemistry in Berlin under William Perkin's former mentor, August Wilhelm von Hofmann, and then, with a brief interregnum for military service and an even briefer period working in his father's business (which convinced both of them that an academic life would be more suitable), he began moving through the scientific ranks at some of the better-known universities: Heidelberg, Jena, and Zurich. Finally, he settled in Karlsruhe, at the city's Technische Hochschule, where he would spend the next seventeen years as a teacher, researcher, and author of numerous papers on aspects of chemistry.

Despite his Jewish background—or perhaps because of it—Haber adopted all the outward manifestations of a Junker aristocrat. His square, shaven head was disfigured by a dueling scar; he had a fondness for military-style tunics and he carried himself as though conscious of his superiority over lesser men. Proud, obdurate, and stiffly patriotic, he seemed the quintessential Prussian. But this steely exterior hid a sensitive soul. Haber was a keen reader of romantic poetry and an amorous suitor, frequently entangled in complex relationships; many counted him a loyal, warm, and devoted friend. He was also a brilliant scientist who could throw enormous energy at cracking problems in the laboratory, happy to put in the long, grinding hours necessary for finding solutions.

In late 1908 Haber's reputation as an original thinker—and the support of influential patrons—won him a plum job. He was appointed director of one of the new Kaiser Wilhelm Institutes in Berlin's Dahlem suburb. These had been established a few months earlier under the German emperor's patronage with the express intention of maintaining German preeminence in the sciences. Haber was given responsibility for the institute devoted to chemistry (Albert Einstein and Max Planck were appointed to similar positions nearby) and it was here that he took up the challenge presented by Sir William Crookes over a decade earlier.

The nitrogen problem wasn't new to him, of course. Like many other chemists around the world he had been applying his mind to possible solutions. But whereas others had focused their energies on duplicating the effects of lightning, Haber believed that the only realistic answer lay in a process known as hydrogenation, combining airborne nitrogen with hydrogen to form ammonia. The chemical composition of ammonia, one atom of nitrogen to three atoms of hydrogen, had been discovered by scientists in the late eighteenth century and chemists had tried unsuccessfully to synthesize it ever since. Haber knew that if this synthesis could be achieved, it would supply nitrogen in a practical fixed form; the ammonia could be combined with phosphates and potash for use as a fertilizer. But he also realized that any such method would necessarily involve very high temperatures and the application of quite extraordinary pressure—about two hundred times the atmosphere at sea level. No one had yet been successful but, typically, Haber was undaunted. Once he had settled himself in at Dahlem, he began work with the help of an English assistant, Robert LeRossignol. After weeks of experiments they had managed to devise a process, but unfortunately it yielded only a trickle of ammonia and even that took an age to form. Something was missing—a catalyst to speed up the synthesis. After several more months, tediously testing likely candidates, Haber finally found one that worked, the rare metal osmium, followed a few days later by a second, uranium. It was time to get in touch with his sponsors.

For much of the previous year Haber's experiments had been financially supported by a grant from BASF. Unimpressed by the prospects for the Norwegian nitrogen project, the company had switched horses when it heard about Haber's work. Now, eager to see what Haber was up to, BASF's general manager, Heinrich Brunck, accompanied by one of his favorite young technical specialists, Carl Bosch, traveled to Dahlem. Brunck came away impressed, although greatly daunted by the enormous technical challenges of a process that had no precedent in the chemical industry. His younger colleague was more optimistic. The son of a Cologne businessman, Bosch had often demonstrated his acuity and determination since joining BASF from Leipzig University in 1899, and now he exercised these talents on his boss. On the way back to Ludwigshafen he persuaded Brunck to continue funding Haber's research. If the scientist could manage to fix nitrogen in the laboratory, a way could probably be found to replicate the process industrially. After all, the potential rewards were enormous—not least from the German government, which could perhaps be persuaded to come up with subsidies.

Thus it was that on July 1, 1909, Carl Bosch, this time accompanied by BASF's catalysis expert, Alywin Mittasch, returned to Haber's laboratory to see a demonstration. Things didn't quite go as planned. A section of the vital pressure apparatus burst and it took most of that day and night to get it fixed. Bosch left in frustration to catch the train home, but Mittasch stayed and was rewarded the following afternoon with an extraordinary sight. Haber's hydrogenation equipment began producing seventy drops of ammonia a minute. At least in theory, one of the world's most serious problems had been solved. Now the only challenge was how to make engineering reality of a remarkable stroke of scientific genius, transforming a few beakers of liquid ammonia into a commercial process that could generate thousands of tons.

As BASF moved quickly to arrange a royalty agreement with Haber and to file the appropriate patents, this seemingly intractable production problem was at the forefront of everyone's minds. The undertaking was enormous (some of the company's directors feared it might even be impossible), and it would take a man with truly remarkable qualities to guide it. Heinrich Brunck was convinced that Carl Bosch was the right candidate. Although he was young, just thirty-five, Bosch had very special skills. He was not just a brilliant chemist but also a highly trained metallurgical engineer, a rare combination, even in that intensely technological industry. Moreover, he had already displayed his decisiveness and foresight in supporting Haber, qualities that Brunck believed would be vital.

Over the next three and a half years, Carl Bosch tried his best to live up to Brunck's expectations. The difficulties were immense. Haber's hydrogenation process relied on extreme pressures and temperatures: scaling up his apparatus into an industrial installation capable of withstanding these extremes—an installation, moreover, that would later have to operate as an efficient mass-production unit—posed scientific and engineering problems that no one had encountered before. Bosch and his team had to identify cheaper and more readily available catalysts than osmium and uranium to speed up the process of ammonia synthesis—extraordinarily laborious work that involved over two thousand experiments—and then develop new heat-resistant alloys to stop the plant from exploding. But their biggest problem was building a high-pressure reactor chamber in which the Haber process could take place. Bosch worked night and day developing prototypes made from steel, which at first seemed to be strong enough. But tests soon showed that the carbon in the steel reacted badly with the hydrogen given off by Haber's apparatus, making the metal brittle and liable to fracture. There seemed to be no way around this obstacle until February 1911, when, during a late-night beer-drinking session with his team of researchers—a rare moment of relaxation in an otherwise relentless schedule—Bosch thought up a method of containing the process in a giant double-skinned tube of iron and steel. Iron, which had no carbon element, was unaffected by hydrogen and Bosch realized that if he used it as an inner sleeve to contain the reactants he could reduce hydrogen's weakening effect on the tube's steel outer skin to a minimum and increase atmospheric pressure throughout the chamber to the levels the process required. A further innovation, putting a few tiny holes in the outer shell, allowed any hydrogen seeping through welding points on the iron inner core to dissipate harmlessly into the atmosphere.

These were significant advances, but, even so, Bosch had to contend with those on the BASF board who were concerned at the huge capital investment the venture required. And when Brunck died unexpectedly at the end of 1912, Bosch had to fight even harder to keep the work going. Finally, however, his vision began to take shape in a huge new plant at Oppau on the Rhine, a few miles from BASF's Ludwigshafen headquarters. By the winter of 1913 the complex was operational, and Bosch's huge double-skinned tubes were producing hundreds of tons of synthetic ammonia for use as fertilizer. It was an extraordinary achievement, an engineering and technical marvel without parallel in the industrialized world, and it won Bosch huge plaudits from across the scientific community. Before long this universal applause had elevated his reputation to near parity with that of Fritz Haber, and the process he had worked so hard to bring to fruition was being identified by their joint names. Carl Bosch, many of his peers declared, was a miracle worker whose skill and determination had quashed fears that the developed world might one day face starvation. In the short term, though, the Haber-Bosch process had other, deadlier consequences. For nitrogen was vital for more than replenishing the soil; it was a key ingredient of high explosives, too, and soon that particular commodity would be in great demand

FOR MUCH OF its comparatively brief existence the German chemical industry had kept clear of national politics. Many of its leaders were members of the Society for the Protection of the Interests of the German Chemical Industry—which assiduously lobbied governments at home and abroad to adopt probusiness policies—and generally they were firm believers in free trade and economic liberalism. But on the whole their active participation in national and international affairs had been industry-specific, restricted to such matters as patent legislation, tariffs, and financial support for the sciences. As time went by, however, and the industry's economic power and influence grew (between 1890 and 1913, for example, exports of dyes and pharmaceuticals provided Germany's largest source of income from foreign trade), they found it harder to stand aloof from the larger questions of the day.

At a local level these were most clearly apparent in the challenges posed by workers' rights and trade unionism. The chemical companies were big employers; tens of thousands of men (it was still an exclusively male world) worked in their factories, often in dirty and dangerous conditions and with little in the way of protection. The industry's extraordinarily rapid growth had brought with it a degree of job security, in that demand for workers, especially skilled ones, was consistently high. But the vast majority (about 75 percent in a company like BASF in 1900) were unskilled or semiskilled. The specialist tradesmen, the foremen, and those with some measure of responsibility (who were all on long-term contracts) were reasonably well paid by the standards of the time, but ordinary shop floor employees most certainly were not. At the turn of the century, the industry's average daily wage was around three marks, barely above subsistence level, and this was for a twelve-hour shift and a six-day workweek, often spent in a poisonous and badly ventilated atmosphere close to hazardous chemicals and complicated apparatus. Accidents and injury were common, fatalities were distressingly frequent, and the long-term consequences of working with potentially harmful substances were largely unknown. Although the chemical companies generally abided by the limited safety standards set by government inspectors, in reality these were woefully inadequate and rarely kept pace with an industry that was constantly inventing new products and developing complicated procedures to make them.

At the same time the heads of the chemical industry were not simply rapacious capitalists, bent on exploiting labor and maximizing profits at the expense of their employees' health and well-being. Most of them had been brought up in a tradition of Christian philanthropy and charity and believed there was some commonality of interests between the worker and the firm. In their view, the employer was obliged to provide an adequate wage and some degree of social benefits, while the employee's duty was to respond with diligence, loyalty, and hard work. Thus firms like Bayer, Hoechst, and BASF built workers' housing next to their plants, donated sums to local schools and hospitals, and established workers' libraries, public baths, and saving associations. Occasionally they also offered health checkups for their employees and families, which, if somewhat basic, were at least free.

Yet when set against the realities of low pay, often fearsomely strict factory discipline, and the dreadfully dangerous working conditions that many workers endured, these provisions are hard to see as outstandingly generous, especially as they were often motivated by self-interest. Companies were keen to avoid industrial strife, to bind employees closely to the firm and hold organized labor at bay. As early as 1884, BASF's board had been horrified by a critical report from the government's factory inspectorate, not because of the serious questions it raised about plant safety but because of its potential threat to "social peace": "Such official pronouncements in the possession of a socialist agitator constitute inestimable material for the promotion of class hatred." If tightening up safety procedures and providing a bit of health insurance for workers could keep the unions outside the factory gates, they were a price worth paying.

By the turn of the century, the relationship between German capital and labor had begun to change: the days when a little corporate patronage could mitigate wider social problems were drawing to a close. For some years the left-wing SPD (Social Democrats) had been the nation's fastest-growing political party and the trade union movement was starting to show its strength. The chemical business was no more immune to these developments than any other industry. Ad hoc workers' associations and committees that emerged in 1900 became powerful enough to strike several times by the end of the decade. Collective bargaining for wages and better conditions was gradually being forced on businesses that had once prided themselves on their ability to fend such things off. In 1903 Carl Duisberg had lectured Americans on the dangers (as he saw them) of organized labor; within a few years he and his peers were facing a comparably difficult situation back home. Fearful of the chaos that industrial unrest would wreak on their businesses, they slowly became more involved in the increasingly complex domestic political situation. They moved toward overt backing for conservative probusiness political groups such as the National Liberal Party, with its manifesto of "the maintenance of the Reich" and its support for those with property and commercial interests. Inevitably, this political engagement attracted more attention from the social democracy movement, which in any case tended to view the chemical industry's attempts at social provision (by 1912 these had extended to workers' pubs, theater groups, and other such sponsored cultural activities) as strategies to shore up the capitalist system and prevent the trade unions from recruiting members.

German society at large was fracturing, too. The 1912 Reichstag elections saw the election of 110 socialist deputies—an unprecedented number that made Chancellor Bethmann-Hollweg's task of liasing between the Reichstag and the autocratic Wilhelm II (with his coterie of aristocratic military advisers) that much harder. The kaiser was growing frustrated by Germany's inability to carve out "a place in the sun," to establish an imperial role that could rival that of Britain, France, and, to a lesser extent, Russia. To Bethmann-Hollweg, increasingly worried by the prospect of civil strife, it seemed as though a short, sharp war in support of Wilhelm's ambitions might be the only way of avoiding a serious political crisis at home. And by now there were many in business—even in export-dependent industries like the chemical trade—who were coming around to the same view. Patriotism, the sense that German aspirations were being stifled by hostile European rivals, and hope that the glorious triumph of Sedan in 1870 could be repeated were now as openly expressed in the Rhineland boardrooms and laboratories of Bayer, Hoechst, Agfa, and BASF as they were in the aristocratic salons of Potsdam, the bourgeois cafés of Berlin's Unter den Linden, and the working-class beer *Keller* of Essen and Hamburg.

So what shape was the German chemical industry in on the brink of war? Its companies had their various preoccupations, of course—Bayer's struggles with pharmaceutical patent issues, BASF's engineering problems with nitrogen—but collectively they were stronger than they had ever been. They had responded to the challenges of internal competition by forming two powerful associations and had planted the seeds of closer future cooperation. Although prices were leveling off, they still controlled over 85 percent of global dye production and they continued to flood the world with other products, from paints to photographic chemicals. Innovation, so amply demonstrated by the Haber-Bosch nitrogen process, was vital and thriving: Hoechst's Paul Ehrlich had developed Salvarsan, a synthetic pharmaceutical product for the treatment of syphilis (a discovery that won him the Nobel Prize), while Bayer had started exploring promising new technologies for making synthetic rubber. The companies had begun to realize they had much to lose if the coming conflict went against them and perhaps much to gain if Germany was able to prevail over its enemies and secure an economic advantage for its industries. Although chemistry was not as obviously crucial to warfare as, say, the Krupp armaments empire, it was clear to those in the industry (if not yet to the German high command) that it might still have some strategically significant role to play. And so in that last golden period of peace, they quietly drew up their own plans for what was to come, attempting to camouflage their financial assets in potentially hostile countries and making arrangements (woefully inadequate though they turned out to be) with likely neutrals in Spain, Portugal, the United States, and elsewhere, in the hope of circumventing any future enemy blockades of essential raw materials.

And then, on June 28, 1914, Archduke Franz Ferdinand, heir to the Austro-Hungarian throne, was assassinated in Sarajevo and the world went to war.

3

THE CHEMISTS' WAR

It was supposed to be a brief campaign, a reprise of Prussia's crushing victory over France forty-four years earlier. When the kaiser's troops marched west in August 1914, they were under orders that had their genesis at Sedan in 1870. The aim of the Schlieffen Plan (named after its principal architect, the late Count Alfred von Schlieffen, chief of the German general staff until 1905) was very simple. While a small force contained Russia, the bulk of the German army would brush aside neutral Belgium and smash into France in an overwhelming assault to bring about its collapse before its allies could come effectively to its aid. Germany's full strength could then be brought to bear on Russia, quickly securing defeat, and Britain, alone and isolated, would have no choice but to sue for peace.

As a blueprint for war it was bold, clear, and seriously flawed. Germany's military leaders had convinced themselves that France's army would be no more able to withstand the destructive power of sophisticated weaponry than it had been a generation earlier and would consequently surrender within a few weeks. But though this optimism initially seemed justified—Brussels fell quickly and Paris soon came within striking distance—the kaiser's generals had badly underestimated the enemy's determination. At the Battle of the Marne in September 1914, the French, supported by a small British expeditionary force, launched a desperate counterattack that stopped the imperial army's advance dead in its tracks. When the same thing happened at Ypres a few weeks later, both sides began digging trenches and the Schlieffen Plan started to dissolve into the Flanders mud.

The war of attrition that now loomed spelled disaster for Germany's armed forces. Their attempt at avoiding a fight on two fronts had failed and, with the Russians pressing hard in the east and the British gaining time to mobilize in the west, a war that was meant to be over in weeks looked set to stretch into years. Germany had prepared meticulously, but it had manufactured and stockpiled only enough arms, ammunition, and equipment for a rapid campaign. With no contingency plans for a more protracted conflict, it was left dangerously exposed to the harsh realities of nature. The fatherland was very poor in essential raw materials. Nitrates, oil, metals, and rubber, all vital for sustaining manufacturing and fighting a longer war, were available only from abroad. But Britain's Royal Navy controlled the sea routes and was already implementing a strategy used successfully against Napoleonic France a century earlier—a maritime blockade aimed at starving Germany of vital resources.

An astute industrialist was one of the first to spot the potential consequences of the general staff's oversight.* Walter von Rathenau was among his country's leading businessmen, a director of dozens of major corporations across Europe and head of the A.E.G., Germany's electrical power combine, and he was used to being taken seriously. Before the conflict reached the end of its first week he forced his way in to see the kaiser's war minister, General Erich von Falkenhayn. The army was heading for catastrophe, Rathenau warned him bluntly. Unless immediate and decisive action was taken to maintain a continuous

---

*Lieutenant General Ludwig Sieger, the head of the imperial army's Field Munitions Service, also warned his superiors at the very beginning of the war that ammunition would have to be used sparingly but he was icily informed that "the campaign would not last so long" and the precaution was unnecessary.

supply of basic materials, Germany's forces would be unable to stay on the battlefield for any length of time. Defeat was certain.

To his great credit, Falkenhayn listened. Although he had his doubts about Rathenau's bleak prognosis, he was not completely convinced by the exhilarating reports he was getting from the Western Front either. He decided to hedge his bets, appointing the industrialist to run a new agency, the War Raw Materials Office, and charging him with making an accurate survey of the supply situation. Much to the minister's disquiet, Rathenau's hastily assembled team of civilian experts uncovered a resources crisis that was even worse than anyone anticipated. The survey questioned almost a thousand businesses engaged in war production; they confirmed that the deficit in raw materials was a disaster waiting to happen. Within six months—perhaps even earlier if the fighting continued at its current level of intensity—strategic stocks would be completely depleted. Particularly worrying was the critical shortage of saltpeter and its precious nitrate, essential for the manufacture of gunpowder. It could be obtained only from Chile, now thousands of miles away across oceans controlled by the enemy.

At first, few of Falkenhayn's peers in the aristocratic upper echelons of the high command seemed very concerned by these reports; the confidence generated by Germany's early success on the battlefield was such that pessimistic forecasts from a civilian (and a Jewish civilian, at that) could easily be dismissed as an attempt by a noncombatant tradesman to interfere in operational matters well beyond his competence. Rathenau must leave such matters to the military, they insisted, and keep his nose out of their affairs. Then came the Battle of the Marne and the horrible dawning realization that perhaps Rathenau was right after all. The industrialist's stock rose dramatically. As the man who had so presciently identified the problem, he was clearly also the man to solve it. Whatever he wanted he could have, he was told, but the fatherland's supply of munitions must be maintained. His response brought the chemical industry right to the heart of Germany's war effort.

RATHENAU'S FIRST ACT was to call on one of Germany's keenest minds, Fritz Haber, now director of the Kaiser Wilhelm Institute for

Physical Chemistry and the creator of synthetic ammonia. Haber agreed to set up a new division within the War Raw Materials Office to address a range of chemical supply matters but suggested that Rathenau also recruit Carl Bosch, the young engineer at BASF whose achievement of mass-producing ammonia had gained him the reputation of being a miracle worker.

At his first encounter with the officials at Germany's War Ministry in late September, Bosch was taken aback at their ignorance about the scale of the saltpeter crisis and their naïve assumption that he could come up with a solution. With so much of his attention in recent years focused on meeting the challenges at Oppau he had almost forgotten that most people knew little about the complex practicalities of industrial chemistry. He was aware of what was going on in the wider world, of course: so many of his key technicians had been called up for military service that his beloved new plant had been forced to shut down temporarily. He was also alert to the gunpowder problem, which he had independently concluded might be just around the corner. Unfortunately—as he patiently explained to the assembled soldiers and civil servants—while it was true that the Haber-Bosch hydrogenation process produced a nitrate in the form of synthetic ammonia, the compound had to undergo a further stage of conversion, to nitric acid, before it could be used in the manufacture of explosives. The principles of doing that conversion were reasonably well understood but to adapt it to mass production would be huge undertaking. He would need a great deal of money, machinery, materials, and men—especially the men who had been drafted from the Oppau plant into the armed forces. Without their expertise, any attempt at producing weapons-grade nitric acid would come to naught. Moreover, it would all take time. He appreciated that this wasn't a plentiful commodity at that moment, but he couldn't work miracles overnight. And even with time he could not guarantee success.

The War Ministry officials agreed to his demands, but they insisted that BASF make a binding commitment in return. The government would give the company the six million marks it needed to build a new plant; for its part BASF must promise to produce at least five thousand tons of nitric acid a month by May 1915. Officially, at least,

Bosch's superiors on the board (including some who had previously questioned the huge capital investment at Oppau) were delighted by the deal and said that they hoped it would lead to a "permanent arrangement extending beyond the war, which would make it possible for us to supply the military for years to come." Bosch himself was far less sanguine. He knew there was every chance that he would fail in the endeavor and he made sure that Haber quietly passed on a more sober assessment to wiser ministry heads.

In truth, some in the War Ministry also had doubts about the arrangement. Even as Bosch returned to Oppau to begin his one-man mission of saving the German high command from the consequences of its shortsightedness, they set about drawing up alternative plans for dealing with the munitions crisis. Strict rationing of agricultural fertilizers was immediately introduced and the country was searched from top to bottom for any nitrogen supplies that could be added to the dwindling reserves. A brief respite came when a hundred thousand tons of Chilean saltpeter were discovered in the holds of ships moored in the occupied Belgian port of Antwerp; a little more was scrounged from the Austro-Hungarians. But it was becoming clear that the unprecedented ferocity of the fighting on the Western Front alone—which now stretched from the North Sea coast to the Swiss frontier—would soon exhaust these stocks.

Military options, too, were under consideration. With the outcome of Bosch's project so uncertain, planners began to cast hopeful and covetous eyes across the world at Chile, the principal source of natural saltpeter supplies. Only the Royal Navy blockade stood in the way of obtaining sufficient quantities to ensure a German victory. Surely something could be done to reestablish such a vital link?

For a few tantalizing weeks this ambition seemed realizable. On November 4, 1914, Berlin received news to lift the spirits of even the gloomiest civil servant: some days earlier, ships of the imperial German navy had won an apparently decisive victory against a major British force at Coronel, off the coast of Chile. The report was greeted with euphoria in the German high command, because it now seemed possible that the vital trade route could be reopened. But the optimism soon faded. One month later, at a battle near the Falkland Islands, the

Royal Navy took revenge and overturned its earlier defeat. Germany's last chance of reestablishing the flow of Chilean saltpeter had gone. Now only Carl Bosch at BASF stood between the kaiser's armies and seemingly inevitable catastrophe.

Things at Oppau, however, were not going smoothly. The production of nitric acid from synthetic ammonia required high-pressure ovens that had to be designed and built from scratch. New catalysts had to be found to make the resultant process efficient. Bosch had sought to speed things up by skipping the normal laborious experimental stage and going straight to build a full works, but the engineering techniques involved were also new and untried. It quickly became clear that BASF could not solve these problems on its own. Blueprints for parts of the plant were sent to the company's allies in the chemical industry and both Agfa and Bayer became involved in the race. But the weeks were slipping by. Every day brought further reports of the dispiriting deadlock in Flanders as the two sides fought bitter local battles, trying to wear each other out. The disappointing news from the South Atlantic only added to the pressure and led to renewed demands for progress reports at Oppau from nervous supply officials at the War Ministry. Repeatedly they worried away at the same old questions: Could Bosch really pull it off? When would he be ready? The replies they got back from BASF were equally predictable: These things cannot be hurried any more than they are already. Given time, it might work, but you'll have to be patient. Time was a luxury that Germany could not afford. Another way would have to be found to break the stalemate.

ON APRIL 22, 1915, Field Marshal Sir John French, commander in chief of the British army, cabled London with disturbing news.

> Following a heavy bombardment the enemy attacked the French Division at about 5 p.m. . . . Aircraft reported that thick yellow smoke had been seen issuing from the German trenches between Langermarck and Bixschoote. What follows almost defies description. The effect of these poisonous gases was so virulent as to render the whole of the line held by the French Division mentioned above practically

incapable of any action at all. It was at first impossible for anyone to realise what had actually happened. The smoke and fumes hid everything from sight, and hundreds of men were thrown into a comatose or dying condition, and within an hour the whole position had to be abandoned, together with about fifty guns.

The use of poison gas as an offensive weapon of modern warfare was the brainchild of the father of synthetic ammonia, Fritz Haber. At the age of forty-six he was too old for active military service and, being Jewish, he was ineligible for any sort of home front reserve commission. But he was deeply patriotic and eager to get involved in the war effort. He had been one of the first signatories to the Fulda manifesto, an inflammatory document signed by many of Germany's intellectual elite—though not Albert Einstein—that insisted Germany wasn't responsible for the war and that the country's militarism was the only thing that prevented the destruction of German civilization. When approached by Rathenau, Haber readily agreed to put his talents to work at the behest of the War Ministry and set up an office, the Bureau Haber, to facilitate cooperation between academic and industrial chemistry and the armed forces. His principal contact in the high command was Major Max Bauer, the military's liaison with industry, an influential but shadowy figure who would go on to form strong personal links with Bayer's Carl Duisberg and other leading industrialists. Although not a scientist himself, Bauer was interested in the role that chemistry might play in the development of new military materials and prompted Haber to see what he could come up with. As the saltpeter crisis worsened and Carl Bosch struggled to find a solution at Oppau, Haber began looking into the potential of weapons that weren't reliant on nitrates.

Chlorine gas was an obvious choice. It was highly toxic and, if inhaled, attacked the mucous membranes of the mouth, nose, and throat, causing asphyxiation, blindness, and eventually death. It was also widely available. The German chemical industry, particularly BASF, Haber's erstwhile partner in developing synthetic ammonia, often used it as an intermediate in the manufacture of indigo and other dyes. As the war had interrupted the export trade in these commodities, the plants that produced chlorine gas were being underutilized and so there would be no problem making sufficient quantities for the armed forces. Of course, there were some risks to be considered. There had been numerous workplace accidents involving the gas over the years and the industry had learned to treat it with great respect. Haber's research work was consequently quite dangerous (one of his assistants at the Kaiser Wilhelm Institute was killed in a laboratory explosion involving pressurized canisters) and his difficulties were compounded by the fact that all his tests were conducted under conditions of great secrecy. But gradually he was able to devise a workable and reasonably safe method of diffusion that he could demonstrate to the senior army officers who crept in at the back door of the institute at strange times of the day and night.

Their discretion wasn't due only to a desire to retain the element of surprise. Poison gas had been proscribed under the Hague Convention of 1907, to which Germany and all the other World War I combatants were signatories. "The Contracting Powers," the relevant article stated, "agree to abstain from the use of projectiles; the object of which is the diffusion of asphyxiating or deleterious gases." In other words, gas weapons were effectively outlawed by the civilized world and their deployment went against all accepted norms of modern warfare. But a Germany alarmed by the dangerous military impasse was prepared to set such troubling ethical questions aside.

In April 1915, Fritz Haber, chewing a cigar, attired in a baggy military tunic, and accompanied by an eager team of young researchers (among them Otto Hahn, a scientist who would later win a Nobel Prize for discovering nuclear fission), arrived at the front line at Ypres in Belgium. With them they brought some five thousand cylinders of chlorine gas in liquid form. Haber supervised the digging of deep, narrow slits just beneath the top lip of the main trench, leaving room for three layers of sandbags to protect the cylinders from enemy shelling and for small sacks stuffed with potash and peat moss to absorb any leaks. A select squad of troops known as the Pionierkommando 36 (most of whom had been secretly trained at BASF's plant at Ludwigshafen) then took up positions along a four-mile stretch of the line, facing a division of the French army. For two days German artillery pounded the enemy lines and the town beyond. Then at 5:00 p.m. on April 22, the order came to attack. After distributing cumbersome protective masks to the assault infantry waiting around them, the operators donned their own, opened the cylinder valves, and watched for ten minutes as a strong westward breeze took the thick yellow and green cloud out over no-man's-land.

The results, as Field Marshal French explained in his cable to London that evening, were devastating. Within a few seconds the throats, noses, and eyes of the unprotected soldiers in the Allied trenches were smarting agonizingly. Shortly thereafter the men began to cough and vomit blood, their chests heaving as they tried to draw breath, but only managing as they did so to suck more of the deadly poison down into their lungs. Those who didn't suffocate immediately broke and ran, terrified and retching, to the rear—and away from the masked Germans advancing through the noxious murk. By sunset an estimated five thousand Allied troops had died and another ten thousand or so were barely hanging on to life in field medical stations. In the courtyard of one Ypres hospital, doctors and nurses watched helplessly as hundreds of gagging, gasping men lay writhing in death throes. Nothing they could do seemed to make any difference; emetics of salt and water, ammonia salves, all failed. Later that night, a Scottish surgeon carried out a postmortem on one of the dead and removed a set of lungs. They were inflated to four times their normal size and full of a watery fluid. The victim had literally drowned in the gas.

The panic and mayhem caused by this first attack allowed the Germans to breach the Allied defenses, but remarkably they had neglected to amass a sufficient concentration of troops to make good their advantage. Within days a Canadian division, at an enormous cost in lives, managed to check the German advance and recover much of the lost territory. The battle continued with great intensity for another three weeks and gas was used again, but the Canadians, who were its next intended victims, were saved when the wind changed and blew the toxic clouds in another direction.

Haber was not the only German chemist involved in developing gas weapons, nor was BASF the only company involved in their manufacture. Weeks before the attack at Ypres, Haber's unit had experimented with a limited release of Bayer-produced bromine (code-named T-Stoff) on the Russian front, although the attempt failed when the severe winter weather froze the gas. Nevertheless, bromine was clearly a potent substance, as a letter from Carl Duisberg to Max Bauer attested: "How well it works you may best gather from the fact that for eight days I have been confined to bed, although I inhaled this horrible stuff only a few times. . . . If one treats the enemy for hours at a time with the poisonous gas-forming product, then in my view he will not be going home."

Any reservations about the use of chemical weapons seemed to be felt more by Germany's soldiers than by her scientists. A few weeks after Ypres, Crown Prince Rupprecht of Bavaria, commander of the German Sixth Army, confided to his diary, "I made no secret of the fact that the new gas weapons seemed not only disagreeable but also a mistake, for one could assume with certainty that, if it proved effective, the enemy would have recourse to the same means, and with the prevailing winds he would be able to release gas against us ten times more often than we against him."

It was a telling point. The Allies reacted to the German attack of April 22 with outrage and disgust, but Fritz Haber had opened the floodgates. Over the following days, Sir John French's furious demand that "immediate steps be taken to supply similar means of the most effective kind for use by our troops" was echoed by newspapers in Paris and London denouncing the way that Germany's domination of synthetic dyestuff production had left the Allied armies vulnerable to gas attack and calling for retaliation in kind. In the event, the Allies' first response to Ypres was more conventional. One morning in late May 1915, the French air force bombed the BASF plant at Ludwigshafen. Aerial military technology was quite primitive and the material damage was light but there were some casualties among the workforce.* Later that summer, however, the British, led by the chemist J. B. S.

---

*From then on, raids increased in frequency and intensity throughout the war, and though the installation of air defenses managed to prevent too much destruction, the frequent shutdowns caused by alarms inflicted much wear and tear on equipment and civilian morale. As a result, BASF began looking around for an additional site for its all-important nitric acid production. In 1916, with the help of government subsidies, it began to construct a new factory at Leuna, near Merseburg, on the Saale River—out of range of the Allied bombers. The man in charge of construction was a young chemist called Carl Krauch, a protégé of Carl Bosch's. Many years later he would head the list of defendants at Nuremberg.

Haldane, established a secret chemical weapons research station at Porton Down and began producing their own poison gases. The French soon established similar facilities, and by the end of the year the Allies were deploying chemical weapons as frequently as the Germans. Some twenty-two different chemical agents were eventually developed during World War I, including mustard gas, arsenicals, and phosgene, and as time went by these became ever more sophisticated and deadly; one form of phosgene, developed by Haber and manufactured by BASF, could even penetrate gas masks.

Inevitably, the Allies justified their own use of these gases on the grounds that the Germans had used them first and that the laws of war allowed them to retaliate. They also claimed that the overall superiority of German chemistry had given the enemy a head start; they were only struggling to catch up. The German chemists had no such defense. After the first Ypres attack, Haber was downcast, but not because he felt he had crossed a moral Rubicon. His disappointment came from frustration that the breakthrough hadn't been supported by sufficient numbers of troops to make it stick. In later years he would counter any ethical questions with the argument that to be injured or killed by gas was no worse, and in some cases better, than being blown up and mutilated by high explosives or shot and killed by a machine gun bullet. He insisted he had merely been doing his patriotic duty.* After the war the Allies tried briefly to bring him to trial as a war criminal, but Haber grew a beard and hid in Switzerland for a few months until the fuss had died down. Eventually he came back to Germany, where he was able to pick up his work as a scientist and play a leading role in the reconstruction of his country's chemical industry. In late 1918 (to the fury of many in the French and British scientific communities) he was awarded the Nobel Prize for his discovery of synthetic ammonia—an honor he accepted as his due.

---

*His wife may have felt differently. Once a promising scientist in her own right, she is believed to have objected vehemently when Haber began his experiments in the first few months of the war and to have tried desperately to persuade him to drop the project. A few days after his return from the Western Front and just before he was due to leave for the East to initiate a similar attack against the Russians, she shot herself.

Of course, as we now know, Germany could have prosecuted the war without the poison gas program. For on May 1, 1915, right on schedule, Carl Bosch was able to tell delighted War Ministry officials that he had succeeded against all odds in mass-producing synthetic nitric acid. The kaiser's army would be able to carry on fighting, its guns free at last of their fatal dependence on Chilean saltpeter. Bosch was lionized throughout Germany as a national hero, and millions of young men who might otherwise have lived were condemned to a premature death—something he would recall with great sadness in later years.

But the overall significance of both the synthetic nitrate program and the development of poison gas weapons lay in the fact that they brought the German chemical industry right into a mutually dependent relationship with the state. Dye companies, which just a generation earlier had prided themselves as much on their commercial independence as on their scientific acumen and aggressive business skills, had evolved into massive entities that, for the moment at least, were umbilically tied to Germany's political and military establishment and, increasingly, financially supported by government loans and contracts. With Bosch's technical brilliance having ensured that the war would continue for some years, these links would only multiply, forming a pattern of collaboration that would be recalled and reactivated many years later. At a time when the country felt in great national peril and in the absence of a buoyant export market, it is perhaps understandable why this degree of cooperation was thought necessary. But habits acquired under such stressful and demanding circumstances wouldn't easily be broken in the difficult times ahead. The German chemical industry was beginning to swim in very dangerous waters.

FEW PEOPLE EPITOMIZED the strengthening links between the chemical industry and the military more than Carl Duisberg. The war was a turning point for Bayer's ebullient boss. As fiercely patriotic as Fritz Haber and as ambitious for his business as the keenest of the kaiser's generals was for success on the battlefield, he both identified with his country's war effort and took advantage of the unique opportunities for profit and growth that it had to offer.

Arguably, Duisberg had little choice. The war had curtailed much of Bayer's overseas expansion. Exports were interrupted, patents held in enemy countries were declared invalid, assets were frozen, and valuable trademarks were abruptly rescinded. In 1915, for example, the British government declared that the aspirin trade name was no longer Bayer's exclusive preserve and that anyone could now make and market the drug under that name. Other Allied governments followed suit, and in Melbourne, Australia, a clever young chemist called George Nicholas came up with a new brand called Aspro, which was soon one of the many versions of the drug competing for an export market that Bayer had once called its own. International dye sales, the company's other staple, also fell through the floor—as they did for every other German producer—and although there was some consolation in the fact that the United States was still neutral, the Royal Navy blockade made any meaningful transatlantic trade almost impossible. Production facilities were falling idle and revenue was shrinking. For the company to survive the war, new customers had to be found.

Duisberg looked to his own country for ways to plug the gap. If the conflict was becoming, as many people were calling it, the "Chemists' War," then surely there should be opportunities aplenty in providing matériel for Germany's armed forces. He approached the authorities through influential and well-connected friends such as Gustav Krupp, the armaments manufacturer, and was welcomed with open arms. During the spring of 1915 government orders began to flow Bayer's way, not just for obvious products such as dye for service uniforms, medicines for the army's military hospitals, and paints for its trucks and guns but also for new types of explosives, poison gases, and intermediate chemicals. Indeed, the flood of orders became so strong that Duisberg was soon moved to write to Major Max Bauer at the War Ministry: "You should see what things look like here in Leverkusen, how the whole factory is turned upside down and reorganized so that it produces almost nothing but military contracts. . . . As the father and creator of this work, you would derive great pleasure."

Nevertheless, Duisberg knew that the long-term future was more problematic. After Ypres, British and French politicians had started channeling massive public subsidies toward their local chemical industries, and Bayer's previously feeble foreign sparring partners were now heavily engaged in research and development.* Even the United States, still officially adrift from events in Europe, had realized that German superiority in chemistry could one day cost it dear, and its government was encouraging businesses such as DuPont (one of America's biggest domestic chemical producers) to catch up. Duisberg had always been contemptuous of the way Germany's rivals undervalued science, but he recognized that their academic institutions were perfectly capable of turning out first-rate industrial scientists if there was enough demand for their expertise. He was under few illusions as to the effect these developments would have on his country's postwar economy. Whatever the outcome of the conflict, it seemed certain that Bayer and the other German chemical firms were going to face a huge increase in competition.

In these circumstances, the hitherto unachievable suddenly seemed possible. Chemical businesses that had once been bitter enemies were being compelled by the exigencies of war to work more closely together, to share technologies and trade secrets that had previously been fiercely guarded. Bayer and Agfa, for example, had been assisting BASF with Carl Bosch's nitric acid program at Oppau, independent companies such as Griesheim Elektron and Weiler-ter-Meer were working much more closely with the Hoechst-Cassella-Kalle confederation than had been envisaged at the time of its creation in 1904, and this group, in turn, was sharing work and know-how with the BASF-Agfa-Bayer Dreibund. Watching these various relationships flourish, Duisberg became ever more convinced that his old idea of a full union of all the groups was no pipe dream but a sensible, realizable objective. It would give the industry the critical mass it needed to withstand the international competitive pressures of the future.

When he raised the matter with his peers in July 1915, they reacted with much the same indifference they had shown back in 1903. After

---

*In both Britain and France dye plants and patents confiscated from the Germans were used to launch big new chemical combines. In France these would lower the nation's dependence on imported dyestuffs from 80 percent of the market in 1913 to around 30 percent by 1919.

all, many of them reasoned, the war must soon end in a victory for the fatherland and then, bolstered by the economic advantages they would have gained, Germany's chemical firms would easily reestablish their global supremacy. But twelve months later, when the British army at the Somme began displaying its astonishing capacity to sustain losses and an apparently inexhaustible reserve of fresh troops and new armaments, a quick German victory no longer seemed so certain. Resistance to Duisberg's proposals began to dissipate amid the recognition that the Allies would probably have the time to improve their own chemical industries to the point where they could pose a serious competitive threat. Something had to be done to guard against this possibility. Although a complete fusion was still out of the question (Bosch, for one, was reluctant to accept that the profits of BASF's new ammonia business should be split with anyone else), there was general agreement that a sort of half merger could be to everyone's benefit. After much discussion among the parties a new body was created, the Interessen Gemeinschaft der Deutschen Teerfarbenindustrie (Community of Interests of the German Dye Industry), with a mandate to establish a common approach to such issues as pricing and supply, research, patents, legal affairs, and insurance, cooperation on the latter taking the form of a joint insurance fund. Some things were left out of the deal—the businesses would retain their commercial identities and much financial autonomy, and BASF's ammonia profits would be shared just with its old partners in the Dreibund, and then only gradually—but it was the first time that the major powers in the German chemical industry had agreed to work together as a single entity. In late August 1916, Bayer, BASF, Agfa, Hoechst, Kalle, and Cassella, along with the smaller Griesheim Elektron and Weiler-ter-Meer, finally became willing collaborators rather than all-out rivals. The complete IG Farben cartel was still some way off, but its shape was beginning to emerge.

Flushed with this remarkable success—a testament to his extraordinary determination to never let a good idea die—Duisberg went on to exercise his growing influence on the national stage. On September 9, along with fellow industrialist Gustav Krupp, he was called to a private conference with the two men who had just been made responsible for Germany's war effort, the new chief of the high command, Field Marshal Paul von Hindenburg, and his most senior lieutenant, General Erich von Ludendorff. The meeting was arranged by Major Max Bauer and took place on board the supreme commander's train on the German-Belgian border, to the accompaniment of distant artillery explosions. Hindenburg had been appointed after his predecessor, General Falkenhayn, was made a scapegoat for the Germany army's setbacks on the Somme that summer. Although a major attack had been expected, the high command had been completely taken aback by the sheer mass of men and armaments that the enemy had at its disposal. If Germany was to continue to defend itself against such massive onslaughts, let alone go on to win the war, it would have to match the enemy's offensive capacity. Hindenburg explained to Duisberg and Krupp how he intended to reach this goal. Fresh drafts of men were to be called up and a significantly expanded munitions program was to be announced—more cannon, more shells, more machine guns, and a big increase in poison gas and chemical products. There would be no shortage of government money to pay for these new armaments—the stakes were too high for financial prudence to become an issue—but, as the country's leading industrialists, Duisberg and Krupp were expected to play their part to bring the plan to fruition.

Although the two businessmen were flattered by Hindenburg's attentions and pleased by the boost his program would give to their industries, they were both realists. They explained to the field marshal that there was no point embarking on a gigantic munitions push without a sufficiently large workforce to carry it through. The army was clearly going to soak up more and more men. Their fathers, wives, and daughters could in some cases replace them in the factories, but there was already a critical labor shortage, and in Germany alone there simply weren't enough of these substitute workers to raise production to the necessary level. If the high command wanted such a substantial increase in weapons production it would have to consider some controversial measures.

The following week, Max Bauer called thirty-nine of Germany's most important manufacturers to the War Ministry to thrash out the workforce problem and achieve a wider consensus on what had to be done. Again Duisberg dominated the discussion. To murmurs of agreement from his peers, he described the woeful state of the labor market and the difficulty of replenishing it from German sources alone. Wages were escalating, yet productivity was falling. Things were reaching crisis point and everyone knew there was only one solution. The occupied territories would have to be tapped for workers.

In November 1916, as a direct consequence of Duisberg's remarks, the kaiser's troops began deportations from occupied Belgium—in essence, the start of a slave labor program. In under a month, more than sixty thousand men were taken from their homes and workplaces at gunpoint and loaded onto trains for transport to factories and mines in the Reich. The abrupt brutality of the move and the widely reported outpouring of grief from families that accompanied it attracted almost universal condemnation around the world. The U.S. government was one of several neutral powers to complain, cabling Berlin to formally declare its "greatest concern and regret" and that the action was "in contravention of all precedents and of those humane principles of international practice which have long been accepted and followed by civilized nations in their treatment of non-combatants." By the spring of the following year, the extraordinary vehemence of such protests—and the steadfast refusal of many of the Belgians to be persuaded by threats and bribes to actually do the work expected of them—brought the program to a close and most of the deportees were allowed home. But it was by no means the only act of forced labor. In late 1916, for example, hundreds of Russian prisoners of war were drafted to work for BASF at Oppau, Ludwigshafen, and Leuna, the company's new nitrate factory on the Saale River, and thousands more were added as the war went on. These moves remained controversial and problematic. At Ludwigshafen, managers became so infuriated by the "insubordination" of POWs and their loud complaints about their poor treatment and inedible food they introduced a "strict regimen" to restore discipline. What this meant in practice for the unhappy Russians can only be guessed at.

In the meantime, the labor shortage forced up production costs because of the enhanced bargaining power it gave German workers and trade unions. At the industrialists' meeting in Berlin, Duisberg had advised the government to combat this trend by introducing harsh regulations against excessive wage demands and strikes, warning that otherwise more price rises were inevitable. The idea that he and his associates might meet some of this burden themselves from the swollen profits brought in by war work was never an option. In fact, on the one occasion the authorities tried to propose such an arrangement, Duisberg took active steps to frustrate them. In 1916, General Wilhelm Groener was appointed by General Ludendorff to run a new office in the War Ministry that was charged with reducing inflation in the procurement economy. Influenced by one of his aides, Captain Richard Merton, Groener proposed to his superiors that any price increases on war materials be absorbed directly by the industrial community. When Duisberg heard that this measure was being given serious consideration he mobilized his fellow industrialists into petitioning the authorities for Groener's removal. It was a measure of the Bayer boss's growing influence—and the German government's reliance on his industry's products—that the general and his "interfering" aide were quickly called up for frontline service.*

It is hard to figure how Duisberg found the time for such activities. He had fingers in a great many pies—as a semiofficial spokesperson for the nation's chemical industry and as chairman of its new Interessen Gemeinschaft, to name but two—and of course he still had his normal day-to-day responsibilities as the head of Bayer. Yet somehow he seemed to be everywhere, one minute calling a meeting of his peers at the Düsseldorf Industrial Club, the next racing back to Leverkusen to oversee production and egg his staff on to ever-greater efforts.

But Duisberg wasn't able to control everything. Throughout the war, one corner of his empire remained beyond his influence. Unable

---

*At the last minute, Richard Merton, who as well as being an aide to Groener was also the head of the Metallgesellschaft concern (a leading player in the German metals industry), was able to pull his own strings. He got himself appointed to a commission investigating industrial bribery in the occupied areas instead. Groener wasn't so lucky.

to shape events directly he could only watch with mounting frustration as others made costly mistakes. Thousands of miles away across the Atlantic, Bayer's most important American assets were slipping out of his grasp.

WHEN FIGHTING BROKE out in Europe the most immediate consequence for America was the disruption to commerce. Germany and the United States were still at peace, and according to various international preconflict treaties aimed at preserving sea traffic between non-belligerents, trade—at least of goods that were not directly related to the war effort—was perfectly legal and allowed to continue uninterrupted. But although Britain had been a signatory to those agreements, the moment it became clear that the war was going to last longer than expected, London unilaterally announced that *all* Germany-bound material was liable to embargo. Initially, only German ships had been targeted by the Royal Navy but soon U.S. craft were also being stopped and searched, their cargoes impounded as contraband and the vessels ordered to turn back for home.

Washington was furious. President Woodrow Wilson believed—as did many of his fellow citizens—that America's interests were best served by staying well clear of any dangerous adventures in the Old World. Neutrality would allow the United States to play the part of impartial mediator when Europe finally regained its senses. Until that time, America would do business with whomsoever it pleased. Trade with the Central Powers was worth almost $170 million a year in 1914, and the United States was hardly about to abandon it to suit the British and the French.

But the Royal Navy, charged with stopping vital war supplies from getting to the enemy, continued its operations despite outraged cables from the State Department. Diplomatic relations between London and Washington cooled to their lowest point in years. The situation improved only when Britain and France's own increased demand for American exports began absorbing and even surpassing the spare capacity caused by the loss of German business. Nonetheless, it took many months to repair the damage.

Meanwhile, the blockade was causing other problems. The United States was now cut off from hundreds of important commodities, including many medicines, dyes, and intermediate chemicals that had hitherto been available only from Germany. Although the American chemical industry had made great strides since 1903, when Carl Duisberg had dismissed it as second-rate, it was still in its infancy compared with its German counterpart, which, of course, had done all it could to keep things that way. Hoechst, BASF, Bayer, and the rest had been no more willing to relinquish their lucrative patents and monopolies in the United States than they had been in Britain or France before the war. A few factories had been built to make pharmaceuticals and other dyestuff products, but more for tariff-busting reasons than anything else; and while the profits they earned had been sent back across the Atlantic, the knowledge flowing toward the United States had always been strictly controlled lest potential American competitors somehow gain access to important trade secrets. These factories had consistently used German know-how and raw materials and even, when it was available, immigrant German-speaking labor—all in the interests of keeping vital techniques and procedures within the family. As a result, America's reliance on German chemical products had been carefully nurtured to a state of dependency, while its own local industry was still struggling to get out of the development stage. When the war interrupted this one-sided relationship, the scientific expertise and technological infrastructure to replace German goods didn't immediately exist in the United States and many important chemicals quickly became unavailable.*

---

*Of course, German sympathizers in the United States lost no time in pointing the finger at who *they* thought was to blame for the shortages—the perfidious British and their infuriating embargo on German-American trade. Curiously, they were equally quick to claim that the enemy wasn't infallible and that the blockade could be broken any time. For example, when a U-boat, the *Deutschland*, dramatically surfaced in Baltimore harbor in July 1916, with a cargo of three hundred tons of concentrated dyestuffs and pharmaceuticals, the event was excitedly seized on by pro-German newspaper columnists (most notably those working for the Hearst empire), who celebrated it as a triumph of Teutonic ingenuity and daring and an example of what could be done if everyone put their minds to it. But although such ventures undoubtedly had their propaganda value (the same submarine returned with a second cargo four months later), they were too infrequent and came too late to prevent America's chemicals shortage at the start of the war.

Ironically, given its fiercely protectionist attitude, Bayer was among the worst hit. Its best-selling product in America was aspirin, protected by a patent until 1917 and now being manufactured at the company's sparkling new plant at Rensselaer in upstate New York. But the mass production of aspirin required specific raw materials and one of the most important of those, the chemical phenol (used to make synthetic salicylic acid), was in desperately short supply. The problem arose because phenol was also used in the manufacture of certain kinds of high explosives and the British, who needed it for themselves on the Western Front, had made it a particular target of their transatlantic embargo. Before the war, the U.S. branch of Chemische Fabrik von Heyden—Bayer's principal supplier of raw synthetic salicylic acid in America—had followed standard practice and imported all it needed for its Rensselaer contract directly from Germany. Now those shipments had stopped and existing stocks elsewhere in the United States were drying up because America's chemical industry wasn't yet capable of making enough of it on its own. By the spring of 1915 phenol prices were going through the roof and Bayer's U.S. production lines were on the verge of shutting down.

In the normal course of events, the executives at Bayer and Company (the firm's U.S. subsidiary) would have turned immediately to their head office in Leverkusen for guidance, but the war and the blockade had made nongovernmental transatlantic communication difficult. Effectively cut off from Duisberg's advice yet determined to keep their production lines going, the managers sought help elsewhere and became embroiled in a deeply embarrassing scandal.

The affair that eventually became known as the Great Phenol Plot involved a conspiracy to corner the market in the only available supply of the chemical left in the United States, the excess capacity of a factory set up by the inventor Thomas Edison, who had just started making phenol for use in the production of gramophone records. With Bayer's encouragement, a plan was put together by a naturalized German American called Hugo Schweitzer, who was using his various public personae—wealthy socialite, chemical industry consultant, and high-profile propagandist for the kaiser's cause—as cover for a role as an agent of the German government.* Relying on front companies and secret funds supplied by the German embassy, Schweitzer bought the phenol from the unwitting Edison, gave Bayer what it needed, and then kept the rest to sell later—happy in the knowledge that he would both make a great personal profit out of the deal and keep the chemical out of the hands of the British, who wanted it for their own armaments purpose. Unfortunately, his contact at the German embassy—who was being followed by the U.S. Secret Service—left a briefcase containing details of the operation on a train in New York. Within days, the details were leaked to the newspapers. The timing could hardly have been worse. A few months earlier, on May 7, 1915, a German U-boat had sunk the British transatlantic liner *Lusitania* with the loss of around twelve hundred—mainly American—lives, plunging diplomatic relations between the United States and Germany into crisis and bringing the prospect of war ever closer. When, on August 15, 1915, the *New York World* accused the phenol plotters of undermining American interests by conspiring to deprive the country of strategically important materials, Schweitzer was hastily abandoned by his German embassy friends and left twisting in the spotlight of public opprobrium, his usefulness as an agent blown.

Bayer and Company, which the press had rightly identified as the ultimate recipient of the phenol, was also tainted by the scandal. But as no one could prove that it had ever done anything more than ask for Schweitzer's help, the public embarrassment didn't last long. The firm's managers moved quickly to disassociate themselves from direct knowledge of the German embassy's machinations and said their only aim had been to continue making an important drug. Privately, they congratulated one another on stockpiling enough phenol in the weeks before the scandal broke to keep production ticking over into the fol-

---

*Schweitzer was known in German intelligence circles as Agent 963192637. His principal role in the early years of the war was as an intermediary between the German embassy and Walter Scheele, an expatriate scientist with a U.S. chemical firm, the New Jersey Chemical Company, and one of Germany's most important moles in the American industry. Scheele provided secret information on British armaments orders to Schweitzer, worked with him on devising a method of disguising American oil so that it could be smuggled past the blockade, and even prepared incendiary devices that Schweitzer arranged to have planted on British merchant ships anchored in New York Harbor.

lowing year. Even when a mortified Thomas Edison announced that from then on he would sell his surplus only to the military, the damage was seen as minor. For all its indignation, the American government didn't ask Bayer to return the phenol (possibly because it was just as keen as the company to see aspirin supplies maintained), and it was fair to assume that by the time Bayer ran out again others in the American chemical industry would have risen to the challenge of producing it in bulk.

Nonetheless, the company had attracted Washington's attention in a most undesirable manner. The authorities were now bound to keep an eye on a foreign-owned business that had benefited from a conspiracy to corner the market in a chemical crucial to the country's military arsenal—particularly as relations between Germany and the United States continued to deteriorate. In early 1917, in an attempt to increase pressure on Britain and France and to gain some relief from the stranglehold of the enemy's blockade, the German high command ordered an all-out U-boat campaign in the Atlantic. Several Allied ships were sunk as a consequence, but so were some American vessels. Extraordinarily, Germany then became embroiled in a half-baked, and embarrassing, attempt to persuade Mexico to attack the United States. As the public mood in the United States soured, Bayer's panic-stricken New York–based executives realized that any day they might be considered enemy citizens running an enemy business. They began a frantic last-minute attempt to disguise the company's American assets and dealings in dummy corporations in the hope that these would appear to any outsiders to be owned by U.S. citizens.*

It was all too late. On April 6, 1917, the United States declared war on Germany. Shortly thereafter Congress passed the Trading with the Enemy Act and created a body to confiscate all enemy assets. The Office of the Alien Property Custodian, as it was called, was to be run by A. Mitchell Palmer, a former congressman from Pennsylvania. Dogmatic,

---

*One typical effort involved the discreet acquisition, through third-party nominees, of a small American dye company called Williams and Crowell. In a complex deal, Bayer's U.S. executives secretly assigned this business some patents, copyrights, and product lines on the understanding that these licenses would be returned to Bayer after the war. Another operation, the Synthetic Patents Company, was set up to operate in a similar way. Both were unmasked by the American authorities.

single-minded, and stridently anti-German, Palmer enlisted a former New York district attorney called Francis Garvan to lead an aggressive investigation arm, and together they went hunting. All told, German holdings and property in the United States were worth around $950 million, much of it hidden away in a deliberately confusing mass of shell companies and trusts. The two officials were determined to get their hands on the whole lot and made no secret of the fact that their first targets would be those businesses they believed had an explicitly anti-American pedigree. Bayer and Company, complicit in the Great Phenol Plot and besmirched by its association with the notorious Hugo Schweitzer, was right at the top of the list. In a move that carried more than a whiff of official retribution for past sins, Palmer announced he was seizing all the company's property, patents, and trademarks and replacing most of its German executives with Americans. Rensselaer, Bayer's lavish New York offices, and the company's best-selling product lines were gone. Back in Leverkusen the news was greeted with dismay. If Germany was to lose the war now, Bayer's property might never be returned.

THEY CALLED IT the "turnip winter," a bleak interlude when the Allied blockade really began to bite and when that hardy but uninteresting vegetable was one of the few foodstuffs in plentiful supply. But for many of the ordinary Germans who survived the long, cold winter months of 1916–17, it was also the start of a brief period of comparative optimism, a time when, for a while at least, the tide of war appeared to be flowing their way. The U-boat campaign, to take one example, seemed to be going especially well. In April 1917 alone, 852,000 tons of Allied shipping were sunk and coming on the back of similar losses in the preceding two months it was easy to believe the claims of government propagandists who said that the enemy was close to economic collapse. The news from the Western Front was reassuring, too. Strong new defenses, dubbed the Hindenburg Line in honor of the man who had organized them, had been built in time to repel the summer's Anglo-French assaults. The enemy had hurled hundreds of thousands of its troops against the concrete bunkers, barbed wire, and machine gun fire of the German defenses and had paid a dreadful price in dead and wounded. When rumors began to circulate that these extraordinary casualties had provoked large sections of the French army to mutiny, there were plenty on the German side who thought that a successful conclusion to all the nation's trials was only a few months away. Even the shocking announcement that America had declared war on Germany was counterbalanced by the encouraging news coming from the Eastern Front. In March 1917, czarist Russia had collapsed as a viable state and the desperate last-ditch summer offensive launched by the Provisional Government was so heavily defeated that Russia's troops were forced to retreat back across its borders. By the beginning of November, the Bolshevik Revolution had taken place, and a few weeks later the new Soviet authorities began suing for peace at Brest-Litovsk. Given that the Italian army had also suffered a shattering defeat that year, when German divisions under Ludendorff came to the assistance of their Austrian allies at Caporetto (a victory that for a while looked likely to knock Italy out of the war), there definitely seemed much to cheer about.

But amid all the good news there was plenty for the pessimists to point to as well. Yes, the British and Canadian armies had lost almost a quarter of a million men in a grotesquely wasteful effort to take the ruined Flanders village of Passchendaele, but Germany had lost almost 200,000 in the same encounter. Casualties of that magnitude might be sustainable for a time because the German divisions that had once faced Russia could now be shifted to the Western Front, but obviously once America's huge resources were fully deployed on the Allied side the added weight of the extra matériel and troops would tip the balance in the enemy's favor. Anyone who doubted the seriousness of the manpower crisis only had to take note of the German army's announcement in September 1917 that it was seeking fifteen-year-old volunteers to swell its ranks. In any case, cracks were appearing elsewhere, too. By the late autumn of 1917, the U-boat campaign, which had once promised so much, had begun to falter. There had simply been too few vessels and too few crews to press home the momentary advantage, and in the interim the British had managed to beef up their convoy system and reduce losses to an acceptable level. Meanwhile, the blockade on German trade continued, placing impossible strains on the country's ability to prosecute the war and feed its people.

For those running German industry, the strains had always been most evident in the manpower shortages they had to endure. Now these shortages were compounded by a growing sense of discontent among the labor force. War weariness and the never-ending lack of food and fuel were taking their toll, and, as Carl Duisberg had predicted, workers were beginning to demand better terms and conditions. In December 1916, the government had bowed to this pressure and introduced the Patriotic Auxiliary Service Law, which forced companies to recognize organized trade unions rather than the tame in-house workplace associations they had once been able to intimidate. For a time this had brought a degree of industrial harmony, but the atmosphere soon soured again as employees began to turn against the war. In August 1917 workers at BASF's new ammonia factory at Leuna went on strike as part of a national antiwar stoppage organized by the radical Independent Social Democratic Party. Similar walkouts took place at Bayer's Leverkusen facility and at the other IG plants. The police managed to keep an uneasy calm but, even so, managers were forced to call upon the military authorities to threaten the workers with mass conscription in order to get them to go back to work. Of course, the unspoken fear at the back of every employer's mind was that Bolshevik revolutionary fervor would prove infectious and that the volatile truce between labor and capital that had sustained the war effort for the past three and a half years would collapse. But even if this didn't happen, *something* would have to give soon. The nation was exhausted and hungry; it had sacrificed too much.

In March 1918, General Ludendorff gambled everything on one last assault on the Somme. Sixty-two divisions attacked on a front of about fifty miles in an attempt to split the Allies and drive the British back to the Channel. At first the campaign appeared to be the most successful German offensive since 1914. By eschewing the customary preliminary artillery bombardment (by now a wearisomely familiar warning that a battle was imminent) and by using the novel tactic of moving small groups of troops forward behind smoke screens and mustard gas, the German forces made remarkable progress, advancing forty miles in less than ten days, capturing over eighty thousand prisoners and a thousand guns, and even beginning to threaten Paris again. But attempts to capitalize on this success in the following weeks failed as the Germans encountered fierce resistance from French and American troops near the River Marne. Slowly but surely, as the Allies counterattacked repeatedly in the late spring and early summer of 1918, the last great German offensive began to peter out. By the middle of August, the high command realized that it was becoming futile to fight on. General Ludendorff even pleaded with Carl Duisberg to say as much to the kaiser. The deeply patriotic Bayer boss refused the request, but his demurral made little difference to the outcome. When the Allies launched their own offensive that autumn, Germany's exhausted armies collapsed, mutiny spread through the imperial navy, strikes broke out on the streets of Berlin, and the Social Democrats in the governing coalition persuaded the kaiser to abdicate. By the beginning of November the war was all but over. For Germany—and its remarkable chemical industry—things would never be quite the same.

4

THE BIRTH OF A COLOSSUS

On the afternoon of November 13, 1924, the leaders of the German chemical industry gathered at Carl Duisberg's palatial Leverkusen home to settle, once and for all, the question that had preoccupied them time and again: should their companies merge? The discussions began positively enough; those with strong reservations about an amalgamation seemed prepared to listen to those who felt passionately about a merger's potential benefits. But as the meeting ground on into the evening, the gap between the opposing factions had not been bridged. The mood turned quarrelsome, voices were raised, and tempers frayed.

At least the pleasant setting provided some respite. Guests needing a diversion or just a few moments on their own in which to calm down could walk outside onto the grand terrace and down some steps into elaborate formal gardens. Yet as they strolled around the grounds, perhaps puffing contemplatively on an after-dinner cigar, they would have found it difficult to let their thoughts stray too far from the matter in hand. The surroundings were against it, for one thing. The bucolic scene extended only as far as the gate at the end of the drive;

beyond it, poking up from behind some trees, a jarring array of factory chimneys dominated the skyline. A glance the other way, back toward their host's brilliantly lit house, would have brought an equally forceful reminder: there was something about its opulence that suggested grandiloquent projects. The place was massive, all verandas and domes and pillars, a monument to one man's drive, achievements, and ambition. Some might have thought it vulgar, others downright ugly, but few would have denied its *presence*.

Of course, nobody would have been given too much time to dwell on such things. Sooner or later, a messenger would have been sent out to round up the stragglers, to bring them back to the discussions in the bar or the billiard room, where the conflicting parties had set up camp and were arguing furiously about who had said what to whom and why. This was a council of the gods, after all, and even the most junior deities were expected to play their part.

The destiny of the mighty German chemical industry was to be decided at these talks. Six years after the calamitous end of World War I—years defined by the Versailles Treaty, political anarchy, hyperinflation, and aggressive international competition—the last tortuous steps toward full union were taken. IG Farben was about to be born.

GERMANY'S DEFEAT HAD been a near disaster for the chemical industry. Its absorption into the wartime economy had made it dangerously dependent on the armed forces for commissions, with a large proportion of its plants given over to the production of munitions and other strategically important materials. In 1917–18, for example, an astonishing 78 percent of BASF's sales had been to the military alone, and the other firms' level of exposure was nearly as bad. The armistice on November 11, had obviously brought all this work to a halt, and even though some of the industry's well-connected executives had been warned the end was coming (on November 4, 1918, BASF's supervisory board was told that the military was on the verge of total collapse and that Ludwigshafen faced occupation by enemy troops), they had only limited time to prepare for it. A few tons of chemical stocks and finished products that might possibly be confiscated were spirited away deeper into Germany, and hundreds of commercially sensitive plans and technical designs that might fall into enemy hands were destroyed or hidden. But the most important parts of the industry's infrastructure—its specialized equipment, laboratories, and buildings—were immovable, rooted to the banks of the Rhine and wide open to Allied retribution. A period of great confusion ensued.

The uncertainty wasn't helped by the fact that in the days immediately following the cease-fire a rumor went around that some of the industry's more nervous bosses had decided to make themselves scarce, called on urgent business to their country estates or to relatives farther to the east. One report, in the *New York Times*, even claimed that Bayer's Carl Duisberg, "generally looked upon as the connecting link between 'business' and General Ludendorff, and . . . one of the most active of the Pan Germans," had fled to Switzerland. The great patriot hadn't, of course. He was still at Leverkusen in early December when a company of New Zealand troops marched in, occupied the factory, and confined him and his family to a suite of rooms in the basement of his house. In truth, most of the industry's senior managers were equally steadfast. When French soldiers took over Ludwigshafen on December 6, several members of BASF's board came out to meet them, determined to protect their business from whatever vengeful measures their former enemies had in mind.

There was little the executives could do. Such stocks of transportable raw materials and finished products as remained were immediately impounded in lieu of future reparations, and hard on the heels of the troops came dozens of French military chemical specialists, charged with unearthing as much technical information as possible about manufacturing processes for explosives, gas weapons, nitrates, and dyestuffs. Other Allied missions followed suit and soon every major chemical plant along the banks of the Rhine was crawling with foreign experts—rifling through filing cabinets, harassing scientists and foremen with questions, and generally making a nuisance of themselves. On the surface, at least, the British and American investigators were more diplomatic than their Gallic counterparts and gave assurances that they were only after technologies with specifically military application, "in order to further disarmament." The French were less bothered about ruffling German feathers and made no secret of the fact that they were also looking for commercial intelligence that might be useful to their domestic chemical industry.

One of the things the Allies were naturally keen to understand was exactly how Germany had managed to produce sufficient quantities of nitrates to keep its munitions factories going. Clearly, part of the answer lay within BASF's Haber-Bosch plant at Oppau on the Rhine, but only the Germans knew how to work it. The French wanted the facility started up so they could see it in operation, but Bosch, who had been appointed to run BASF in early 1918, refused on the grounds that the processes involved were of purely commercial interest and that to reveal them would seriously compromise the company's viability. The French petitioned the joint Allied peace commission (responsible for overseeing the implementation of the armistice agreement) to order BASF to get Oppau going. To the French government's fury the commission sided with Bosch: nitrate synthesis might result in the production of materials that could be used for explosives, but the process itself had many other, more peaceful uses and so could justifiably be deemed a commercial secret.

While such isolated triumphs were undoubtedly good for morale, in the grand scheme of things they didn't do much to help the wider German chemical industry get back on its feet. The British blockade was still in effect to keep pressure on Germany in the forthcoming peace treaty negotiations, and shortages of food, coal, and important raw materials were making it impossible for factories to return to full capacity. With orders canceled, workers laid off, and many plants barely ticking over, it must have seemed that the situation couldn't get any worse.

Then it did. Germany, like almost everywhere else that winter, succumbed to disease. The great influenza pandemic of 1918–19 was one of the twentieth century's great tragedies—a plague of almost biblical proportions that swept across the world in just a few months and killed at least five times as many people (around fifty million) as had died during the preceding four years of armed slaughter. The death toll was astounding, especially among populations suffering from the other privations associated with wartime, and the pandemic made the postwar recovery of those societies that much harder. Germany was particularly badly hit, with over 400,000 recorded deaths and over a million sufferers forced to take to their beds. With so many workers and managers laid low by the *Blitzkatarrh*, it soon became impossible for industrialists to keep their businesses functioning.

Ironically, one of the few beneficiaries was Bayer's pharmaceutical division. There was no cure for the flu (scientists at the time didn't know that it was caused by a virus and had no hope of developing an effective vaccine), and so people turned to whatever palliative treatments they could find to mitigate its symptoms. Aspirin, Bayer's most successful invention, was barely two decades old but its ability to ease aches and pains and reduce fever was already widely known. With few effective alternatives it quickly became the medicine of choice for millions around the world. Although it was now available from other suppliers, there was such great demand for the drug over the winter of 1918–19 that Bayer's Leverkusen plant actually managed to double its production. And of course, the more that people used it and found it helpful the more customers Bayer lined up for the future. For a time, the rush on aspirin was a lonely shining beacon in an otherwise bleak landscape.

There were no such bright spots in the political situation. During the relatively bloodless prodemocracy coup of November 9–11, 1918, the majority Social Democrats in the German parliament successfully pressed for an armistice, forced the kaiser to abdicate, and declared their intention of forming a republic. The new chancellor, Friedrich Ebert, had won the reluctant support of the military hierarchy (on condition that he uphold the authority of the traditional officer corps and oppose the spread of Bolshevism) and managed to push through Germany's surrender. But then things became more difficult. That winter the country degenerated into sectarian class conflict and violence as political extremists took their ideological hostility to one another—and to the new government—into the streets. A Spartacist revolt in Berlin was suppressed only with the help of the Freikorps (a hastily assembled posse of demobilized servicemen, nihilistic counter-revolutionaries, and university students), while elsewhere soldier soviets and anarcho-syndicalists created havoc and threatened rebellion.

Ebert's hold on power was tenuous at best and though his interim government of Social Democrats was made up of pragmatic men who wanted to get on with the business of demobilization, restoring the economy and reaching a peace settlement with the Allies, there were plenty of others, on the left and the right, who persisted in the belief that more fundamental political change was necessary.

It was remarkable in this climate that anything could be achieved at all, but once the immediate threat of revolution had receded with the defeat of the Spartacists, the authorities found a brief opportunity to hold elections to the new National Assembly and then gather its delegates together in the Thuringian town of Weimar to draw up a republican constitution. On February 11, 1919, Ebert was elected president (with the power to dissolve parliament and issue emergency decrees) and a shaky center-left coalition of Social Democrats, the Catholic Center Party, and the liberal German Democratic Party quietly took up the reins of government. If, as some contemporary critics complained, this national regenesis lacked crowd-pleasing luster and ceremony, at least it seemed to offer some measure of stability in which the nation could begin preparing for the forthcoming peace negotiations. These were still febrile times, however, colored at one extreme by nationalism, anti-Bolshevism, and the rage of the disenfranchised elite of the old regime and at the other by support for Communism and fury that the revolution had failed to turn the country into a dictatorship of the proletariat. Thus, the new republic had to find its feet amid antiparliamentary subversion from the left and the right and a recurring stream of attempted paramilitary putsches. It was not the best atmosphere in which to build a democratic consensus or indeed to run a business—as the chemical industry soon found.

During one such attempted coup, the right-wing Kapp putsch of March 1920, the government was obliged to decamp to Dresden. Thousands of workers from chemical factories across Germany took part in the national strike that followed, forcing the putschists to back down but seriously disrupting production in the process. The episode put Carl Duisberg in an awkward position. His old friend General Ludendorff was one of the leaders of the revolt, and Duisberg, whose political sympathies were generally in tune with the coup's aims of restoring the monarchy and the old order, might have been expected to express his support, especially as he also distrusted organized labor and was usually forthright in condemning strikes, whenever they occurred. On this occasion, however, he kept his criticism of the unions to a minimum and directed his public statements of disapproval at the putschists. The plotters' impetuosity had unnerved him because it seemed destined to end in violence and chaos, whereas the strikers, for once, had acted in support of the status quo. Like most industrialists, Duisberg hated anarchy more than anything; social instability was bad for business and, when it loomed, even old friendships and personal political preferences had to take second place. Of course, Duisberg and his peers in the industry had no such qualms about condemning left-wing actions that were aimed at overturning the status quo. In March 1921 an attempted workers' uprising was staged by the VKPD (an alliance of Communists and the Independent Socialists), and BASF's Leuna works erupted into violence. During ten days of bloody clashes, two thousand workers armed with machine guns occupied and barricaded the factory until it was stormed by police with artillery support. Thirty workers and one policeman were killed and hundreds more were carted off to prison. Afterward, BASF's board ordered the dismissal of the whole factory workforce until they could be rehired with all the radical elements weeded out.

Against such a politically volatile background, it was never going to be easy for the Weimar government to negotiate a peace treaty with the Allies that was acceptable to everyone in Germany. In the event, the process proved to be exceptionally intractable, so difficult and controversial that it widened the country's political divisions still further. The unrealistically optimistic expectations shared by many Germans in the immediate aftermath of the armistice were undoubtedly a factor. Even quite level-headed people believed that achieving a fair settlement would be merely a matter of turning up at the peace talks. In their view, Germany had lost the war, but not by much. As evidence, they pointed out that, prior to November 11, 1918, not a single Allied soldier had crossed the country's borders and its territorial integrity was as intact as it had been in August 1914. Furthermore, in relative terms, Britain and France had suffered equally grievous human losses and the latter had sustained great structural damage as well, and to the east, Russia was arguably even worse off, its devastation magnified by violent revolution and civil war. Had it not been for the intervention of the United States on the Allies' side, the final chapter of the war's story might have been very different. As it was, with things so finely balanced between winners and losers, it didn't make sense to distinguish between them or to ask that Germany pay an unduly harsh price for its surrender. The kaiser was gone, his aristocratic clique of generals was consigned to history, and surely things should just be allowed to return to normal. After all, had not America's President Wilson made it plain that he was in favor of a fair peace for everyone?

This was wishful thinking to a remarkable degree. The idea that Britain, Belgium, and France—especially France, which had lost so much—were going to allow Germany to emerge from the war relatively unpunished was nonsensical. From the victors' perspective, Germany had been solely responsible for the conflict, its militarism, nationalism, and greed the cause of millions of deaths. Germany had invaded the sovereign territories of its peace-loving neighbors and, with the help of perfidious allies in Austria-Hungary, had sought to redraw the map of Europe to its advantage. Now the Germans were beaten and down and the only way to make sure they stayed that way was to keep kicking them until they stopped twitching. Germany had been a menace before the war; it was still a menace now. Before the nation could be trusted, it had to acknowledge its guilt and pay for its sins—and redemption was not going to be cheap.

THUS THE STAGE was prepared for the circus of Versailles. On the one side there were the victors, hoping to ensure fair play (the United States) or determined with varying degrees of vengefulness to extract as much penance from their former enemy as possible (Britain, France, and Belgium). On the other side were the principal losers, the Germans, singled out from their unhappy camp followers in the Austro-Hungarian and Ottoman Turk axis who had negotiated separate peace terms. (Bulgaria had surrendered on September 29, 1918, the Ottoman Turks on October 31, Austria on November 4.) The German delegation traveled west in uncertain spirits, the more optimistic among them believing that the Allies might help their nation through the civil chaos that was unfolding at home, the others speculating gloomily on the unpalatable demands they would be asked to swallow—but none of them were prepared for the exercise in humiliation that followed. For several days after the delegates' arrival at Versailles on April 29, 1919, they were simply ignored, separated from the main proceedings by wooden fences and barbed wire, officially to protect them from being attacked by irate French citizens but in reality to rub their noses in their lowly status. And there they waited, anxious, perturbed, and increasingly frustrated, for the Allies to deign to inform them of Germany's fate.

Carl Bosch was among them. The new German government had put together a peace delegation composed of politicians, lawyers, bureaucrats, and business leaders. It had first asked Duisberg to represent the critically important chemical industry, but he had declined, perhaps recognizing that the appearance of one of the old regime's most publicly stalwart supporters would be inflammatory. Bosch, reluctantly, stepped into the breach and joined the others on the train to Paris, hoping that he might be able to help secure the return of patents, trademarks, and factories impounded by the Allies over the last four years. This was no insignificant matter. The companies in the chemical industry's expedient wartime coalition—the Interessen Gemeinschaft—had all lost assets in these confiscations and desperately wanted them back. Bayer, for instance, had seen its American assets—offices, cash, production and distribution facilities, rights to dyestuffs, chemical and pharmaceutical goods, stockpiles of manufactured product, and trademarks and patents—all seized by A. Mitchell Palmer's Office of the Alien Property Custodian. This indignity had been compounded in December 1918 when the whole lot, including Bayer's state-of-the-art factory at Rensselaer, was auctioned off for $3.5 million to a firm of quack-remedy manufacturers. BASF, by comparison, hadn't done quite so badly in the United States—its prewar American importers, Kutroff and Pickhardt, had survived the conflict intact—but it had lost many important dye patents and assets in France. The other members of the IG—Weiler-ter-Meer, Kalle, Griesheim Elektron, Hoechst, and Agfa (especially the last two, which had to hand over significant assets in dyes, medicines, and photographic technology)—had all been hit as well. One of the reasons they had been persuaded to work together in 1916 was because they had seen that one day there might be strength in numbers. Now they looked to Bosch to exercise that strength—and recover their property.

He did his best to prepare for the task, marshaling his thoughts in a paper he circulated to his fellow delegates entitled "The German Chemical Industry and Its Desires during the Peace Negotiations." In it he mounted a persuasive argument, based on morality and international legal precedent, for the return of the confiscated property. If patents had been suspended, he said, they should now be reestablished and extended to make up for lost time.

Bosch and his colleagues back home would be bitterly disappointed. From the beginning of the delegation's second week at Versailles, when its members were presented with an agenda for the negotiations (an agenda they had had no part in drawing up), it was clear that German sensitivities were the last thing on Allied minds. There was no provision for any meetings between the parties, negotiations were to take place through an exchange of notes, and, in an ominous portent of what was to come, the Germans were given an eighty-thousand-word draft of the treaty document that demanded their country acknowledge its guilt, sacrifice territory and the larger part of its armed forces, and pay massive reparations. Not only was nothing said about returning seized assets, the Allies (driven by the French) also insisted that they wanted to see the closure and demolition of all establishments responsible "for the manufacture, preparation, storage or design of arms, munitions or any other war materials." This, they made plain, included all the German chemical plants that had produced nitrates or poison gases. As most of the factories of the Interessen Gemeinschaft had been involved in such work, the demand threatened the very foundations of their industry.

Appalled and humiliated but determined to try to make something of a stand, the Germans issued their counterproposals on May 29 with a plea that in future the talks take place face-to-face: "This peace is to be the greatest treaty in history. It is without precedent to carry on such vast negotiations by means of written notes." Two weeks later, their request completely ignored, they received a second draft of the Allied version, with only a few minor amendments inked into the margin and an order that it should be signed by June 28. Twenty-four hours before the deadline, after agonizing debate, the German parliament agreed to ratify everything except for clauses that acknowledged responsibility for the war and provided for the extradition of the kaiser and his former advisers. The Allies insisted the conditions be reinserted and threatened to renew hostilities if they weren't. On the final day, with only two hours to go before the deadline expired, Germany agreed to all the terms.

The headline provisions of the Versailles Treaty are well known. Germany lost about 13 percent of its territory, including Alsace-Lorraine and all its overseas colonies. Its army was reduced from its wartime height of around three million to a rump of a hundred thousand men, its officer corps was decimated, its navy's ships were to be scuttled and most of its heavy weapons confiscated. The Rhineland was to be temporarily occupied and permanently demilitarized and the industrially rich Saarland, a small region to the west of the Rhine, was to be placed under a French mandate with a promise that its people would eventually be able to decide whether they wanted it to become a permanent part of France. Perhaps worst of all, Germany would now have to meet massive reparations demands—far in excess of its capacity to pay.*

For the companies of the Interessen Gemeinschaft the most dreadful news was buried in the small print. The treaty required Germany to immediately surrender 50 percent of its stocks of dye, pharmaceutical, and other chemical products to its former enemies. Until January 1, 1925, the Allies would have the right to buy up to a quarter of the

---

*France tried to get these valued at 269 billion gold marks but, under pressure from the Americans and British, eventually agreed to 132 billion—about $30 billion.

industry's output of those products at prices well below market rates.*
None of the confiscated patents or assets would be returned and there
would be no retroactive compensation for their loss. Moreover, the
dreadful French-inspired demand that German chemical plants be
destroyed was still extant.

Carl Bosch had one last ace up his sleeve. After the main terms
had been signed he participated in supplementary negotiations at
Versailles to iron out the fine details of the settlement. One night, he
sneaked out of the German delegation's quarters and scaled a wall
for a secret meeting with Joseph Frossard, a civil servant in charge of
the German chemical industry's prewar factories in France, which
the French government had confiscated in 1914 and subsequently
consolidated into a state-owned corporation.† Bosch had a dramatic
proposal to make. If the French dropped their demand that the Interessen Gemeinschaft's major plants in Germany—Ludwigshafen, Oppau, Leverkusen, Hoechst, Leuna—be demolished, the IG companies
would share with them the technology behind the Haber-Bosch process. This would allow the French to begin making synthetic nitrates
for themselves. Frossard agreed to relay the offer to his masters.
Two days later Bosch was allowed out (this time through the front
gates) to attend more detailed talks with ministers in the center of
Paris. He spoke passionately about the essential role that the main
German nitrogen plants (especially BASF's facilities at Oppau and
Leuna) played in manufacturing fertilizer, crucial to the production
of food for Germany's desperately hungry population. If they were

---

*Although it seemed draconian at the time, this particular provision was something of a
double-edged sword in that it kept the IG companies' products in exactly those markets from
which their foreign competitors were trying to exclude them. Furthermore, the sudden availability of large quantities of cheap German chemicals depressed global prices and undermined
profitability. In 1921, realizing that their own industrial growth was being retarded, the Allies
were forced to modify their terms. The Germans were told to supply products to order instead.
This brought some stability back into the market but, as some chemical manufacturers in
Britain and France pointed out, it helped the IG companies recover, too.

†How Bosch arranged this meeting isn't known but he must surely have done it with the
connivance of the French authorities. Nevertheless, it caught his guards by surprise. The next
morning the head of the German delegation received a note from the commander of the French
army security detail at Versailles: "Last night in violation of law Professor Bosch left the German quarters surrounded by barbed wire and scaled the wall of the Versailles Park. After two
hours and five minutes he returned the same way." But it wasn't much of a rebuke and no further action was taken.

destroyed, the country faced famine. Saving them would be an act of humanity.

The French government was probably moved less by this plea than by the notion that it could get its hands on the strategically important technology that had allowed Germany to sustain the war for so long. But it agreed to the deal, on condition that BASF hold back no secrets, build new nitrate plants on French soil, and provide all the necessary training for the scientists who would run them. It even unbent sufficiently to accede to Bosch's request that Germans be given back a 50 percent share of the factories that France had confiscated in 1914.

It was a measure of Bosch's utter desperation that he even thought of striking such a bargain. Sharing profitable technology had always been abhorrent to his industry and he would never have considered it had he not been absolutely certain that the IG factories faced destruction. Oppau, his own particular glory, was of immeasurable value to him and he knew that his colleagues, particularly Duisberg, felt the same about their own prize facilities; the plants symbolized the very best of German science and technology and protecting them from harm was worth a high degree of sacrifice. However, securing the factories' immediate physical safety was one thing; securing the German chemical industry's long-term future was something else entirely. The draconian rules laid down by Versailles jeopardized everything he and his industry had worked for, and he wasn't looking forward to explaining the conditions to his colleagues back home. As he began the dismal return journey he probably sensed that his gleeful foreign competitors were already rubbing their hands over the plight of the Rhineland concerns. At last the Interessen Gemeinschaft companies seemed vulnerable, their previously invincible status as masters of the industry in peril. Perhaps now their long domination could be overturned.

In those bleak days after Versailles, Bosch's peers were very worried about this threat. While they'd accepted that some postwar bitterness was inevitable, they had hoped that it would be short-lived and that after a brief hiatus for the peace negotiations they'd be able to pick up their profitable export businesses just where they had left them in 1914. Instead, they now faced a torrent of aggressive new competitors, many of them equipped with confiscated German products and patents and protected by a new range of tariffs that were expressly designed to keep the Germans out—by making their goods more costly than those manufactured by domestic producers (by 1920, for example, tariffs in Belgium had made some imported German dyes 15 percent more expensive than equivalent goods made locally). Getting back into those markets and recovering some of their assets would take ingenuity, patience, money, monotonous and expensive legal proceedings, lobbying, and ceaseless negotiation. Even worse, as Bosch's example had shown, it would mean coming to terms with some of those foreign rivals, striking deals and forging partnerships—by sleight of hand, if necessary—which in turn would mean sharing profits, technology, and science. To men whose pride in their achievements was matched only by their disdain for the competence of their foreign counterparts, this was a deeply galling prospect. Nonetheless, it had to be faced.

CARL DUISBERG WAS one of the first to bite the bullet. Bayer had lost many of its most significant overseas assets, among them trademark rights to its crown jewel, aspirin, which was even then proving its worth as the key palliative treatment for influenza. In Britain, where the wartime authorities had declared open season on the drug, numerous suppliers were now beginning to make it and call it by the famous name that consumers were used to.* The situation was the same in France, Belgium, Italy, and Poland—even in those parts of Bolshevik Russia where an industrial economy still functioned. In short, Bayer had lost one of its most important prewar monopolies; where it still had access to European markets or could hope to force its way back in, it was now having to compete as just one among many.

Things were even worse in the United States. There, Bayer and Company was now the property of Sterling Products Inc., a patent medicine business run by one William E. Weiss, a carpetbagging

---

*After Bayer's exclusive trade name rights were revoked in Britain in February 1915, any UK manufacturer could call its acetylsalicylic acid aspirin and Bayer's USP (unique selling proposition) was gone. Consumers became less discerning and more open to advertising from competitors.

opportunist from Wheeling, West Virginia. Sterling was best known for Neuralgine, a quack analgesic marketed through newspaper advertisements of questionable veracity, but by paying $3.5 million to the Office of the Alien Property Custodian, Weiss had been able to get his hands on the U.S. rights to sixty-four best-selling Bayer drugs, including aspirin, Phenacetin, and Sulfonal, and at Rensselaer, New York, the sophisticated production plant to manufacture them.* He knew he'd hit upon something big and was determined to use all his patent medicine seller's panache to exploit it to the full. As he told his board, "The field has merely been scratched on the surface and there are tremendous possibilities ahead." Indeed, it wasn't long before he came round to the view that, having got hold of all these tremendous Bayer properties in America, Sterling should try to exploit them overseas as well.

Weiss had a major problem, however. He no more idea of how to run a state-of-the-art pharmaceutical plant than he had of how to speak a foreign language. Indeed, linguistic deficiencies were a significant part of his predicament, because the U.S. government, when it seized the property, had fired, deported, or interned most of its managers and overseers as enemy aliens. Reasonably enough, these men hadn't been disposed to leave a set of instructions behind them and the few technical blueprints and patents that did remain were written in German and couched, as usual, in the most arcane scientific terms. Much as Weiss wanted to swing into action, to mass-produce aspirin and the other drugs, he simply couldn't get more than a fraction of the vast modern Rensselaer plant going. There was still a large stockpile of completed product on-site, but it wouldn't last forever. Unless Sterling Products found a way to operate the factory, its $3.5 million purchase could turn out to be one of the worst bargains in history. Weiss would have to get some expert help—and the only logical source for that was at Bayer Leverkusen.

Help was very difficult to obtain. Although Weiss was able to call on the services of an intermediary, Ernst Möller (one of the few former Bayer and Company managers to hang on to a job with the firm

---

*Sterling also acquired Bayer's U.S. dyestuffs business but Weiss had no interest in it and quickly sold it.

after the war), their joint letters to Leverkusen asking for assistance were met with only the curtest acknowledgments. Exasperated, Möller wrote independently to Rudolf Mann, Bayer's pharmaceuticals chief, warning that if Sterling wasn't able to reach an agreement, then two companies with the same name and the same products might soon be competing in the same markets around the world. Surely, that was in no one's interest. Once again, only a brief, noncommittal reply came back. Eventually, fed up with waiting for a positive response to these approaches, Möller and Weiss decided to force the issue. They booked a passage to Europe and cabled Leverkusen to say they were on their way. The gambit worked: in late September 1919, at a small hotel in Baden-Baden, William Weiss and Carl Duisberg finally met.

It was not a happy meeting. Duisberg was a very angry man. A few weeks earlier the German chemical industry, under the terms of the Versailles Treaty, had been forced to surrender half its stock of drugs, dyes, and other chemicals to the Allies. Now this arriviste, this upstart, this *non*chemist had the temerity to come to Germany to ask for help. Duisberg was prepared to listen, but Weiss had to understand that Bayer wanted him to return all its property—but especially aspirin—forthwith. This, of course, Weiss refused to do. Wiry and dynamic and streetwise, his plainspoken manner in stark contrast to Duisberg's bombast, the American knew the value of what he had bought and he wasn't going to relinquish any of it on the say-so of an arrogant German technocrat. On the contrary, as the discussion continued, he saw how Duisberg's anguish over Bayer's lost U.S. assets could be turned to Sterling's advantage. Bayer was obviously desperate to regain a foothold in America and Weiss realized he could probably satisfy some of that desire by giving the Germans a share in the profits that Sterling Products was going to make from its ownership of Bayer's U.S. name and goods. However, the price for this could be set very high, certainly far higher than just the provision of some technical advice on how to run a factory. Weiss was convinced that if he handled the situation carefully he could extract from Bayer the rights to sell its drugs in many more parts of the world than just the United States.

Thus began three years of bitter transatlantic bargaining. Meeting followed meeting, sometimes making progress, at other times collapsing back into bad-tempered stalemate. On one such occasion, Sterling Products tried to bluff the Germans into a deal by threatening to export its U.S. Bayer medicines to Europe and Asia, putting them in head-on competition with the output of Bayer Leverkusen in those markets. Of course, with its Rensselaer plant barely operational, Sterling could not yet make enough Bayer drugs to service the American market, let alone produce any for overseas, but Weiss knew that the Germans would be worried that this situation might change. The threat provoked Duisberg into a tirade. He stood up, banged on the table, and shouted: "Everywhere in the whole world, except in the United States, people will know that we are the true Bayer. Laws can say what they want, but this situation contradicts global morality. They can't use our prestige for their advantage. . . . No money is good enough!"

It says a great deal about William Weiss's character and negotiating skills that he refused to be cowed by such outbursts, particularly as, privately, he was very impressed by Bayer's German operation. His first visit to Leverkusen, in April 1920, had been a revelation. Everywhere he looked, Weiss saw signs of his opponent's power and accomplishments. The factory was enormous—ten times the size of the plant at Rensselaer—and even though it wasn't yet back up to full production it still bustled with all the energy of a small city. Huge barges came and went from Bayer's riverside wharves, and steam engines shunted between vast sheds and laboratories where dyes and medicines were made and tested, while thousands of workers and scientists and technicians moved purposively about, engaged in tasks that Weiss could only guess at. Even the company's library was on a jaw-dropping scale, housing tens of thousands of books, journals, and papers on chemical procedures gathered from around the world. There was also Duisberg's own extraordinary house to take in, with its reflecting pools, manicured lawns, formal Japanese-style gardens, and battalion of servants and gardeners.* And if all that wasn't remarkable

---

*The great man even arranged for a Bayer flag to be raised outside the building when he was in residence.

enough, there was the Great Hall where the meetings between the two sides took place, a vast, echoing neoclassical structure with carved marble columns and two massive front doors with brass handles bearing the Bayer logo. New visitors sometimes likened the experience of walking through those doors to that of a slave being brought to ancient Rome for the first time. Here was the seat of power, the heart of the empire, where decisions were made and the *Untermenschen* did as they were told.

But Weiss was made of sterner stuff. Impressed though he was, he was a consummate salesman, well able to hide his feelings. In his view, Duisberg's anger merely underlined Bayer's impotence. The Germans could bluster all they liked, but to reestablish an American business they would have to make a deal with Sterling. Help with running Rensselaer was only a start. For that Weiss was prepared to relinquish some of Sterling's lesser holdings, perhaps by sharing rights on the Latin American aspirin trademarks that had been among the subsidiary acquisitions of his North American purchase. If Duisberg and Bayer wanted something more, they would have to offer more in return, to collaborate in other territories and in other fields.

Eventually, of course, they came to terms. In reality, neither side had much choice: Bayer's bosses couldn't envisage a future without a strong presence in the United States and Sterling's board knew its investments didn't have much of a future without Leverkusen's technical assistance. On April 9, 1923, they agreed to divide the world between them. Sterling (through a subsidiary called the Winthrop Chemical Company) would manufacture all of Bayer's products in North America and would get all the help it needed to put Rensselaer back into full production. It would have the exclusive rights to sell those products in the United States, Canada, Britain, Australia, and South Africa but 50 percent of the profits would be handed back to Leverkusen. Sterling could also continue to sell aspirin in Latin America, with Bayer getting the lion's share of a 75–25 profit split. In return Sterling would refrain from using the Bayer trademark on any of its own products (Weiss had successfully played on Duisberg's fear that Bayer's proud name might be used to legitimize some of Sterling's dodgier merchandise) and would stay out of Bayer's markets in the rest of the world.

Unquestionably, Weiss got the better of the deal. He had parlayed an initial outlay of $3.5 million into rights to sell some of the finest chemical and pharmaceutical products in some of the most profitable markets of the world, a spectacular return on a relatively modest investment. But there was some compensation for Leverkusen, too: an aggressive new competitor had been kept at bay and a foothold (albeit through a share in profits rather than ownership) had been reestablished in the United States. To Duisberg's great chagrin, however, he hadn't been able to get back the thing he'd most set his heart on, his company's American aspirin business. Weiss, resisting all attempts to pin him down, had managed to keep that particular cherry out of the pie, denying Leverkusen even the 50 percent profit share he had conceded on other products. The failure would haunt Duisberg for the rest of his life.

Of course, Sterling had been able to push the deal through only because it had something to offer the Germans. Other American companies found it harder to twist the IG companies' arms—particularly once the Allies had withdrawn their demand that key German installations be destroyed. The DuPont Corporation, for example, had bought up dozens of confiscated dyestuff patents from the alien property custodian in the belief that they contained the secrets of Germany's success. After spending a great deal of money in futile attempts to follow the specifications laid out in the patents, DuPont realized how devilishly complicated the whole process was—and how deliberately vague the Germans had been when drawing up technical documents for overseas publication. So, taking a leaf out of Weiss's book, the company's executives arranged a meeting with Carl Bosch—whom DuPont's executives thought would be more amenable than Duisberg—to see if he would facilitate a joint venture between the American firm and some of its German counterparts. Unsurprisingly, Bosch refused to help.

DuPont was forced to resort to subterfuge. One of its executives, a Dr. Kunze, was sent to Germany on a secret recruiting mission. He arrived in Cologne in October 1920 and quietly set about suborning Bayer's dyestuff scientists with the promise of lucrative contracts. Four of them took the bait: Max Engelmann, Joseph Flachslaender,

Heinrich Jordan, and Otto Runge, a descendant of the famous Fried-lieb Runge, the first scientist to isolate aniline from coal tar back in 1834. They signed deals that guaranteed each of them an annual salary of $25,000 for the next five years. This was an extraordinary sum at the time (about ten times what they were getting paid at Bayer) and perhaps helps explain why they were also persuaded to load up a crate with stolen blueprints, formulas, and other sensitive material. Thus equipped, Kunze and the four chemists took off for the Nether-lands. Dutch customs officials weren't in on the plan, however, and when they opened up the party's baggage and found the incriminating technical data they tipped off the police in Cologne. German prosecu-tors immediately issued an arrest warrant and asked that the four men be held in Holland on suspicion of industrial espionage, pending ex-tradition proceedings. Legal technicalities allowed two of the chemists, Flachslaender and Runge, to be released on bail and Kunze managed to get them out of the country and back to America. The other two were less fortunate: ignominiously deported back to Ger-many, they were kept under police surveillance while awaiting trial.

As might be imagined, the German press had a field day, accusing the men of treason and the United States of espionage, which in turn led the new Weimar government to refuse passports to all German sci-entists. But DuPont would not be denied. A few months later, with the active help of American army agents, Engelmann and Jordan were spirited out from under the noses of the German police and smuggled into the United States. By the middle of July 1921 all four chemists were hard at work in DuPont's Delaware laboratories.

The British watched all this with interest. The UK chemical indus-try was a little more advanced than America's at this stage (the coun-try had been at war with Germany for longer than the United States, and the UK government had invested more heavily in research for poi-son gases and other war materials), and its businesses were initially more successful in unraveling confiscated German technical data. But the BASF patents for synthetic nitrate foxed them completely. A firm called Brunner Mond and Company had bought the license to use them from the Board of Trade but, like DuPont, Brunner found the specifications impenetrable. So the British firm, too, went looking for

German expertise and eventually bribed two Alsatian engineers who had worked in the IG during the war to bring their know-how to the UK. Not every such effort was successful. An Italian attempt to smuggle two scientists formerly employed at Cassella into Switzerland in May 1919 was foiled when one of them fell ill and had to be taken to the hospital en route. The German police were notified and the men were "persuaded" to return home.

ON THE MORNING of September 21, 1921, the great fury aroused by the Germany chemical industry's involuntary brain drain was temporarily forgotten in the face of a much more immediate disaster—a massive explosion at BASF's plant at Oppau on the Rhine. The blast, which was felt and heard as far away as Munich and Paris, occurred in a silo used to store ammonium sulphate saltpeter. Over six hundred people were killed and another two thousand were injured, many seriously. The structural damage was immense. A crater, a hundred meters wide and twenty meters deep, was torn into the earth at the heart of the works and many of the factory buildings around it were irreparably damaged. The nearby village of Oppau was also largely destroyed, with over 80 percent of dwellings rendered uninhabitable and many bigger civic buildings, such as the school, church, and town hall, completely flattened. For miles in every direction windows had been smashed, doors blown in, and tiles ripped from roofs. One witness, over five miles from ground zero, described seeing a flock of geese blown clean out of the sky by the shock wave.

The explosion was devastating for BASF. Financially the losses were colossal; the cost of plant and equipment alone was estimated at nearly 600 million marks. There was also a strong chance that the company would have to cover an estimated 200 million marks' worth of structural damage to local communities. Then there was the matter of financial compensation for victims and their families, which was bound to be high. One of the advantages of belonging to a coalition of businesses now became abundantly clear. Almost a third of the plant and equipment costs would be covered by an insurance fund set up jointly by all the Interessen Gemeinschaft companies, and its constituent firms now agreed to raise additional funding by issuing an emergency rights offer of shares onto the German stock market. Although this extra cash could not cover all of BASF's liabilities, it helped the company through a very difficult patch.

Carl Bosch was enormously grateful for this assistance, but no amount of money could ease his personal anguish. Oppau had been his grand project, the place where he had made his reputation during the war, where the Haber-Bosch process had been perfected to provide the all-important nitrates for the German military, and where fertilizer was produced that helped feed the whole nation. He had only just managed to save the facility from destruction by the Allies. Now the explosion had shattered his achievements and left him facing the possibility that his famous process had in some way been responsible for one of the worst industrial accidents in history. On September 25, the day the funerals began, he gave a moving speech in Oppau and aired his private fears: "The very material that was destined to create nourishment and bring life to millions . . . has suddenly proven to be a savage foe, for reasons we do not yet know." He promised to do everything he could to establish the reasons for the blast, to provide assistance for the survivors, and to rebuild the works as soon as was humanly possible.

Inevitably, there were rumors: a clandestine store of German munitions had become unstable; the Allies, frustrated in their efforts to dismantle the German chemical industry, had sent in an undercover team to bring down one of its most famous landmarks; BASF had been secretly testing new and deadly weapons and the project had gone horribly wrong. An opinion piece in the *New York Times* was typical of the speculation: "When the fact is well known that there is an unrepentant and revengeful military party in Germany that looks to another war to restore her baleful power, and when the world believes that these dangerous reactionaries would welcome the discovery by their chemists of annihilating gases of enormous power, it is not inconceivable that the disaster at Oppau may have been due to covert experimenting by those chemists." One British newspaper, the *Daily Mirror*, even suggested fancifully that BASF's scientists had been trying to manufacture an atomic bomb.

Although the absolute cause was never fully established (it was impossible to be definitive because all the workers and technicians in the silo that day were killed in the explosion and nothing remained of the storage facility itself), the truth was almost certainly much more prosaic. BASF's own investigators concluded that the disaster was probably due to poor quantity-control procedures: apparently, incorrect concentrations of ammonium nitrate and ammonium sulphate had been brought together in the wrong place and at the wrong time (in the right combination the two ingredients produced a nonexplosive fertilizer). Exactly why this had happened no one knew but the company moved quickly to ensure that the movement and storage of potentially dangerous materials was monitored more effectively in the future. There was one bright spot, though. One of the few buildings still standing at Oppau was the main ammonia plant, proof that, whatever else was the cause, the Haber-Bosch process was not responsible.

As BASF's lawyers began haggling with the authorities and with victims over compensation, this latter news at least was very welcome. Carl Bosch breathed a deep sigh of relief and felt able to start thinking about the plant's reconstruction. Clearly it was a massive task and needed an energetic and bold executive in charge, not least because a huge construction workforce would somehow have to be pulled together from all over Germany. He chose Carl Krauch, one of the company's rising stars and the man who had been responsible for building BASF's second nitrate plant, at Leuna on the Saale River, in the last year of the war. Money was no object, Bosch told him. Although the explosion was going to cost the company dearly, without Oppau the firm's very future was in doubt. With foreign competitors already breathing down its neck, and a need to manufacture goods for use in reparations payments, the critical thing was to get the plant back into profitable production as quickly as possible.

Krauch rose to the challenge. He cajoled, bullied, and persuaded all the other Interessen Gemeinschaft companies (and several other German manufacturers) to suspend parts of their own operations and to lend workers to the project. Some of them were assigned to rebuilding parts of the town but most were dedicated to the factory itself. In an extraordinary demonstration of hard work, ingenuity, and cross-industry cooperation, ten thousand workers labored day and night to get the plant back on line. A mere three and a half months after it was blown apart, Oppau was back in business. Unfortunately, its reopening was almost immediately overshadowed by another national crisis.

AT THE END of the war, most of Europe was on the verge of bankruptcy. To meet the cost of their mushrooming military commitments, the combatant nations had been forced to raise huge loans, levy increasingly burdensome taxes, and print money. But all this extra cash in circulation had dramatically increased inflation—both of domestic prices and of national currencies. When peace returned, harsh measures were deemed necessary to restore long-term economic stability. One of the principal methods followed by the Allied governments was managed deflation, that is, taking money out of circulation, which theoretically at least was supposed to gradually reduce prices and restore the value of currencies.

But economics is an imprecise science, and achieving exactly the right effect proved an elusive goal. Instead of a slow and careful return to economic normality the world was plunged into a depression. Industrial output, no longer stimulated by military demands, fell dramatically in Britain, France, and the United States, with a consequent and dramatic rise in unemployment. Of course, prices fell, too, and things eventually corrected themselves as demand recovered, but during 1920–21 the economic contraction was very severe.

Germany, though, had followed another route. Its economy had been just as dreadfully battered as those of its enemies and, of course, it faced the additional burden of an impossibly large reparations bill. But the Weimar government, grappling with political anarchy on the streets, was unwilling to take any measures that would increase unemployment or otherwise jeopardize social peace. Rather than managed deflation, Weimar sought instead to stimulate the economy. In a desperate attempt to get German businesses back on their feet and generate enough revenue to meet the Allies' demands, it printed money, staggering amounts of it, that the central bank pushed out into the economy. In the short term, demand increased, productivity recovered, and unemployment fell, but inflation, fueled by all this extra cash, began to spiral upwards. By January 1922, the cost of living was twenty times what it had been in 1914. By that autumn it was out of control, a runaway train of hyperinflation that was saw prices rise to absurd levels month by month. Still the German central bank continued to pump out cash, until the mark lost any realistic value and the economy began to self-destruct.

Over Christmas 1922 Germany twice defaulted on reparations obligations, missing scheduled deliveries of telegraph poles and coal to France and Belgium. Previously, both countries had complained that Germany's currency depreciations were being deliberately engineered to minimize its obligations; now they decided enough was enough. In January, seventy thousand French and Belgian troops were sent across the border into the Ruhr, ostensibly to lay their hands on the missing commodities and protect some of their nationals but in reality to establish by force and occupation the full economic control they had sought and failed to gain at Versailles. The German government responded by suspending reparations entirely and ordering the Ruhr's inhabitants to engage in a campaign of passive resistance. The move enraged the French. Cutting the region off from the rest of Germany, they imprisoned or deported over forty thousand civil servants, police, railway men, and other local officials for supposed infractions of occupation regulations or for their refusal to cooperate. When things began to turn nastier, with low-level sabotage and minor acts of terrorism, the French retaliated with shootings, hostage taking, and massive fines.

The German chemical industry's plants on the banks of the Rhine, deep in the heart of the occupied territory, ceased operations during these months. One by one their managers stopped production, and the factories were seized by foreign troops in search of dyestuffs and fertilizers—much as they had been back in December 1918. In early May 1923, Carl Bosch found out from an informant that the French army was planning to enter BASF's Ludwigshafen and Oppau works. He just had time to oversee the dismantling of his Haber-Bosch equipment and its shipment to Leuna, in unoccupied Germany, before he and the rest of BASF's managing board fled to safety in Heidelberg. In August a French military court in Landau convicted them in absentia for impeding the delivery of reparations goods. Bosch and his finance director, Hermann Schmitz, were sentenced to eight years in prison and fined 150 million marks, but the longest sentence went to August von Knieriem, the company's chief legal counsel. He was given a ten-year term for signing the orders that forbade the company's workers from cooperating with the enemy. Of course, all these men were well out of the reach of the occupying authorities and had no intention of returning until the coast was clear, but in their absence it was difficult, if not impossible, to keep the factories going. Furthermore, one thing was now plain: Carl Bosch's personal concord with the French government was well and truly over.

The wider financial consequences of the occupation were catastrophic. As companies that had been manufacturing goods for reparations closed plants, laid off workers, and ceased trading, unemployment rose to 23 percent and tax revenues fell so low that they no longer covered even the costs of the national postal system. Meanwhile state expenditures were on the rise as the Weimar government was forced to import expensive coal from Britain and Poland and to pay dramatically higher social security benefits. To fill the hole in the government's coffers, even more money was printed—in increasingly absurd denominations—and inflation exploded into the stratosphere. By the summer of 1923, the mark was worth one five-hundred-billionth of its value in 1918, workers were famously using wheelbarrows to cart their daily wages to the bank, middle-class women were taking up prostitution in exchange for a bowl of soup, and householders were paying off their mortgages for less than the price of a bottle of aspirin.* That autumn, the first 1-trillion-mark note was issued, followed days later by the first 100-trillion-mark note. Money—or at least the official German version of it—had ceased to have any meaning.

---

*The courts had declared that in legal terms "a mark was a mark." If you had debts to pay this was terrific news, but anyone relying on a fixed income or a pension or savings was plunged into poverty. Suicide became increasingly common among the middle classes.

People got by either through bartering their possessions, their labor, or their bodies or, if they were very lucky, by getting hold of unofficial scrip—promissory notes issued by companies such as BASF and Hoechst and backed by foreign bank deposits and corporate bonds—that had gone into general circulation.

It couldn't continue. In late September 1923, the government (led by a new chancellor, Gustav Stresemann) abandoned passive resistance to the occupation of the Ruhr. Shortly thereafter, Hjalmar Schacht, the head of a new central bank, the Reichsbank, stopped printing the now worthless mark. It was replaced briefly by an interim currency, the rentenmark, and then in early 1924 by the reichsmark. Slowly, businesses began to recover, people went back to work, and the economy showed signs of settling down.

But it was an uneasy calm. Stresemann was a member of the liberal German People's Party, which had formed a "Grand Coalition" with the Social Democrats (SPD). His government, like the previous SPD–led administration, was forced to devote much of its time to addressing various paramilitary conspiracies aimed at undermining the new republic's fragile democracy. Threats from the left, such as the Communist-led siege of Hamburg's police stations in October 1923, were relatively easy to deal with because the government could generally call on the enthusiastic support of the army. But right-wing plots were more difficult to put down: the Reichswehr (the predecessor of the Wehrmacht) could not always be relied upon to forget its political predisposition for the old order.

In November, a loose consortium of these *volkisch* putschists, under the nominal leadership of General Ludendorff, planned another coup, a "March on Berlin" from Munich, in the hope of enlisting the support of Gustav von Kahr, an extremist Bavarian politician.* Kahr, already something of a local dictator and an advocate of regional secession, was willing to help but he wanted first to secure the backing of the Black Reichswehr, paramilitary groups set up with the connivance of the army to circumvent Allied restrictions on German mil-

---

*The title "March on Berlin" was inspired by Benito Mussolini's "March on Rome" in October 1922, which had led to the Fascist leader's appointment as prime minister of Italy.

itary strength. For the conspirators, Kahr's vacillation was too much and on November 8 one of Ludendorff's leading associates, a former army corporal, took matters into his own hands. His name was Adolf Hitler and his small political cadre, the National Socialist Party, would one day invest the comic opera events that followed with the status of grand mythology. Hitler hijacked a meeting that Kahr was addressing in the Bürgerbräukeller in Munich, bursting through the doors with a group of armed men in brown shirts and shouting that the national revolution had begun. Unfortunately for the conspirators, Kahr had decided against lending his support, and his allies in the army were even less inclined to get involved. The putsch collapsed the next day when a march of two thousand supporters, led by Hitler and Ludendorff, was met by a volley of gunfire from the Bavarian state police. Hitler, lightly wounded, slunk away and was later arrested and put on trial with Ludendorff.

As it happened, this feeble affair was the last coup attempt against the Weimar Republic. When the extreme right next reached for power it would use more sophisticated tools. In the meantime, Stresemann and his successors were finally free to concentrate on more mundane matters, such as wrestling with inflation and revitalizing the Germany economy. In 1924, a new agreement with the Allies, called the Dawes Plan, made the reparations burden more manageable, and newly elected governments in Britain and France began to adopt a less hostile tone. In November, the Franco-Belgian occupying force withdrew from the Ruhr. Stability, of a sort, was returning.

Germany's chemical industry was also beginning to regroup. The companies of the Interessen Gemeinschaft had been battered by blows that should have crippled them beyond recovery: a huge growth in foreign competition, the loss of vital patents and assets, the debacle at Versailles, the flu pandemic, the constant political uncertainty, the occupation, hyperinflation, the explosion at Oppau—the list was painfully long. Yet somehow the industry had managed to survive. Indeed, on balance, the industry's accounts for the period contained a surprising number of positive entries. Against all expectations the inclusion of dyestuffs and fertilizers in the Allies' list of reparations goods had actually helped created a secure export market for the IG's goods in tough trading years. The collapse in the value of the mark had paradoxically made many products cheaper and more attractive to foreign consumers, and in those nations where the IG companies had been able to reestablish their sales operations, a healthy increase in profits was the welcome result. Even the hyperinflation had had its upside, allowing the industry to repay for a pittance the massive wartime loans it had gotten from the government and banks for factory expansion.

But survival wasn't enough. Piecemeal deals with individual rivals, such as Bayer had concluded with Sterling, would not in the end hold other competitors at bay. Temporary benefits gained during currency depreciation would diminish as the mark was stabilized. Technology needed updating, new products had to be invented, and somehow new capital had to be found. Unless the IG companies came to grips with these issues and changed the way they organized their business, they would have to accept that the future belonged to others. If they were ever going to reassert their global dominance they would have to do something many of them had shied away from until now—come together in one all-powerful, financially secure group and meet the opposition head-on.

CARL DUISBERG HAD always been the most fervent supporter of full union. In 1904 and in 1916, he had tried to get his peers to accept the idea that salvation lay in togetherness but had had to settle for less ambitious agreements on purchasing, financing, insurance, and legal affairs instead. In truth, the wartime Interessen Gemeinschaft had never really developed into more than a loose federation of related businesses. It allowed their bosses to present a united front to the outside world when necessary and to help one another when confronted with extraordinary events such as the Oppau explosion, but it also left them free to act autonomously when their interests diverged. In the difficult months and years immediately after the war, the firms had frequently taken independent action as they sought to maintain their relative position in the industry and to avoid layoffs and factory closures. IG companies had even found themselves fiercely competing for orders again. But by 1924, faced with the bitter new reality, the industry's leaders were finally beginning to accept that autonomy was a costly luxury. It might have been expected, then, that Duisberg would have seized this moment to force through the full coalition he had always dreamt of. That year he became chairman of the IG General Council for the second time in his career and he certainly had all the necessary authority to bang heads together had he so wished.

But, strangely, Duisberg began to get cold feet. Now in his early sixties, he was becoming more cautious, and something made him balk at the prospect of totally subsuming his beloved Bayer into a larger organization. Possibly it was because he had seen too many grand designs come apart in the war or maybe he just disliked the idea of ceding control to younger men. Whatever his motives, he now decided that a full merger was no longer required. All that was needed, he declared, was a new central holding company to manage sales and investments—a slightly more powerful Interessen Gemeinschaft than had existed before.

Carl Bosch felt otherwise. Thirteen years younger than Duisberg, he had been running BASF for only four years and where the older man saw difficulties he saw opportunities. The tax system in Germany had just been made more favorable to amalgamation and he believed that a merger could significantly reduce costs. Though he had previously been reluctant to relinquish BASF's independence, he could see that there was now too much duplication of effort, too many unnecessary staff. Duisberg was correct in targeting sales as an area where efficiencies could be introduced (overseas, for example, the IG companies were represented by eight separate and competing sales agencies) but Bosch was certain much more could be achieved. He had visited the United States in late 1923 and, just as Duisberg had done twenty years earlier, returned with the conviction that a single unified corporation was the best foundation for success. The IG companies needed to recapitalize to finance a new range of products—in particular an extraordinary new project for developing synthetic fuel that he had up his sleeve. The best way to do so was by offering investors a chance to get in on the ground floor of something with momentum and critical mass, a single company that would dwarf its opponents and be able to dictate terms to the marketplace and the banks.

Thus, the two godfathers of the IG took up positions directly contrary to those they had held only a few years before, with the rest of the IG companies lining up behind them according to their bosses' individual prejudices and ambitions, the smaller firms in the antimerger camp, the larger ones—with the exception of Duisberg's Bayer—in favor of total fusion. The arguments began in early 1924 and continued throughout the year, culminating in a two-day conference in November at Duisberg's extraordinary house.

The location was deeply symbolic of all the grandiosity of the old days, of the age of commercial barons and their great aspirations. The industry owed its early success to the entrepreneurial talents and commercial ingenuity of the men who had started dyestuff companies along the banks of the Rhine in the nineteenth century. Some had fallen by the wayside, but those who had survived and those who followed on their heels had achieved much through their single-mindedness and determination. Now that individualism was being pressed to give way to corporatism. For men who had spent their lives in the comfortable embrace of small, sometimes family-dominated enterprises, the prospect of abandoning their identities and merging into one indivisible union was disconcerting, to say the least: they were anxious about gambling all their past achievements on one uncertain project. Those who had always been skeptical of the merits of a merger were now pleased, if a little confused, by the sudden appearance of Duisberg as an ally. Those who had supported the idea in the past couldn't understand why he had changed his mind, especially as the economic climate was much more conducive to a full union than it had ever been before.

From the outset it was obvious that the pro-merger camp had all the best arguments. Carl Bosch was a convincing and persuasive advocate, and he was supported by a clever group of rising BASF stars, including Carl Krauch, who had rebuilt Oppau, and Hermann Schmitz, the company's finance director. They were on hand with compelling statistics and diagrams to support their chief's case that a merger would produce significant cost savings, increase the industry's collective influence over pricing and supply, and make it easier to raise investment capital. Gradually Bosch began to win the waverers over, to the fury of Duisberg, who had always seen himself as the Interessen Gemeinschaft's natural leader. To be outargued and outmaneuvered in his own home was maddening. By the time Duisberg's guests sat down to dine on the evening of November 13, the discussion had degenerated into personal squabbles and name-calling. After the meal, Duisberg, with friends from the Kalle and Cassella companies, retired to the billiard room in a rage; Bosch and his supporters from Hoechst, Weiler-ter-Meer, Agfa, and Griesheim went off to shut themselves in a downstairs bar, and for the rest of the evening mediators ran up and down the stairs trying to get them all to see reason. The next day, in a hardly more positive vein, the discussions continued until it became clear that opposition to a merger had all but dissipated and only Bayer's boss was holding out. When a vote confirmed this near unanimity, Duisberg was devastated and resigned his chair in favor of his opponent. Just before he left that evening, Bosch took his host to one side, assured him of his everlasting respect, and tried his best to smooth things over by promising to appoint Duisberg's son Curt to an important job in the new IG. But that was scant compensation. Although Duisberg had no choice but to concede defeat, the rejection of his authority was a massive blow.

It would be over a year before the details of the deal agreed in principle at Leverkusen were completely hammered out. In early 1925 Carl Bosch fell ill and negotiations were stalled for a while. Then there was haggling over what the new organization was to be called. Bosch wanted to lose the IG designation because an *Interessen Gemeinschaft* (or community of interests) would not properly reflect the status of the new company. Duisberg felt that the commercial value of the IG name was too great for it to be abandoned entirely, and it was vital that it be included in the new identity. In this at least he got his way, winning the unanimous support of the other businesses' heads. They decided the new entity would be known as the IG Farbenindustrie Aktiengesellschaft, or, as everyone soon began calling it for short, IG Farben.

On December 2, 1925, representatives from BASF, Bayer, Hoechst, Agfa, Weiler-ter-Meer, and Griesheim signed the deal. The two smaller IG businesses, Kalle and Cassella, remained legally distinct but wholly owned subsidiaries of the new company. To assimilate the rest, BASF, as the previously largest single firm, increased its capitalization to equal that of the five other signatories, exchanged its stock for theirs, and legally assumed the new entity's name.* IG Farben headquarters would be at Frankfurt am Main. Thirty-nine directors of the various contracting firms joined BASF's existing board to form a new supervisory board, the *Aufsichtsrat,* and Carl Duisberg was elected its first chairman with a brief to look after broad policy. The actual day-to-day running of the company was entrusted to the *Vorstand,* a managing board led by Carl Bosch. For all intents and purposes he was now chief executive of the new enterprise and, insofar as anyone could be said to be in overall control of such a massive organization, his word carried the most weight.

And so IG Farben was born. Sixty years after the first German synthetic dye concerns opened for business, the bulk of the nation's chemical industry had at last resolved all their differences and joined together in a single corporate body. It was to become one of the mightiest companies in the world.

---

*In a narrow technical sense, BASF took over the other companies, but this was just legal mechanics, the most efficient way under German law of bringing the firms together.

5

BOSCH'S PLAN

Although a quiet and unassuming man, Carl Bosch was not someone to shy away from obstacles. He had made his reputation by finding an engineering solution to one of chemistry's most intractable problems—the mass production through hydrogenation of synthetic ammonia—and he had burnished it in wartime by helping his embattled nation find a way to make explosive-grade nitrates. Time and again throughout his career he had shown that he had the patience and determination to leap the highest hurdles. But now, at the age of fifty-two, he faced a truly monumental challenge: to devise an organizational structure that would turn IG Farben into something more than the sum of its parts.

There were plenty of positives to build on. The firms that had joined the combine all came from the same industry, made many of the same products, and shared many of the same customers. Their bosses had agreed to set aside old rivalries, to pool the science and technology they had once jealously guarded and work harmoniously toward economies of scale that would yield higher output at lower costs. All that mattered now, they declared, was the furtherance of the common good.

Yet it would take more than goodwill and grand declarations to make IG Farben successful. There were still considerable differences among the combine's constituent firms, which could not be swept away overnight. Each business had its own board of management whose members' egos needed to be massaged; each had its unique traditions and areas of specialist expertise. The companies used different procedures for bookkeeping, purchasing, paying taxes, and applying for patents and had separate agreements with trade unions about pay and conditions, all of which had to be brought into line with those of their partners. For plants and factories used to operating as semiautonomous entities, responsible for their own production and research processes, coordinating their work, or at least avoiding too much duplication, would require an unprecedented degree of planning. The firms had entered into the agreement as equals—notwithstanding the legal mechanics that had seen BASF acquire their stock—and time was needed to come to terms with the new reality of being just part of a greater whole.

That whole was vast, multifaceted, and already rapidly expanding. On the day the merger deal was concluded IG Farben was capitalized at RM 646 million. Just one year later the figure had grown to almost RM 1.2 billion as the German public, the banks, and international financial institutions rushed to invest in the new industrial giant. Within a few more years this mountain of capital was financing a program of acquisitions that saw the IG take stakes in chemical, steel, coal, and fuel firms such as Dynamit AG, Rheinische Stahlwerke AG, Köln-Rottweil AG, the Westfalische-Anhaltische Sprengstoff AG, and the Deutsche Gasolin group. By 1929 it employed over 120,000 people who worked in 106 different plants and mines, producing 100 percent of Germany's dyes, 85 percent of its nitrogen, 90 percent of its mineral acids, 41 percent of its pharmaceuticals, a third of its rayon, and nearly all its explosives. The IG's growing product range would eventually include a number of other inorganic and organic intermediate chemicals, glues and industrial adhesives, detergents, bleaches, insecticides and pesticides, fire-retardant materials, photographic supplies, artificial fibers, plastics, cellophane, synthetic rubber, and light and nonferrous metals. It had the second-largest brown coal holdings in the country and controlled around 15 percent of Germany's lignite supply and a substantial share of its briquette production. The combine's portfolio also included strategic investments in banking, high-pressure chemistry, and oil research and sales; minority interests in newspapers, shipping, and transport; and a slew of partnerships with, and holdings in, chemical businesses overseas.

Finding a management recipe to meld this disparate collection of ingredients was never going to be easy. Even the most basic issues of corporate governance were complicated by the necessity of keeping the various stakeholders happy. For the first four years of IG Farben's existence Bosch was content to go along with a blueprint suggested by Carl Duisberg. This approach followed the federal model of the old Interessen Gemeinschaft, with a few tweaks here and there to allow for a centralized sales operation and the allocation of specific markets and areas of production to individual factories or regional groups of factories. These "work groups," as they were called, were based on the old individual company identities and their geographical location. The Lower Rhine, Central Rhine, and Upper Rhine work groups thus corresponded to Bayer (Cologne/Leverkusen), Hoechst (Frankfurt am Main), and BASF (Ludwigshafen and Oppau).* But while Duisberg's plan recognized autonomy and individual responsibility—good principles in a business so dependent on innovation—it also established a pattern of informal, and at times uneasy, collegial leadership that dogged IG Farben's operations for some years to come. Without a clear chain of command (an issue that would never be properly resolved), decision making was sometimes painfully slow, mired in committee procedure and bureaucracy. The more impatient or more independently minded managers were occasionally moved to act on their own initiative, which threatened to undermine the coherence of the business as a whole.

By 1931, however, Bosch had begun to implement a new organizational structure (see diagram). His most important decision was to create three product divisions, or *Sparten*, into which all of the IG's

---

*There were exceptions. The Central Germany group, for example, included the factories of the Berlin-based business of Agfa but not the former BASF works at Leuna, which were still directed from Ludwigshafen and were therefore included in the Upper Rhine work group. Eventually, to complicate matters still further, Berlin became a work group in its own right.

main technical and commercial groupings were placed. *Sparte* I, chaired initially by Karl Krekeler and then by Bosch's protégé Carl Krauch, was responsible for everything to do with high-pressure hydrogenation chemistry, including the combine's synthetic nitrogen installations, coal mines, and oil interests. *Sparte* II, under Fritz ter Meer, was responsible for most of the company's traditional product range—its dyes, pharmaceuticals, solvents, and various other inorganic and organic chemicals. *Sparte* III, run by Fritz Gajewski, looked after the manufacture of explosives, photographic materials, and specialized paper products, artificial fibers, and cellophane—most of which were produced in Berlin and central Germany.

Given their disparate manufacturing priorities and markets, each *Sparte* had its own unique identity, as well as its own way of conducting business, coordinating policy, and setting goals. This work was usually conducted through dozens of project-specific subcommittees before it was passed to larger divisional management committees for assessment and review. In *Sparte* II, which had the widest and most complex product range and the biggest number of plants and feeder subsidiaries, this supervisory role was divided among three powerful bodies—the Chemicals Committee, the Dyes Committee, and the Pharmaceuticals Committee. In the other two *Sparten* the structure was more straightforward, with smaller coordinating committees to set production targets. All three *Sparten*, however, also had to coordinate their work with two companywide bodies—the Commercial Committee and the Technical Committee. Of these, the latter was the more important. Attended by the IG's most senior technical specialists and by engineers and managers of key plants, its meetings examined production plans, research and development initiatives, and requests for construction funds put forward by more than three dozen subcommittees. Two further organizational changes completed Bosch's shake-up. The first involved the creation of five separate sales and marketing groups, known as "combines"—for dyestuffs, chemicals, pharmaceuticals, photographics and fibers, and nitrogen and oil. The second saw the expansion of a complex of satellite departments (first established in 1927), which were known collectively as Berlin NW7 after their postal-code district in Germany's capital. These departments would handle press relations, market re-

I.G. FARBENINDUSTRIE A.G.

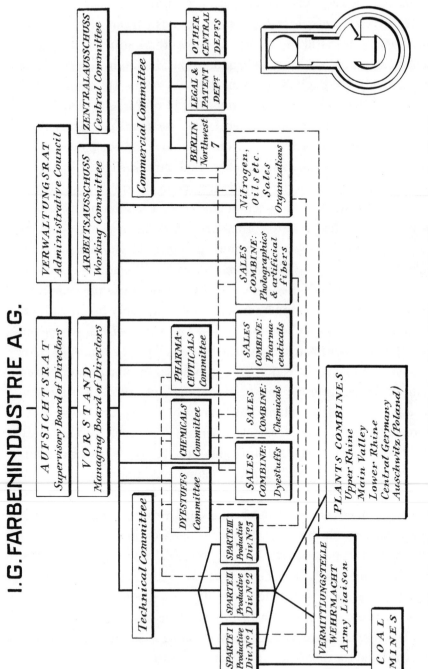

The administrative structure of IG Farben from 1933 to 1945. *(Illustration by Neil Gower)*

search, legal and tax matters, economic negotiations with foreign customers and partner firms, and contacts with the government.

IG Farben's *Aufsichtsrat* (supervisory board) and the *Vorstand* (managing board) still sat above this labyrinthine structure and were theoretically responsible for all final decisions. But both were overlarge and unwieldy. On the IG's creation, the *Aufsichtsrat* was composed of all the members of the supervisory boards of Farben's constituent firms, some fifty-five people, whereas the *Vorstand* had eighty-three full and deputy members drawn from the individual companies' managing boards. Though these numbers had shrunk slightly by 1931, Duisberg and Bosch, as the board's respective chairmen, struggled to find ways of making them function efficiently. The solution seemed to lie in confining their role to formalities and delegating much of their work to yet another layer of committees. Thus the *Aufsichtsrat*'s administrative council, the *Verwaltungsrat*, with only eleven members as opposed to its parent's fifty-plus, took over most of its duties, meeting about four times a year and leaving the full supervisory board with little more than honorary responsibilities. The *Vorstand* had to operate through two subordinate bodies. The first was the *Arbeitsausschuss*, or Working Committee. It had around two dozen members at any given moment, drawn from the *Sparte* bosses, the ranks of plant managers, the heads of the sales combines, a few lawyers and accountants, and occasional representatives from elsewhere in the business. This body quickly came to be regarded throughout the IG as the principal management group, responsible for formulating and implementing general policy and making decisions on such matters as acquisitions, relationships with other cartels, plant openings and closures, political contributions, and so on. For Bosch, though, the Working Committee was still too clumsy and whenever he could he preferred to operate through an even smaller body, the *Zentralausschuss*, or Central Committee. Usually gathering a day before the Working Committee, its half a dozen members (including Carl Duisberg in an advisory role) worked with Bosch on advance tactics and formulating a common line on matters scheduled for discussion in the larger meeting.

This extraordinary plethora of boards, committees and subcommittees, commissions, and working groups had one very obvious drawback—the onerous workload they placed on the shoulders of the IG's most senior executives. Because operations at many of the larger plants and sales combines cut across neat divisional structures, managers' functions and responsibilities frequently overlapped and they often had to sit on several bodies as once.* Understandably unwilling to add to their burdens, managers were reluctant to interfere too much in one another's principal areas of business and jealously guarded their own fiefdoms. The unfortunate consequence was that unless they seriously blotted their copybooks, managers were largely unaccountable for their actions (certainly to the *Aufsichtsrat*, whose function was increasingly ceremonial) and often went unchallenged. Nor was there any meaningful outside scrutiny. The IG controlled all its own preference shares and therefore a clear majority of stockholder votes. No other individual investor or institutional shareholder had a big enough stake to demand changes, and annual general meetings were generally rubber-stamping affairs. For the most part, whenever the combine needed additional capital it usually either turned to the Deutsche Länderbank, in which it had a large stake, or raised cash through debenture and rights issues, sales revenue, and reserves. As a result, the IG was insulated from unwarranted external interference, a state of affairs that pleased its managers but did nothing to provide effective oversight of the company's dealings. In principle, Carl Bosch, as chairman of the *Vorstand*, could use his authority to intervene in or overturn the decisions of those below him. But the larger IG Farben grew, and the more complex its expanding network of divisions, committees, holdings, and subsidiaries became, the harder it was for one man, no matter how driven or scrupulous, to keep an eye on everything. With his own interests in the field of high-pressure chemistry occupying more and more of his attention, Bosch had no choice but to hope that his equally overburdened subordinates were doing their jobs properly.

So who were those men? Insofar as it's possible to generalize, the average IG Farben senior executive (as exemplified by members of the

---

*Many of the more senior executives also sat on the boards of other companies—either IG Farben subsidiaries or businesses with which the combine had close commercial relations.

Vorstand in the mid-1930s) was in his late forties or early fifties and was married with children. More likely than not, he came from western or southwestern Germany, had received a doctorate—usually in chemistry, though other sciences, mathematics, and engineering were represented, too—and had risen to his present position through one of the IG's constituent businesses. Usually Protestant and from a bourgeois background, he would have had all the conventional middle-class attributes and aspirations of the time; he was hardworking, law-abiding, respectable, community-minded, patriotic (around half the IG's senior executives had fought in World War I), and conservative in both politics and social outlook.

But this rather bland overview conceals a number of intriguing exceptions and powerful personalities, people such as Fritz Gajewski, the chief of *Sparte* III, who as one of eleven children born to a humble elementary schoolteacher had to scrimp and save and work part-time in a suburban drugstore to raise the money to get to the University of Leipzig. Or Hermann Schmitz, the IG's chief financial officer and one of Bosch's principal assistants in the concern's creation, who came from a very poor working-class family in Essen and had received only the most basic schooling. At his first job, as a lowly clerk in the Frankfurt offices of the Metallgesellschaft (a nonferrous metals business), Schmitz's extraordinary intelligence had quickly brought him to the attention of William Merton, the firm's owner, and within five years he had been put in charge of all the company's foreign operations. Commissioned into the army on the outbreak of war, he was badly wounded in the first few weeks of fighting. Rather than return directly to his old job, he accepted a post at Walter Rathenau's War Raw Materials Office and it was there that he met Carl Bosch. Their friendship began in the aftermath of the first Allied air attacks on Ludwigshafen and Oppau when Schmitz helped Bosch successfully lobby the government for subsidies for a new nitrate plant at Leuna, and it continued at Versailles, where Schmitz was one of two Metallgesellschaft representatives in the German delegation. When Bosch finally persuaded him to come over to BASF as its top financial officer in 1919, he kept his seat on the metal firm's board and thus cemented a close link between the two companies that would continue for many years.*

Baron Georg von Schnitzler, the IG's commercial chief (and chairman of its influential Dyes Committee), came from the other end of the social scale. He was related to the vom Raths (ennobled by Wilhelm II for their services to industry) and had married Lily von Mallinckdrodt, a noted society hostess. Cosmopolitan and urbane, habitually attired in English tweeds, he collected fine art and enjoyed fine wines and divided his time between his industrial responsibilities and his extensive private estates. As far removed from the median at one extreme as Hermann Schmitz and Fritz Gajewski were at the other, he was one of the *Vorstand*'s two aristocrats. The other (from less distinguished lineage) was August von Knieriem, the IG's clever legal counsel and patents expert, whose dueling scar and stiffly formal manners hinted at his Prussian background. When on the run from Ludwigshafen's French occupiers in 1923, he had taken up residence in the same Heidelberg hotel as Carl Bosch.

A number of the executives had a particular genius for scientific innovation or for motivating others, men such as the bullish and bespectacled Nobel Prize–winning Heinrich Hörlein, who had followed Arthur Eichengrün as chief of Bayer's pharmaceutical research laboratories and who went on to invent a whole new class of antiepilepsy drugs. Or Fritz ter Meer, the rather snooty scion of the Weiler-ter-Meer family business and head of the influential *Sparte* II, who was convinced that IG Farben's future lay in manufacturing synthetic rubber and spent his spare time hiking energetically through the Swiss Alps. And then there was Carl Krauch, who by force of sheer personality and will had overseen the reconstruction of Oppau in the aftermath of the devastating explosion a few years earlier. His reward was the chairmanship of *Sparte* I,

---

*Bosch and Richard Merton (William's son and successor as head of the Metallgesellschaft) also took up seats on each other's boards. Interestingly, this was the same Richard Merton who had so infuriated Carl Duisberg during the war by recommending that industrialists bear the burden of any price increases in procurement materials. On that occasion Merton's reward had been ejection from the War Ministry and a dangerous posting to the Western Front, rescinded only at the last minute. But that wouldn't be the last time he tangled with the establishment. With four Jewish grandparents, Merton's connections with IG Farben were destined to end in grim circumstances.

where he could use his privileged status as one of Bosch's key lieutenants to push through Farben's interests in high-pressure chemistry.

Even those among the IG's senior executives who were well connected via family had largely earned their places in the upper ranks through merit and determination. Wilhelm R. Mann, for example, had dyestuffs running through his veins. His father, Rudolf, had headed Bayer's pharmaceutical department and had been instrumental in arranging the first difficult meetings between Carl Duisberg and Sterling Products in the early twenties. Young Wilhelm had been just another company chemist at the time, quietly recovering from his experiences in the trenches of the Western Front while he learned the ropes, but on his father's retirement his profound grasp of the intricacies of the international drugs and medicines scene and a capacity for clever deal making had sent him shooting up the ladder. Now he was chairman of the IG's powerful Pharmaceuticals Committee and chief guardian of the combine's hugely profitable aspirin business.

There were plenty of others—scientists, engineers, production chiefs, sales specialists—each commanding a little bit of the IG Farben empire and all eager to flex their muscles in the new regime. Carl Bosch, thoughtful, academic, and prone to savage bouts of melancholic introspection, had the difficult task of fostering their often conflicting ambitions while, at the same time, maintaining the combine's coherence. In the early years, when the founding families of the constituent businesses still exercised a significant degree of influence (if not active management), that juggling act was relatively straightforward.* As time went by and the IG began to expand, the balance became harder and harder to maintain. "Decentralized centralism," as the company's organizational ideology was known, was fine so long as everyone remained focused on the IG's principal mission of maximizing efficiency and profits. Any deviation from that mission, and the empire threatened to fall apart.

Perhaps had Bosch devoted more of his time at the outset to resolving the IG's structural contradictions, to keeping a firmer hand on the management tiller, as it were, the company might have proved less

---

*The original *Aufsichtsrat* contained members of the Bayer, Meister, Bruning, Kalle, vom Rath, and von Weinberg families, who had all been owners or principal shareholders in the IG's constituent businesses.

vulnerable to some of these weaknesses later on. But throughout the venture's early years much of his attention was elsewhere—fixed on a venture so gargantuan in its implications and potential that the day-to-day running of the business must sometimes have seemed like a distraction. That project had been one of the principal reasons behind Bosch's desire to bring the concern into being and he was prepared to gamble everything on its success. The world was about to run out of one of its most important commodities, and if Bosch had his way IG Farben was going to provide the solution.

WHEN FUTURE HISTORIANS come to look back at the late twentieth and early twenty-first centuries the search for oil is sure to be seen as one of the defining political and economic motifs of our age. Many wars have been fought over it, calamitous consequences for the planet are expected because of our addiction to it, even more dire catastrophes are predicted for when we finally run out of it. After the air we breathe and the food and water we consume, oil has become the most important and sought-after commodity on the planet. Who controls its supply now and who will control it tomorrow are questions of the greatest strategic significance. But one thing is certain: the world's oil reserves are finite and irreplaceable. When they eventually dry up—and some believe we are already well past the point where this has started to happen—it is not too difficult to imagine some of the possible consequences: rationing, the shutting down of vital industries, and the gradual collapse of those economic infrastructures on which modern societies depend.

But remarkably we've faced this prospect before. Back in 1926 the world was told it was running out of oil. Of course, economic reliance on it then was nowhere near as absolute as it is now and people would have been better able to cope with its sudden disappearance, but the shock and the concern were profound nonetheless. The crisis was a consequence of society's growing love affair with the car. The automobile boom was just getting under way, yet already the internal combustion engine had begun to exert its terrible logic; there couldn't be more cars on the roads without the fuel to drive them and that fuel had to come from somewhere. Unfortunately, those resources were very limited. By the early 1920s governments had begun to get nervous about whether oil discoveries could keep pace with this accelerating demand and sought reassurances from the petroleum industry. The answers they received were alarmingly contradictory, so vague in fact that America's president Calvin Coolidge was forced to set up a special body, the Federal Oil Conservation Board, to determine the exact level of global oil reserves. Its report, delivered on September 6, 1926, sent jitters around the world. "Total present reserves in pumping and flowing wells . . . are estimated at about four and half billion barrels, which is theoretically but six years' supply." Sometime in 1932, the experts warned, the ground would yield its very last drops.

In these circumstances, anyone with a solution stood to gain a great deal, which was where IG Farben and its technically brilliant boss came in. Carl Bosch had a plan that promised to resolve the looming oil crisis and provide a much-needed alternative focus for one of the IG's core businesses. The scheme had grown out of his concern that Germany's domination of global synthetic nitrate production was coming to an end. Despite his efforts at Versailles and during the French occupation of the Ruhr, he had been unable to keep the Haber-Bosch process out of the hands of foreign competitors. Now the largest of those rivals, Britain's recently formed Imperial Chemical Industries and America's DuPont and Allied Chemicals, were beginning to make synthetic nitrogen in bulk, and it wouldn't be long before the world was awash with it.* Bosch knew that this glut could spell the end for the IG's plants at Leuna and Oppau, unless an alternate use for their expensive high-pressure equipment was found.

Bosch may have had his failings as a manager but no one could accuse him of shortsightedness where business opportunities were concerned. In the early 1920s he had realized that the world's dependence on oil was about to become critical and that German expertise in hydrogenation chemistry might provide the answer. Of all the leading industrialized nations, Germany was the most deficient in key natural resources. It had a few things in abundance—coal especially—but for

---

*IG Farben had tried to get these firms to agree to export quotas in an attempt to limit their access to the market, but the move failed when ICI and DuPont concluded a bilateral patent- and market-sharing agreement.

the most part the country had had to import raw materials from abroad or learn how to develop them synthetically. Oil was at the top of that list and naturally German chemists had long sought a way of making the fuel themselves. One of those scientists, Friedrich Bergius, had come up with a promising laboratory procedure and Carl Bosch was eager to exploit it industrially.

Like many of his contemporaries, Bergius was fascinated by coal, or, more precisely, by the possibility of obtaining synthetic fuel from it, using the high-pressure processes so much in vogue in Germany. In 1909, while on staff at Hanover University, he began by experimenting with artificial coal developed from cellulose and then, as his skills and experience grew, he went on to use the ordinary brown and bituminous varieties. It was a complicated procedure but in essence he was looking for a way of liquefying coal and increasing its hydrogen content under pressure so that its properties would be close to that of oil. He would certainly have been mindful of the fact that Germany was about to go to war and that the country was woefully short of this vital commodity. He was therefore especially pleased to be able to announce in 1913 that he had cracked the problem and was filing a patent for his invention. Two years later, he set up a plant in Rheinau, near Mannheim, to develop the process industrially.

Translating laboratory techniques into industrial-scale production proved much harder and more expensive than Bergius had envisaged. As the months went by and the project began to flag, his financial backers became restless and began drifting away. Then Germany captured oil fields in Romania, removing some of the immediate necessity for a synthetic product and draining his work of some of its urgency. Meanwhile, other scientists had begun making progress in the same area. In 1914 Franz Fischer and Hans Tropsch at the Kaiser Wilhelm Institute for Coal Research came up with a procedure that involved passing a mixture of carbon monoxide and hydrogen over a hot catalyst to produce liquid hydrocarbons. BASF scientists were on the same track and had even filed their own patent for a process around the same time as Bergius in 1913. All of these procedures, however, suffered from much the same problems—the difficulties of finding effective catalysts and of converting theoretical principles into viable, cost-effective factory production.

The break came only in 1923, when Matthias Pier, one of Carl Bosch's scientists at Oppau, devised a commercially viable process for synthesizing methanol from coal, relying on high-pressure hydrogenation equipment similar to that which BASF had used to make synthetic nitrates. A valuable chemical in its own right, methanol could also be used as a crude fuel for motor vehicles. But more important was that the process pointed to a way in which Friedrich Bergius's discovery could be made to work on an industrial scale. Bosch, vividly aware of the great potential of synthetic fuel technology, quickly acquired Bergius's patents and his company's assets for around RM 10 million.*

The IG, with its vast capital, technological expertise, and extensive holding in the coalfields of the Ruhr, was now well placed for getting into the oil game. Indeed, that prospect had been one of the principal reasons behind Bosch's determination to bring the combine into being in the first place. He knew that the project would require resources far beyond anything that BASF could command on its own and that only the IG's critical mass could provide the necessary economies of scale. Of course, anything involving such a massive degree of investment carried great risks and would demand enormous effort on the part of all the scientists and engineers involved. But if they were successful the payoff would be huge.

Bosch's gamble led to one of the IG's first commercial decisions: to invest hundreds of millions of marks in the assembly of a new plant at Leuna.† The aim was to eventually manufacture a hundred thousand tons of synthetic oil a year, which would sell for around twenty pfennigs per liter in Germany—a highly competitive price at a time when natural oil sold for between twenty-three and twenty-five pfennigs per liter, and one that could ensure IG's profitability for years to come. But that was only the beginning. Bosch also had ambitions of exploiting the process worldwide, of forging partnerships that would take

*The deal was finessed by Hermann Schmitz, Bosch's chief financial officer, and completed just prior to the IG's formation.

†The scale of the investment was staggering. Between 1925 and 1929 more than RM 250 million were poured into Leuna, mostly into the synthetic fuel program. To put this figure into perspective, it was three times as much as was given to Ludwigshafen during the same period and around four times more than was put into the Bayer plant at Leverkusen and the Hoechst plant in Frankfurt.

the combine's technology into new markets and help to reestablish its domination of the global chemical industry. As corporate initiatives go, the synthetic fuel program was about as big, bold, and ambitious as it was possible to be. The combine's very future was riding on it.

The gamble was not universally popular. Though Bosch had a great deal of authority as IG's new boss, he was still only primus inter pares; he had no automatic fiat to push things through without consultation and had to listen patiently to the grumbling of several senior colleagues about the potential risks. He mollified them by pointing to the American government's predictions about an impending oil crisis; even if the forecasts were only half right, he argued, the price of oil was going to shoot up and a synthetic alternative would eventually pay great dividends. But Bosch knew that not everyone at the IG was convinced.

There were potential external opponents to placate, too. From the start Bosch had realized that by embarking on a program of fuel production IG Farben ran the risk of coming into conflict with the traditional oil industry. Previously the oil barons and the chemists had been able to keep out of one another's way, their products, technology, and markets being separate and distinct. That was clearly going to change and Bosch knew that unless he came to some sort of accommodation with the oil industry—especially with one or more of the half dozen companies that controlled it—the combine was going to find itself in a competitive minefield. On the other hand, if a deal could be achieved—perhaps by selling some of those oil firms a license to use the IG's new fuel technology—the funds could help defray some of the heavy costs of Leuna. So in 1925, while his plan was still in its embryonic stages, Bosch had cautiously made contact with the largest of them, Standard Oil of New Jersey—or Esso, as it was more colloquially known—by sending a group of executives under Wilhelm Gaus, Oppau's production head, on a goodwill visit to Standard's refineries around New York. Gaus was under strict instructions to drop hints throughout the trip about the acquisition of the Bergius patents and the IG's plans to develop them. If Gaus could also find an opportunity to invite Standard's managers back to Germany on a reciprocal visit, then so much the better. Either way, he had to make sure the Americans took the bait.

Standard's bosses duly obliged. The company was very interested in any process that allowed it to better refine leftover heavy oils and tars into premium liquid fuel products, and it already knew from conducting its own research that hydrogenation and the Bergius process might offer a way. But it was the prospect of extracting crude oil equivalents from coal that really caught the Americans' attention. More aware than most of the looming shortfall in oil reserves, Standard had already begun searching for alternatives. In the early 1920s the company had bought several thousand acres of farmland in Colorado because it hoped to extract oil from the shale beds there if and when the technology became available. The news that IG Farben might have acquired this capacity was intriguing but also slightly alarming. If the world did run out of oil or if the IG truly was planning to make synthetic fuel at prices competitive with natural petroleum, then clearly Standard had to gain access to such technology before anyone else.

In March 1926 Frank A. Howard, who ran the Standard Oil Development Company, arrived in Ludwigshafen to see for himself what all the fuss was about. He was given a grand tour of the huge plant and its glistening laboratories, with his IG guides making absolutely sure he saw enough of the hydrogenation procedures to whet his appetite. As they had intended, Howard was staggered by the scale and ambition of all the research and development on display, especially the work being carried out on synthetic fuel—demonstrated to him on a small pilot installation because Leuna had yet to go on line. That evening, Howard sent a cable to his boss, Walter C. Teagle, the president of Standard Oil, describing his epiphany in suitably dramatic terms: "This matter is the most important which has ever faced the company. . . . [IG] can make high-grade motor fuel from lignite and other low quality coals in amounts up to half the weight of the coal. This means absolutely the independence of Europe in the matter of gasoline supply. Straight price competition is all that is left." A few days later Teagle, who had been visiting Paris, came rushing to Ludwigshafen. He went on the same tour as his subordinate and was just as stunned. The implications of the fuel technology were simply breathtaking. Unless Standard found a way to control, or at least to cooperate with, this new competitor, the commercial foundations of the global oil industry could be completely undermined.

Bosch had hooked his fish. Now he had to reel it in. The first moves, on both sides, were cautious. The Standard executives believed that the Germans were unlikely to sell their Bergius patents outright—or at least not for any price that the American oil company could afford—and suggested instead a limited partnership to bring the new fuel to market. Bosch provisionally accepted the offer, subject to negotiations on the level of Standard's investment, but realized that if he pushed the Americans too hard and too quickly he could still scare them off. He forced himself to be patient and put his energies instead into getting Leuna operational.

That work had gotten off to a promising start. There were some teething problems with the Bergius technology, to be sure—it was difficult to find the right catalysts and build the new high-pressure installations—and progress was slower and more expensive than the company wished. But in April 1927 the first Leuna gasoline went on sale. That year one ton of the fuel was produced. By the end of the following year, output had risen to twenty-eight thousand tons. By 1929 more than sixty-seven thousands tons of oil products would be coming out of the factory gates and the company would be well on its way to meeting its target level of a hundred thousand tons.

In the meanwhile, the negotiations between Standard and the IG waxed and waned. In an attempt to force the pace, Bosch went to the United States to meet Teagle and Howard but returned, in low spirits, without a conclusive agreement. Then in August 1927 there was a small breakthrough. In return for the American rights to use the Bergius process to improve the quality of its natural crude oil, and a 50 percent share in the profits from selling licenses to use this technology to other partners, Standard agreed to invest in a joint research and development program with the IG and to build a plant for this purpose in Louisiana.

The agreement still didn't quite satisfy either partner. By now Standard was convinced that the Bergius process was one of the most significant scientific developments in the history of the oil industry. When it had begun applying the IG hydrogenation technology to crude oil, it had come up with extraordinary results—more than doubling the amount of petroleum that could be refined from one barrel of crude. Standard naturally wanted to use the technology in all its refineries, not just those in the United States, but was prevented from doing so by the terms of the deal with the IG. When its executives considered what could potentially be done with coal—as abundant in America as it was in Germany—they salivated at the possible returns. They simply had to broaden the agreement.

Bosch, on the other hand, needed Standard's money—and lots of it. Despite the early successes, the new plant at Leuna was proving ruinously expensive, as continual breakdowns and technological failures pushed operating costs through the roof. Synthetic fuel was being produced and the IG's publicity machine was doing a fine job of convincing the outside world that all was going well, but the truth was markedly different. The fuel was costing far more to produce than anticipated and only by selling it at a massive discount could the IG could keep its price competitive with that of traditional gasoline. The losses were piling up—reaching RM 85 million by 1929—and the fuel was still nowhere near commercial viability. Every month the figures seemed to worsen and with every gloomy report the complaints of the skeptics on the combine's management committees grew harder to ignore. There were even muted suggestions that the project be abandoned before it began jeopardizing the IG's financial stability. Bosch realized that he would have to find a solution before his colleagues withdrew their support.

In November 1929, accompanied by Wilhelm Gaus, August von Knieriem, the IG's lawyer, and Hermann Schmitz, the combine's financial genius, Bosch returned to the States to make Standard an offer they couldn't refuse. Although he knew that his government would never let the IG completely surrender the German rights to a process that promised to secure the nation's future economic self-sufficiency, he could still sell Standard the rights to the rest of the world.

As he'd expected, the Americans leapt at the opportunity. In return for 2 percent of Standard's stock—546,000 shares with a cash value of around $35 million—Bosch gave up all the IG's rights to fuel hydrogenation technology outside Germany. The two giant businesses set up a joint firm, Standard-IG (80 percent owned by the Americans, 20 percent by the IG), to exploit the patents and know-how arising from any future research and development in the field. Howard Teagle would also join the board of the IG's new U.S. subsidiary, the American IG Chemical Company.*

Emboldened by the partnership, Bosch dangled another tempting carrot. Oil wasn't the only product that could be extracted from coal, he told Standard's bosses. It could also be turned into synthetic rubber, a product known as buna. So far it was proving too expensive to produce commercially compared with natural rubber, but these costs could be reduced significantly if buna was made from oil, which Standard obviously had in abundance. Given buna's potential as a raw material for motor tires *and* Standard's close links to the U.S. automobile industry, there was a clear synergy to be exploited. Would they be interested in cooperating on this project, too?

They were. A few months later Bosch sent Carl Krauch to the United States to close negotiations. Another new business was to be formed. Called Jasco (the Joint American Study Company), it would be owned jointly by the IG and Standard and would develop new processes in the oil-chemical field, especially any that led to the production of buna.

Bosch was pleased. Yes, he had handed over most of the global rights in the technology to the Americans but he had kept the right to make synthetic fuel in Germany, which, given his country's oil deficiency was bound to bring in enormous profits eventually. With $35 million worth of Standard stock now resting comfortably in the IG's accounts—and contracts with a powerful possible competitor safely signed—Bosch felt he could focus on the combine's other concerns.

And then the wheel turned yet again. Bosch had based his whole synthetic oil strategy—indeed the IG's very future—on the premise that oil

---

*In June 1928 Farben had begun reviewing its American holdings, which encompassed all the agreements between its constituent businesses and American partners—such as that between Bayer and Sterling—and had placed them into a Swiss holding company, IG Chemie, in Basel. The following April it set up the American IG Chemical Company, which then exchanged its shares against the Swiss IG's shares of the old American subsidiaries. These maneuvers were complicated but they had three big advantages: they helped insulate IG Farben against possible countermeasures and confiscation of its assets if Germany again defaulted on its reparations; they helped disguise the American IG's German parentage at a time when anti-German feeling was still strong in the United States; and they thus made it easier to raise money in the U.S. capital markets. In the years to come, American IG would raise around $30 million through bond issues, making Wall Street one of IG Farben's biggest lenders.

was going to be in short supply and that demand and prices would soar. But in late 1930, to the astonishment of all who had predicted an oil famine, massive new reserves were discovered in Texas. The finds came as the Great Depression began sending demand for automobiles (and the fuel that drove them) into rapid decline. When new oil reserves were found in the Middle East the following year, oil prices collapsed and the future for Leuna suddenly looked very bleak. In 1931, after almost RM 300 million of investment in Leuna, the cost price of synthetic oil stood at around forty-five pfennigs a liter. The world sale price for a liter of natural petroleum was around seven pfennigs. The differential made the IG's product impossibly uncompetitive. As the IG's losses began spiraling once again, its financial stability was badly shaken. Soon even some of Bosch's closest collaborators were openly calling for the closure of the fuel project. Unless he could find yet another solution, the IG's boss faced the stark prospect that the combine's synthetic fuel project—and his career with it—would end in ignominious failure.

The solution, when it came, lay far beyond the IG's clinically clean laboratories and comfortably appointed committee rooms. It was sometimes easy to forget from that vantage that there was a world outside—and that this world was changing. Germany was once more in political and economic turmoil. Its street corners had become battlegrounds, its beer cellars and meeting halls the setting for fierce demagogy, vicious bigotry, and angry brawls. The IG's leaders watched these developments with aloof distaste, only reluctantly getting involved when the turmoil threatened to spill over their factory walls and rational words were needed to calm things down. But the combine was too big, too powerful, and too central to the national interest to be allowed to remain on the sidelines for long. At a time of growing economic crisis, German self-sufficiency had become a key maxim in a revolutionary and violent new ideology. The IG's control over one of the secrets of that self-sufficiency, and its enormous financial exposure to the costs of developing it, had made it uniquely vulnerable to pressure and persuasion. Soon Bosch and his colleagues would be faced with a choice: to oppose the revolution that threatened to sweep over Germany and risk financial disaster or to join it—and so ensure IG Farben's survival.

6

STRIKING THE BARGAIN

For most of the middle years of the Weimar Republic, IG Farben's involvement in politics was largely a matter of tactical expediency. If the IG had a unifying corporate political philosophy (as distinct from the individual convictions of its senior executives), it was simply one of supporting whichever party believed in letting the combine get on with making money. With much of its revenue coming from exports, the IG was keen that the Germany authorities maintain good relations with the country's former enemies, while lobbying steadily and quietly for the revision of the most hateful parts of the Versailles Treaty. Domestically, the company wanted stable government that didn't interfere in its affairs, low taxes, low inflation, limits on the power of organized labor, and support for agriculture, the main consumer of its synthetic nitrate output. Farben's position was straightforward economic liberalism; anything else, be it excessive red tape or political extremism, was thought to be bad for business. The eventual restoration of German power was something to be hoped for, as it would strengthen the IG's long-term fortunes, but patience and diplomacy were the best way to bring it about. Even when there were disagreements between the firm's leaders (Carl Duisberg was notably more nationalistic than Bosch, for example), these usually had little bearing on their common approach to running the company.

To a degree, then, it made sense to try to advance the IG's corporate agenda by giving support to politicians and groups that were friendly to business. But in Weimar's fractured coalition politics it wasn't always easy to identify who these might be. The left, of course, was problematic: as the party of the workingman and the trade unions, the Social Democrats (Sozialdemokratische Partei Deutschlands, or SPD) would hardly be likely to advance policies that quashed the power of organized labor. Moreover, though pillars of the republic's democracy, they were also the architects of its tax-funded social and welfare system, which big business detested on principle. Farther to the left, the Communists (Kommunistische Partei Deutschlands, or KPD) were completely beyond the pale. Evidently bent on undermining Germany's political stability, importing Bolshevism, and destroying capitalism and private property, they were ideological anathema to everything the IG stood for.

The right had its problems too. In theory, Alfred Hugenberg and the conservative German National People's Party (Deutschnationale Volkspartei, or DVNP) might have qualified for support as they were undoubtedly probusiness and opposed to organized labor, but they were too doctrinaire and intemperate to be relied upon. In any case, Hugenberg's unfortunate habit of leveling accusations of treason against anyone who had been involved in the Versailles settlement didn't exactly endear him to Carl Bosch, one of the treaty's leading negotiators. The extreme right was even more objectionable. For most of the middle years of Weimar, the various small splinter parties of ex-monarchists, extreme nationalists, and beer hall xenophobes were simply too fanatical to be taken seriously. Even when the Nazis (Nationalsozialistische Deutsche Arbeiterpartei, or NSDAP) began to emerge out of this herd in the late 1920s—largely because of their better organization, their paramilitary violence, and the growing cult of personality around their leader, Adolf Hitler—their hate-filled anti-Semitism and contempt for democracy were still a long way from gaining mainstream respectability. In parliamentary terms they were scrabbling away on the margins, competing for a few Reichstag seats with better-supported fringe groups such as the Economy Party (Wirtschaftspartei).

This left the bourgeois parties of the center right and center. The most worthy of consideration was Gustav Stresemann's German People's Party (Deutsche Volkspartei, or DVP). In many ways Stresemann was IG Farben's model politician. Statesmanlike, moderately conservative, but liberal in his attitudes toward big business, he believed in working toward solutions gradually and in restoring German power through patient negotiation. He was also one of the concern's greatest supporters, at one time famously declaring, "Without IG and coal I can have no foreign policy." But unfortunately, though he served in ten coalition administrations (once, briefly, as chancellor in 1923 and thereafter through nine successive terms as foreign minister), his party was never able to command enough support to form a government on its own. Clearly, if the IG was to see its interests protected and advanced it would have to spread its largesse across some the Reichstag's other centrist groups—such as the liberal-minded Democratic Party (Deutsche Demokratische Partei, or DPP) and the Catholic-influenced German Center Party (Deutsche Zentrumspartei, or Zentrum)—and hope they could maintain a stable alliance.

Carl Duisberg had begun the process of political engagement back in the last days of the old Interessen Gemeinschaft, setting up an informal committee (carried over into the new concern in 1925) with responsibility for coordinating political donations and influencing the legislative agenda. Among its members—all drawn from the *Aufsichtsrat*—were several well-connected parliamentarians. Two of them, William Kalle and Paul Moldenhauer, belonged respectively to the left and right wings of Stresemann's DVP. Another member, Hermann Hummel, was a deputy for the Democratic Party from 1924 to 1930, while a fourth, Clemens Lammers, sat in the Reichstag for the Center Party. With Duisberg and Bosch at the helm, this group of IG executives handled the IG's political links from 1925 until 1932, dispensing quite large sums of money in the form of annual grants and donations,

such as RM 200,000 a year to the DVP and RM 70,000 to the Center
Party. Smaller, ad hoc sums were given to other groups and individuals as necessary.*

Party donations were not the only way to influence political opinion,
of course. The press came in for attention, too, albeit with mixed results.
In 1922, for example, the premerger Interessen Gemeinschaft invested
two million marks in the launch of *Die Zeit*, in the hope that the newspaper might provide an outlet for Stresemann's views, although little actually came of the venture because the politician severed his connections
to the publication within a couple of years. A much smaller grant, made
in 1925 to a highbrow economic and political periodical, the *Europäische Revue,* was more rewarding in the sense that some of the combine's
senior figures were subsequently invited to write essays for it on business subjects, but the journal's limited circulation meant that its impact
on national affairs was minor. More was expected of an investment
made in February 1929, however. As public opinion began to radicalize,
Carl Bosch spent RM 1.4 million of his discretionary funds to acquire a
35 percent share of the *Frankfurter Zeitung*, one of the country's leading liberal dailies. The paper was in financial difficulties and Bosch
hoped (wrongly, as it turned out) that keeping it going would help
strengthen public support for the probusiness programs of the democratic center and center-right parties. A few months later the IG also
bought three-quarters of the shares of the *Frankfurter Nachrichten*, a
paper closely associated with the DVP. This was followed by smaller investments in the Deutsche Allgemeine Zeitung, two syndication and
wire services, and the UFA movie studios.

The effectiveness of these activities is debatable. Had the IG's sole
aim been to shore up the moderately conservative elements of Germany's democratic system, then its efforts were clearly a failure. The
political donations were sizable enough and no doubt extremely welcome to the recipients, but in the end they did little to stop the erosion
of support for bourgeois parties or the drift of public opinion to ex-

---

*Most notably a grant in 1929 of RM 20,000 to a dissident faction of the Nationalists,
who split away from Alfred Hugenberg's DVNP to form the Conservative People's Party
in 1930.

tremes. The investments in newspapers, even the later ones, were of similarly questionable value because in reality the IG exercised little control over the papers' editorial policies. But, of course, the combine's engagement in politics wasn't purely altruistic. Its main purpose—during the relatively stable third quarter of the 1920s, at least—was to ensure that the IG's voice was heard along Berlin's corridors of power and that its interests were protected. On that score its activities were more fruitful because they bought influence, which reinforced the IG's behind-the-scenes lobbying of ministers and civil servants and cemented its leading role in pressure groups such as the Chemical Industry Association (Verein zur Wahrung der Interessesen der chemischen Industrie Deutschlands), chaired by Duisberg until 1924 and by Bosch from 1927 to 1933.

When business conditions began to deteriorate, however, the IG was forced to take political affairs more seriously. In 1928–29 an agricultural and industrial recession hit home and then the Wall Street crash triggered the most serious economic crisis in German history. For a business that was laboring to bring a hugely expensive synthetic fuel project into profitability, the Great Depression couldn't have happened at a worse time. How the government responded to the crisis was of the utmost importance.

GERMANY'S ECONOMIC RECOVERY after the great inflation of 1923 had been largely financed by foreign loans, especially from the world's biggest economy, the United States. Even though most of these loans were short-term, the flood of readily available cash had tempted many in German industry into borrowing huge sums to finance their expansion and mechanization. German banks got into the act, too, drawing on foreign credit to finance their own investments back home and relying on the growing economy to provide the necessary revenue to service the debt.

In 1928 the taps were turned off. In the face of a burgeoning recession, the major industrialized nations, led by the United States, began to impose strict monetary restrictions, cutting back on their foreign lending to protect their gold reserves—at that time the basis for financial stability and international currency values. Businesses around the world felt the effects, especially in countries like Germany that were dependent on a flow of external capital to keep their economies moving. As investment dried up, industrial production slowed, unemployment began to grow, and tax revenues shrank. The German administration found it increasingly difficult to raise money through selling bonds (the usual recourse for governments in financial difficulties), because of concerns about the return of inflation.

Then in October 1929, a bad situation suddenly became much worse. An outbreak of panic selling on the New York Stock Exchange turned into a flood: share prices began to plummet—more than $10 billion was wiped off the value of U.S. businesses on October 29 alone—which triggered yet more panic selling. American companies tumbled into insolvency, drawing the financial institutions that had invested in them down as well. As the banks' exposure to this domestic emergency grew, they began calling in their short-term foreign loans to bridge the gap. Germany, already suffering from a sharp reduction in incoming investment, now experienced a massive outflow of capital.

The effects were swift and devastating. Within months the country was in the grip of a deep depression. Businesses failed as owners and managers were unable to fund production. Unemployment rose to extraordinary levels, climbing to five million within a year and six million a year later. By 1932 one worker in three was out of a job, with around thirteen million people (if all their dependents are taken into account) thrown into desperate straits. Farmers lost their land as government subsidies were cut and the banks foreclosed on the loans that had kept the farms going; some half a million white-collar workers—clerks, technicians, civil servants—suddenly found themselves on the dole; even lawyers and doctors struggled to survive. Those who managed to hang on to their jobs had to accept savage cuts in their wages as employers reduced their hours to adjust to the collapse in demand. Government finances, already weak, buckled under the strain, as an unemployment benefit system that had been intended to provide temporary relief for three-quarters of a million claimants at any one time now had to cope with seven or eight times that number and for much longer periods than anyone had anticipated.

Day after day, month after month, the crisis deepened. Crowds of young men took to Germany's roads hunting for work. Others hung listlessly about town and city centers, hustling for spare cash from passersby, and it became commonplace to come across men with placards around their necks pleading for a job. The signs of economic catastrophe were everywhere to be seen—boarded-up shops and factories, ragged and malnourished children, soup kitchens, beggars, prostitution, and spiraling criminality. In many working-class urban areas there was an atmosphere of palpable menace and despair. German society seemed to many to be on the verge of collapse, its leaders apparently helpless and bereft of solutions. If any situation was likely to turn people toward the political extremes, this was it.

IG Farben, now far and away Germany's largest company, was theoretically better placed than most to cope with financial problems: it had large cash reserves and a substantial part of its income came from overseas. But no business could remain unaffected by an economic collapse on this scale, especially not one that had mortgaged much of its future to develop an expensive and highly speculative new technology. By the time the Depression, coupled with the discovery of new oil reserves, sent oil prices tumbling, the IG had already sunk hundreds of millions of marks into its synthetic fuel project. Its capacity to absorb these huge R & D costs was dependent to a large part on the profits it earned from its other products, most notably synthetic nitrogen, which as recently as 1926–27 had contributed over 40 percent of the concern's sales revenue. But by late 1928 the synthetic nitrogen market had begun to fall apart. Now prices fell as international demand for commodities slumped. With the enormous capital costs for the development of the IG's high-pressure facilities at Oppau and Leuna still on the books, the concern's vast new headquarters at Frankfurt still to be paid for, and a massive wage load for its 120,000-strong workforce to meet, something had to give.* In such circumstances, even the injection of cash the IG had received from the sale of synthetic fuel rights to Standard Oil was going to make little difference.

---

*The Frankfurt building, designed by the architect Hans Poelzig, was the largest company headquarters in the world on its completion in 1930.

As Carl Bosch and the IG's management team began casting around for ways to weather the crisis, their options seemed fairly limited. The company was rich in assets that might be sold but in such an economic climate there would obviously be few takers. Efforts could be made—and were made—to trim nonessential expenditures and managerial salaries, to cut R & D spending to the bone, and to make production more cost-effective. It was now that Bosch drew up plans for dividing the IG into separate production *Sparten*, to organize the concern more efficiently. But mass layoffs were unavoidable. Between 1929 and 1932 the concern shed 46 percent of its workforce—dwarfing the 33 percent fall in the German workforce as a whole. The social consequences of this move, which disproportionately affected blue-collar workers, were appalling. In Ludwigshafen and Oppau, employee numbers fell from over twenty-six thousand people in 1928 to around twelve thousand four years later—putting impoverished families on the breadline and sending the already battered local economy into freefall. The company attempted to mitigate some of the worst effects of the crisis by setting up workshops for the unemployed and dispensing free food and medical care, but, though well meant, this assistance made little difference to the dreadful situation many loyal former IG Farben employees now found themselves in. Not that those who kept their jobs were much better off: by December 1930, 85 percent of the remaining workforce saw their working hours, and therefore their wages, severely reduced.

The IG survived the Depression in better shape than most German companies; sales of dyes and pharmaceuticals had continued to generate some export revenue and had seen the business through the worst years. Still, its losses were considerable. By 1932, most, if not all, of the gains it made as a result of the merger had been wiped out. The IG had liquidated much of its cash reserve, sales had slumped to 85 percent of what they had been in 1926, and overall profits diminished by more than half (although in such circumstances it is remarkable that the company made any profits at all). Perhaps more importantly, however, the crisis refocused the IG's attention away from overseas sales toward its internal markets. The dye and pharmaceutical sales could not be relied on forever. Protectionism and tariffs were going to feature strongly in the post-Depression era, and then all exports, of whatever sort, would suffer. Carl Bosch was convinced that the IG would have to look to its domestic market to provide a much greater share of future revenue and that this would be forthcoming only if the concern was making something Germany could not afford to do without. Inevitably, therefore, his attention turned once again to synthetic fuel.

EVEN IN BETTER times, Bosch had only just managed to stave off the complaints of others in the firm who thought fuel hydrogenation a colossal waste of time and money. As the depression ate into the company's financial security these critics became harder to ignore, especially when Carl Duisberg took up their cause and declared his open hostility to the project. To him it seemed absurd that Bosch was still throwing resources at a scheme that now seemed unlikely to ever show a profit, especially when there was good money to be made from dyes and drugs. Surely, he protested, the money would be better spent on developing new products in these areas, which would have a better chance of success.

Quarrels between the IG's two leading figures were much less frequent than they might have been given the disparity in their temperaments, and it was a sign of how bad the situation had become that their difference of opinion now threatened to break out into a full-scale row. The dispute reached its height when Duisberg used his authority as chairman of the *Verwaltungsrat*, the administrative council of the *Aufsichtsrat*, to commission a report on the future of synthetic fuel. A group headed by Friedrich Jaehne, IG Farben's chief engineer, was asked to examine the prospects for the project and in February 1931 concluded that the only way to continue fuel hydrogenation at Leuna was with large government subventions. As most senior people in the combine immediately understood, this evaluation was tantamount to saying that the whole project should be abandoned, because it had always been an axiom of faith at the IG that public subsidies would unacceptably compromise the concern's independence. As Jaehne put it in his report, public funding would "necessarily lead to influence by the state. It would be better to close down the plant."

But Bosch, supported by his principal allies, Carl Krauch and

Hermann Schmitz, wasn't so easily outmaneuvered. After another fierce debate in the *Vorstand* he managed to get an alternative evaluation under way, this time led by his old friend Fritz ter Meer. As expected, ter Meer and his team loyally arrived at a different conclusion from that of Jaehne. To shut the project down would slice over RM 161 million from the company's asset sheet and throw many thousands more people out of work. It would also substantially increase the costs of making nitrogen (the engineering components of the various Haber-Bosch-Bergius manufacturing processes were so closely intertwined that closing one would seriously affect all the others), and it would deprive the IG of its best chance of generating income and jobs when better times returned.

The resulting stalemate was actually a short-term victory for Bosch because it meant that fuel production at Leuna limped on. It is hard, nevertheless, to understand what made him so stubborn about a venture that posed such a serious risk to the whole of the IG. Perhaps his mulishness grew out of the many battles he had fought and won at BASF over synthesizing indigo and fixing nitrogen, reinforcing his conviction that the fuel project was just another problem to be overcome with patience and hard work. He may also have drawn strength from the Nobel Prize for Chemistry that he received jointly with Friedrich Bergius in 1931, "in recognition of their contributions to the invention and development of chemical high-pressure methods."* Bosch was the first engineer to win the award and it made him, yet again, something of a national hero. But such extraordinary validation can do powerful things to a man's ego—even that of someone as unassuming as the IG boss—and it may have inspired him to hold his nerve. After all, the prize confirmed that the world's top scientists considered high-pressure chemistry and fuel synthesis to be of supreme importance. If they could see its value, why couldn't his colleagues?

Typically, Bosch pressed ahead. In May 1931, determined to find a way out of the deadlock, he decided to lobby the government for substantial tariff increases on natural petroleum imports. Either Bosch was

---

*Fritz Haber had been awarded the Nobel Prize in 1918 for discovering a method to synthesize ammonia. The 1931 prize acknowledged Bosch and Bergius's success in building on Haber's work to create new applications for high-pressure chemistry.

lucky or his political antennae were very finely tuned, because his timing couldn't have been better. The Grand Coalition—of Social Democrats (SPD), the People's Party, the Center Party, and the Democratic
Party—which had been in power since 1928, had collapsed in March
1930 after the SPD refused to continue serving in government with
conservative parties committed to reducing public spending by slashing
unemployment benefits. Chancellor Heinrich Brüning of the Center
Party led the new minority coalition administration that followed, in
which the small far-right Economy Party took up the place vacated by
the Social Democrats. Although it was undermined by internal rivalries
and was to become infamously authoritarian in its brief term, the new
government seemed full of promise. To Bosch and to Duisberg (who
rated Brüning as the best German leader since Bismarck), the new
chancellor seemed to have a grasp of the economic fundamentals that
had escaped his immediate predecessors. At the time of Bosch's approach, Brüning and his finance minister, Hermann Dietrich, were
preparing a series of radical deflationary measures, including big cuts
in government expenditure, to try to bring the economy back under
control. But it seemed they weren't averse to a bit of protectionism either. Heavily influenced by the IG boss's appeals, the Brüning cabinet
issued an emergency decree on June 5 that raised German customs duties on imported oil products by 70 percent and then, to Bosch's delight, went on to block imports of nitrogenous fertilizers as well.*

The financial relief offered by these measures was potentially very
significant. Increasing the cost of imported natural petroleum promised to make the IG's synthetic version far more attractive to German
consumers. The prohibition on imported nitrogen was even more beneficial because, without the competitive presence of the foreign product, domestic synthetic nitrogen prices could be substantially increased.
Over time, the additional revenue generated by these price rises might
be sufficient to help the IG finance its fuel project. The news was certainly enough to convince Duisberg and the other skeptical members

---

*The IG's enthusiasm for Brüning increased after this decision, and in October 1931 it lobbied for the inclusion of IG representatives in his cabinet. One, Hermann Warmbold, a member
of the *Vorstand*, was actually appointed as economics minister and served ineffectually during
the government's last six months in office, having resigned from the IG to take the position.

of the *Vorstand* that a fresh and hopefully definitive study on the future viability of Leuna should be carried out. Yet again it seemed that Bosch might be about to pull his beloved hydrogenation process back from the brink of disaster—provided, of course, that the report was to his advantage.

He entrusted the task to Wilhelm Gaus, from *Sparte* I, who had to find a way both to reconcile the competing interests of some of the most powerful figures in IG Farben and to come up with a series of recommendations acceptable to everyone. Presumably Bosch hoped that because Gaus had been involved in the synthetic fuel project in the past—most notably by helping to arrange the Standard Oil deal—he would enthusiastically endorse its continuation, just as Fritz ter Meer had done. But though Gaus admired and respected Bosch—most of the managers at IG Farben were fond of their boss, infuriating though he could be at times—and wanted desperately to make the sums work out in his favor, it quickly became clear to him that even with the government's protectionist measures the Leuna project was still going to make a huge hole in the company's finances. Like many of his colleagues, he could not shake off the feeling that it was somehow wrong to hang the company's well-being on trade embargos and tariffs. Internationally IG Farben had always been in favor of free trade and against trade barriers. Was it not hypocritical, then, for the concern to rely on them at home when it had always campaigned vigorously for their abolition abroad?

After much agonizing, Gaus felt he had no choice but to come down against the project, and in June 1932 he wrote to tell Bosch the bad news: "After a careful consideration of all the factors affecting the calculation of profits I do not see any reason at all to support the expansion of gasoline production. I have therefore decided to recommend the complete shutdown of gasoline production. Whether it should be resumed again in better times is a question to be decided later." Bosch was infuriated by the letter and responded by shuffling its unfortunate author off to less interesting work in *Sparte* II. In the short term, Gaus's report had little impact, because Bosch immediately produced a contrasting set of figures from the IG's accountants (calculations that he had probably kept up his sleeve for just such a time), which showed that it would actually cost more to shut Leuna than it would to keep the plant running at a loss.

But he knew he couldn't keep pulling rabbits out of the hat. The fuel project's balance sheet was becoming too dreadful to ignore and Bosch was in danger of losing the support of even his most faithful colleagues. There was only one option left. The time had come to act on the unthinkable proposal raised by Friedrich Jaehne over a year earlier, an idea that everyone had rejected many times over because of its implications for the concern's autonomy. IG Farben would have to swallow its pride and ask the government for subsidies. Unfortunately, with Germany in political turmoil, it was an inauspicious moment to go begging for favors.

THE DEPRESSION HAD fatally undermined the Weimar Republic. As successive governments failed to find solutions to Germany's economic plight, more and more people gravitated toward the political extremes. On the left the Communists were the principal beneficiaries. They welcomed the economic collapse because they saw it as the beginning of the end of the capitalist system. The new millions of proletarian jobless were ripe for recruitment to the cause, and in industrial areas such as the Ruhr and in the larger cities, the party had massively boosted its membership. Inevitably, the result was more ostentatious parades, violent demonstrations, rent strikes, and hunger marches, which all ratcheted up the fears of the propertied classes. When some of the poorer areas of Berlin were declared "red districts," to be defended at all costs against the despised bourgeoisie and their agents in the police, the threat of revolution suddenly seemed very real. But the increase in social tension was made a great deal worse by the fact that the Communists directed much of their venom and violent rhetoric toward the Social Democrats, whom they saw as compromisers and collaborationists. This antagonism was reciprocated, needless to say, because the SPD viewed the Communists as rabble-rousing agitators whose paramilitary Red Front Fighters' League was just a Soviet-inspired cover for anarchy, treason, and disorder. Rather than unite to present a common front against the extreme right, the two parties of the left sought constantly to undermine each other.

At the opposite end of the political spectrum, the Nazi Party had been gathering strength. The NSDAP had come a long way since the failed comic-opera putsch of 1923, for which Adolf Hitler was sentenced to five years in Landsberg Fortress. Paroled after a mere ten months of soft living and visits from well-wishers, Hitler had made good use of his imprisonment. Not only had he been able to dictate *Mein Kampf* to his chauffeur, Emil Maurice, and his ever-willing drudge Rudolf Hess, he had also had time to ponder the importance of bringing the disparate elements of ultranationalism together under his sole leadership and of gaining mass support. Over the subsequent five years he met the first of these aims, largely through his own speaking ability, the talents of his tireless administrator Gregor Strasser, and the propagandizing of his newest recruit, Joseph Goebbels, a failed novelist from southwest Germany. The party had created an elaborate and formidable organizational structure with numerous subdivisions and specialist groups (from the Hitler Youth to the National Socialist Factory Cell Organization) and of course it had recruited heavily into the ranks of its brown-shirted paramilitary wing, the Sturmabteilung, or SA, whose members fought, with increasing regularity and enthusiasm, their opposite numbers on the left. After Hitler had swatted away a small internal challenge to his authority in 1926, these factions had bonded together around unconditional loyalty to his cult of leadership and began to extend the reach of their power.

The Great Depression gave Hitler the opportunity he was looking for. The economic failings of successive Weimar administrations, allied to fears about a Communist uprising, alarmed the petit bourgeoisie particularly, and the Nazis were able to harvest their support. White-collar workers anxious about losing their jobs, farmers bankrupted by loans, civil servants, teachers, and small businessmen—all were increasingly attracted to a movement that seemed to project an image of youth, dynamism, and strong, decisive action. The Nazis became a catchall party for protest votes, transcending social boundaries to a degree never seen before in Germany. Hitler's solutions, propagated through speeches, slogans, and imagery, were vague and inchoate, but what mattered was they were expressions of opposition to the weakening republic. People read into his program whatever they wished, even writing off brownshirt hooliganism as a justifiably arduous response to the Marxist menace. The Nazis promised an end to vacillation and incompetence and a better, safer future. For now, for many people, that seemed to be enough.

This support began to pay extraordinary electoral dividends. In May 1928 the NSDAP had won only 2.6 percent of the vote and a derisory 12 seats in the Reichstag, but in the election of September 1930 the Nazi Party gained 107 seats and 18.3 percent of the votes. This breakthrough had transformed the political landscape and brought the Nazis into even starker opposition to the Communists, who had also increased their numbers of delegates. Parliamentary proceedings frequently degenerated into uproar as both sides shouted each other down, raised interminable points of order, and challenged one another to fistfights. Outside on the street, knuckle-dusters, truncheons, and belt buckles were more the norm.

With the Reichstag in periodic chaos and suspended more often than it was in session, Chancellor Heinrich Brüning ruled increasingly by emergency decree. But despite his efforts to assert control—with decrees that banned political uniforms and curbed the freedom of the press—his authority was waning. The economy was still failing and Brüning's harsh prescriptions for rescuing it weren't working. Measures such as cutting government expenditure, suppressing demand, and raising domestic interest rates may well have been popular with large firms like IG Farben because they reduced prices and made German exports more attractive overseas, but in the short term they only increased the suffering of the economically marginalized and gave more ammunition to the extremists. Even Brüning's patient negotiations toward ending reparations (he laid the groundwork for a deal to be agreed on at the Lausanne Conference of July 1932) went largely unheralded. The street violence went on, and with the police increasingly shaky in their allegiance to Weimar democracy (yet institutionally more prone to direct their attentions toward the disorder coming from the left rather than from the right), the situation was rapidly deteriorating. The chancellor's allies began deserting him.

Brüning's resignation on May 11, 1932, a mere two years after his taking office, marked the effective end of parliamentary democracy in Germany. His replacement as chancellor, Franz von Papen, was a member of the landed gentry and an old friend of Germany's octogenarian president, Field Marshal Paul von Hindenburg. He had previously sat in the Prussian parliament as a member for the Center Party but had fallen out with them and been drifting to the far right ever since. Now Papen was to preside over a cabinet of largely unknown aristocratic reactionaries who disdained party affiliations and were bent on erasing the last vestiges of the Weimar Republic. Believing that this could be achieved only with the support of the Nazi Party (which Papen's coterie believed could be manipulated and controlled), they quickly persuaded Hindenburg to dissolve the Reichstag and call fresh elections to give the suspension the cover of legitimacy. In the meantime Papen lifted Brüning's ban on paramilitary uniforms in an attempt to get Hitler on his side and deposed the minority SPD-run state government of Prussia on the grounds it was no longer able to maintain law and order. When the Social Democrats failed to call out their supporters to resist this obvious coup or even to mobilize their power base in the labor movement for a general strike (the unions had been emasculated by three years of unemployment and it had become plain that the SPD could expect no help from the Communists), both the conservatives and the Nazis realized that the way was now opening to some kind of authoritarian regime. The only question was what flavor of dictatorship it would be.

It would take nearly another year for the answer to emerge. But first came the election of July 1932, which was fought amid almost uncontrolled hysteria. The Communists portrayed it as the last dying twitch of capitalism before the revolution; the SPD urged its supporters to rise up and overcome the threat of fascism from right and left; the bourgeois parties appealed desperately for calm and stability. Hitler, meanwhile, was flying around the country in a specially hired airplane tantalizing massive crowds with his utopian message of national unity and the restoration of German power, while denouncing the betrayal and humiliations of the Weimar era in ever more frenzied terms. It was an election dominated by slick propaganda, torchlight parades, symbols and imagery, apocalyptic warnings, and racial hatred—fought amid escalating paramilitary violence and the disintegration of civil society. In the aftermath of his failed putsch in 1923, Hitler had told his subordinates, "Instead of working to achieve power by an armed coup, we will have to hold our noses and enter the Reichstag. Sooner or later we will have a majority, and after that—Germany." Now he was determined to deliver on that promise.

The results were almost—but not quite—what he had hoped for. It was true that the Nazis received a massive boost in parliamentary influence, more than doubling their vote from 6.3 million to 13.8 million and becoming the largest party in the Reichstag, with 230 seats. But still Hitler could not translate these gains into actual power. Immediately after the election he declared that he would enter an administration only as Reich chancellor. Anything else would involve being a junior partner in a coalition government led by others, something he refused to countenance. But President Hindenburg wasn't yet prepared to give way. Increasingly uneasy about the violence on the streets, he was reluctant to be seen as endorsing any sort of return to full parliamentary rule by appointing the leader of the largest party to the most senior role in government. The stalemate wouldn't be broken until the Reichstag met in September. Having failed to win a decisive majority on his own part, Papen hoped to get the parliament dissolved on the day it opened so he could carry on ruling by emergency decree. But instead the Nazis responded by cynically supporting a Communist-led motion of no confidence in Papen's leadership. Overwhelmingly defeated, the administration was compelled to seek a fresh mandate through another election.

As the weary parties geared up for the poll in November, Hitler climbed back on board his campaign plane. But this time his messianic appeal seemed to be fading. Enraged by Papen's refusal to accept immediate defeat in the previous election and by new decrees banning political and paramilitary demonstrations, Hitler launched a series of vitriolic attacks on the government that alarmed some of his more moderate followers. To make matters worse, Nazi propaganda methods that had once seemed fresh and interesting had long since been copied by the opposition and had lost their capacity to surprise—a problem exacerbated by the fact that the party's coffers had been all but drained by the July campaign and there was less money to spend on torchlight parades, posters, flags, and all the other paraphernalia that the Nazis held so dear. At a time when the Nazis needed to spend heavily to attract the attention of an increasingly disillusioned electorate, Hitler found himself giving speeches to half-empty meeting halls because there had been no cash available to advertise his appearances.

It is perhaps not surprising, then, that the Nazis did badly. Their share of the popular vote fell to 11.7 million and the party lost thirty-four of its Reichstag seats. They were still the largest party in the chamber but now they had fewer seats than the combined ranks of the SPD and the Communists. Indeed, the latter had actually done rather well, gaining another eleven Reichstag deputies, and were now only just behind the Social Democrats in number. For Franz von Papen, of course, the election was a complete humiliation; his government still faced an overwhelmingly hostile majority in a chaotic legislature. After trying and failing to persuade the Nazis and the Center Party to join him in a coalition, he toyed briefly with the idea of getting the army's backing for an outright coup, before accepting the inevitable and standing down.

Von Papen's replacement, Kurt von Schleicher, the minister of defense, fared little better. His administration lasted a mere seven weeks, collapsing after he revealed economic proposals that included nationalizing the steel industry and distributing bankrupt Junker estates to the peasantry. As a former adviser to President Hindenburg, he had kept these disturbingly socialist-style ideas to himself. When he brought them to light as chancellor, they were enough to sow seeds of uncertainty in his patron's mind. When Schleicher approached Hindenburg with a request for extraconstitutional powers to govern the country, he was refused and had no option but to resign.

Negotiations to choose his successor were already under way. The president and his circle had recognized that with every passing week in which street violence continued unabated Hitler's claim to some sort of government post had become stronger. The belief was still that the Nazis, crude and vulgar though they were, could be tamed, but only if they could be brought into the fold. Thus, unable to find any alternative way out of the political deadlock, Hindenburg and his advisers now made one of the more unfortunate decisions in history. On January 30, 1933, Adolf Hitler was finally sworn in as Reich chancellor.

THE BOSSES OF IG Farben had kept a watchful if somewhat disdainful eye on all these developments. Initially, they had been most worried by the growth of support for the Communist Party because of its implications for their holdings and its potential for causing industrial unrest. In 1929 the firm held elections to its works councils and for the first time the Communist-led Revolutionary Trade Union Opposition (Revolutionäre Gewerkschaftopposition, or RGO) put up candidates. Although the more moderate SPD-influenced unions won most of the seats, in some plants, to the *Vorstand*'s considerable alarm, the RGO won around 20 percent of the vote. Management-worker relations had never been perfect within the IG and there had been moments, especially during the company's earliest years, when anxieties over rationalization and job losses had made the atmosphere quite tense. These pressures had dissipated between 1925 and 1928 as the economy improved, not least because the company was able to grant wage increases well above the rate of inflation, which went a long way toward easing workers' concerns and kept strikes at bay. But the economic downturn of 1929, with its resulting redundancies and drastically reduced working hours, had brought radicalism back to the shop floor. The RGO vote was a clear sign to IG Farben's management that the dangerous politics of the outside world had entered the factory gates.

Up until this point, the Nazis had been seen as much less of a problem in the workplace than the Communists. There were far fewer of them, for one thing—the party didn't put forward any candidates for works councils until 1930, when they won less than 10 percent of the poll—and although their taste for political activism made them noticeable, it initially consisted of little more than putting up posters in prominent places to annoy their opponents. But from that autumn things began to get markedly more heated. Despite company policy that national politics should be left at home, fighting broke out between extreme left- and right-wing factions in one of the canteens at Leverkusen. Then, in June 1931, a group of Nazi workers at Oppau stole explosives from a company store. Their intention, it later tran-spired, was to make bombs and grenades that could be used against the Communists in the event of a civil war. One of the weapons went off prematurely and the police were able to identify and arrest the ringleaders, but the IG's managers took the episode as a clear warning that Nazi influence in the workplace was increasing.

What was commanding most of their attention, however, was the worryingly extreme rhetoric of the Nazi leader. As Hitler grew in po-litical strength, the supposedly dangerous influence of Jews at the top levels of the nation's leading industrial concerns became a regular theme in his speeches and in the party's propaganda. Although IG Farben was by no means the only business singled out, it was targeted because sev-eral of the members of the *Aufsichtsrat* were Jewish, among them Arthur von Weinberg, Kurt Oppenheim, Max Warburg, Alfred Mer-ton, Otto von Mendelssohn-Bartholdy, and Ernst von Simson. Their presence on the supervisory board, the Nazis claimed, was clear evi-dence that the concern was part of an international Jewish conspiracy of financiers intent on destroying Germany. Perversely enough, when these slurs were first made in 1927, they came from one of the firm's own employees. Robert Ley was a chemist working at the old Bayer plant in Leverkusen but in his spare time he was also a local Nazi gauleiter. During one of his speeches he launched a fierce denunciation of Max Warburg, whose family had banking and investment interests in the United States as well as in Germany. The IG board sacked Ley when he refused to apologize but the incident presaged what was to come. By the summer of 1931 the IG was being regularly traduced in the Nazi press for its "disgraceful" susceptibility to Jewish pressure.

The concern's senior executives were made deeply uneasy by these at-tacks and tried their best to defuse them. Duisberg thought a direct ap-peal to the Nazis might help, so he enlisted his press secretary, Heinrich Gattineau, to contact Karl Haushofer, one of Hitler's favorite intellectu-als and, as it happened, Gattineau's old university professor.* In June

---

*Haushofer had supervised Gattineau's doctoral thesis, "The Significance of the Urbaniza-tion of Australia in the Future of the White Race," and was known to be close to Rudolf Hess, Hitler's factotum.

1931, Gattineau wrote to Haushofer, explaining that the attacks on the IG were unfair because its leadership was actually composed of hardworking and patriotic German Christians who had only the country's best interests at heart. He added, "If you could talk sometime to Herr H. about our situation . . . I would be most grateful."

Whether Haushofer did so or not isn't clear, but the attacks diminished for a while. In an attempt to take advantage of the friendlier climate, Gattineau set up a tour of Leuna later that autumn for a group of Nazi economic specialists so they could see the concern's famous synthetic fuel project for themselves. The experts were impressed and before they left they assured Gattineau that the IG's work accorded completely with the goals of their movement. But the good relations didn't last very long. The combine was too big and juicy a target. By the summer of 1932, the Nazi press was complaining again, only this time its theme was that the concern's stranglehold on synthetic fuel, coupled with its internationalist tendencies, made a potentially vital technology dangerously vulnerable to foreign influences.

This was exactly what Bosch didn't want to hear. Just as he realized that the IG would have to approach the government for subsidies to keep Leuna going, the Nazis had substantially increased their presence in the Reichstag and were tightening their grip on the levers of power. Bosch *had* to find out what Hitler thought of the fuel project. He asked Gattineau to approach Haushofer and Rudolf Hess about arranging a meeting between Hitler and Heinrich Bütefisch, a young technical director at Leuna and—after Bosch himself—one of the IG's most knowledgeable hydrogenation specialists.

When Hitler arrived for the meeting in September 1932, both Gattineau and Bütefisch were immediately struck by how exhausted he looked and doubted whether they could hold his attention. They needn't have worried. Hitler seemed eager and interested and quickly told them why: "Today an economy without oil is inconceivable in a Germany that wishes to remain politically independent. Therefore German motor fuel must become a reality, even if this entails sacrifices. . . . It is urgently necessary that the hydrogenation of coal be continued." Germany's deficiency in raw materials during World War

I had been a decisive factor in its defeat, in Hitler's view. Self-sufficiency in oil was therefore vital to reverse the country's fortunes.

As the discussion progressed, Gattineau was astonished by the Nazi leader's apparent grasp of the scientific complexities. He recalled later that Hitler "surprised me again and again by his amazing understanding of technical matters." In truth, Gattineau was probably a little overawed by the situation and took Hitler's apparent ease with the jargon as evidence of knowledge that didn't exist.* Nonetheless the interest seemed to be genuine and although the two-hour conversation never got as far as specific commitments, the IG men went away impressed. Carl Bosch's feelings were more those of relief. After Bütefisch had told him what had happened, he said, "The man is more sensible than I thought."

Over the next few months, as the last acts in the Weimar drama were played out, there were no further official encounters between the two sides. The Nazis carried on complaining about the undue influence of Jews in key German industries but backed off from specific attacks on the IG; Bosch continued to fight a rearguard battle against those who were skeptical of his beloved fuel project. Support for the Nazis at the top levels of the cartel was limited to Wilhelm Mann, the head of the IG's pharmaceutical interests and the only director on the *Vorstand* to join the NSDAP. He had obtained his party card in February 1932 but allowed his membership to lapse later in the year. Until the political situation became clearer, no one else, it seemed, was prepared to make an open commitment to Germany's most popular party.

Then came Adolf Hitler's appointment as Reich chancellor and his prompt decision to hold fresh elections. The Nazi leader had not yet achieved the absolute authority he craved. In the Reichstag, he was short of a majority and had to rely on the support of the nationalist DNVP. In the cabinet, men from Hindenburg's circle of aristocratic reactionaries, including Franz von Papen, who had been appointed vice chancellor, continued to occupy key posts. With the DNVP's Alfred Hugenberg holding the Economics Ministry and the army's Gen-

---

*Hitler was fond of expatiating grandly on scientific matters but as Albert Speer, his architect, was to say many years later, he "depended on unreliable, incompetent informants to give him a Sunday-supplement account." He added bitingly that Hitler lacked "any real understanding" of fundamental scientific research.

eral Werner von Blomberg at the Defense Ministry, the Nazis were left with only one other major office of state, that of minister of the interior, which went to Wilhelm Frick.

Admittedly, the judicial powers of this latter post—augmented with those held by Hermann Göring as Reich minister without portfolio and acting Prussian minister of the interior—allowed the NSDAP considerable control over the forces of law and order, which could surely be used to the party's advantage, but it wasn't yet the out-and-out victory that Hitler had promised his supporters.*

The window of opportunity for securing that victory was closing. For the past three years the Nazis had been riding a wave of popular discontent fed largely by economic failure and fears of a Soviet-style uprising. But the Depression was bottoming out and much of the rest of the world was already on the way to recovery. With the end of reparations having been secured at Lausanne, it would not be long before better times returned to Germany, too. When that happened, widespread anxiety about a Marxist revolution would surely dissipate and protest voters who had once flocked to the Nazis would soon revert to more moderate habits. Hitler knew that the elections, called for March 5, 1933, could be his last chance of obtaining a mandate and consolidating his position.

And so, as the Nazis stepped up their marches and parades and began using their newly acquired police powers to suppress their opponents' political activities, Hitler's election apparatus geared up for one last surge. All that remained was to find someone willing to pay for it.

TWO AND A HALF weeks after Hitler's appointment, twenty-five of Germany's leading industrialists received a polite but pointedly worded telegram. It told them that they had been:

INVITED RESPECTFULLY TO A CONFERENCE IN THE
HOME OF THE PRESIDENT OF THE REICHSTAG,

---

*Göring also held the honorary position of president of the Reichstag, as representative of the largest party.

FREIDRICHEBÈRT STRASSE, ON MONDAY, FEBRUARY
20, 6 O'CLOCK AFTERNOON, DURING WHICH THE
REICH CHANCELLOR WILL EXPLAIN HIS POLICIES.
(SIGNED) PRESIDENT OF THE REICHSTAG GÖRING,
MINISTER OF THE REICH.

This wasn't the first time the Nazis had tried to engage the interest of
the business community, but until recently few bankers or industrialists had bothered to pay much attention. There had been some notable
exceptions, of course. Fritz Thyssen, the steel manufacturer, had been
an early supporter, as had Hjalmar Schacht, the banker who had overseen the stabilization of the mark back in 1924. Others were Friedrich
Flick, a coal mine owner and a director of the Dresdener Bank; Robert
Bosch, the electrical manufacturer (and Carl Bosch's uncle); Hugo
Stinnes, Otto Wolff, and Ernst Poensgen, all owners of Ruhr coal
mines and steel plants; the influential financiers Kurt von Schroeder
and Walter Funk; and Wilhelm Keppler, a minor industrialist. But
even the most passionate of these supporters had been hedging their
bets, flirting with other right-wing political groups and handing out
discreet donations here and there until they could feel which way the
wind was blowing. They were all committed nationalists, and pro-
foundly conservative ones at that, but they were also businessmen—
pragmatic, self-interested, and opportunistic—and not yet convinced
that the Nazis were capable of running the country or the economy.
Nevertheless, modest as they were, their donations had given the party
at least the tincture of respectability during times when others of their
class had seen only an ill-disciplined rabble and an outspoken Austrian
parvenu.

By 1932, however, the Nazi election machine required more money
than this small core group of benefactors could supply. It had also become clear the party needed more influential sympathizers in the
higher echelons of society if Hindenburg and his associates were ever
to take the NSDAP seriously. Walter Funk and Kurt von Schroeder
were thus charged with spreading the word among their fellow businessmen and arranging for Hitler to meet wealthy potential backers,
while Wilhelm Keppler was asked to gather together a circle of like-

minded individuals who could advise Hitler on how to win the support of the wider financial community.

The Nazis' hopes that this approach might pay dividends were given a small boost on January 27, 1932, when Fritz Thyssen invited over six hundred members of the Industrie Klub to a meeting at Düsseldorf's Park Hotel. To the astonishment of many present, who had not been warned what to expect, Hitler made a dramatic entrance with a bodyguard of brownshirts and then proceeded to give a two-and-a-half-hour address. Despite the theatrics it was one of his more platitudinous speeches. He denounced Bolshevism, as he always did, and told them of his belief in the merits of private property and hard work. But he said nothing at all about the Jews and gave little if any detail of how he actually planned to revive the economy. Such things were principally a matter of national unity, he said. Marxism was the main obstacle to economic recovery. The National Socialists were working hard to overcome that threat and once it had been dealt with better times would follow.

It would take more than vague generalities to impress such a knowledgeable audience. Although the meeting was hailed as a triumph by the party's propagandists and there was a small increase in donations from the business community in the weeks that followed—Siemens, the Dresdener Bank, and United Steel were among those companies who gave money around this time—the flow soon dried to a trickle again and then the party's accounts at the J. H. Stein bank in Cologne were as exhausted as they had been before. If the industrialists had been mildly reassured by the emollient nature of Hitler's address (his rare omission of anything anti-Semitic was presumably carefully calculated to avoid alienating a group of people that might have Jewish friends and business associates), they were still not ready to give their support to a man who thought that patriotism and ideological ardor were the only remedies to Germany's economic ills.

Just over a year later, however, the situation had changed entirely. Hitler was now chancellor—albeit with a very tenuous hold on power—and, like it or not, business leaders were going to have to live with that fact. When the most powerful among them received telegrammed invitations to a select gathering at the official residence of the new president of the Reichstag, they therefore felt compelled to attend.

The identities of many of those present that February evening have been lost to history (the event was meant to be confidential, after all, and later on there was little incentive for the attendees to own up to their presence), but the group was led by Gustav von Krupp, the head of the eponymous armaments concern that had been a central player in German military-economic circles since the Franco-Prussian War. As president of the Reichsverband der deutschen Industrie (RDI) and perhaps not yet fully attuned to the new realities, von Krupp had prepared a memorandum in advance of the meeting. In it he had set out some of his federation's concerns about the Nazi Party's fiscal program and the importance of keeping a "clear demarcation between the state and the economy." It was clear that he expected a two-way discussion and as he took his seat in the front row he was probably reassuring his neighbors about what was to come.

In the row immediately behind him sat four representatives from Europe's largest corporation, IG Farben. Although the identities of two of the quartet are still a mystery, we do know that the concern's two leading figures were not in attendance. That evening Carl Duisberg was at the IG plant at Leverkusen, near Cologne, preparing to flick the switch on the world's largest electrical sign—a 236-foot-diameter Bayer Aspirin logo strung with thousands of lightbulbs. It is not clear whether his absence was due entirely to his legendary love of flummery and symbols (of which the giant sign was a perfect expression) or because he simply thought it wise to keep his distance from the Führer, but his nonattendance was noteworthy. As a hugely influential figure in German industry, Duisberg would normally have been expected to play a key role in such a gathering. He also had a reputation as one of the IG's most ardent nationalists. As early as 1925 he had been telling the RDI that Germany needed "a strong man," something "always necessary for us Germans, as we have seen in the case of Bismarck"; a year later he publicly called for "leaders who can act without concern for the caprices of the masses." But though his instincts were undoubtedly authoritarian, they were always more Hindenburgian than Nazi and it is doubtful that such a patrician figure would ever have had much time for the Austrian upstart.

Carl Bosch was absent too. The IG boss had his obsessions but they tended to be scientific rather than political. Though he certainly would have been invited, it was more his style to avoid making personal political commitments unless absolutely necessary. In such matters his normal boldness gave way to caution. He left the grand statements to others and sat back to watch events unfold.

The two IG attendees whose identities are known were both members of the *Vorstand*. One, Gustav Stein, was a relatively minor director who was also head of the Gewerkschaft Auguste-Victoria, an IG subsidiary. The other, Baron Georg von Schnitzler, was a much more significant figure, the IG's commercial chief and head of its Dyes Committee. Although formally the leader of the concern's four-man party, he later claimed to have had only a watching brief. His role was to listen and observe and then report back to Bosch with a confidential account of what had transpired.

At the outset, Hitler made a point of shaking everyone's hand. This was one of his standard gambits in small gatherings because it allowed him to stare straight into the eyes of the person he was talking to—a disconcerting experience for those who hadn't met him before and a useful trick for influencing people. Then, speaking without notes, he addressed the assembled group for the next ninety minutes.

The first half of his speech was in keeping with most of his previous statements to business audiences. Again avoiding any mention of Jews, he restated his commitment to private property and his belief in the merits of enterprise. He touched on rearmament, Germany's right to self-determination, and the importance of a martial spirit in resolving economic questions. Other familiar themes followed: the threat of Marxism, the failures of democracy to combat it, and the Nazis' historic struggle to provide "salvation from the Communist menace." Then he hit his stride and spelled out the message that he wanted delivered loud and clear: only one chance remained to work within the system, one final election to restore national unity and power. Should it fail, he assured his listeners, "there will be no retreat. . . . There are only two possibilities, either to push back the opposition on constitutional grounds . . . or the struggle will be conducted with other weapons, which may demand greater sacrifices."

Hitler's meaning was plain: if the Nazis didn't win at the polls there would be all-out civil war. Leaving this stark ultimatum ringing in his audience's ears, he sat down.

After a moment's dazed silence, Gustav von Krupp rose to thank him, having clearly decided that the chances of dialogue were slim and that the proceedings should therefore be brought to an end. But before he could speak, Hermann Göring took to the floor. In order to fight the next election the NSDAP needed money, he told the audience, and they were going to have to provide it. It was only right that "business should carry the burden of this struggle, as befits its position." Then, in words heavy with sardonic consolation, he added, "The sacrifices asked for will be easier for industry to bear if it is realized that the election of March 5 will surely be the last one for the next ten years, probably even for the next hundred years."

As Hitler and Göring left the room to the whispering executives, the Nazi financier Hjalmar Schacht got to his feet and administered the final sting. "And now, gentlemen, pay up!" Three million reichsmarks were required and the sooner they were handed over the better. Most of those present reached for their checkbooks, but Georg von Schnitzler told Schacht that he lacked the authority to pledge an immediate contribution. He would have to speak to his colleagues first. Two days later he sat down with Carl Bosch to report on the meeting. The IG's boss heard him out in silence and then "shrugged his shoulders in reply." To Schnitzler it seemed that Bosch had already come to a decision.

On February 27 the IG deposited RM 400,000 in the Nazi Party's accounts, far and away the largest donation made by any firm. Interestingly, Bosch does not seem to have discussed the payment in advance with his colleagues (presumably because he couldn't see the point). It certainly did not come up at the next scheduled meeting of the company's Central Committee, the most appropriate forum for any retrospective debate; the minutes from March 2 show only that a general political discussion took place. Bosch's feelings can therefore only be guessed at. He was presented with a clear choice—back a promised return to stability and a climate in which business could carry on or face a devastating civil war. Hitler's threat was blackmail, but there didn't seem to be any option other than to pledge the IG's support.

That night the Reichstag building burned to the ground. A young Dutch vagrant, Marinus van der Lubbe, was found alone on the premises with matches and lighters. Loosely affiliated with the Communist Party, he had decided on his own initiative to strike against one of the supreme symbols of the bourgeois order. During the resulting public hysteria, whipped up by a barrage of Nazi propaganda, a Marxist revolution suddenly seemed imminent. Angry mobs took to the street with the brownshirts to the fore, keen to vent their fury against their hated opponents. Protected and encouraged by the police—now controlled by the Nazis—the storm troopers were freed of all restraints and the violence quickly escalated into a bloodbath. All over Germany, Communists, Jews, and Social Democrats were attacked and beaten in their homes and in the street, before being arrested and imprisoned. It was a time for settling old scores and anyone who had ever spoken out against Hitler was now a target.

The election that followed took place in an atmosphere of manifest terror. While the parties of the left were more or less paralyzed by state-sponsored intimidation, the Nazis were able to blanket the nation with propaganda and mount huge rallies, thanks to the massive largesse bestowed on them by IG Farben and others. The result was only ever going to go one way. The Nazi share of the vote increased to 44 percent and its number of Reichstag delegates rose from 196 to 288 (in a parliament of 647 seats). This still wasn't the absolute mandate that Hitler wanted, but the Nazis now had far more popular support than any other party. When the party's seats were combined with the 52 won by its coalition partner, the nationalist DVNP, Hitler's government had a slim majority. It was enough, Hitler reassured his cabinet two days after the vote, and in any case, his lack of an absolute mandate would soon cease to matter. The nature of the current "emergency" was such that he felt confident of pushing through the constitutional changes that would allow the government to bypass the president and the Reichstag.

A few days later, standing beneath a giant swastika banner in the Knoll Opera House, a temporary home for the country's fatally wounded legislature, Hitler introduced the Enabling Act, which would allow the government to rule by decree. It was a coup de grace to the old order. A desperately brave but doomed attempt by Otto Wels, the chairman of the Social Democrats, to mobilize his fellow deputies against the proposed legislation was howled down by massed ranks of Nazi storm troopers.* With the Communists nullified (as presiding officer Hermann Göring had illegally declared their votes to be invalid) and the depleted and demoralized ranks of the Center Party unwilling or unable to do any more than try to preserve the independence of the country's Catholic Church, it was left to the SPD to oppose a law that would see the permanent suppression of civil rights and democratic liberties. The act was passed by 444 votes to 94. From that moment on, Germany's descent into the repressive and brutal dictatorship of the Third Reich was inevitable.

Having played such a significant part in the final chapter of Weimar democracy, IG Farben now set out to solidify its relations with the new regime. A few weeks later the cartel increased its financial donations, responding with alacrity to requests for money from local and national Nazi Party officials. By the end of 1933 the IG had handed over RM 4.5 million in contributions to one fund or another. In the meantime, Bosch began looking for ways to extract a dividend from the company's investment. After all, having sold its soul to the devil, the combine should at least get something in return—and what Bosch wanted more than anything was to save the IG's synthetic fuel program.

In less than a year the ink would be drying on a deal of truly Faustian proportions.

---

*Wels carried a cyanide tablet in his pocket against the eventuality that he would be arrested that day and tortured by the Nazis.

7

ACCOMMODATION
AND COLLABORATION

On March 29, 1933, William Mann, head of pharmaceuticals, wrote to executives at all IG Farben's offices abroad and overseas. Marked "personal" and "strictly confidential," his letter said:

The national revolution in Germany, which represents a natural reaction to the muddled state of affairs of recent years, and not least to Marxist-Communist agitation, has developed with unparalleled peace and order. The present German government has a right to claim that it has won a victory against Bolshevism, the enemy of the entire world, a victory which will benefit not only Germany but all civilized peoples of the earth. It carried out this battle in a manner which clearly demonstrated the will for self-discipline and the readiness to submit to firm leadership. It is all the more regrettable that some—very few—unimportant incidents which, practically speaking, were unavoidable in view of a government revolution of such tremendous proportions, have been taken up by a large part of the foreign press as an occasion to disseminate atrocity propaganda against Germany, with the slogan "Combat German Goods!"

Since our immediate business interests have also been affected by these political developments, we feel it is important, for this reason, but especially because of our duty as Germans, to tell you explicitly for our part as well, *that the contents of all atrocity tales being spread abroad about mistreatment of political opponents and Jews are in no way in keeping with the facts.*

We therefore *urgently request you*, immediately upon receipt of this letter, to contribute to the *clarification of the actual facts* in a manner which you deem suitable and adaptable to the special conditions of your country, either by visiting leading personalities of the country and editors of influential papers or by distributing circulars to doctors and the rest of your clientele. We request in particular that you emphasize as effectively as possible the part of this letter that states there is *not a true word* in all the lies and atrocity stories being disseminated abroad.

Signed MANN
Head of the Pharmaceutical Sales Combine
IG Farbenindustrie Aktiengesellschaft

For all its size and complexity, the IG could be surprisingly nimble when its interests were threatened. Within a fortnight of the Nazis' assumption of power in March 1933, the concern—or at least one part of it—was taking steps to insulate itself from the international fallout.

This looked set to be considerable. Foreign newspapers had been watching events in Germany with alarm and their reports about the anti-Semitic violence of the storm troopers and the systematic arrest and torture of the Führer's political enemies had generated such widespread public outrage abroad that many were now calling on their governments to place an embargo on German exports. Typically, Hitler reacted to these protests by blaming his opponents for spreading false and malicious propaganda and got his retaliation in first by scheduling a preemptive nationwide boycott of Jewish businesses for April 1. Concerned about the looming cycle of reprisals and counterreprisals, and its implications for trade, which was just beginning to recover after many lean years, some exporters were anxious to try to defuse the situation and the more enterprising among them wrote re-assuring letters to their contacts overseas.*

Few of these correspondents can have showed as great a disregard for the facts as the IG's pharmaceuticals chief. By any stretch of the imagination Wilhelm Mann's analysis was a whitewash of events. Cir-culated to seventy-five Bayer sales agents around the world, his letter's central message—that Nazi persecution of political opponents had been exaggerated to the point of invention—was patently absurd, bor-dering on the kind of black-is-white doublespeak that George Orwell would later hold up to ridicule. The letter begs important questions about whose interests Mann thought he was serving—his own or his employer's.

To a degree, the document probably reflected Mann's personal concerns and prejudices. The previous year he had been the first IG di-rector to join the Nazi Party, and although he had let his membership lapse, he hastily rejoined when Hitler became chancellor. It is possible that he was embarrassed by his temporary loss of faith and wanted in some on-the-record way to compensate for any damaging impression his recusancy might have caused. It is also conceivable that he gen-uinely believed what he was saying, that the foreign media's stories about the mistreatment of political opponents and Jews were really nothing more than the smears and slanders and atrocity propaganda that Hitler claimed them to be. But if this is what Mann felt, it amounts to willful blindness. As Victor Klemperer noted in his diary at around this time, evidence that the new regime was ruthlessly ex-ploiting its power was hardly difficult to find: "Day after day . . . provincial governments trampled underfoot, flags raised, buildings taken over, people shot, newspapers banned, etc., etc. Yesterday the dramaturg Karl Wolf dismissed 'by order of the Nazi Party'—not even in the name of the government—today the whole Saxon cabinet, etc., etc. A complete revolution and party dictatorship. And all opposing forces as if vanished from the face of the earth." If a minor professor

---

*Some businesses, including several Jewish organizations, were undoubtedly pressured by the authorities into writing in encouraging terms to contacts abroad, but there is no evidence that IG Farben was put under such pressure.

in Dresden could see so clearly what was going on in Germany, then a senior executive of the nation's largest and most powerful company could hardly avoid noting it, too.

Nor could the rest of the IG's management team. The cartel had already given large sums of money to the Nazis and was in the process of giving more, which in theory (if not yet in practice) made it one of the party's most important sponsors. At the same time the company had reason to feel vulnerable to official measures the government took against the Jews, since there were still several in senior positions around the firm. In the circumstances, any action that affirmed the IG's stand with the government made sense. In any case, the letter must have been authorized. Although, as a senior executive, Mann enjoyed a large degree of autonomy within the IG's labyrinthine administrative structure, he would certainly have had to obtain clearance from at least some of his fellow directors for a communiqué of this sensitivity. The fact that this was forthcoming speaks volumes about the situation the company was now in and the uncertainty that many of its top managers were feeling about the best way to move ahead. Perhaps more disturbingly, it raises the distinct possibility that some of them sympathized with Mann's point of view.

Carl Bosch, however, did not share these sympathies. The IG boss may have had his faults but he was no anti-Semite. Many of his closest colleagues were Jewish or of Jewish ancestry, including his secretary, Ernest Schwarz, several members of the concern's supervisory board, and many of its top scientists. So was one of his oldest friends, Fritz Haber, who discovered synthetic ammonia and whose work had led to one of Bosch's greatest personal triumphs during the Great War. Indeed, Haber's treatment at the hands of the Nazis would have already brought home to Bosch how bad things were getting.

A few days after Hitler's speech in the Knoll Opera House and the passage of the Enabling Act, uniformed Nazis had begun taking up senior positions in all areas of public life. Their immediate aim was to purge German society and culture of Jewish and socialist influences and they set about forcing the resignation or dismissal of non-Aryan civil servants, hospital doctors, academics, administrators, teachers, and anybody else of Jewish descent (a classification so narrowly defined as to include even those with only one Jewish grandparent) who held a publicly funded post. One of their principal targets was the world of science and technology and in a matter of weeks thousands of Jewish university lecturers and researchers and hundreds of professors were thrown out of their jobs and deprived of their livelihoods, in a program of racial cleansing that was shamefully uncontested by most of their Aryan colleagues and students.

In April 1933, despite his conversion to Christianity and the faint possibility that his war service might grant him an exemption from dismissal, Fritz Haber realized that he had no choice but to yield to the growing pressure and stand down from his chair at the University of Berlin. In a brief and dignified letter of resignation he stated that although he had always done his best to be a good German and had tried to put his country first, he accepted that now he had no choice but to go abroad. In truth, he felt totally betrayed. Once one of the nation's most revered scientists, he had been ignominiously rejected by the fatherland he had served so diligently. Even a tree planted in his honor by his colleagues in the courtyard of the Kaiser Wilhelm Institute was chopped down and burnt by the Nazis. As he wrote to a friend, "I am bitter as never before. I was German to an extent that I feel fully only now and I find it odious in the extreme that I can no longer work enough to begin confidently a new post in a different country." Two months later, a broken man, he left for England.* He was part of an extraordinary exodus of scientific talent that included Albert Einstein and sixteen other Jewish Nobel laureates.

Carl Bosch saw Haber's departure and the loss of other leading scientists as a dreadful blow to Germany's prestige and capabilities and was determined to try to persuade the new authorities that their policies were misconceived. Academic research had always been fundamental to the nation's scientific achievements and the IG had regularly sponsored, promoted, and benefited from the work of the various

---

*Haber found it difficult to settle in England because of the hostile reception he got from some in the British scientific community who never forgave him for his work on poison gases during the war. As a result, he decided to accept an offer from the Hebrew University in Palestine. According to one account, he was also considering trying to return to Germany but was dissuaded from doing so by IG Farben's Hermann Schmitz, who warned him that the Nazi terror was continuing unabated.

bodies run under the auspices of the Kaiser Wilhelm Institute. A policy that deprived the country of its finest talent was nothing short of lunacy. But Bosch's attempts to lobby the various ministries came to nothing and in the absence of an official change of heart he could do little to persuade the Jewish scientists he knew personally that it was worth staying to ride out the storm. His only recourse was a direct appeal to Hitler himself.

As it turned out, the opportunity was not long in coming. Bosch had wanted to meet the Führer in order to follow up on Hitler's September 1932 discussion with the IG's Heinrich Gattineau and Heinrich Bütefisch on the subject of synthetic oil. Having sanctioned a large donation to the Nazi Party prior to the election, Bosch thought it now made sense to find out if the new chancellor was still as keen on man-made fuel as he had previously seemed to be. In May Bosch finally got a call inviting him for talks.

At first the meeting went smoothly. Hitler reiterated his interest in IG Farben's great project and to Bosch's relief promised that his government would give it its full backing. The IG could go ahead with expanding Leuna safe in the knowledge that German self-sufficiency in strategically important raw materials was at the heart of the regime's plans for the future. Then Bosch, as delicately as he could, raised the "Jewish question." Perhaps the Führer didn't realize the potentially damaging consequences of his policies, he suggested. If more and more Jewish scientists were forced abroad, German physics and chemistry could be set back a hundred years. To his alarm, Hitler erupted in fury. Obviously the businessman knew nothing of politics, he snarled. If necessary, Germany would "work one hundred years without physics and chemistry." Bosch tried to continue but Hitler rang for an aide and told him icily, "The *Geheimrat* wishes to leave."*

From that moment on Bosch was persona non grata in Hitler's circle. The two never met again and the Führer refused to attend any events where he knew the IG boss would be present. Some men would have found this state of affairs deeply disturbing and would have tried to effect a reconciliation or at least keep a low profile, but to Bosch's

---

*The term *Geheimrat* is an honorific, meaning privy councillor or "great man."

great credit, he refused to let it bother him. Secure, perhaps, in the belief that Hitler's antipathy toward him personally was not going to get in the way of the Nazis' support for the IG's synthetic fuel program, he continued quietly with his efforts to defend Jewish scientists and even tried to persuade some non-Jewish Nobel laureates to argue on their behalf. His labors met with little success. A timorous attempt by a few Aryan scientists to organize a petition against the dismissals petered out in the face of widespread Nazi hostility and Hitler's intractability. When Max Planck, the physicist, by no means a fervent anti-Nazi, tried to persuade the Führer of the merits of hanging on to Fritz Haber and the others—by explaining that it was only sensible to distinguish between those Jews with value and those without—Hitler again flew into a rage. "A Jew is a Jew," he said. "All Jews cling together like burrs. Wherever one Jew is, other Jews of all types immediately gather." Slapping his leg repeatedly to emphasize his points, he shouted so violently that Planck left, emotionally drained by the experience.

Unable to do much more on the national stage, Bosch sought instead for ways to look after his closer Jewish associates, discreetly paying compensation to some of those driven out of the country and arranging overseas postings, within the company, for some key IG staff in the hope that saner times would return. Ernest Schwarz, for example, was sent to work in New York, while Edwin Pietrkowski, Bosch's deputy chairman at the Chemical Industry Association, was given a job in Geneva. When Fritz Haber died, unexpectedly, in January 1934, while visiting family in Basel, Switzerland, Bosch thumbed his nose at the authorities by helping to organize a memorial service at the Kaiser Wilhelm Institute—in defiance of an explicit government prohibition—and then asked as many of the country's leading scientists and academics as he could think of to attend. The invitees included government officials and military servicemen who had worked with Haber, although very few of the civil servants now employed in Nazi-controlled ministries turned up. Max Planck, who gave a valedictory address to the audience of five hundred or so, had no choice but to open the proceedings with a Nazi salute—a hesitant one, it should be noted.

Bosch's recalcitrance aside, however, IG Farben was adjusting with remarkable ease to the demands of a government that was already showing the hallmarks of an absolute dictatorship. The events of May 1, 1933, were a case in point. Hitler had declared that this traditional workers' day should be celebrated as an explicitly Nazi holiday of industrial achievement. At the concern's Leverkusen plant, the manager, Hans Kühne, rushed out an enthusiastic statement calling on all his colleagues to join in the proceedings "and thus prove our will to cooperate." Sullenly or otherwise, most of the workforce obliged. The scene was the same at Ludwigshafen, where the entire staff, including all the plant's senior executives, assembled at 8:00 a.m. alongside uniformed detachments of the local SA and the National Socialist Factory Cell Organization. Only a year earlier, May 1 would have been a decidedly left-wing celebration; now the workers were all lined up docilely in front of Nazi banners to listen to speeches extolling the merits of the "people's chancellor." They were even urged to give three rousing "*Sieg Heils*" at the end of the rally.

Needless to say, the former Communist and SPD trade unionists among them kept their heads down. One young Ludwigshafen employee, twenty-one-year-old Horst Wolff, later wrote his mother that the events of that day had sickened him deeply and that he had wanted to complain formally to management. Older workers in his section told him to keep his counsel and bide his time because "the Nazis wouldn't be around for long." Their advice turned out to be wise: on May 2, brownshirts and SS men smashed into every trade union office in the country, taking over newspapers and periodicals and confiscating funds. Hundreds of leading officials were attacked and humiliated and the management and assets of the whole labor movement were placed under Nazi control. A few weeks later, the regime began the final stage of its "revolution" by banning the Social Democrat Party outright and arresting its officials all over Germany. More than three thousand SPD functionaries were thrown into prison or hastily formed concentration camps, where many were beaten, tortured, and even murdered. Not long afterward all the remaining bourgeois political parties—including the Nationalists, Hitler's erstwhile coalition partners—were bullied or manipulated into dissolution. By July 1933 Germany was indisputably a one-party state.

Given the breakneck speed of these events, which demonstrated the regime's increasingly sophisticated understanding of how to use fear and intimidation to get people to conform, it is perhaps not surprising that the IG and its directors slipped so readily into collaboration—not, of course, that any of them apart from Carl Bosch and one or two others of the concern's founding generation had so far shown any real appetite for dissent. Carl Duisberg provided an interesting example. Despite his undoubtedly strong belief in the importance of strong government and the need for Germany to regain its place in the world, the IG's godfather never had much time for the Nazis. Now in semiretirement he returned to his lavish house in Leverkusen to write a memoir in which he pointedly failed to mention either Hitler or the new regime. In any case, many of the old guard were on their way out. Between 1930 and 1933 dozens of IG veterans had died, retired, or otherwise left the business, including twenty-nine members of the *Aufsichtsrat* and thirty-one members of the *Vorstand*. Of the latter, around a dozen had been regular attendees at meetings of the *Arbeitsausschuss,* or Working Committee, the principal management body at the IG.

The newer generation of IG leaders took a much more cynical and pragmatic view; whatever its drawbacks the new government clearly had a firm grip on power and it was important, both for their shareholders and for the future of the company, to maintain good relations. Inevitably, some viewed this cooperation in a more idealistic light. Georg von Schnitzler, for example, was later to claim that he had made an accord with the Nazis only because they were better than the alternative: "The collapse of the liberal bourgeois parties in Germany to which I adhered convinced me that Germany had to choose between national socialism and bolshevism. Under these circumstances I considered it right to make the attempt to come to terms with national socialism in order to save the German people from chaos." Of course, idealistic or not, the practical consequences of such a justification were the same.

The most obvious manifestation of the company's growing compliance was the number of senior IG executives who followed Wilhelm Mann into the NSDAP at this time, eager to sign up before an announced freeze on new recruits (which was to last until 1937) came into effect. Hans Kühne, the manager at Leverkusen, joined after being sponsored by Robert Ley (a former Bayer chemist and Nazi gauleiter who was now head of the German Labor Front), although he was kicked out the following year for being a Freemason. Years later, he said that he had been attracted only by the regime's promises to create jobs and political unity. Fritz Gajewski, the head of *Sparte* III, signed up along with Wilhelm Otto, his division's head of sales. Friedrich Mullen, a deputy member of the *Vorstand*, joined on April 1, the day of the Nazi-inspired nationwide boycott of Jewish businesses, while Erwin Selck, the director in charge of the IG's influential Berlin NW7 offices, got in by virtue of his personal financial contributions to a mounted Sturmabteilung detachment; he later joined a cavalry unit in Heinrich Himmler's SS. Others had to wait until loopholes in the party rules allowed them in. Heinrich Hörlein, the Nobel Prize–winning head of the IG's pharmaceutical department, joined in June 1934 but was able to get his party card backdated to May of the previous year. Heinrich Gattineau applied for membership immediately after the Nazis came to power but had to wait two years for acceptance, as did Ludwig Hermann of the Hoechst plant in Frankfurt.

Actual party membership was not the only way to gain friends and influence people in Nazi circles. There were plenty of proxy organizations to belong to as well. For example, both Christian Schneider, one of the most eminent scientists at Leuna (and later in charge of *Sparte* I), and Heinrich Bütefisch, the hydrogenation expert who had met Hitler, eventually followed Erwin Selck into the SS as honorary colonels, while Heinrich Gattineau took up a part-time commission in the SA as he waited for his party card. Others were a little more circumspect—for now. Hermann Schmitz, the IG's financial chief, declined to seek party membership in 1933, though he did accept a nomination in November as a Nazi-sponsored delegate to the Reichstag, which gives some indication of where his sympathies lay. Georg von Schnitzler was another who wasn't quite ready to put his cards on the table; for the moment he restricted himself to maintaining a "salon" in Berlin at which high-ranking Nazis could mix with other political and industrial dignities.

These men were still in the minority among IG executives. For some years to come, many remained skeptical about the Nazis or at least unconvinced that an overt expression of support was yet advantageous or necessary. It is also true that such levels of support as the IG's managers did evince were not especially unusual when compared with those in other leading German firms, such as Krupp, Siemens, AEG, and the steel giant Vereinigte Stahlwerke. In time, though, more and more came to feel that some sort of affiliation was necessary. In 1937,when the party opened its doors to new members, a further fifteen members of the IG's *Vorstand* rushed to sign up.

The small handful that remained aloof beyond that date had a very different rationale. Carl Bosch never joined. For all the concessions the IG's chief executive made to the regime's demands, he always maintained that they were the unfortunate by-product of commercial expediency rather than the consequence of ideological commitment. In any event, Hitler's fury over his attempts to intervene on behalf of Jewish scientists would hardly have helped Bosch's application. Fritz ter Meer, the haughty chief of *Sparte* II, also stayed out, although his reasons were more about class than politics. He later claimed that he had decided not to apply because he had no intention of "attending meetings of local party members and listening to lectures by people far below me socially."

One of the most curious cases of agnosticism—curious in the sense that it was potentially prejudicial to his career and therefore completely out of character—was that of Max Ilgner. Young, deeply ambitious, and often exasperatingly self-promoting, Ilgner came from an unusual background for an IG Farben executive. His father and grandfather had both been middle-ranking army officers and he grew up expecting to follow in their footsteps. In 1918, after a spell in a Prussian cadet school, he saw a few weeks' active service as a subaltern on the Western Front and then, during the chaos at the end of the war, joined the Freikorps. He had hoped to return to the army, but the Versailles Treaty imposed restrictions on the size of the Reichswehr and so, like many other young officers, Ilgner was forced to look for another way to earn his living. As it happened, his uncle was Hermann Schmitz, then Bosch's financial lieutenant at BASF, so in 1924, after obtaining a doctorate (in political science rather than chemistry), Ilgner used the connection to get a job as a salesman in Ludwigshafen. Only twenty-five years old, he energetically began climbing the ladder to greater things.

In 1926 he was sent to work for his uncle at the IG's new central finance and public affairs section, based in the Deutsche Länderbank building on Unter den Linden in Berlin's NW7 district. His task initially was to act as a liaison between Schmitz and the rest of the concern, a role that was not as grand as it sounded; he was actually a glorified messenger boy. But Ilgner was determined and competent and, perhaps more importantly, was able to rely on his uncle's patronage. By late 1934 he had significantly expanded his area of responsibility—and that of the NW7 operation—and risen to become a deputy member of the *Vorstand* with a large degree of authority over press and public relations, market research, financial administration, and, crucially, the IG's contacts with the government. Much of this influence was exercised through his control of two important NW7 subsections. The first, established in 1929, was called the Department of Economic Research, or *Vowi* (a short form of *Volkswirtschaftliche Abteilung*), and was responsible for producing reports on developments overseas that might affect the IG's commercial interests. The second, the Department of Economic Policy, or *Wipo* (*Wirtschaftspolitische Abteilung*), was set up in 1932 (initially under Heinrich Gattineau) and had a more specific brief: to review matters that bore directly on IG Farben's relationship with government, such as the law, taxation, and foreign economic policy. Of the two bodies it was the *Vowi* that was at first most influential. Drawing heavily on the IG's global network of sales offices and foreign contacts as well as its own research staff in Berlin, the department gathered commercial and economic intelligence and produced reports that were often passed on to government ministries, in much the same way that modern think tanks pass on advice today. Conveniently, of course, they also provided Ilgner with a means of access to the corridors of power.

While Ilgner's activities propelled him into the higher reaches of the IG, they also earned him the enmity of several of his peers. Contemporaries on the *Vorstand* were deeply distrustful of his hunger for influence and his apparent determination to use his position to increase his profile in the outside world. As one of his subordinates, Kurt Krüger, was to say of him later: "Ilgner had great ambitions, but greater still was his conviction that he was destined to do great things, as well as his unusual desire for acclaim and acknowledgment, which drove him to try to play a role in public life." However, with Hermann Schmitz always on hand to lend his support, Ilgner's critics had to put up with him.

Given the opportunity for self-aggrandizement that official association with the regime would have presented, it is therefore a little odd that Ilgner chose not to join the Nazi Party. Offered an exemption from the recruitment freeze in 1933, he declined on the mundane grounds that he didn't want to have to resign from the Rotary International, a necessary requirement because Joseph Goebbels, Hitler's propaganda chief, had taken a bizarre dislike to the Rotary and banned its members from joining Nazi ranks. Possibly Ilgner believed Nazi membership would make little or no difference to his career in the long run. In any case, his decision did not signify a refusal to deal with the regime. On the contrary, he showed no reluctance to trying to cement personal alliances with leading Nazis or doing all he could to advance the IG's cause in government circles. According to Krüger, Ilgner, like others on the concern's management team, believed that a pragmatic approach was the best way to secure influence.

> After Hitler took over the government, Ilgner followed the new trend with "banners and coattails flying" and tried to make connections in order to be "in on things" and to be able to take part. However, it cannot really be disputed that he hoped to influence developments in a way favorable to the German economy. Accordingly, he made haste to conform to the official party line and observe the institutions and outward forms of the Nazi regime. . . . However, this was not only Ilgner's endeavor, but that of the whole leadership of IG, who, in this way, tried to secure the interests of the company, which they thought threatened under the new regime and with which they felt they had a bad name. The tendency to ingratiate oneself with the new powers showed itself everywhere.

From the Nazis' point of view, individual expressions of loyalty by IG Farben managers were far less important that the company's wholesale cooperation. The IG, in common with other businesses, was expected to play a central role in the process of national renewal and, if necessary, to place its own interests second to those of the state. As a consequence, at home and abroad, the cartel was about to be pulled in several conflicting directions.

Overseas, the IG's immediate objective was to repair the harm done to sales by the political fallout from the Nazi takeover and the boycott of Jewish businesses. Wilhelm Mann's letter was an early and overzealous attempt at damage limitation, but as the months went by such efforts became commonplace. In July 1933, for example, when the DuPont Corporation sent two executives to Frankfurt to arrange to sell back its small stake in IG Farben, a move prompted in part by the U.S. firm's unease over recent events, several of the IG's leading figures went out of their way to try to convince the Americans that things in Germany were returning to normal and that some of the stories they had heard were not true. Among them, remarkably, was Carl von Weinberg, the Jewish deputy chairman of the *Aufsichtsrat,* who told the DuPont executives that the Nazi movement had his full approval and that he was keeping his money in the country. Even Bosch unbent sufficiently to explain that Hitler had recently been curbing the more extreme elements of his party. The Americans were unconvinced, and the sale went ahead as planned.

Max Ilgner rose to the task of damage control with particular enthusiasm. He appreciated better than most just how much harm the Nazis' harsh rhetoric had done to Germany's reputation abroad—and therefore to the IG's exports—and took it on himself to form a Circle of Economic Advisers to Goebbels's Propaganda Ministry in the hope that its output could be made less strident. At first, he had some modest successes. He persuaded Goebbels to attend a few meetings of the circle and managed to explain frankly to him how the outside world now saw the country. "I didn't paint a rosy picture as was customary in the Third Reich. Trade was dropping off and we were worried about German exports," he later said. "We were tried and proven economists and we knew well the reaction of the world to propaganda." Eventually, though, Goebbels took exception to Ilgner's claims that his officials were harming German interests and left in a huff, never to return.

Undeterred, Ilgner decided—again on his own initiative—to enlist the services of Ivy Lee, one of America's most famous public relations and advertising experts, to improve Hitler's unsavory reputation overseas.* When the American arrived in Berlin in early 1934 (after spending a few days in Rome on a similar mission with Mussolini), Ilgner arranged for him to meet the Führer.

Although the notion of hiring one of Madison Avenue's most gung-ho practitioners to give Adolf Hitler public relations advice might now seem quite bizarre, it was an amiable enough occasion, by all accounts. The meeting even appears to have survived the moment when Lee blithely suggested that, since the Jewish boycott wasn't going down very well with the American media, Hitler should consider dropping it. Regrettably, there is no record of the exact words with which the Führer declined to take this counsel, but presumably they can't have been too bruising, because afterward Lee was happy to give Ilgner several tips on how IG Farben could help spin the dramatic changes taking place in Germany: foreign journalists could be entertained at press receptions featuring moderate speakers from German public life; influential Americans could be invited to take guided motor tours through the country to see how conditions were improving; Germany's culture, beautiful landscape, and fascinating people should always be emphasized over the unpleasant rhetoric of the Nazis. Probably Lee's most important proposal, however, was that he and Ilgner should discreetly arrange for positive articles about the new Germany to be placed in U.S. newspapers and magazine, copies of which could then be sent on to leading American opinion makers.†

Ilgner's enthusiastic adoption of such tactics, in addition to his

---

*Standard Oil's chairman, Walter Teagle, had introduced Ilgner to Lee a few years earlier when IG Farben was looking for ways to combat negative publicity generated by its formation of the American IG Chemical Company.

†Ivy Lee's work on behalf of IG Farben in particular and Nazi Germany in general didn't go unnoticed back home in the United States. In the summer of 1934 Lee was interrogated by the House Special Committee on Un-American Activities, during which he freely admitted that the material he had disseminated on behalf of the IG was authorized by the official German propaganda apparatus. He was pressed particularly on why he had advised the IG to respond to foreign media concerns about the dangers of Germany's 2.5 million Nazi paramilitaries with the claim that they were unarmed and organized only in case of Communist peril. Wasn't it strange that a chemical company should be interested in such things? After vacillating for a while Lee was forced to admit that IG Farben was effectively acting as an advocate for the German government. The inquiries didn't lead anywhere, however, because a few months later Lee fell ill and died.

frequent trips overseas to promote the notion that Nazi Germany was a misunderstood land of peaceful intent and impressive accomplishments, sat uneasily with some of his *Vorstand* colleagues. Georg von Schnitzler complained at one point that "we now appear as the champion of the German cause in general and as auxiliary government agents without even knowing whether the government considers this desirable. . . . The less one mixes business matters with questions of sympathy or antipathy to various forms of government or with the national psychological attitude the better it will be for our business." But such criticism made little difference. Ilgner was indefatigable, and in any case the party's Foreign Organization was also now beginning to insist that the IG's overseas sales apparatus be used to disseminate propaganda. Although that idea was not implemented overnight (in the summer of 1933, for example, the Bayer field office in Montevideo was still independent enough to fend off a request by the German embassy that it include Nazi literature in its mailings to the local medical community), resistance soon began to crumble. By February 1934 the concern's foreign staff had been told by managers to cancel any advertising in publications overtly hostile to the Third Reich and to swear an oath guaranteeing their personal political allegiance.

The IG was to be just as susceptible to pressure at home. In its factories it struggled to come up with an appropriate response to the Nazification of working life, not least because individual plant managers had differing attitudes toward such questions as whether or not to make the Hitler salute mandatory or if collections for party funds could take place on company premises. The absence of clear-cut guidance from IG headquarters in Frankfurt (where senior executives were often so confused and divided about such things they issued conflicting instructions) caused endless hours of anxiety farther down the line as local bosses tried to decide on the wisest course to follow. Not surprisingly, therefore, they often erred on the side of safety and did what they thought the party would most want.

The IG's various internal newspapers are a particularly good example of how Nazi influence spread. Prior to May 1933 these papers (each plant had its own version) were full of the usual cheery and anodyne workplace stories about orders won and various individuals' achievements. But from that point the publications began to take on an overtly political character. For example, the November 1933 issue of the Ludwigshafen *Werkszeitung* carried an account of a speech given by the Nazi Robert Ley—head of the German Labor Front—on the virtues of an authoritarian state that pretty much set the tone for what was to follow. The next June, a swastika began appearing on the paper's masthead, and in early 1935 all the different dedicated plant papers were combined in one monthly, companywide journal, *From Works to Works*. The stated purpose, an editorial revealed, was to fulfill the "National Socialist challenge" by bringing everyone in the company closer together. But, of course, the consolidation also created a centralized vehicle for ideological indoctrination.

The cartel's labor relations policies had to be reconsidered, too. With the old trade unions replaced by the Nazi Factory Cell Organization and the German Labor Front, management had to work out its responses to the issues these organizations began raising over pay and conditions. Was it best, for example, to accede to local party requests that workers be allowed paid time off to attend rallies or paramilitary training sessions? To say yes would be to relinquish yet another slice of managerial control. To say no risked alienating Nazi activists who might have powerful friends. More often than not, managerial control lost out.

Sometimes the regime's interference took on a more surreal form. In April 1933 the IG was ordered to conduct full-scale air raid exercises at Ludwigshafen and Leverkusen. As Germany wasn't at war with anyone at the time these events struck many employees as a little odd, but true to form, Hans Kühne at Leverkusen encouraged everyone to play along and not make too much of them.

The IG was also wrestling with scientific questions. In August 1933 Hermann Göring banned the use of animals in experiments, a somewhat ironic directive given Göring's well-known love of hunting. The ban was a matter of the utmost concern to the IG's pharmaceutical and pharmacological departments. Bayer scientists had been using animals in the laboratory since the end of the nineteenth century (Heinrich Dreser, for example, had tested aspirin on rats, frogs, goldfish, and guinea pigs before he was satisfied it was safe for human use) and the practice was now an integral part of preparing drugs for the market. A prohibition against it threatened to bring much of this work to a standstill, and the IG's chief pharmacist, Heinrich Hörlein—Nazi Party member though he was to become—felt compelled to campaign publicly against it. He was eventually able to get the ban partially lifted but not before the Nazi press had thoroughly enjoyed itself by publishing cartoons portraying evil "Jewish scientists" torturing animals to prepare noxious substances for sale to good Aryan folk.

Gradually, however, the concern's anxieties about how to deal with the new regime began to fade. Insulated to a large extent from the brutality, discrimination, and general disenfranchisement that was the daily lot of Jews, socialists, Communists, and other enemies of the state, the *Vorstand* and the *Aufsichtsrat* took note instead of the perceptible improvements in the IG's balance sheet. The company's main aim, after all, was to make money and the figures were definitely getting more robust. By the end of 1933, the IG had paid off a lot of debt, increased its workforce by over 15 percent, and started spending on R & D again. More importantly, it had worked out ways of responding to pressure on exports caused by foreign disquiet over the Jewish boycott (Max Ilgner's efforts, combined with heavily increased overseas advertising for IG goods, were yielding results), and it had posted a net profit of around 65 million marks, up 32 percent on the previous year. Even the company's shares were on the rise.

It is questionable, of course, how much of this improvement was due to the new government's economic policies—namely, to reduce some taxes on industry, increase spending on armaments, and push ahead with make-work schemes (which that autumn saw 300,000 of the unemployed put to work building *Autobahnen*). The settlement of Germany's reparations problem a year earlier and the gradually recovering global economy were probably far more significant to IG Farben's profitability in 1933 than anything the Nazis had yet managed to accomplish. Indeed, given that the concern had made substantial political donations to various Nazi funds that year—some 4.5 million reichsmarks in total—it might be said that the party had so far gained more from the IG than the other way around. But calm, albeit of a poisonous sort, had returned, and to businessmen deeply concerned by the threat of continuing chaos that stability was priceless.

IN THE MIDST of the upswing in its fortunes, one part of Farben's empire still gave cause for concern: Leuna, the home of IG's synthetic fuel program, was continuing to lose money. The tariff protection measures against natural petroleum that Bosch had extracted from the Brüning government back in 1931 had provided a temporary respite, but to many in the company the project was still a costly white elephant that should be abandoned. To avoid that fate, Bosch knew that something more substantial was needed. His meeting with Hitler in May, despite its explosive ending, had given him strong grounds for supposing that a Nazi government committed to self-sufficiency would provide the necessary guarantees. He still had to find a way, however, to turn that expression of interest into tangible support.

The strain on Bosch was increased by the fact that the IG's monopoly on synthetic fuel had recently come under challenge. During the latter years of the Depression, coal producers in the Ruhr, looking for ways to boost their dwindling sales, had become interested in the prospect that synthetic fuel might be made from the by-products of coke, using a procedure known as the Fischer-Tropp process. Bosch had long been aware that this method might one day prove more competitive than the IG's own technique, but because the company was so heavily committed to the Bergius process, he chose not to pursue the alternative. Now Bosch began hearing reports that the coal magnates were considering going into production for themselves. The concern moved quickly to minimize the threat, offering the Ruhr producers assistance in adapting the IG's own hydrogenation process for manmade fuel, as well as more advantageous terms of access to the German Nitrogen Syndicate (some mine owners had also tried branching out into nitrogen manufacture only to be undercut in pricing by this IG-dominated association). These bribes brought the coal industry "inside the tent" and ensured its support for the overtures the IG was making to the government for financial assistance, but they also intensified the pressure on Bosch to deliver some genuine gains.

In June 1933 Bosch stepped up his efforts by contributing to a twenty-page paper authored mainly by his lieutenant Carl Krauch, the head of *Sparte* I. Written with ministers, civil servants, and the military firmly in mind, "The German Fuel Economy" spelled out the stark choices facing the country. Germany already imported about 75 percent of its fuel. If demand continued to grow (all those new autobahns would undoubtedly mean more thirsty cars), its dependence on foreign supplies would only increase. This dangerous situation could be avoided by expanding the IG's synthetic fuel production to the point where it could meet most of Germany's needs, but doing so would require massive levels of capital investment—far beyond anything that the company and its shareholders could be expected to risk on their own. The only solution, therefore, was for the state to underwrite the costs of the increase in production capacity and guarantee a minimum price for the finished product.

Yet again Max Ilgner was to prove instrumental, ensuring that this document found its way onto the right desks in Berlin. For some years he had been consolidating friendships in the Reichswehr's Weapons Office (responsible for arms procurement), especially with Georg Thomas, a bright young lieutenant colonel on the commercial liaison staff whom he had kept informed about the IG's development of synthetic raw materials like oil and rubber. As a result, Thomas had become something of a convert to the notion that autarky—or economic self-sufficiency—was of great strategic importance, and he had written several confidential memoranda to his superiors recommending that the armed forces should consider supporting the IG's work. Now that evangelism bore fruit. Shortly after the Nazis came to power in 1933, Hermann Göring, in his new role as minister of aviation, had been ordered by Hitler to begin covertly building up an illegal military air force—in direct contravention of the terms of the Versailles Treaty.* To keep this black Luftwaffe secret it would obviously be necessary, among other things, to arrange for dependable supplies of aviation

---

*Göring combined the aviation minister's role with various other official duties. He was still president of the Reichstag, head of the Gestapo, and minister-president (prime minister) of Prussia.

fuel that didn't appear on the sales manifests of overseas oil companies. Informed of the problem, the army's Weapons Office had passed on Thomas's memos to state secretary General Erhard Milch, Göring's deputy in the Aviation Ministry, and in August 1933 Milch got in touch with Carl Krauch to explore the potential of the IG's project.

The general's most immediate concern was whether synthetic oil was suitable for conversion into a high-octane aviation product. Krauch assured him it was and furthermore that it could be made into vital engine lubricants, too. When Milch asked whether synthetic oil could be produced in sufficient quantities, Krauch arranged to send him a copy of "The German Fuel Economy." Milch read the paper through and discussed its conclusions with the head of the Weapons Office, General von Bockelberg (and his eager subordinate Lieutenant Colonel Georg Thomas). Convinced of the merits, Milch proposed that both armed services should work together to persuade the Economics Ministry to grant financial assistance to the IG. The cartel had independently been lobbying Gottfried Feder, an undersecretary at the Economics Ministry, for subventions, but it had encountered resistance. Feder had favored stockpiling imported natural petroleum (international oil prices were especially low at the time) and increasing Germany's capacity to refine crude oil, on the grounds that these measures were considerably cheaper than subsidizing Leuna. He even won Hitler's support for his proposals but backed down when the army and the air force joined ranks with the IG.

The result was a groundbreaking agreement known as the *Benzinvertrag* (gasoline contract), which was signed in Berlin on December 14, 1933. In exchange for the IG's promise to raise production at Leuna to 350,000 tons per year by 1935, the Reich agreed to buy all of the factory's output that could not be sold on the open market. It also guaranteed a ten-year price that corresponded to the costs of production (including taxes), with a return of 5 percent interest on the IG's investment. Any profits above that amount would go to the government.

Carl Bosch's relief when he was invited to put his name to this deal must have been beyond measure. For the best part of eight years he had nurtured a dream that one day the IG's synthetic fuel program, based on technology that he had been instrumental in developing, would be in a position to free Germany from its dependence on foreign oil. He had fought many battles and faced many hurdles in pursuit of this goal and on several occasions he had been thrown into deep depression by the reverses he'd encountered. Now at long last his dream was turning into reality. His beloved Leuna was safe and, with sales of licenses to other producers interested in the synthetic fuel process bound to follow (any such royalties lay outside the terms of the *Benzinvertrag*), it looked set to be hugely profitable, too. At that moment, with such an extraordinary prize secured, it is doubtful if he gave the political implications of the deal much thought.

From now on the IG's fate and fortunes would be inextricably tied to those of the Third Reich. The future was not yet visible but the cartel had in essence committed to providing Hitler with the means to launch the most devastating conflict in human history. The agreement Bosch had signed was far more than the fulfillment of his long-held ambitions. It was also a pivotal moment in a sequence of events that would lead inexorably to the blitzkrieg, to Stalingrad, and to the gas chambers at Auschwitz. Many years later the U.S. Army's General Telford Taylor would accuse IG Farben's bosses of making World War II possible, of being "the magicians who made the nightmare of *Mein Kampf* come true." On that interpretation at least, the magicians had just cast their first spell.

8

FROM LONG KNIVES
TO THE FOUR-YEAR PLAN

The surroundings were not intended to be especially welcoming, of course, but to someone accustomed to the perks and privileges usually accorded to an executive at one of the world's largest companies, the bleak accommodation of a Gestapo prison cell must have come as a particular shock. If Heinrich Gattineau's racing mind gave him any peace at all that night, then it is possible he spent some of the time reviewing the circumstances that had brought him to such a place. But he would have spent a great deal longer in communion with his God. A man in fear of imminent execution is unlikely to waste too much energy on anything other than prayers for a reprieve.

He wouldn't have been the only one praying. On June 30, 1934, hundreds of previously faithful Nazi adherents discovered that their loyalty counted for less in the new Germany than Adolf Hitler's determination to prove that he was its only master.

The Röhm purge—or the Night of the Long Knives, as it came to be known—took place at the end of an extraordinarily tumultuous period in German history. In little over a year Hitler had destroyed the democratic Weimar Republic and replaced it with his personal dictatorship. In the process he had smashed all the political parties but his own, suppressed the trade unions, abolished freedom of speech, stifled the independence of the courts, driven the Jews out of most areas of public and professional life, and placed the economic, political, and cultural framework of an entire nation under the suffocating influence of a corrupt and repressive ideology. Astonishingly, however, he continued to retain the approval of the German people, winning overwhelming popular support (95 percent) in a plebiscite held on November 12, 1933, for his decision to withdraw Germany from the League of Nations, and a 92 percent share of the votes in an election for the Reichstag—albeit for a single-party Nazi slate—that was held on the same day.

Nevertheless, Hitler's consolidation of power was incomplete: he had not yet secured the support of the army, the one unifying national body of the previous era that had remained outside his direct control. He had tried wooing its senior officer corps with promotions, promises of rearmament, and ingratiating gestures of respect to their titular head, Field Marshal von Hindenburg (who, though now senescent and virtually powerless, was still clinging on to the office of president). But it was clear that he hadn't yet done enough to win over the generals completely. This worried the Führer greatly. He was acutely aware that the old reactionary forces represented by Kurt von Schleicher and Franz von Papen continued to lurk in the shadows and had lost none of their appetite for intrigue.* If they were ever able to stir up trouble in the armed forces, especially by playing on the mutual jealousy and resentment felt by the Reichswehr and the Nazi Party's powerful paramilitary wing, the SA, there was a very strong possibility they could mount a plot against him.

To compound the problem, the SA was becoming restless. Having spent the previous year brutalizing the party's left-wing opponents and the Jews, the brownshirts were now making noises about the need for a "second revolution" to curb the prerogatives of the old Junker classes. Ernst Röhm, their piratical, headstrong, and homosexual

---

*Unable or unwilling to fade into decent obscurity, Schleicher had begun to dabble in politics again.

leader, had long been one of Hitler's most devoted supporters—and perhaps the closest thing he ever had to an intimate friend—but as the ranks of the Sturmabteilung had swollen to over two and half million, Röhm's ambitions had become correspondingly grandiose. Once a Nazi government had been secured, the SA chief made it plain that he would not be satisfied with a sinecure in Hitler's cabinet. He wanted to reorganize the military, to place his brownshirts at the head of a vast new People's Army into which the Reichswehr, denuded of its stuffy, anachronistic officer corps (which Röhm despised unreservedly), would be totally absorbed.

The military establishment recoiled in horror at this idea. Disgusted by the gossip that was circulating about corruption, drunkenness, and sexual depravity within Röhm's circle and worried that his flamboyant posturing might draw foreign attention to the army's plans for clandestine rearmament, the generals quietly made it clear to Hitler that if he wanted their support the SA and its plebeian generalissimo would have to be suppressed; in the process, they found common cause with two of Hitler's other lieutenants, Reichstag president Hermann Göring and SS leader Heinrich Himmler, who both loathed Röhm as a dangerous rival.

As a former corporal, Hitler shared some of Röhm's proletarian distrust of the military establishment and sympathized with his political radicalism. But he needed the army's support and was alert to whispers from Göring and Himmler about the SA leader's loyalty and ambitions. Moreover, it was becoming obvious that Hindenburg was ill and wouldn't last long. When he died there would be a vacancy for the Reich presidency and there were still worryingly unresolved questions about how his successor would be chosen or who it would be. Hitler was determined to take the role for himself, though he doubted he could succeed without the Reichswehr's backing. But what if some other rival emerged to try to gain the army's allegiance in the meantime? With Hitler prey to suspicion, the atmosphere in Berlin became more poisonous by the day. To the outside world the new Nazi regime appeared strong and unified. Behind the scenes it was a maelstrom of jealous hatreds and distrust. Something or somebody would have to give way.

In the early hours of June 30, 1934, the tension boiled over into violence as Hitler cynically took the one step that was almost guaranteed to win the Reichswehr's approval. At the head of a group of Himmler's SS men, he descended on Röhm's temporary headquarters at the Hanselbauer Hotel in Wiessee, near Munich. Having surprised the SA boss and his associates in their sleep (and, infamously, a couple of men together in bed), Hitler ordered the execution of his once most devoted follower and several of Röhm's lieutenants.* At the same time in Berlin, Göring and Himmler were coordinating the arrest and murder of his other subordinates. That night SS and Gestapo firing squads brought 150 SA leaders to the Lichterfelde cadet school and shot them. The pretext—almost certainly invented—was that a plot had been uncovered, a mutiny that would have involved Röhm and other SA leaders launching surprise attacks on government buildings and even assassinating Hitler himself. But it quickly became an excuse for settling old scores as the SS hunted down other supposed enemies of the regime. Kurt von Schleicher was shot with his wife as they opened the front door of their Berlin villa to a plainclothes SS detachment. Also murdered were two of Franz von Papen's closest confidants, his secretary, Herbert von Bose, and an adviser, Edgar Jung; both men had been urging the former chancellor to speak out against Nazi terror.† Estimates vary on how many others were killed in the course of the next few hours, but it was probably around five hundred in total. Hundreds more were arrested, beaten up, and taken off to Gestapo headquarters in Prinz Albrecht Strasse for questioning.§

For Heinrich Gattineau, the IG Farben press chief who had once spent an exhilarating few hours discussing synthetic fuel and German self-sufficiency with Adolf Hitler, the Night of the Long Knives was a

---

*Röhm was taken into custody for a few hours before being shot in a cell at Stadelheim prison, near Munich.

†Papen himself survived; indeed, after a brief period of house arrest, he accepted the post of German ambassador to Vienna from the people who had murdered his friends. Former chancellor Heinrich Brüning was equally fortunate. He had slipped out of the country in May after being tipped off that he was marked for murder.

§The SA continued after the Röhm purge under different leadership but it was never the same force again. The SS, of course, emerged from the SA's shadow as an independent organization under the leadership of its Reichsführer, Heinrich Himmler. It would eventually become a much stronger rival to the army than the brownshirts had ever been.

stark lesson in the wisdom of choosing one's friends carefully. Having joined the SA while waiting for his full Nazi Party card, he had gained the rank of *Standartenführer*, or colonel, and quickly become one of Röhm's key economic advisers. Now, bewildered and terrified, he was dragged out of his bed by the secret police and taken into custody to answer charges that he had financed Röhm's supposed plot with IG Farben money.

The allegations were untrue, of course. There had been no conspiracy to finance, and even if there had been, it is highly improbable that Gattineau would ever have been able to use IG funds for such a purpose; although he was authorized to dispense small political donations, he rarely did so without seeking his superiors' permission. But at the best of times the Gestapo was not particularly disposed to worry about such trifles as proof. At this moment of crisis, it was enough that someone somewhere had made the allegation. Several of the SA commanders with whom Gattineau had most closely associated were executed that night or over the following days and in each case the evidence was equally fanciful. As he sat before his interrogators, desperately pleading his innocence, the IG man must have been certain he was next on the list.

Something stayed his accusers' hands that night. It may have been that IG Farben called in a few favors on Gattineau's behalf; many years later Max Ilgner would claim that he had come to the hapless executive's aid. Or it might simply have been that with so many other "conspirators" to dispatch, the SS and Gestapo put off dealing with the small fry until later and focused elsewhere as the wave of violence spent itself. Whichever it was, after a few days Gattineau emerged shakily into the sunlight as a free man. He immediately resigned from the SA and other prominent public posts he held and vowed to be more careful in the future, but that didn't save him from a furious reception back at NW7. His immediate superior, Erwin Selck, who had his own connections to the SA to worry about, tried to get Gattineau dismissed or at least banished from the Unter den Linden offices on the grounds that he was now a dangerous liability who could only draw unwelcome attention to the IG. Carl Bosch intervened and restored calm, but even he had to agree that the executive should keep a low profile for a while. Gattineau's position as head of the *Wipo* research office was made subordinate to Max Ilgner, and a short time later he surrendered all his press duties to him, too. Remarkably, he achieved some degree of rehabilitation a year later when he finally won admission to the Nazi Party (if he bore any grudges, he kept them to himself) and gradually worked his way back into its good graces, but his career never fully recovered.

Though the immediate consequences were slight, the incident was confirmation to anyone in the IG who needed it that the Nazis had to be taken seriously. Indeed, although it can only be speculation, a reminder to that effect may even have been the authorities' real purpose in arresting Gattineau. Despite the number of senior IG executives who had joined the NSDAP, there were still many in the party who viewed the giant cartel as a bastion of pro-Semitism, run by arrogant and unpatriotic nonbelievers. The temptation to rattle their composure may have been too strong to ignore.

But if this was their intention it had little apparent effect on Carl Bosch. Having momentarily swallowed his antipathy to the Nazis in order to secure a deal for Leuna, he soon returned to his usual stance. Not long after the Gattineau affair he was arranging Fritz Haber's controversial memorial service and making disparaging remarks about the party at the concern's board meetings. To those who knew him well, the IG boss's mood was darkening. He had always been subject to periodic bouts of depression and now they were becoming longer and more frequent. There was still plenty of fight in him and his judgment was still sharp but his consumption of alcohol and painkillers was increasing. The stresses and strains of trying to run a massive business in Hitler's Germany were taking their toll.

The death of his sparring partner and colleague Carl Duisberg (at the age of seventy-four) on March 19, 1935, did little to improve his mental state. For all their many differences, Bosch had deeply respected the elder man, not just as a visionary whose determination to end the German chemical industry's self-destructive internal competition had done so much to bring IG Farben into being but as a committed scientist whose love for the laboratory and what it could produce had brought so many wonderful discoveries to light. To be sure, the two had had fierce arguments over the direction the IG was going and Bosch, a humble man in many ways, had often shaken his head over Duisberg's vanity and ostentation. Nevertheless, he knew there had been no sharper business brain in Europe when it came to cutting a deal or finding a way out of an impasse. It was a great blow to be deprived of his advice at so difficult a time.

Duisberg's passing was mourned throughout the whole of Germany but at Leverkusen, the scene of his greatest achievements, it had a special significance. The huge Rhine-side factory that had dazzled his rivals was closed for the day and thousands came from the company town and from nearby Cologne to pay homage. His monumental house, where the excruciating negotiations to create the IG had taken place, was shuttered and silent and the flag that had once proudly proclaimed the master's presence was hauled down for the last time. It was a fitting way to say good-bye to someone who had always enjoyed ceremony and pomp. That night, however, the giant aspirin logo over the Bayer factory was turned on as usual, its thousands of electric lights a brilliant reminder of Duisberg's most remarkable legacy. An assessment of his wider historical significance came a few weeks later—fittingly enough in a foreign newspaper: "Germany is deprived of one of the greatest and most valuable citizens she has ever had," wrote the London *Times*. "In the legend of the future, he may well come to be considered the most efficient and effective industrialist the world has yet known."* But given what was to happen to his company and his country over the years that followed, it was probably just as well that Duisberg died when he did. Though his patriotic heart might have rejoiced at the restoration of German power, the grand old man would have been devastated by the IG's growing entanglement with the criminal new regime.

Duisberg was not the only significant German to die that year: on August 2, Field Marshal Paul von Hindenburg, the eighty-seven-year-old guardian of the Hohenzollern legacy, passed into history. He had

---

*Duisberg's legacy to the IG wasn't restricted to drugs, dyes, and scientific discoveries. He also left three sons. Carl Jr. served on the IG's supervisory board, Curt followed in his father's footsteps in the pharmacy department at Leverkusen, and Walter, an American citizen from 1933, became vice president and treasurer of the American IG.

been debilitated for some months, retiring to his sickbed at his ancestral estate in Neudeck, from where he dispatched a last telegram to Hitler to thank him for having recently "nipped treason in the bud." He probably knew a little of the true events of the Röhm purge and the fate of his once favored adviser Kurt Schleicher, but he kept the knowledge to himself. His political testament endorsed Hitler as his successor, for the Führer had "led the German nation above all professional and class distinctions to internal unity."

With all possible opponents out of the way and the army's unease erased by his suppression of the SA, Hitler was able to grasp the opportunity on offer. The presidency and Reich chancellorship were immediately consolidated by emergency decree into one office held by the Nazi leader.* A few weeks after Hindenburg's death Hitler was in a position to demand that the armed forces swear allegiance to his person rather than to the state. On August 20 all officers and men paraded and took a pledge that was used to justify many terrible acts in the years to come: "I swear by God this sacred oath, that I will render unconditional obedience to Adolf Hitler, the Führer of the German Reich and people, supreme commander of the armed forces, and will be ready as a brave soldier to risk my life at any time for this oath." The last remaining barrier to the Nazi revolution had been removed. Hitler was the unchallenged master of Germany. Now, buoyed by the public's adulation and with the help of the IG's synthetic wizardry, he could prepare to take on the world.

VITAL THOUGH OIL undoubtedly was to the Führer's ambitions for military self-sufficiency, it was only part of the equation. As the IG plowed ahead with its expansion of the Leuna synthetic fuel program, it also began to develop plans for another crucial material. Synthetic rubber, or buna, had first become a target of Bayer and BASF during World War I, when the British naval blockade hindered imports of the

---

*Actually, Hitler had persuaded his compliant cabinet to prepare this decree the day *before* Hindenburg's death, a treasonable and illegal act according to the German constitution as it then stood.

natural product from the Far East.* Since then the project had followed an uncertain course, being variously taken up and abandoned as world rubber prices rose and fell and the investment required to take buna beyond the experimental stage seemed either more or less likely to deliver a decent return. In 1933, however, the combination of a Nazi government keen on achieving autarky and the rapidly improving economy had suddenly made the synthetic rubber program more attractive—an impression that was reinforced in August of that year when Fritz ter Meer, the head of *Sparte* II, managed to persuade military procurement officials in Berlin to buy a thousand buna tires for testing on the Reichswehr's vehicles.

The IG proceeded cautiously. Having come so close to catastrophe with its investments in synthetic oil, the cartel was nervous about making a big financial commitment to yet another experimental product until there was proven demand—or enough of a safety net in the form of subsidies. As ter Meer and his colleagues made clear in a memo to the authorities, "Before we resume our efforts on a large scale, it is necessary that the government decide whether it is sufficiently interested in the manufacture of synthetic rubber in Germany to be prepared to support the project."

Unfortunately, the Reich's economics experts, led by Hjalmar Schacht, were far from convinced. They pointed out that a natural rubber tire cost around eighteen marks to produce, while its buna equivalent cost over ninety. To overcome such a massive price differential and qualify for subventions, the synthetic product would have to be of markedly better quality than the natural one—something that the army's tests quickly found not to be the case. With no apparent depletion of natural rubber supplies on the horizon, there didn't seem much point in discussing subsidies any further.

It took a direct intervention from the Führer to get things moving again. In this instance, Hitler had little interest in economic niceties. Always aware of the lessons of the Great War, he was determined to make Germany self-sufficient in strategic resources: the fatherland

---

*The word *buna* was an amalgamation of the first two letters for the molecule butadiene and Na, the chemical symbol for the element sodium.

must never again be put in jeopardy because of its dependence on foreigners for raw materials. Rubber was especially vital to Hitler's plans for rearmament and a secure nationally controlled supply was essential; if that meant paying a higher premium, then so be it. Informed that the IG's program had stalled, he appointed his personal economic adviser, the Ruhr industrialist Wilhelm Keppler, as a plenipotentiary for raw materials and synthetics and told him to sort the problem out. The Führer assumed the production of synthetic rubber was now taken care of and announced to a Nazi rally at Nuremberg on September 11, 1935, that "the erection of the first factory in Germany for this purpose will be started at once."

In truth, Keppler had a much harder time than he expected. Although Hitler had given the go-ahead, no formal commitment to subsidies had been made. Schacht, by now economics minister, was thus able to continue dragging his heels, protesting that uncompetitively priced buna tires would generate none of the foreign exchange revenue the country so desperately needed—a reasonable concern given the investment the state was being asked to make. The army also remained resistant because its tests showed that buna tires fell apart under rigorous military conditions. Indeed, even the IG still had cold feet. The concern was willing in principle to invest money and energy in buna, Fritz ter Meer told Keppler, but without the assurance of public funds, the project was not financially viable. Commercial manufacturers were reluctant to make tires with buna because it was so expensive. To bring them on board, production costs would have to drop significantly—something that could not be achieved without state subsidies. It was only when Keppler went back to Hitler and obtained his explicit and unqualified backing for an agreement on government support that Carl Bosch and his colleagues were persuaded to move forward. In late 1935, under the direction of a promising young chemist called Otto Ambros, the IG began building another new plant, this time at Schkopau, a few miles from Leuna. The company announced that once production tests were out of the way the works would expand its capacity to a thousand tons a month.

The decision to proceed with buna was one of Bosch's last acts as chairman of the *Vorstand*. The death of Duisberg had left the chair of the *Aufsichtsrat* vacant and now, at the age of sixty, the IG's boss decided to fill it. He was exhausted and depressed by the day-to-day pressures of the business, and though he had every intention of playing an important role in IG Farben for years to come, he was glad to let someone else take responsibility for dealing head-on with the government. Having won the Nobel Prize and secured his beloved fuel hydrogenation project at Leuna, he had a great many extraordinary achievements to his credit, but he was also made uneasy by the IG's now irrevocable association with the Nazis. The recent deals he had sanctioned were commercially right for the concern but they were good for Hitler, too, and that must have been increasingly troubling. It was time to move off center stage.

To those in the IG who were accustomed to Bosch's dominant presence at the top of the firm, the announcement of his successor came as a shock. Fifty-six-year-old Hermann Schmitz sprang from an entirely different mold. Reticent, cautious, and almost obsessively secretive, he had been headhunted by Bosch for BASF after the war because of his expert knowledge of banking and accounting procedures. During the period following the IG's creation, these skills had proved to be a great asset: Schmitz had quickly mastered the company's complicated financial affairs and gone on to become one of Bosch's most useful lieutenants. But as a leader of men Schmitz was to prove woefully inadequate. He had none of his predecessor's charisma, let alone any scientific training or experience of running a big plant, and though his stolidity and circumspection gave the impression of calm competence— qualities sufficient to recommend him to the IG's board members and major shareholders—they would turn out to be far less significant than his flawed political and moral judgment. He had already shown he was susceptible to Nazi blandishments by becoming a party-sponsored delegate to the Reichstag during the rigged November 1933 election. In the years following his appointment as *Vorstand* chairman, Schmitz's misguided opportunism, idiosyncratic decision making, and weak management would contribute in a major way to the cartel's downfall.

Crucially, his promotion came as the IG—reassured by the return of civic stability, the improvement in its financial performance, and, most significantly, the benefits already accruing from the *Benzinvertrag* with Göring's Air Ministry—showed signs of a shift in its position, moving away from tactical and semipassive support of government policies to an active role in shaping and implementing Nazi programs for self-sufficiency. Hitler's stated aim was the restoration of German power: it was no secret to his coterie that his plans included—indeed, would inevitably lead to—armed conflict at some point in the future. But such a step could be taken only after meticulous preparation and rearmament and the mobilization of significant parts of German industry. The covert Luftwaffe program was an early phase of this rearmament; now the effort would be expanded across all the armed services. Key businesses were expected to become full partners in the enterprise, sharing its aims and the Nazis' sense of urgency. With the Nazi-sympathizing Schmitz in the driver's seat, the cartel would become fully engaged in this process, creating an infrastructure that would allow it to respond directly to the government's demands for strategic autarky—in effect, taking a lead role in getting Germany ready for war.

Carl Krauch, the head of *Sparte* I and one of the combine's most ambitious and influential figures, was to be the principal architect of this new partnership. A visiting professor of chemistry at Heidelberg University and a leading figure at the Kaiser Wilhelm Institute (like several other IG executives, Krauch maintained close links with the academic community), he had originally been another of Bosch's protégés back at BASF. He had first shown his energy and organizational skills in 1921 when he had managed to get the explosion-torn Oppau works back on line in less than four months. Subsequently he had played a key part in helping his chief persuade the Interessen Gemeinschaft companies to join together and, as head of *Sparte* I, had responsibility for all the cartel's activities involving hydrogenation, a process he understood as well as, if not better than, anyone else in the company. Understandably, he had always been a staunch supporter of Bosch's determined efforts to keep Leuna alive and he had been delighted when his paper on the German fuel economy had led to the IG's synthetic gasoline contract with the government. Now he was to follow that deal to its logical conclusion and become one of the most important men in Nazi Germany.

Given his contacts with the Air Ministry over the *Benzinvertrag* it is perhaps not surprising that Krauch appreciated the real significance of the regime's drive to self-sufficiency long before anyone else in the IG: General Erhard Milch's inquiries in the run-up to that deal had clearly stemmed from Hermann Göring's desire to find a secure source of aviation fuel for the new Luftwaffe and implied that the government was preparing for armed conflict in the near future. The question of when and how the cartel was explicitly informed of this objective would later be the subject of much debate, but Krauch evidently knew enough in 1934 to begin planning an office to coordinate the IG's relations with the military. The *Vermittlungstelle Wehrmacht*, or Army Liaison Office, was not formally established until September 1935 but by then, as a memo from Krauch to his colleagues in *Sparte* I demonstrated, its purpose was unambiguous.

> The newly founded *Vermittlungstelle Wehrmacht* has as its task the simplifying and building up of a tight organization for armament within the IG. . . . In case of war, the IG will be treated by the authorities concerned with armament questions as one big plant, which in its task for armament, as far as it is possible to do so, will regulate itself without any organizational influence from outside.

The *Verm. W.*, as it was known, was housed in a small suite of rooms at the rear of the Berlin NW7 offices. Its six staff members worked under Krauch's supervision and were responsible for monitoring and coordinating the relationship between the IG's various *Sparten* and the armed forces. Judging from Krauch's memo, the concern seems to have hoped that by creating its own liaison infrastructure it could avoid government interference that might one day threaten its commercial independence. But years later the timing of the move would lay the IG open to charges that it had helped initiate a process that could only have had an aggressive intent. Its executives would claim at Nuremberg that the IG of 1935 was just an ordinary private company: large, powerful, and strategically important, to be sure, but no better informed of the government's intentions that any other business. Prosecutors would suggest otherwise. To them, a decision to set up a department tasked with ensuring the company's effective contribution to a future war economy—at a time when the vast majority of people in Germany were ignorant of any need for a war economy—could be interpreted in only two ways. Either the concern's executives had displayed a truly remarkable degree of prescience or, more likely, they had had inside knowledge of what was to come and were early and willing participants in bringing it about. The defendants' case was not helped by the fact that within its first few months the *Verm. W.* prepared a *Mob-Kalendar*, a planning document for mobilization that addressed such issues as how to ensure adequate energy supplies for the IG's factories in wartime, enforce transportation and workforce requirements, and organize air raid protection procedures. Sensible defensive precautions though these may have been, they seemed to have almost nothing to do with the state of the country at that moment. Hitler was still six months away from marching troops in to the Rhineland (a move that surprised most of his countrymen as much as it did the rest of the world) while the Anschluss with Austria, the annexation of the Sudetenland, and the invasion of Poland were some years in the future.

Suspiciously prescient or not, having set this process in motion Carl Krauch soon went one step further. He went to work directly for the government, joining a newly formed commission for coordinating government policy on raw materials and foreign exchange. The commission was a consequence of an ongoing conflict between Hitler's two economic experts, Hjalmar Schacht and Wilhelm Keppler, about the cost of the rapidly accelerating rearmament program. The German harvests of 1934 and 1935 had been poor and Schacht wanted to use some of the country's limited foreign exchange reserves for importing vital foodstuffs. Keppler, in line with the Führer's wishes, wanted to use those reserves to buy and stockpile strategic raw materials. With neither adviser willing to give way, the dispute dragged on until March 7, 1936, when, in flagrant violation of the Treaty of Versailles and the subsequent Locarno Pact, Hitler sent troops into the Rhineland to reclaim the territory for the Reich. The incursion was a huge gamble because had France and Britain retaliated (as they were legally entitled to do), the Wehrmacht, still unprepared for war, would have been quickly overwhelmed. In the event, neither nation was willing to accept the challenge, but the Soviet Union and Romania responded by limiting oil exports to Germany, which led to a supply shortage and dramatic price rises. Hitler asked Göring to deal with the fuel problem and also to mediate between his bickering economic advisers.

Convinced that the former air ace knew nothing about financial matters and would therefore be easily manipulated, Schacht then approached Göring with a proposal that he should lead a commission for coordinating government policy on raw materials and foreign exchange. The economics minister had intended that he himself would retain control of this organization, but the move backfired badly on April 27 when Hitler's official communiqué put Göring in charge, effectively sidelining Schacht. With that the economy was firmly yoked to the government's military ambitions.

After appointing Colonel Fritz Löb, one of his Air Ministry aides, to run the commission's administrative staff, Göring went looking for a pool of technical specialists to provide expert advice. His first call was to Carl Bosch and Hermann Schmitz at IG Farben to see if he could obtain the services of Carl Krauch as his head of research and development. Though uneasy about the request, Bosch and Schmitz were worried that, if they didn't accede, others in the regime might seize on their refusal as an excuse to set up a rival state-owned synthetic fuel operation. So they agreed.

Krauch was delighted. A fiercely ambitious man—whose hopes of succeeding Bosch as chairman of the *Vorstand* had been dashed by the appointment of Schmitz—he was now about to enter into the highest circles in the land. Moreover, there was no suggestion that he should give up any of his key positions or privileges at the IG. He would continue as head of the newly formed *Vermittlungstelle Wehrmacht* and as chief of *Sparte* I, with its all-important hydrogenation production. He was also allowed to keep drawing his comfortable IG salary, to retain his place on the *Vorstand*, and to take two of his closest associates at the *Verm. W.*, Johannes Eckell and Gerhard Ritter, with him onto Göring's team. He was aware, of course, that retaining his connections with the IG would attract some adverse comment from other companies (something that also concerned influential *Vorstand* members such as Georg von Schnitzler), but if his move helped cement the concern's relations with the government that would be a price worth paying. For one thing, he'd be able to see to it that the Reich's plans for fuel and rubber self-sufficiency continued to complement the IG's interests.

As Krauch settled into his work, he quickly realized that the poisonous internal politics of the Third Reich added layers of complication to his job. Göring proved to be even more intent than Keppler on spending the Reich's hard-pressed resources on rearmament and synthetic strategic raw materials, and just as unconcerned about the effect it would have on the economy. "If war comes tomorrow we will have to rely on substitutes," he said. "Then money won't play any role at all." Inevitably, Göring clashed with Schacht. The economics minister had nothing against synthetics in principle but he continued to voice his concern that they were significantly more expensive than natural products. At a meeting of ministers at the end of May 1936, he cited buna as an example. Natural rubber could be obtained cheaply on the open market, he declared. What was the point of wasting money on a substitute that cost several times as much? He also furiously protested against a plan to adapt the blast furnaces of all Germany's steel factories (by means of a procedure called the Renn process) to allow them to use domestic low-grade iron ore rather than premium imported materials from Sweden and elsewhere. Schacht insisted that the investment required would greatly increase production costs, making it impossible to sell German steel overseas. Millions of marks worth of vital foreign exchange would be lost as a result.

The rows eventually grew so heated they began appearing in the foreign press. That summer the *New York Times* twice reported that the minister of defense, General Werner von Blomberg, had been called in to mediate and calm things down. But the two sides proved intractable. Göring wanted to dramatically increase public borrowing to finance Germany's push to rearmament and strategic self-sufficiency; Schacht held to his insistence that doing so to subsidize the production of expensive substitutes—instead of importing more affordable natural materials from abroad—could lead to an overheated German economy and a return to the hyperinflation of 1923.

Schacht had failed to take account of his opponent's well-honed political skills. Even as the country was preparing to give itself up to celebrating the Berlin Olympics that August—an event that was carefully stage-managed by Joseph Goebbels to present an acceptable face of Germany to the world—Göring's team of economic experts was working away on a set of proposals to confound his rival. After throwing a number of lavish welcoming parties for foreign dignitaries in his capacities as president of the Reichstag, air minister, and minister-president of Prussia (each one a glorious opportunity to parade in an elaborately gold-braided full dress uniform), he set off to brief the Führer at his mountain retreat on the Obersalzberg.

As might have been expected, Hitler needed little persuasion to come down on Göring's side of the argument. Drawing heavily on his minister's ideas, he dictated a confidential memorandum setting out his reasons for initiating a four-year plan to prepare Germany for war by achieving strategic self-sufficiency. In the long term, he said, the Reich's need for raw materials would be answered by increasing its *Lebensraum,* or living space, through military conquest. In the short term, a solution had to be found within its existing borders. Rearmament had to take precedence over everything else and that meant aggressively pursuing a program of developing synthetics—whatever the cost. Stockpiling was not an alternative because no country could possibly accumulate enough raw materials for more than a year of conflict. Even maintaining strong foreign currency reserves was little more than a distraction. Germany had enjoyed substantial currency assets in World War I, after all, but had been unable to buy sufficient fuel, rubber, copper, and tin.

Hitler also made it perfectly plain that the only purpose of industry—and indeed of his stubborn minister of economics—was to serve the needs of the Reich. Both had to understand that concerns about costs and production difficulties were secondary to the greater requirements of the state: "The minister of economics has only to set the tasks of the national economy; private industry has to fulfill them. But if private industry considers itself unable to do this, then the National Socialist state will know by itself how to resolve the problem."

Although Schacht was not sent an advance copy of Hitler's memo, he was informed that Hitler was planning to use the Nazi Party's annual rally that September as the launching pad for a vast new program for national self-sufficiency. Realizing that such a public declaration would effectively make the policy irreversible and fearing that the economic consequences would be atrocious, Schacht tried desperately to get General Blomberg to warn their leader that he was about to make a grave mistake.

> If the Führer emphasizes this in front of the masses in Nuremberg he will receive a great amount of applause from the audience, but he will bring failure to the entire commercial policy. There is only one thing in our present needy position: the promotion of exports. Every threat against foreign countries, however, will bring about contrary results. We have had reverses in the field of fuels. . . . There will not be large amounts of rubber. The Renn process in the field of ores is meeting great difficulties. If we shout our decision to make ourselves economically independent, then we cut our own throats because we can no longer survive the necessary transition period. . . . If the people's food supply is not to be endangered, the Führer must refrain from his plan.

But Blomberg, sensing which way the wind was blowing, declined to get involved. The following day Göring appeared at an economic cabinet meeting, triumphantly waving a copy of Hitler's memo and insisting that the matter was now settled beyond doubt. If the economics minister still had any qualms, he said sarcastically, he could console himself with the thought that Frederick the Great had been a strong inflationist. A few weeks later, as expected, Hitler announced the Four-Year Plan at Nuremberg, and he followed it up on October 18 with an announcement designating Göring as its plenipotentiary, with authority to issue decrees for the "strict coordination of all competent authorities in party and state."*

Of course, all of these developments had significant implications

---

*Göring was not slow to exploit the many opportunities for personal enrichment that his new responsibilities opened up—in the form of bribes and inducements from manufacturers and financiers. He wasn't the only one to benefit. Because so much of Göring's time was to be devoted to the Four-Year Plan, Hitler decided to pass his ministerial responsibilities for the police to Heinrich Himmler. With a portfolio that now encompassed the SS, the Gestapo, and concentration camps for political opponents, Himmler was becoming a force to be reckoned with—and someone with whom the IG would eventually have to work.

for IG Farben and Carl Krauch. One of Göring's first acts was to transfer his entire staff at the raw materials and foreign exchange commission to the newly formed Office of the Four-Year Plan, with Krauch continuing in his role as head of research and development and one of his *Verm. W.* subordinates, Johannes Eckell, taking specific responsibility for rubber.* It quickly became apparent just how important Krauch's role was to be. Strategic self-sufficiency had to cover three main areas of industrial activity—coal, steel, and chemicals (including synthetic fuel, buna, nitrogen for explosives, plastics, and synthetic fibers). Coal production was going smoothly; the Ruhr could provide as much as the country required. The steel industry needed some attention because manufacturers were proving resistant to the idea that they should work with low-grade domestic iron ore.† But for the moment, the only area requiring large-scale investment was the chemical industry, making it the principal beneficiary of the Four-Year Plan's largesse. Around one billion reichsmarks had been earmarked for industrial investment in the first six months of the program and the German chemical industry was to receive over 90 percent of it. The IG's share of this money (reflecting its total dominance of the sector) came to around 72 percent—almost two-thirds of a billion reichsmarks for just one company and its products. Even if the Four-Year Plan had not been set up—as was later suggested—purely for the benefit of IG Farben, with the cartel's very own Carl Krauch now in a position to influence the allocation of these funds, it would soon begin to look that way. Having already profited hugely from the overall expansion in domestic and international trade that had followed since the end of the Depression, one of the world's most prosperous businesses was about to get a great deal richer.

That this increasing wealth was a result of the Nazi regime's determination to use military might must by now have been blatantly obvious to even the most blinkered IG Farben executive. On December 17, 1936, during a secret speech at the Preussenhaus in Berlin, Hermann

---

*Unlike Krauch, Eckell resigned from the IG and became a full-time civil servant on the government payroll.

†In 1938, frustrated by the steel industry's opposition, Göring set up a state-owned steel manufacturer, the Hermann Göring Werke.

Göring left an audience of industrialists and government officials—including the IG's Carl Bosch, Hermann Schmitz, Georg von Schnitzler, and Carl Krauch—in little doubt of what the Nazis expected from them.

> The struggle we are approaching demands a colossal measure of production capacity. No limit on rearmament can be visualized. The only alternatives are victory or destruction. If we win, business will be sufficiently compensated. . . . We live in a time when the final battle is in sight. We are already on the threshold of mobilization and we are already at war. All that is lacking is the actual shooting.

RIGHT: BASF's founder, Friedrich Engelhorn, was one of the nineteenth century's most successful dyestuff entrepreneurs. *(BASF Aktiengesellschaft)*

LEFT: A determined looking Carl Duisberg, shortly after he joined Bayer in 1884. *(Bayer Business Services GmbH, Corporate History & Archives)*

ABOVE LEFT: Fritz Haber won a Nobel Prize for the fixation of nitrogen; he also developed chemical weapons and, at Ypres, pioneered the combat use of poison gas. *(Nobel Museum)*

ABOVE RIGHT: Carl Bosch. BASF's engineering and chemistry genius became IG Farben's first chief executive. *(BASF Aktiengesellschaft)*

British poison gas casualties on the Western Front in France, 1918. *(Imperial War Museum)*

ABOVE: The huge Ludwigshafen plant on the banks of the Rhine. Such facilities made the German chemical industry envied throughout the world. *(BASF Aktiengesellschaft)*

A Bosch-Reactor. The design of this huge double-skinned iron and steel tube made possible the industrial synthesis of ammonia nitrate. *(BASF Aktiengesellschaft)*

On September 21, 1921, a huge explosion tore apart BASF's nitrate factory at Oppau on the Rhine. The blast was heard as far away as Munich and Paris. *(BASF Aktiengesellschaft)*

A few hours after the explosion, dazed survivors stand outside their wrecked homes. The disaster was one of the worst industrial accidents in history. *(BASF Aktiengesellschaft)*

Carl Duisberg, pictured around the time of IG Farben's creation in 1925. *(Bayer Business Services GmbH, Corporate History & Archives)*

Duisberg's villa at Leverkusen, where agreement to establish IG Farben was reached in November 1924. Note the flag signifying Duisberg's presence in the building. *(Bayer Business Services GmbH, Corporate History & Archives)*

Leuna, center of IG Farben's revolutionary synthetic fuel production. *(BASF Aktiengesellschaft)*

A stylised image of a Leuna filling station. German self-sufficiency in strategic raw materials such as fuel was to become a key objective for Nazi military planners. *(BASF Aktiengesellschaft)*

On its completion in 1930, IG Farben's headquarters in Frankfurt was said to be the largest office complex in the world. Today it forms part of a university campus.

Carl Krauch in the early 1930s. One of IG Farben's most ambitious executives, Krauch would become a central player in Hermann Göring's Four Year Plan to re-arm Germany. *(BASF Aktiengesellschaft)*

An IG Farben float in a German Workers Day parade in Ludwigshafen, May
1, 1935. *(BASF Aktiengesellschaft)*

9

PREPARING FOR WAR

The three years running up to World War II were to prove the most commercially successful that IG Farben had yet experienced. As a consequence of its dominant role in Hermann Göring's Four-Year Plan, the company enjoyed a period of unprecedented growth and prosperity, selling more products, employing more people, making more money (and paying more tax) than ever before. By 1939 turnover had reached almost RM 2 billion, with gross profits rising by 50 percent (to RM 377 million) and net profits increasing by 71 percent (to RM 240 million). Well before Adolf Hitler finalized his secret plans for the invasion of Poland, the IG labor force had doubled in size, with over 230,000 workers striving in an expanding network of factories, offices, laboratories, and mines to meet the regime's voracious appetite for strategic raw materials.

Not all of this growth came from sales to the military. The IG was able to exploit the fact that many of the new synthetic chemicals it was making for the Wehrmacht had potential for civilian use as well. When Germany's worsening foreign relations adversely affected export markets and the cartel had to look for domestic customers instead, its adaptable range of ersatz products helped make up the shortfall. Indeed, by 1939 the company was addressing these new opportunities so effectively that a citizen of the Third Reich, had he so wished, could have risen each morning to the chimes from a plastic IG alarm clock, washed and shaved using IG soaps, and then sat down at a table covered with an IG synthetic cloth to eat a breakfast cooked in IG synthetic fats and drink coffee sweetened with IG saccharine. As he left for work, aboard a bus fitted with IG buna tires and powered by IG synthetic gasoline, his wife (Nazi ideology having scant sympathy for the notion that a married woman should ever be employed outside the home) could have cleaned the floors with an IG polish, treated the dog's fleas with an IG pesticide, and then perhaps have taken an IG aspirin to relieve the headache brought on by her tedious life as a hausfrau. It mattered little that some of these synthetic substitutes were not as good as the real thing, because for many patriotic Germans they were symbols of the Reich's scientific prowess. That every one of them had been made from materials originating from within the fatherland represented a remarkable turnaround for a country that had always been woefully deficient in natural resources—a triumph that Nazi propagandists were keen to celebrate.

> What the chemical industry is today is evident from the fact that it, above all, has succeeded in securing national independence in raw materials, an accomplishment that previously had frequently been considered impossible. The value of chemistry to the German national economy cannot be expressed in terms of money, anymore than can the price of a glass of water to a person who needs it urgently for the preservation of his life.

Without Hitler's rearmament programs, however, there would have been far fewer IG products to sell. Synthetic oil and other materials had gone into full-scale production only because the government was prepared to subsidize them for strategic reasons; indeed some 40 percent of the IG's sales increases between 1936 and 1939 came from five areas of production directly stimulated by the Four-Year Plan: nitrates for explosives, fuel, metals, buna, and plastics.

At Nuremberg many years later the origins and dual-use potential of some of these products would became the focus of heated debate, with prosecution and defense citing numerous examples to prove that the IG's motives had been either deliberately militaristic or merely opportunistic. Thus the court was variously invited to consider that the fuel which drove a bus, for example, could also with some adjustment be made to power tanks and Stuka bombers, or that buna could be used in military vehicles as easily as in civilian automobiles, or that ersatz fiber could be turned into uniforms, or that the methanol found in shaving lotion was an essential component of military antifreeze.

But interesting though these debates were, they were always going to be of less significance than two rather more straightforward, and unarguable, propositions—namely, that in the three years prior to World War II the IG proved more than willing to provide the expanding Nazi military machine with the materials it needed and that without the concern's synthetic chemistry Germany would have been unable to fight for long. Because whether its science was the chicken or the egg, IG Farben was clearly indispensable to the Führer's plans from 1936 onward, and the company's leading executives, with very few exceptions, were content that this should be so and collaborated without reservation. With barely a demur, and certainly no resignations out of principle, they provided Hitler's government with economic intelligence on Nazi Germany's future enemies, while conspiring to deny those enemies the synthetic resources they would need to defend themselves; they acceded enthusiastically to the regime's demands for more output and more factories, often building secret plants that produced *exclusively* military materials; they embraced the regime's Aryanization program with a lack of protest that was truly shaming, given the IG's previous tradition of employing Jews; and they joined the Nazi Party in increasing numbers until only a few brave skeptics were left.

At Nuremberg the defendants argued that many of their actions were of peaceful, commercial intent, or, at most, designed for their nation's defense, and that they were often acting under duress; but there is no gainsaying that they were happy to take the money they were offered and raised no discernible moral or practical objections to where it was coming from. Had the IG's managers found the courage to oppose doing business with the Nazis in the late 1930s, or had they been even marginally less compliant, Hitler would have struggled to get his war machine moving. Instead, their cooperation drove the machine forward, as the cartel's own Georg von Schnitzler was eventually forced to acknowledge: "IG took on a great responsibility and gave, in the chemical sector, substantial and even decisive aid for Hitler's foreign policy which led to war and the ruination of Germany. . . . I must conclude that IG is largely responsible for the policies of Hitler."

HAVING GAMBLED SUCCESSFULLY that the reoccupation of the Rhineland would be unopposed by Britain and France, Hitler proceeded in 1936 to cement alliances that would allow him to consolidate Germany's gains and prepare the way for his next forays on the European stage. Thus Mussolini's Italy was drawn into an axis that was defined as much by the need of the two countries for foreign friends (Italy having fallen foul of the League of Nations over its invasion of Abyssinia) as by their common political philosophy and mutual hatred of Bolshevism. This association was soon extended to include imperial Japan, whose expansionist foreign policy had already involved it in a savage conflict in China.

In the meantime, Spain had also attracted the Führer's attention. The outbreak of civil war in July 1936, between the left-wing Republican government and General Franco's fascist Nationalist movement, had all the elements of a dress rehearsal for the greater clash between the era's two dominant ideologies that many now saw as inevitable. Hitler was naturally predisposed to support the Nationalists, not least because he believed an extended conflict would increase tensions in the Mediterranean and move Italy (which also supported the Spanish rebels) closer toward Germany and farther away from Britain and France—as indeed happened. But it also gave him an ideal opportunity to test some of the blitzkrieg tactics that Germany's military strategists had been developing. In defiance of an international noninvolvement agreement among the European powers (which Soviet Russia also ignored), Germany and Italy sent planes, tanks, troops, and technical "advisers" to the Nationalists in considerable numbers—

along with the Condor Legion, an air force unit that became infamous for its bombing of the Spanish town of Guernica.*

In these circumstances, the IG's executives can hardly have needed the stimulus of Hermann Göring's martial speech at the Prussenhaus in December 1936 to appreciate the seriousness of the government's drive for rearmament. Nonetheless, after years of patiently lobbying authorities for subventions and concessions, they must have been taken aback at the speed with which the Four-Year Plan began to affect their business. As 1937 got under way the concern came under intense pressure to increase its productive capacity to meet the regime's demands.

Carl Krauch—who still attended IG *Vorstand* meetings and retained leadership of *Sparte* I—was the principal conduit for this pressure. Göring had made him responsible for ensuring that Germany reached self-sufficiency in more than two dozen key products, from fuel and rubber to sulphur, phosphates, nonprecious metals, resins, and textiles, and since the IG was the major producer of most of these materials, he naturally directed the government's orders and investment back to his old firm. By February 1937 his office had commissioned more than RM 500 million worth of special projects and was anticipating investing RM 8 billion more—a significant part of which was destined for areas in which the IG had a special interest.

But Krauch's role went far beyond merely allocating funds and identifying likely suppliers. He also took it upon himself to gauge whether the Four-Year Plan was setting its targets high enough, clashing repeatedly with his immediate superior, Colonel Fritz Löb, who though formally responsible was out of his depth when it came to assessing the Wehrmacht's likely needs and industry's ability to meet them. The troubled relationship between the two dated back to 1935 and the early days of the raw materials commission (Göring's first attempt at stimulating synthetics production), when Krauch had gone behind Löb's back to quadruple the size of an IG contract for buna from fifty to two hundred tons a month. Once the Four-Year Plan was

---

*For the IG, the Spanish civil war was an opportunity to assess the performance of its synthetic aviation fuel, supplied to the Luftwaffe as part of the 1933 *Benzinvertrag*.

up and running, Krauch called a meeting of IG managers and army ordnance officials (to which he didn't invite Löb), where it was decided to increase the IG Farben buna contract to a thousand tons a month—an order that was pushed through over Löb's objections. The two clashed again early the following year when Krauch managed to win Göring's approval for a second IG buna plant, at Hüls (by now Schkopau was producing its maximum capacity of two thousand tons a month), despite the colonel's insistence that it was unnecessary.

This pattern was repeated several times as Krauch sought to raise production levels for a variety of different commodities. In December 1937, for example, Paul Körner, Göring's state secretary in the Office of the Four-Year Plan, asked him to review some estimates for synthetic fuel production that Colonel Löb had submitted for synthetic fuel. Krauch, immediately seeing that they had been set far too low to meet the military's targets, revised them. To Löb's considerable fury, Körner passed the new estimates on to Göring. A few months later the same thing happened when Krauch scrutinized his superior's estimates for explosives. His dual role within the IG meant he was better placed than anyone else to know whether the concern was making enough synthetic nitrate to hit the targets set by Löb, and he could see quite clearly that the necessary production capacity didn't exist. Yet again he passed his concerns on to Körner, who raised them directly with Göring. The latter was so disturbed he called his bickering subordinates to a conference at Karinhall, his palatial country estate.

Krauch was at his most formidable in such situations. With years of committee experience at the IG behind him, he was easily able to demonstrate his mastery of the figures and demolish his rival's projections. Göring was deeply impressed and Krauch left the meeting with a license to reexamine all of Löb's estimates. The result was the Krauch Plan, a systematic revision of Germany's productive capacity for strategic raw materials coupled with a new program for achieving the desired objectives. In the summer of 1938 Göring made Krauch plenipotentiary general for special questions of chemical production and gave him complete responsibility (which, remarkably, included authority over army ordnance) for putting the plans into effect. In less than two years Carl Krauch had evolved from part-time government adviser to become the most important industrial figure in Germany's war preparations.

The concern's response to the huge flood of orders coming from Krauch was mixed at first. On the one hand the IG welcomed the surge in business and profits; on the other it found that working for the government involved a huge growth in bureaucracy and a remarkable degree of secrecy—both of which made the management of an already complex organization increasingly convoluted. When Carl Bosch had been in day-to-day charge, he had just about succeeded in keeping track of its affairs through the labyrinthine network of committees that held the IG together. His successor, Hermann Schmitz, found that this fragile cohesion suffered considerable strain as more factories, offices, and subsidiaries started working directly for government agencies—often under terms of the strictest confidentiality. While this lack of transparency was an inevitable consequence of dealing with military officials intent on concealing the extent of Germany's rearmament from the outside world, it meant that the IG's central offices in Frankfurt and Berlin were less and less able to monitor the concern's development and keep an eye on all its output.

Even when the central departments *did* manage to retain control and oversight of the production and sale processes, the complexity of the task was staggering, not least because IG products emanating from one plant were often not the finished articles but intermediates in the production stage of a range of others, which could be made in different factories by other parts of the combine, by its subsidiaries, or indeed by other manufacturers entirely. Keeping track of what was being made where and for whom called for degrees of planning and coordination that would have stretched the most efficient business—a challenge compounded by military paranoia and, as the thirties wore on, by the fact that the Reich's boundaries were expanding and the plants dependent on the concern's supplies were growing in number and increasingly far-flung.

Take, for example, the synthetic nitrate, methanol, diglycol, and other intermediates and stabilizers that were essential for the manufacture of high explosives such as TNT, hexogen, and nitropenta. Krauch's office would decide that a given month's quota of explosives

222 · HELL'S CARTEL

production needed to be increased and would issue a contract to the *Vermittlungstelle Wehrmacht* office at Berlin NW7. There, staff would allocate the production of the necessary intermediates to major IG plants at Ludwigshafen, Leverkusen, Oppau, and elsewhere. Once made, the materials would then be loaded onto barges, trucks, and trains for shipping to the factories of explosives manufacturer Dynamit AG or its subsidiaries (the DAG itself, of course, being majority-owned by the IG). DAG plants could be at any of a number of sites: Pressburg, Troisdorf, Mannheim, Hachenburg, Kummer, Schlebusch, Oberf, Schönebeck, St. Ingbert, Haslock, Gnaschwitz, Sömmerda, Braunsfeld, Fürth, Silberhutte, Empelde, Düneberg, Wurgendorf, Ferde, Saarwelligen, Vecker, Munde, Reichsweiler, Hamm, Bölitz, or Adolzfurt. These facilities might be within twenty-five miles of the intermediate-producing IG plant or several hundred miles away in Austria or Czechoslovakia. Then, of course, the finished explosives would have to be delivered back to army ordnance depots for distribution to the relevant military units. And this was just one category of products. Given that the IG produced everything from fuel for the Wehrmacht's tanks to bottled oxygen for the Luftwaffe's pilots—not to mention the myriad materials it made for civilian customers—it is a wonder the concern's planning and coordination sections didn't completely collapse under the strain. As Georg von Schnitzler would tell his interrogators after the war, "A survey of what the IG really did or did not make for the Wehrmacht became more and more a matter of guesswork."

As a result, individual executives came to enjoy more influence and independence than they had ever had before. This was a potentially positive development for those who were able to handle the responsibility, but it may also have led to a greater degree of militarization than the IG was required to embrace. Because managers were no longer obliged to defer government armaments contracts upwards for approval, the IG lost its ability to discriminate between projects that had at least some semblance of peaceful legitimacy (that is, for products with dual civilian-military applications) and those with an unmistakably belligerent purpose.

The IG's involvement in the development and manufacture of poison gases offers a case in point. Having been so badly tarnished by the international outcry over the creation and deployment of chemical weapons in World War I, the concern might have been expected to steer clear of such projects. But, in late 1936, under the stimulus of the Four-Year Plan, the IG assumed responsibility for the production of mustard gas—which would eventually be made at Hüls, Trostberg, and Schkopau—and then went on to develop two of the world's most dangerous substances.

The first of these was tabun, an organic phosphorous compound that attacks the central nervous system by inhibiting muscular movement, especially in the lungs, and leads to devastating and fatal contractions. Gerald Schrader, a leading IG research chemist, had stumbled upon the compound during his work on insecticides and promptly reported the discovery to his superiors. Heinrich Hörlein, the IG's pharmaceutical genius, immediately recognized the gas's military potential and passed the information to army ordnance via Krauch's office. A Colonel Rudriger, in charge of the Wehrmacht's poisons unit, called the researcher up to Berlin to demonstrate the substance on animals and was so impressed by its lethality he asked Schrader to develop it into a weapons-grade material. Nine months later, during the course of this top-secret work, Schrader found a second and even more deadly nerve toxin. Known as sarin (its generic chemical description, isopropylmethylphosphrofluoridate, was too complicated for anyone but a chemist), it was so powerful that even the tiniest inhalation could bring about a gruesome and agonizing death. The Wehrmacht wanted this product in its arsenal, too, and was prepared to pay handsomely for it. An ambitious IG executive, Otto Ambros, assumed responsibility for the program (Ambros's star was firmly in the ascendant) and began negotiating finances for the construction of a large production plant at Dyhernfurth in Silesia.

Projects of this kind were the inevitable consequence of the pressure the regime was now exerting on the IG. It is possible that under more normal circumstances shareholder scrutiny might have forced the company to pause and reflect on its activities, but the Nazis had already taken steps to prevent this. In January 1937, determined to let nothing get in the way of its ability to orchestrate industry's response to mobilization, the government had published the German Corporation Law, which removed stockholders' rights to examine balance sheets and allowed governing boards to conceal the details of their business dealings from investors—if national interests dictated these should be kept secret. In theory, of course, this provision should have increased the obligation of managers and board members to act ethically and responsibly. However, few seemed up to the challenge. Instead, as Hitler's hold over Germany and its people strengthened, many of the country's business leaders set their integrity aside and surrendered their companies to Nazification. Unfortunately, the IG was no exception.

IN 1937, after a four-year moratorium on new members, the Nazi Party opened its ranks once more. The *Vorstand*'s Heinrich Hörlein, Wilhelm Mann, Fritz Gajewski, and Heinrich Bütefisch were already full members, while one or two others had joined various ancillary bodies such as the SA or SS. Now almost all of the IG's managing board signed up, including Hermann Schmitz, Georg von Schnitzler, Christian Schneider (who would shortly take over Carl Krauch's job as head of *Sparte* I), Otto Ambros, Carl Lautenschläger, and Ernst Bürgin. Krauch joined, too, although in his position it would have been hard not to, and even the fastidious Fritz ter Meer condescended to send in an application, although he later claimed it wasn't endorsed. Of the two *Vorstand* members who stayed out, August von Knieriem, the IG's lawyer, eventually joined in 1942, while Paul Haefliger, the concern's leading international dealmaker, was excluded as a Swiss citizen. A small group of nonexecutive directors on the *Aufsichtsrat* continued to withhold their allegiance (among them, of course, Carl Bosch, who was to demonstrate his dogged independence of spirit as late as May 1939, when he criticized the Führer in a speech in Munich).* But the supervisory body's power to influence the concern's day-to-day affairs, never very great in the first place, had waned considerably since the

---

*Bosch questioned the Führer's grasp of economics during a speech at the Deutsches Museum in Munich on May 7, 1939. As punishment he was removed from the institution's board and prohibited from making speeches without permission.

death of Duisberg and was now about to be weakened even further, challenged by the regime's insistence on a full Jewish purge.

The government's anti-Semitic program reached a new level of intensity during 1937–38. Until this point, Nazi racial policies aimed at business had been concerned with making life difficult for solely Jewish-owned firms (limiting their access to raw materials, denying them foreign exchange and export licenses, and scaring off their customers with vicious propaganda) in the hope that the proprietors either would be forced to sell their assets at bargain basement prices or would collapse into bankruptcy. In January 1938, however, the regime (through decrees issued by Hermann Göring) began defining "Jewishness"—and Jewish firms—in ever more narrow terms. By July of that year, the presence of even one Jew on a firm's board or executive committee made it a "Jewish" company.

As a consequence, all the remaining Jewish executives at the IG were forced to resign. Those at the lower levels had mostly gone by then, and there were none left on the *Vorstand*, but Bosch's *Aufsichtsrat* was still something of a non-Aryan haven. As late as 1935 he had invited his old friend Richard Merton of the Metallgesellschaft onto the supervisory board, and its ranks still included several other men of Jewish origin: Otto von Mendelssohn-Bartholdy, Carl von Weinberg, Arthur von Weinberg, Wilhelm Peltzer, Gustaf Schlieper, Ernst von Simson, and Alfred Merton. Many of them were influential and powerful, with a proud tradition of serving Germany; Carl von Weinberg, for example, was a former owner of Casella, one of IG Farben's constituent businesses, who had been ennobled by Kaiser Wilhelm II for his contributions to German industry. In 1934, as a loyal son of the fatherland, Carl had even reassured visiting DuPont executives about the Nazi government's intentions toward the Jews, declaring that he was happy to keep his money invested in Germany. But his patriotism counted for little now and he lost his position, along with the rest.

On this occasion, at least, there was probably little the IG's Aryan executives could have done to protect their colleagues and, though they made no official protest, they did, to their credit, try to mitigate the consequences in a number of cases. Neither of the Weinberg brothers, for example, was completely abandoned by the company. With the backing of Schmitz, Krauch, von Schnitzler, and Fritz ter Meer, Carl was eventually helped into exile in Italy, where he was sustained throughout the Nazi years with an annual IG pension of RM 80,000, routed secretly through a subsidiary company's bank account in Milan. His older brother, Arthur von Weinberg, elected to stay in Germany and wasn't quite so lucky. Although Hermann Schmitz reportedly gave money to the Weinbergs to bribe a Nazi official so that Arthur wouldn't have to wear a yellow star, he was nevertheless arrested and incarcerated at Theresienstadt concentration camp. Schmitz and Krauch approached Heinrich Himmler and persuaded him that the eighty-two-year-old could be safely allowed to live out his remaining years in Mecklenburg, with his daughter, the Princess Charlotte Lobkowicz. Unfortunately, the decision was conditional on the approval of the local gauleiter and Arthur von Weinberg died in captivity before it could be obtained.

In the overall scheme of things, these few small acts of humanity demonstrated none of the courage of someone like the businessman Oscar Schindler, who was prepared (double-edged though his motives may have been) to take enormous risks to save the lives of the Jews who worked for him. While it is commendable that a few IG executives had the conscience and loyalty enough to stand by a former senior colleague or two who had helped create their company, it seems a tepid sort of gallantry when one considers that the concern made little or no effort to mitigate the effects of Aryanization on its prewar blue-collar Jewish employees, who were mostly summarily dismissed without any regard to their future welfare. In any case, even the help the cartel gave senior Jewish staff seems to have been selectively tendered.

An episode involving Gerhard Ollendorf, head of the IG's Agfa film factory at Wolfen until his retirement from the *Vorstand* in 1932, was clear evidence of the IG's selectivity. In November 1938 Ollendorf approached Fritz Gajewski, the chief of *Sparte* III, and told him that he was trying to get permission to leave Germany because the situation for Jews was becoming intolerable. The *Sparte* chief commiserated, wished him well, and said good-bye. Then he wrote a letter to the Gestapo.

We wish to inform you that according to our interpretation Dr. Ollendorf has knowledge of secret matters and that, therefore, it would serve the general interest of the economy not to permit Dr. O. to go abroad for the time being. Since Dr. Ollendorf may still be in possession of papers, we would consider it advisable to have his home searched as a precautionary measure and any documents sent to us for study and analysis. We request that this matter be treated in complete confidence.

Of course, Gajewski said nothing of this to Ollendorf, who was subsequently arrested and prevented from emigrating until Gajewski relented and sanctioned his release. Indeed, until 1947, all that Ollendorf knew about the affair was that he had remained in Nazi custody until Gajewski somehow managed to secure his freedom and that his former colleague had then supported his application to leave, permission for which was finally granted in the early summer of 1939. Ollendorf was so impressed by the efforts that Gajewski had apparently made on his behalf that after the war he agreed to repay the favor and wrote an affidavit on the IG man's behalf for his trial at Nuremberg. Unfortunately for the hapless Gajewski, his 1938 letter to the Gestapo was discovered by the prosecution and read out in court.* But at least Ollendorf had managed to get away. Other Jewish IG officials were not so lucky. The company did nothing for Ernst Baumann, a hydrogenation expert at Leuna who was picked up by the Gestapo in late 1939 and died in Buchenwald in 1940, or for three Jewish middle managers from the IG's plant at Piesteritz, who suffered the same fate.

In the meantime, the IG's official response to the enforced resignation of its Jewish *Aufsichtsrat* directors was to apply immediately for a certificate declaring the company to be a "German firm" in accordance with the Reich's race laws. Without such a document, the IG could not have carried on its work for the government, and by the increasingly distorted standards of the wider German business

---

*What effect the revelation had on Ollendorf's opinion of his "old friend" isn't recorded, but there is a strangely satisfying symmetry in the fact that, not long after Ollendorf managed to get out of Germany, Gajewski was himself interrogated by the Gestapo. According to the historian Peter Hayes, during a tour of local Nazi officials at the IG's Wolfen plant in September 1939, Gajewski made some injudicious remarks about the viability of a plan that the Führer had endorsed to make paper and fabric from potato skins. The words were reported and Gajewski was hauled in for a few hours' questioning. He was warned to watch his behavior in the future.

community the cartel's request for clearance was not exceptional. Nevertheless, it was a sad footnote to the truncated careers of the concern's senior Jewish personnel.* But the IG was becoming quite hard-nosed about such matters; any reservations its executives might have felt about the regime's anti-Semitism were not strong enough to stop the opportunistic purchase of a number of formerly Jewish-owned businesses. In 1936 the combine took over the firm of Weinessigfabrik L. Hirsch, and in 1938 it snapped up IFC Mertens and the Halle-based company Braunkohlenwerke Bruckdorf AG, establishing a pattern of questionable acquisitions that would later be repeated in occupied Europe.

Even for those Jewish staff the company *had* managed to spirit abroad (in the early and mid-1930s Carl Bosch had been successful at placing some people in overseas subsidiaries), life was now more complicated. By 1937 the Nazi Party's Foreign Organization (Auslandorganisation, or AO) had become particularly troublesome. The AO's leader, Ernst Bohle, a fanatical anti-Semite and a close associate of Rudolf Hess's, was determined to increase the NSDAP's influence overseas and rid all foreign branches of German businesses of any Jewish connections. The size of the IG's overseas operations was always going to make it a target, but Bohle, who had grown up in South America, where the concern was strongly represented, seemed

---

*All of this, of course, was in stark contrast to the steadily improving conditions being enjoyed by the IG's "German workers" as a consequence of the cartel's work for the Four-Year Plan. The rapid expansion in the IG's manufacturing capacity led to great labor shortages and in concert with the regime, which was desperate to maintain industrial productivity, the company set up various incentive schemes to motivate and reward staff. Foreign holidays, weekend breaks at Strength through Joy (*Kraft durch Freude*) camps, cinema and theater tickets, mystery tours, and prizes of sports equipment were all on offer to "comrades" who showed especial dedication to the cause of meeting the firm's targets. Organized by Labor Front representatives within each plant, these trinkets were nominally awarded on the recommendation of the factory boss and the personnel department, but they seem to have been less popular or significant than the increased pay the company was forced to offer to hang on to its most skilled staff. The IG wasn't the only large manufacturer striving to meet onerous targets in the later 1930s, and though the Nazi bureaucracy was beginning to limit labor mobility, it was still possible for specialist workers to shop around for the best job. The situation became critical in some IG plants and managers were forced to ask for drafts of conscript labor—the Nazi Party's remedy for the habitually unemployed—to fill in the gaps. The cartel even abandoned its long-standing reluctance to hire women. In 1938, for example, out of a combined workforce of seventeen thousand at Ludwigshafen and Oppau there were just over one hundred female employees. A year later this number had grown to over a thousand.

to take a particular dislike to the cartel. For the first few years after the Nazis' seizure of power, the IG had sometimes been able to contest the AO's insistence that it dismiss its foreign Jewish employees and cease doing business with Jewish communities and businesses abroad. But in early 1937, when the AO became an adjunct of the German Foreign Office, Bohle gained official backing to enforce his views. By September 1937, Georg von Schnitzler's Commercial Committee had ordered the preparation of "lists of the non-Aryan employees working abroad, together with a proposal for a gradual reduction of their numbers." Five months later, in the aftermath of Hermann Göring's decrees defining "Jewishness," the concern's memoranda became infused with more than a whiff of panic: "The few remaining foreign Jews have to be systematically eliminated from our agencies," urged one, adding that department heads were responsible for the speedy execution of the order. As a result, seventy Jewish foreign employees lost their jobs between February and November 1938 and the remaining thirty-seven were dismissed or forced into retirement by the end of the following year.

IF IG FARBEN'S executives believed that sacking Jewish overseas staff would be enough to satisfy the AO's insistence that the cartel conform to Nazi ideals, they were clearly mistaken. The AO wasn't finished with the IG yet. Next, it required the company to change its overseas advertising policy, asserting that commercial logic was of less importance than the need to avoid giving German money to newspapers that published "insulting and abusive" articles about the fatherland. In January 1938, Max Wojahn, the head of the Bayer sales operation in South America, was exasperated to be told that he had to pull the IG's aspirin advertisements from *La Critica*—a mass circulation Argentinean tabloid that was also notably anti-Nazi—and place them instead in the pro-German *La Razon*, which had a readership of only a few thousand. Wojahn cabled his bosses at Leverkusen, pointing out that he was in the middle of a campaign to sell one of the company's most profitable export items (known in South America as Cafiaspirina) and that by refusing to advertise in papers that ran anti-Nazi articles the IG would inevitably sacrifice ground to the competition. He was told to obey orders.

But Bohle also wanted the IG to act as a propagandist for the Nazi cause and again his attention was drawn to the concern's extensive marketing operation in South America, where the AO had long had ambitions of establishing a German sphere of interest. There was no reason, he insisted, why the company should not send copies of Hitler's speeches to those on its commercial mailing lists or why its local managers and those posted to the region from Germany could not be used as agents of influence on the party's behalf. With no apparent reluctance, the Commercial Committee hastened to agree.

> Gentlemen who are sent abroad should be made to realize that it is their special duty to represent National Socialist Germany. They are particularly recommended as soon as they arrive to contact the local or regional [Nazi Party] group and are expected to attend its meetings regularly as well as those of the Labor Front. The sales combines are to see that their agents are adequately supplied with National Socialist literature. Collaboration with the AO must become more organized.

It is perhaps no wonder, then, that the IG's traveling road shows in Argentina and Brazil (mobile cinema units that set up screens in remote towns and villages to show advertisements for Bayer drugs in between cartoons and popular movies) were soon playing Nazi propaganda films or that the promotional flyers its salesmen handed out during the intermissions were richly decorated with swastikas.

At this remove it is hard to gauge the sincerity with which these activities were carried out.* It is unlikely that the IG was fully behind the propagandizing, not least because in many parts of the world the company was better served commercially (in terms of tariff duties and

---

*As for the efficacy of these efforts, Nazi propaganda—from a variety of sources—certainly played a part in keeping Latin America neutral during much of the Second World War and the large and wealthy expatriate German community to which IG staff belonged was effective at influencing government policy, but the concern was not the only German business with interests in the region.

local taxes) by concealing the true ownership of local subsidiaries rather than flaunting their German origins. Waving the swastika attracted attention and won the combine some relief from the pressure of Nazi officials but it also drove revenues down and that was never popular with managers. In truth, the IG was happier acting on the German government's behalf in more discreet ways, such as gathering intelligence.

Max Ilgner's *Vowi* operation (*Volkswirtschaftliche Abteilung*, or Department of Economic Research) at Berlin NW7, which had been established in 1929 to produce reports on foreign developments that might affect the concern's commercial interests, became especially useful in this regard. Ilgner's personal trips abroad throughout the mid-1930s had often provided him with titbits to pass on to the Nazi authorities, and his account of a visit to China and Japan—"an extensive study of the economic development of the Asiatic countries"— had reportedly been read "with pleasure" by Adolf Hitler himself. But in 1937–38 Ilgner began to use the concern's economic intelligence apparatus to greater effect, turning many of the IG's overseas executives into quasi-agents (Ilgner called them his *Verbindungsmänner*, or liaison men) and asking them to pass back any information on Germany's foreign rivals that might be of value to the regime and— though this was never explicitly expressed—might boost his own and the IG's standing. Inevitably, much of this material was the kind of low-grade business intelligence that German embassy staff could have easily gleaned from cocktail party gossip and a careful perusal of trade journals and the local media. But occasionally it strayed into more strategic areas. For example, one report from a *Verbindungsmann* in Central America offered a tour d'horizon of the region's political and military pressure points, with speculation about the Uruguayan government's ability to act independently of the United States and England, the disposition of its air and naval bases in relation to those of neighboring states, and the willingness of the Argentinean armed forces to defend themselves "against a coup de main of the United States of America at the La Plata estuary or against any possible cession of the Malvinas by England to the U.S." While this information was of little importance to the IG's pharmaceutical sales operation in the region, the Nazi government's military analysts lapped it up and pressed for more.

IN THIS CLIMATE the various foreign partnerships the IG had entered into during the 1920s and early 1930s were bound to come under special scrutiny. Many of these ventures—such as a 1930 deal with Switzerland's Ciba and France's Kuhlmann over dyestuffs or a later agreement with Britain's ICI over nitrogen—were relatively straightforward cartel arrangements, aimed at minimizing competition. Although there had sometimes been a trade-off whereby IG know-how had been exchanged for investment capital and market access, there was usually a clear and demonstrable commercial logic behind them. But there were other, more secret deals where the logic was not so apparent, in which it appeared as though the IG had passed technology and patents to foreign rivals for no apparent gain. To the cartel's disquiet, the Nazis now began to probe into these transactions.

In late 1937, for example, the German government learned of the contracts Bayer had made with William E. Weiss and Sterling Products in 1920 and 1923. In return for the U.S. rights to Leverkusen's drugs, Sterling had agreed to hand back 50 percent of the sales revenue the medicines generated and (later) to give the IG a minority share in the company. It had been in both parties' interests to keep these matters secret at the time because of the soured relations between Germany and the United States, and so the money had been funneled through the IG's U.S. subsidiary to accounts in Switzerland—making considerable tax savings for the IG in the process. To the Nazis, however, it looked as though German patents and trademarks had been handed over to the Americans for nothing—and they wanted to know why. In March 1938 the IG tried to come up with a solution that would satisfy the regime without jeopardizing the company's earnings. It so happened that Earl McClintock, one of William Weiss's deputies, was due to visit Leverkusen on a routine business trip. Much to his surprise, on his arrival in Cologne McClintock was immediately taken to Basel, Switzerland, instead. There he was astonished to find Hermann Schmitz, the IG's chief executive, waiting in his hotel room.

After apologizing for the cloak-and-dagger nature of their meeting, Schmitz came to the point. The Nazis were asking awkward questions about the arrangement between their two companies, and the Americans would have to help out by paying the IG for its products and technology. McClintock protested that Sterling had already paid with its stock and a percentage of its U.S. sales revenue and that there was no question of giving the IG any more: a deal was a deal and if the Nazis didn't like it, that wasn't Sterling's concern. Well then, Schmitz suggested hopefully, perhaps the Americans might *pretend* to pay, sending Leverkusen an annual check for $100,000, which the IG would later find a way to return to them secretly. McClintock agreed to discuss the matter with his colleagues back in New York, although he knew what their response would be—the proposal was almost certainly illegal and might be construed as an attempt to defraud the company's stockholders. Under pressure from the government, the IG refused to let the issue drop, however, and was still trying to persuade Sterling to go along with the plan nine months later. In January 1939 Wilhelm Mann, head of the IG's pharmaceutical sales combine, wrote to William Weiss and told him that the concern was in desperate need of a $100,000 check, threatening that the "acute state that the matter had reached . . . might possibly not leave our original agreements unaffected."

The IG's troubles with Sterling paled next to its other foreign problems. The Nazis had also been delving into the cartel's agreements with Standard Oil and now were putting pressure on the IG to bring them to an end. Pharmaceuticals were one thing but synthetic oil and rubber were strategically important commodities and controlling them was a matter of vital national interest. If information and money connected with these programs had been flowing overseas, it would have to stop—immediately.

But of course, like so many of the regime's other rulings, this one was far from absolute. It soon became apparent that the Nazis were more than happy to allow the IG to extract advantages from its special relationship with Standard, providing they were of benefit to Germany. The IG's acquisition of substantial stocks of tetraethyl lead

234 · HELL'S CARTEL

from a Standard subsidiary in 1938 was a case in point. Tetraethyl
lead was an important element in the manufacture of high-octane
gasoline. When added to the *benzin* that the IG produced at Leuna, it
significantly increased the fuel's performance to a level that was suitable for use as an airplane propellant—clearly a matter of great interest to the Luftwaffe. The Ethyl Gasoline Corporation, a jointly owned
subsidiary of Standard Oil and General Motors, had developed the additive in America during the late 1920s and had since become its principal producer. As Nazi rearmament began to gather pace, government
officials decided that Germany should also have the capacity to make
it. Having just signed the *Benzinvertrag* with the IG, they asked the
concern to obtain the relevant licenses.

The IG approached Standard Oil, its partner in hydrogenation
projects, and Standard approached its subsidiary with a proposal
that the IG and Ethyl Gasoline form a joint company to build and operate tetraethyl lead plants in Germany. The board of Ethyl Gasoline
was keen to go ahead, despite the objections of DuPont, which
protested vigorously that any such transfer of technology might have
military consequences. On December 15, 1934, for example, a DuPont
official wrote to E. W. Webb, the president of Ethyl Gasoline: "It has
been claimed that Germany is secretly rearming. Ethyl lead would
doubtless be a valuable aid to military aeroplanes. . . . Under no condition should you or the board of Directors of the Ethyl Corporation
disclose any secrets of 'know-how' in connection with the manufacture of tetraethyl lead in Germany." Nevertheless, Ethyl Gasoline
eventually managed to obtain the necessary permissions from the
U.S. government.

All this took time: to the German government's frustration, the IG
didn't begin constructing its first tetraethyl lead plant, at Gapel, near
Berlin, until early 1936 and the first modest quantities of the additive
didn't come off the production line until 1938. The Air Ministry was
keenly aware that the international situation was rapidly deteriorating
and that a crisis might come sooner than anticipated. Desperate that
the Luftwaffe's planes should be in a position to sustain a long campaign if necessary, the ministry asked the IG, through Carl Krauch, to
obtain tetraethyl lead from its overseas contacts.

The IG knew that both the timing and the scope of the request made this mission especially delicate. One year earlier Krauch, Hermann Schmitz, and August von Knieriem, the IG's chief attorney, had met Standard Oil officials in London to negotiate the purchase of $20 million worth of ordinary aviation fuel.* Quite what the Americans had made of the deal is hard to say but they must have appreciated that the fuel was destined for the Luftwaffe and not the IG. As von Knieriem acknowledged later, "It is quite unusual for IG to purchase oil in the amount of 20 million dollars. Our business is to make oil by the hydrogenation process and not to purchase gasoline." On that occasion, the Standard executives approved the sale without question, but the IG knew that rumors about the deal must have spread. If the IG now went looking for tetraethyl lead, particularly at a time of growing international tension, no one was going to be deceived about its likely destination. Nevertheless, Krauch, Schmitz, and von Knieriem set off for London once more and this time met executives of the Ethyl Export Corporation, another Standard Oil affiliate, to ask if they could "borrow" five hundred tons of the all-important additive. Once again they were particularly careful not to mention any Luftwaffe connection, but five hundred tons was a huge amount and the men on the American side of the table could not have been in any doubt about what it was for. Still, Ethyl Export agreed to go ahead with the "loan," and on July 8, 1938, Krauch was able to tell the Air Ministry that the tetraethyl lead was about to be shipped.

In all likelihood the Standard executives looked the other way because their company was then desperately trying to persuade the IG to live up to its side of their agreements on synthetic fuel and rubber, which obliged the two companies to exchange scientific and technical information. However, the high premium the Nazis placed on protecting trade secrets was proving a formidable barrier to this exchange. In March 1937 the IG's Berlin office issued a memorandum reminding

---

*The Luftwaffe was not yet totally dependent on the IG's synthetic fuel and the Air Ministry continued to add to its stocks of traditional aviation gasoline by purchasing abroad through neutral agencies for as long as it was able. These stocks were quickly diminishing, however, because the Luftwaffe's fleet of planes was constantly expanding, more aerial training was being undertaken, and combat missions were still being flown on General Franco's behalf in Spain.

all staff of the strict punishments (including the death penalty) that awaited anyone who leaked details of scientific or technical work being carried out for the state. Then, on July 14, the German authorities, worried that that the Americans might catch on to the true extent of their rearmament program, ordered the IG to be as disingenuous as possible with Standard: "IG Farbenindustrie is permitted to inform its partners in the agreements, in a cautious way, shortly before the start of large-scale production, that it intends to begin production of isooctane and ethylene lubricant. The impression is to be conveyed, however, that this is a matter of large-scale experiments. Under no circumstances may statements on capacity be made."

Synthetic rubber was even more problematic. Under the terms of the Jasco (Joint American Study Company) agreement that Carl Bosch, Carl Krauch, and Fritz ter Meer had negotiated on the IG's behalf in 1930, Standard was committed to handing over the patents and expertise connected with any new advances its scientists made in the synthetic rubber field. There was no reciprocal requirement for the IG to share knowledge on the buna process—its own version of the technology—merely an understanding that the two companies might jointly exploit any discoveries should they ever move from the drawing board to the manufacturing stage. The deal had suited the oil giant at the time because its attention had been focused on the apparently greater prize of securing the IG's synthetic fuel technology, and buna had seemed a long way off. Now, though, IG buna was a commercial reality. In defiance of initial expectations the product was beginning to sell well in Germany and had already begun to appear in other markets. Understandably enough, Standard wanted to exploit buna in the United States, either on its own or by selling licenses to local tire manufacturers, and turned to the IG to get the technology and the necessary patents. But the combine seemed strangely reluctant to cooperate.

Standard's disquiet was compounded by the fact that its experts had meanwhile discovered another synthetic rubber process. Although it was still at the early development stage, the procedure—for a product called butyl—looked very promising. Because the IG held exclusive rights in the field, however, Standard was legally obliged to hand the technology over to the cartel. Unless the IG let the oil company share in its buna success, Standard faced being cut out of the synthetic rubber business altogether. There was a broader political anxiety, too. Standard's executives knew that war in Europe was becoming more likely. In that event the oil company's agreements with the IG would inevitably be scrutinized by the U.S. government, and lurking in the back of their minds was the uncomfortable thought that Standard might one day be accused of having given the Germans a strategic advantage. It was imperative, therefore, that the balance be restored in its favor.

GERMANY'S FOREIGN POLICY had become steadily more aggressive since Britain and France had failed to resist the reoccupation of the Rhineland. At a top-secret meeting on November 5, 1937, Hitler discussed some of the reasons for this increased belligerence with five key individuals: Field Marshal Werner von Blomberg, minister of war and commander in chief of the armed forces; Colonel General Baron Werner von Fritsch, commander in chief of the army; Colonel General Hermann Göring, commander in chief of the air force and president of the Reichstag; Admiral Erich Raeder, commander in chief of the navy; and Baron Konstanin von Neurath, Germany's foreign minister. Hitler's military adjutant, Colonel Friedrich Hossbach, attended to take notes and later produced a famous account, the "Hossbach Memorandum," which remained secret until after the war. Hitler began by telling the assembled group that what he had to say was the fruit of "thorough deliberation and the experiences of four and a half years of power." Over the next four hours, he then explained his ambitions for the years ahead: the rights of Germany to more living space, his plans for military conquest to acquire it, the likely response of Britain and France, the need to strike no later than 1943—although the opportunity might arise sooner—and much more. Crucially, the Führer left no one in any doubt that he intended, sooner rather than later, to add Austria and Czechoslovakia to the Reich. On March 11, 1938, Hitler achieved the first of these objectives, when he sent troops into Austria to effect the Anschluss (union) of Austria with Germany. As expected, Britain and France protested vociferously but took no action. Nevertheless, with German ambitions in Czecho-slovakia becoming more apparent by the day, the political tempera-ture was rising rapidly.

Standard, increasingly anxious at the turn of events, immediately redoubled its efforts to wrest the buna rights from the IG. Three days after the annexation of Austria, Frank Howard, Standard's head of de-velopment, met Fritz ter Meer in Berlin to ask for the licenses. The IG man promised to do all he could but explained that in the current cli-mate the government would have to give permission. He hinted that the Nazis would be more likely to agree if Standard handed over the butyl processes first. Howard felt he was in no real position to argue. He knew the pressure the IG was under and believed that ter Meer was genuinely trying to help. In any case, what did Standard really have to lose? Buna was a going concern, whereas butyl was still at the devel-opment stage. He agreed to pass on the information and returned to New Jersey to await developments.

He would come to regret his naïveté. If anyone had a motive to guard the IG's buna secrets it was Fritz ter Meer. The head of *Sparte* II had been a proselytizer for synthetic rubber since the formation of the combine in 1926 and had maintained his faith through the years of economic uncertainty that followed. When his peers had lost interest in the project, he had somehow found the money to keep it going, even sending his protégé Otto Ambros on an expensive fact-finding trip to the natural rubber plantations of Java and Sumatra. In 1931 the De-pression had forced ter Meer to cut spending on buna development, but from the moment the Nazis expressed an interest in supporting the technology he had worked tirelessly to get it up and running. His dream was to make buna manufacture so efficient and cost-effective that it could compete with the natural product even without govern-ment subventions. But until that day the IG would have to rely on mil-itary subsidies, which meant that good relations with the authorities were imperative. Sharing buna with the Americans would perhaps have been acceptable in less turbulent times, provided the IG had es-tablished an unassailable commercial lead; doing so now would risk alienating the Nazi regime. And that simply couldn't be allowed to happen.

A few days after his meeting with Howard, Fritz ter Meer sat down with Colonel Löb of the Four-Year Plan and two other procurement officials. There was only one question on the agenda, how "to halt the development of a synthetic rubber capacity in the U.S.A." Ter Meer, recounting his conversation with Howard, explained that there was no doubt that the United States would get the technology sooner or later because the science behind it was not that complicated. Nevertheless, that moment could be delayed, he felt, by letting the Americans believe that the IG was just about to hand over the buna processes. The stalling couldn't go on forever, of course: "We are under the impression that one cannot stem things in the United States for much longer without . . . the risk of being faced all of a sudden with an unpleasant situation." But if Standard could be left dangling for a while, Germany could gain valuable time. With Colonel Löb's backing, ter Meer therefore wrote to Howard on April 9, explaining that he had "taken up negotiations with the competent authorities in order to obtain the necessary freedom of action in the United States with regard to rubberlike products. As anticipated, these negotiations have proved to be rather difficult and the respective discussions are expected to take several months. . . . I will not fail to inform you of the result in due course."

Ten days later Howard replied. He understood ter Meer's problems and wished him well in his negotiations, but in the meantime could the IG let Standard approach rubber producers and tire manufacturers and begin discussing how they might be organized into a consortium for exploiting the buna technology? A slight delay was probably acceptable but the matter really needed to be resolved in the next few months. What Howard didn't say was that Standard was coming under pressure from those same tire manufacturers and that it was hard-pressed to stop them from going off and developing synthetic rubber on their own. That very day he had had to write to Fred Bedford, a producer of rubber products, to explain why it was necessary to wait for the IG's permission: "We know some of the difficulties they have, both from business complications . . . and from a national standpoint in Germany, but we do not know the whole situation and since under the agreement they have full control over the exploitation of this process, the only thing we can do is continue to press for authority, but in the meantime loyally preserve the restrictions they have placed on us."

The exchange of letters between Standard and the IG continued in much the same vein for another six months, at the end of which Howard made another fruitless trip to Berlin to try to persuade ter Meer to relinquish the buna rights. The *Sparte* boss's excuse this time was that Germany's annexation of the Sudetenland in Czechoslovakia (which took place on October 1) had thrown up some unexpected problems, but he promised to visit the United States soon to sort the whole thing out. He arrived in New York at the end of November 1938 and, after an inconclusive meeting with Standard's board, spent a couple of weeks touring tire factories, reassuring the manufacturers that negotiations between the IG and the oil giant were in their final stages and would soon be resolved to everyone's satisfaction. Then he abruptly returned home—with the matter still up in the air. As the political situation in Europe became more difficult by the day, Howard and his colleagues got the uneasy feeling that their relationship with IG Farben was running into the sand.

TER MEER WAS RIGHT about one thing: Germany's annexation of the Sudetenland *had* given rise to problems, though they were perhaps not as much of a surprise as he made out. While it is unlikely that the IG had any official advance warning of Hitler's plans for the Sudetenland, or indeed of the Anschluss with Austria that had taken place six months earlier, its executives undoubtedly had some intimation of the move. By the spring of 1938, when the general thrust of the Führer's expansionist ambitions became plain to anyone in Europe who could read a newspaper, the IG had been working on mobilization contracts for almost two years; developing and producing thousands of tons of materials, from explosives and poison gases to synthetic aviation fuel and military tires, all of which manifestly contributed to the aggressive capacity of Germany's armed forces. Many of the IG's leading figures had been in regular contact with senior members of the Nazi hierarchy: Carl Krauch was about to be made Hermann Göring's special plenipotentiary for chemical production; Georg von Schnitzler, the chief of the IG's Commercial Committee, was regularly wining and dining Nazi officials in Berlin. As war had been a theoretical possibility ever since Germany had reclaimed the Rhineland, it is hard to imagine that the IG bosses didn't speak to their associates in government to try to get an inside edge on exactly how, when, and where the Führer was likely to make his next move. Indeed, given that the combine had long since become the regime's leading financial backer, pouring millions of marks into Nazi coffers, they may even have told themselves that their duty to shareholders demanded the acquisition of such intelligence.

Something must surely have been conveyed, because by 1938 the IG was remarkably well prepared for the dramatic events that were about to unfold.* Sometime prior to the Anschluss, for example, the cartel suddenly reaffirmed its interest in acquiring Austria's leading chemical and explosives firm, Skodawerke Wetzler AG, whose parent company, the Creditanstalt, was owned by the Rothschild banking family. The IG had actually considered taking a minority stake in Skodawerke as early as 1927, but because it already controlled Austria's next two largest chemical producers, Carbidwerke Deutsch-Matrei AG and the Dynamit Nobel AG, it decided to negotiate joint marketing agreements instead. As the IG was only concerned with ensuring that Skodawerke was kept out of its markets in Western Europe, a limited arrangement was deemed sufficient.

In late 1937, however, the combine took the unusual step of sending Paul Haefliger to Vienna to put pressure on Skodawerke's owners to sell their majority stake. This new move was almost certainly a defensive gambit motivated by fears, or well-informed gossip, that some sort of union with Austria was in the offing. The IG must have known

---

*Several days before the Anschluss, Paul Haefliger, the IG's principal international negotiator, warned a colleague in Paris to get out of France, apparently because the imminent German takeover of Austria might trigger a more general war. At Nuremberg, prosecutors suggested that Haefliger's prescience was clear evidence that the IG had advance knowledge of what was about to happen. They also alleged that on the day before German troops crossed the border, the IG executive had attended a company mobilization conference and recommended moving the concern's headquarters from Frankfurt to Berlin because of the dangerous proximity of the French. Haefliger responded that he had been working on "assumptions" until the Anschluss and then "we realized suddenly that—like a stroke of lightening from a clear sky—a matter which one had taken more or less theoretically could become deadly serious."

that once Austria was part of a Greater Germany there was a strong chance that an independent Skodawerke (providing it had been thoroughly Aryanized) would be eligible to begin competing for the Reich's Four-Year Plan chemical contracts. The concern had come to regard these contracts as its own and saw it had no option but to try to protect them. Frustratingly, the Rothschilds, possibly confident of Austria's continued independence, refused to sell. Nevertheless, they did agree to consider a compromise proposal for a joint venture.

But before this deal could come into effect the Anschluss changed the situation. Within a few days of Nazi troops crossing the border on March 11 and with a suspicious degree of efficiency, Max Ilgner's office produced a lengthy document for government officials entitled "A New Order for the Greater Chemical Industries of Austria" and suggested to all and sundry (including Wilhelm Keppler, Hitler's personal economic envoy to Germany's newly acquired territory) that allowing the IG to take over Skodawerke in its entirety would speed up the Aryanization of Austrian industry. The Rothschilds were Jewish, Creditanstalt's chief executive, Josef Joham, was Jewish, and Skodawerke's general manager, Isador Pollack, was Jewish. Someone would have to take over from them and who better than the company that had maintained an interest in Skodawerke over many years and had proved so reliable an ally back in Germany?

Keppler, who had tangled with IG Farben before, took some convincing, at one point telling Haefliger that "it was not desirable that the IG should buy all the chemical plants in Austria," although, of course, his reservations didn't make much difference to the Rothschilds, who now had to give up their company whether to the IG or to someone else. But Keppler's arguments did hold up proceedings for a few months. By the time he and his subordinates finally gave in to the IG's lobbying and approved a deal in late 1938, Josef Joham had fled the country and Isador Pollack had been kicked to death by SS thugs during a search of his house. A few months after the IG acquired the business for a pittance (in return for a loose promise to pay shareholder dividends for twenty-five years), the firm was merged with the IG's two other Austrian companies into one wholly owned subsidiary, Donau-Chemie AG.

If the IG had been a relatively passive observer of the Anschluss, it was to take a much more active role in fomenting the conditions that led to Germany's next territorial gain. Czechoslovakia had been created under the provisions of the Versailles Treaty in 1919 and, as its name suggests, was preponderantly populated by Czechs and Slavs. But there were large minority groups as well and some of these were unhappy about having been corralled into the new state. The most vociferous were the three-and-a-quarter-million ethnic Germans of the Sudetenland region, who wished to be reincorporated into the fatherland. Led by Konrad Henlein, a devoted Nazi, they intensified their protests in the aftermath of the Anschluss and within weeks, backed by Berlin, were inundating the authorities in Prague with demands for "self-determination." Eduard Benes, Czechoslovakia's president, refused to countenance the splitting up of his recently formed country and the stage was set for a confrontation with Hitler.

On May 24, 1938, Georg von Schnitzler's Commercial Committee, with the full backing of Hermann Schmitz and the IG's *Vorstand*, sanctioned a scheme (later fleshed out by Max Ilgner) to provide financial support to the region's pro-German newspapers and to put its sales agents in Czechoslovakia to work campaigning for "reconstruction according to the German pattern." In the meantime, the IG proceeded to Ayranize its interests in the country in accordance with the combine's new policy toward its foreign holdings.

As the political tension heightened, Hitler subjected Eduard Benes and his government to a set of increasingly impossible demands, gambling again that France and Britain, Czechoslovakia's principal allies, would be unwilling to go to war (as Britain's Neville Chamberlain was later to say so memorably) "because of a quarrel in a far-away country between people of whom we know nothing." Flush with money from IG Farben advertising, Sudeten newspapers upped the ante still further by running "atrocity stories" recounting imaginary attacks on ethnic Germans by Czechs and Slavs, praising the racial homogeneity of the Nazi state, and appealing for help from the international German diaspora.

The IG's motives were mixed. On the one hand, there was genuine sympathy in the *Vorstand* for the plight of the Sudeten Germans, but the concern also wished to demonstrate its suitability to take over one of Czechoslovakia's greatest companies. The Aussiger Verein was the fourth-largest chemical firm in Europe and it had managed (with the help of Britain's ICI) to keep the IG's involvement in Czech chemical manufacture to the bare minimum. As a result, the IG considered the Verein an astute and potentially dangerous rival. Although its head-quarters were in Prague, most of its productive capacity was in the Sudetenland. If the region was incorporated into the Reich, it was pos-sible that the Verein might be forced to sell its plants to a German firm. The combine was keen to be the new owner, because if a non-IG firm took over the factories, it could pose a serious challenge to the IG close to its domestic heartland—especially in the dyestuffs field, where the Verein was particularly strong. Hence the cartel openly supported Hitler's attempts to bring the Sudetenland under the Reich's wing.

So while von Schnitzler, Ilgner, and ter Meer turned their attention to lobbying the government, Hermann Schmitz's office arranged a contribution of RM 100,000 to the Sudeten German Relief Fund and the Nazi-dominated Sudeten-German Free Corps, which was busy in-citing civil unrest along the border with Czechoslovakia. In the mean-time, the IG's sales offices went looking for former German employees of the Aussiger Verein, so that if and when the Czech firm was forced to sell, there would be suitable replacements available for its Jewish personnel.

Events moved quickly. At a hastily arranged peace conference in Munich on September 30, to which Eduard Benes's government was not invited, it was decided by Hitler, Mussolini, Edouard Deladier, the French prime minister, and Britain's Neville Chamberlain that the Sudetenland should be handed over to the Reich. The IG reacted with speed and determination. Even before Chamberlain had time to fly back to Britain to wave a copy of the agreement and declare "peace in our time," the *Vorstand* had appointed von Schnitzler, ter Meer, Ilg-ner, and Hans Kühne, the production chief for organic and inorganic chemicals, as its special representatives to the Verein's Sudetenland plants. Hermann Schmitz then uncharacteristically broke cover by committing himself to print. He sent a telegram to Hitler: "Pro-foundly impressed by the return of the Sudetenland to the Reich that you, my Führer, have achieved. The IG Farbenindustrie AG puts a sum of half a million reichsmarks at your disposal for use in the Sudetenland territory."

In an equally bullish mood the concern's special representatives contacted the Aussiger Verein and began negotiating the "purchase" of its Sudetenland plants. As they had feared, there were other interested parties. Both the Ruettgerswerke AG and the Chemische Fabrik von Heyden were desperate to get their hands on the factories. Of the two, the latter was the bigger threat. Stubbornly independent, Heyden had been troublesome to the IG ever since it had caused Bayer to be stripped of its British aspirin patent in 1905. Now it lobbied the authorities assiduously, putting forward the claim that it was the only possible counterweight to the "power hunger of the IG and the strengthening of its monopoly position." The Aussiger Verein, meanwhile, was doing its best to avoid selling at all and began appealing to the Czech government for help in hanging on to its property.

However, von Schnitzler hadn't risen to his senior position merely by virtue of his aristocratic charm. He quickly arranged a compromise with Heyden whereby the two companies would put in a joint bid for the plants, then he threatened the Aussiger Verein board that he would complain to the German government that "unrest and a breakdown of social peace" in the Sudetenland were becoming inevitable. Desperate to avoid giving Hitler any more reasons for intervening in the affairs of their country, the authorities in Prague advised the Verein to sell the plants on the IG's terms—for a little over half of what the Czechs thought they were worth. The deal was signed on December 7, 1938.

Of course, Hitler was never short of reasons for military action. Three months later he sent the Wehrmacht into the rest of Czechoslovakia and captured Prague, where the Sudeten-German leader, Konrad Henlein, was appointed head of a new Nazi administration.

WHILE THE IG was busy positioning itself to take over Austrian and Czech chemical firms, Standard Oil's request for buna technology was still unresolved. Fritz ter Meer's involvement in the Verein negotiations may have gained him some temporary respite, but Frank Howard and his colleagues couldn't be stalled indefinitely. As the new year began, however, the IG had a more pressing problem to discuss with Standard: how to protect their agreements, and the rest of the IG's U.S. interests, from the consequences of the deteriorating international situation. It was becoming clear that war in Europe was inevitable. In Britain, the initial relief that had greeted Neville Chamberlain on his return from Munich was turning into widespread disgust that Hitler had been allowed to get away with too much for too long. The public mood was darkening in France as well. Having suffered so grievously in 1914–18, the French had never ceased to be mistrustful of their neighbor to the east. At Munich, Prime Minister Deladier had been less convinced than Chamberlain about Hitler's willingness to stop at the Sudetenland and had warned the British that giving in would only encourage more aggression. Within a few months his pessimism was proven justified. First the Nazis took over the rest of Czechoslovakia; then they forced the Lithuanian government into handing over the port of Memel. By early April 1939, Hitler's Spanish ally, General Franco, had won the civil war to the south and Benito Mussolini had ordered the Italian army into Albania. Faced with potential belligerents on three sides, France redoubled its efforts to strengthen the Maginot Line fortifications on the border with Germany and joined with Britain in offering guarantees of military aid to Poland, Greece, and Romania in the event of a Nazi attack. By the end of April most Western European politicians privately acknowledged that it was a question not of whether war with Hitler was coming but of how and when it would begin.

The IG had been in this situation before. In the months running up to the start of the Great War, the cartel had taken steps (which later turned out to be ineffective) to safeguard its foreign assets from seizure by hostile powers. This time it was determined to do a better job. Fortunately, Hermann Schmitz was a master of corporate camouflage. In late 1938, encouraged by Nazi officials, he began devising complicated schemes to disguise the true ownership of the IG's overseas holdings by transferring them temporarily to apparently unconnected subsidiaries and partners. Schmitz knew his plans would work only if the IG could find compliant partners—either neutrals or citizens and businesses in potential enemy nations—who could be trusted to play along and allow the concern to reclaim its assets later. The subterfuge was easier to accomplish in some countries than in others. In the United States, for example, Standard was the obvious partner. Although the oil giant had not yet got its hands on the IG's buna technology, it would still be keen to prevent their joint synthetic fuel operations (incorporated in the United States as the Standard-IG Company) from being seized by the U.S. government in the event of a conflict and to shield their prewar cartel agreements from scrutiny by the U.S. Anti-Trust Division. In other words, Hermann Schmitz had a nice mix of carrot and stick to ensure Standard's cooperation: lend a hand and enjoy the benefits of some of the IG's U.S. assets for the next few years or risk losing everything to an alien property custodian.

In July 1939 Schmitz called in Walter Duisberg to formalize the arrangement. The eldest son of the famous Carl Duisberg, Walter worked for the concern in the United States and had become a naturalized American citizen. He was told to approach Standard's Walter Teagle with a suggestion: the IG's share of their joint holdings should be sold either to a U.S. citizen such as himself or to an American enterprise such as Standard. As Schmitz had expected, Teagle immediately grasped the idea and told his colleagues that "in view of the unsettled conditions" Standard should cooperate. On August 30, a deal was hastily hammered out whereby Standard agreed to acquire the IG's 20 percent share of the Standard-IG Company (for a mere $20,000), while the concern's 50 percent share of Jasco would be bought by Walter Duisberg (for an even more paltry $4,000). In theory, thereafter both Standard and the IG were protected should the U.S. alien property custodian ever have reason to go looking for the IG's American assets—although it was perhaps a little ludicrous to suppose that the U.S. authorities wouldn't spot Walter Duisberg's antecedents. Standard's executives were delighted, of course, because on the face of it the agreement gave their company ownership or control of a large part of the IG's U.S. empire. Some things remained unsettled, though. The oil giant still hadn't managed to get its hands on the concern's buna technology, among other significant patents. If the IG didn't come through with this information soon, Standard would have lost its chance.

But in those final few months of peace the IG was even less responsive than before, its attention increasingly elsewhere, its managers preoccupied, its factories working overtime to fulfill a last-minute blizzard of orders from the German military. Krauch, who had finally relinquished his day-to-day responsibilities at the IG (though he had kept his seat on the *Vorstand*), was determined to wring every last drop of productive capacity from his old company and make sure his new masters had all the materials necessary to wage war on a grand scale: synthetic oil and rubber, aluminum, magnesium, high explosives, nickel, plastics, lubricating oil and greases, tetraethyl lead, methanol, poison gases, pharmaceuticals, photographic materials, dyestuffs, and thousands of other products indispensable to modern mechanized armed forces. Hermann Schmitz, Fritz ter Meer, Georg von Schnitzler, Wilhelm Mann, Fritz Gajewski, Max Ilgner, Heinrich Hörlein, Heinrich Bütefisch, Hans Kühne, Christian Schneider, Otto Ambros, Carl Lautenschläger, and Ernst Bürgin were doing their best to meet those needs. The IG still made aspirin and margarine, silk dye and household detergents, fertilizer, paints, and pesticides, but the company was now on a war footing and its civilian markets were fading to a shadow of what they had once been. The concern's major scientific and technological breakthroughs were henceforth reserved for the military, its sales agencies abroad transformed into unofficial bankers for the Foreign Ministry, its economic intelligence put at the disposal of the Abwehr (the military's intelligence office) and the SS. The IG continued to make money, of course—doubling its profits in the years to come and benefiting from almost a billion reichsmarks in additional government loans, subsidies, and tax breaks—but its independence had gone.

By now, this level of militarization was not unique to the IG. Across the industrialized world, large corporations were hastily being transformed into executors of government policy. In Britain, for example, Imperial Chemical Industries had been gearing up for military production since late 1937, establishing the factories that would eventually produce nearly all the UK's wartime explosives, light metals, and basic chemicals. Within Germany, too, other corporations were involved in the war effort. But the IG had been at this game for far longer and was much more practiced in responding with alacrity to a regime with aggressive intent. There was certainly no doubt about the importance of IG Farben products to the German armed forces as they prepared to invade Poland. The Heinkel and Junkers Stuka bombers that would launch attacks on Warsaw, Kraków, Lodz, and Lublin were largely made from the IG's light metals. Around 75 percent of their engines were produced from high-grade IG nickel, their fuselages from IG aluminum, their wings from IG magnesium. Even the windshield wipers were tipped with IG buna. Their engines weren't just fueled with IG aviation *benzin*; they were lubricated by the company's oils and greases. Over 90 percent of the phosphorus incendiaries they carried were made from materials supplied by IG factories. The Wehrmacht invasion force of 1.5 million men was similarly in the IG's debt. An estimated 25 percent of a foot soldier's equipment, including mess kits, belt buckles, webbing, and helmets, came from the company's materials—a proportion that was to increase as the war went on. Mechanized units were, of course, highly dependent on IG buna and fuel, but several vehicles had also been armored with specially strengthened Farben light metals. Eighty-five percent of the high explosives contained in their shells came from the IG or its subsidiaries, and amid the second wave of troops there were units equipped with IG mustard gas. The list goes on and on—from the buna boats that assault troops were to use to cross rivers to the plastic keys on the Enigma machines that signals units used to encrypt their messages, the IG's synthetic materials were woven into the very fabric of the advancing army. No other company, be it Krupp, Siemens, Thyssen, Zeiss, Flick, or any of the other German industrial giants, could claim as much. By the eve of war, the mighty IG had become Hitler's cartel.

IN THE EARLY hours of September 1, 1939, as Frank Howard was making desperate efforts to contact Fritz ter Meer and put flesh on the bones of the oil giant's "purchase," the first waves of Luftwaffe dive-bombers were flying eastward, high above the trucks and half-tracks that rode on the IG's artificial tires and the artillery units that were loading shells containing its explosives. Other armies could now worry about Chilean nitrate and Asian rubber and Anglo-American oil. The blitzkrieg—given teeth by IG Farben's genius for synthetic chemistry—was about to be unleashed.

10

WAR AND PROFIT

A strange air of unreality settled over the Reich during the first few days of war. The American correspondent and author William Shirer, who was in Berlin at the time, later described the peculiar apathy he encountered in the streets on September 1, with newsboys "shouting their extras" that no one wanted to buy and construction laborers working on the new IG Farben building on the Unter den Linden "as if nothing had happened."

But had Shirer been able to look into the IG offices he would have found a more purposeful calm—born of the fact that the concern's senior executives had known well in advance about the attack on Poland: indeed, they even had a pretty fair idea of the date on which it would commence. The tip-off had come from Claus Ungewitter, a dedicated Nazi with close ties to the top ranks of the SS, who had been appointed Reich commissioner for chemistry at the Economics Ministry. Back in June, he had spoken to the IG's Georg von Schnitzler and left him in no doubt as to what the government intended. As Schnitzler later recalled:

Dr. Ungewitter told me in the summer of 1939 that war with Poland would not begin until harvest time, September 1939. I was a very worried man. Even if we hadn't been told directly that the government intended to wage war, it was impossible for officials of IG to believe that the enormous productions of armaments and preparation for war, starting with Hitler's coming to power, accelerating in 1936, and reaching unbelievable proportions in 1938, could have any other meaning but that Hitler and the Nazi government intended to wage war come what might. We of the IG were well aware of this fact. . . . In June or July 1939, the IG and all heavy industries were completely mobilized for the invasion of Poland.

Von Schnitzler wasn't the only one to get the message. At around the same time Ungewitter had an almost identical conversation with Carl Wurster, director of the IG's Ludwigshafen and Oppau plants, telling him that the war would start "at harvest time." Wurster later said that he had immediately relayed these remarks to his superiors, Otto Ambros and Fritz ter Meer, and told them that the Nazi official had suggested they shift manufacture of vital commodities away from Ludwigshafen (presumably because its location on Germany's western border and renown as a production center for synthetics made it vulnerable to air attack). Ernst Struss, Fritz ter Meer's assistant and office manager, later recalled a further meeting with Ungewitter, this one actually attended by Ambros and ter Meer, at which the Nazi commissioner, clearly doing his official best to make his point understood, had once more repeated his warning.

The IG got the message and readied itself to play its part in the war effort. A couple of weeks after these meetings the company agreed to set up an Association for Sales Promotion, which the Abwehr intended to use as a cover for its agents abroad. Meanwhile, Max Ilgner handed over to the government the IG's extensive collection of maps, photographs, and documents that detailed the whereabouts and productive capacity of chemical and explosives factories across Europe and the United States. There were also discussions in the *Vorstand* about the vulnerability of the IG's huge Frankfurt headquarters and the Rhine plants to air attack and what could be done to protect them. By mid-August senior managers had begun implementing their mobilization plans and were discreetly letting staff on foreign business trips know that they should be making their way home.

The Poles, needless to say, were not so well prepared and quickly succumbed to the juggernaut that swept over the border. Within days of the invasion, Poland's major cities had been devastated by bombs, its air force destroyed, its soldiers overwhelmed by the crushing power of the German army. Kraków fell on September 6; Warsaw was surrounded a few days later. As the shattered nation staggered under these repeated blows, its misery was compounded by the arrival of Soviet forces from the East, occupying half the country up to a line secretly agreed on by Stalin and Hitler a few weeks earlier. By the third week of September Poland had been effectively dismembered.

WITH ALMOST WOLVERINE speed, the IG moved in. A small team led by Georg von Schnitzler followed hard on the heels of the Wehrmacht, armed with a comprehensive survey of the enemy's chemical industry that Max Ilgner had compiled two years earlier and a determination to pick the juiciest plums before anyone else could get to them. The document, entitled "The Most Important Chemical Plants in Poland," had been updated in recent months with information from the IG's network of traveling sales agents (probably with this very eventuality in mind) and listed dozens of potential targets. But three in particular stood out: Boruta, the country's largest dye maker and intermediate producer; Wola, which was owned by three Jewish families; and Winnica, with which the IG already had a connection through its Swiss holding company, the IG Chemie. Of course, these firms were mere minnows compared with the German giant: the Polish dye and intermediates market was worth only around RM 20 million in total and even before the war the IG had controlled almost a quarter of it. But von Schnitzler and his colleagues were concerned lest the Wehrmacht take possession of any stockpiles of completed product before the IG had a chance to stake a claim to them, because if those goods were impounded and then dumped onto the market all at once prices across the industry could be seriously depressed. Furthermore, as in Austria and Czechoslovakia, the IG did not want any possible competitor acquiring the companies as a way to muscle into its domestic market.

So even before the country was completely subdued, von Schnitzler was finding his way through burning rubble and along the refugee-clogged roads. Presenting himself and his associates at the gates of each factory, he curtly informed owners and managers that, as part of "the former Polish state," their enterprises were now subject to his inspection. Then he cabled Berlin, suggesting that an immediate meeting be arranged with the Ministry of Economics. "We consider it of primary importance that the above-mentioned stocks be used by experts in the interests of the German national economy," he wrote. "Only the IG is in a position to make experts available. . . . We intend to present ourselves in the middle of next week to the competent authorities in Berlin for further deliberation."

But when von Schnitzler called at the ministry on his return he found that officials were unwilling to be pushed into hasty decisions. Although they agreed that the IG could manage the plants on a temporary basis and that two of its employees, Hermann Schwab and Bernhard Schoener, could be appointed as trustees for the three companies, there was outright hostility to the concern's brash assumption that it could take over the businesses in their entirety. The ministry's General von Hanneken wrote to the IG on September 21 to emphasize that "there will be no changes in the conditions of ownership of the plants concerned" and that this interim appointment should not be seen as "preparation for a change in the ownership conditions."

Von Schnitzler was not easily put off, however, and he soon made a direct appeal to Hermann Göring, whose Four-Year Plan Office had set up an organization, the Main Trusteeship Office East, to confiscate, and dispose of, Polish property. As his petition was being considered, other IG executives made sure that the important "assets" of the three target companies were "secured" and began surveying Poland's smaller chemical factories. Carl Wurster set off in a vast Mercedes, with a chauffeur, an interpreter, and a representative from the Reich Office of Economic Expansion, to determine which of these lesser plants could be dismantled and shipped back to Germany.

In the meanwhile, Maurcy Szpilfogel, one of the Jewish partners at the target firm of Wola, who owned two country estates as well as a large property in the Polish capital, was finding out exactly what the IG meant by "securing assets."

> When the Germans crossed the border, I fled first to my brother's house at Orwick and later to my own house at Warsaw, where I had stored part of the dyestuffs manufactured in Wola. In September 1939, [the IG's] Schwab and Schoener visited me in this house. After introducing themselves as IG commissioners, they stated that all my dyestuffs were confiscated, along with all my houses. They prohibited my use of any article in any of these houses. They confiscated my cars. The dyestuffs were then put under seal. In accordance with the German "laws" then in existence, the "trustees" were permitted to allot 500 zloty per month, per family, to the Jews who had been robbed of their property. But Schwab allotted only 500 zloty for all three families; that is, for myself, my wife, and her aged mother, who was living with us; for my married daughter and her husband; and for my sick son, who was in a sanatorium. Then I had to pay 150 zloty to the IG for so-called rent. At that time, one family, even living at the most modest level, could not survive on 350 Zloty a month.

If Szpilfogel, an honors graduate of the famous Karlsruhe Polytechnic in Germany, found this treatment hard to swallow, it was nothing to what was coming. Within a few months the pitiful allowance was stopped altogether and he and his family were thrown out of their homes and told to find shelter elsewhere. By 1940 they had been moved to the newly established Warsaw ghetto. From there, in desperation, Szpilfogel wrote to Georg von Schnitzler, whom he had known before the war, pleading for permission to go back and work at the Wola factory he had once owned and managed. Von Schnitzler didn't reply, and as Szpilfogel later recalled, what happened next marked the beginning of the tragedy that was about to befall Poland's Jews.

> The ghetto was ostensibly administered by its inmates; the purpose of this was to force the Jews themselves to introduce the measures that were intended to lead to their extermination. When the liquidation of the ghetto began, it was the task of the president of the Jewish Council, among other things, to segregate, by order of the SS, a

certain number of ghetto Jews—5,000, to begin with—and have them taken to a collection point. . . . The inhabitants were given to believe that they were being assigned to work on a farm.

Another time, the Germans rounded up Jews intended for extermination by having single houses, blocks of houses, or whole rows emptied, ordering everyone to gather on the street, which was surrounded by soldiers. Anyone who went back into the house was immediately shot. Those who had been assembled in the street were taken to the collection point, loaded onto trucks, and sent to meet their fate. My wife and children went onto the street one day and never came back.

While Maurcy Szpilfogel was struggling to stay alive, the IG was working hard to impound his factory. The concern's appeal to Göring about the Polish plants had failed because responsibility for confiscated enemy property was shifted to Heinrich Himmler's SS before the matter was settled. Von Schnitzler therefore set about cultivating the friendship of Himmler's deputy in Poland, SS Brigadeführer Ulrich Greifelt (later shown to be responsible, among many other things, for the mass murder of Polish hostages).* Eventually they struck a deal: the IG succeeded in obtaining full ownership of the Boruta plants in return for a promise to Himmler to invest five million marks in the newly defined Nazi-Polish province of Warthegau. The cartel also bought the technical equipment of Winnica and Maurcy Szpilfogel's Wola from the government for a further seventy-two thousand marks, before shutting down both premises. The concern went on to acquire three further confiscated Polish properties: a French-owned coal mine in Silesia and two small oxygen plants, all at similarly knocked-down prices. Although these were minor gains in comparison with the IG's earlier acquisitions, they, too, were made with the assistance of the SS and cemented a working relationship that was already proving highly productive.

Not everyone at the IG could stomach the concern's strengthening

*Von Schnitzler wasn't alone in establishing links to the SS leadership. Heinrich Bütefisch, the IG's synthetic fuel genius and part-time SS colonel, became a member of Himmler's Circle of Friends, a group of around thirty-six influential individuals from industry, party, and government who gathered regularly to discuss matters of interest to the Reichsführer.

links to the Nazi hierarchy. Back in Germany Carl Bosch had had enough. For many months he had been sunk in the depths of depression and alcoholism, unable to shake off the feeling that he was, in some way, personally responsible for his country's aggression. His sense of guilt had been growing since 1933, when he sanctioned the IG's first massive donation to the party. The prize then had seemed to be a return to political and economic stability and, more important, a chance to get the new regime's financial support for his cherished high-pressure programs. But stability had long since given way to a repressive dictatorship, and the technology, though it had made huge profits for the IG, had also provided Hitler with the tools to wage war. When the burden of dealing with the Nazis had finally become too difficult to bear Bosch had relinquished day-to-day control of the IG and assumed the chairmanship of its supervisory board instead. From that lofty but increasingly ineffectual position he had watched his Jewish colleagues be stripped of their jobs and his business become one of the world's greatest producers of military matériel. In May 1939 he had made a speech at the Deutsches Museum in Munich in which he had openly questioned the Führer's decisions and poured scorn on his economic policies. In the past, the opprobrium of Carl Bosch would have made politicians tremble; now the Nazis merely booted him off the museum's board and banned him from making public statements. Prevented from sniping at his enemies, even from the margins, Bosch took refuge in his house at Heidelberg, locked the door, and started drinking. By February 1940 his physical and mental state had deteriorated to such an extent that his friends and family insisted he take himself to Sicily for a rest. In early April he returned to Germany to live out his last weeks. His final words to his doctor were to predict that Hitler's insanity would lead to the destruction of Germany and the downfall of IG Farben. On April 26, aged sixty-five, he died.

Though many at the IG mourned Carl Bosch, the concern moved rapidly to find his successor. The *Aufsichtsrat* wasn't the force it had once been, but it still played a role in influencing policy and it was vital to have one of the IG "family" in the high-profile chairman's seat. The most obvious candidate was quickly selected: Carl Krauch, Hermann Göring's plenipotentiary general for special questions of chemical production. With this new addition to his workload, Krauch finally had to give up his place on the *Vorstand*, but he was generously compensated for his trouble. Apart from his normal director's fees, he received a onetime special payment of RM 400,000 and was allocated a further monthly allowance of RM 5,000. For its part, the IG considered the money well spent. The new role made Krauch an even more significant figure in Germany than he had been before and it maintained the company's connections at the highest level.

Those connections were to prove vitally important in the months ahead. In early April 1940 the Germans overwhelmed Denmark and Norway. On May 10 the Nazi war machine began tearing through the Low Countries, while launching a simultaneous and massive attack on France through the Ardennes. By June 22 the campaign in the West was all but over; the bulk of the defeated British Expeditionary Force had been evacuated from Dunkirk, and the Netherlands, Belgium, and France had capitulated. With all of continental Europe under his control—or in the hands of cowed neutrals and compliant allies—Hitler had won an extraordinary victory.

NATURALLY, THE WEHRMACHT'S successes were wildly celebrated in Germany, but the conquest of France was especially savored at the IG's Frankfurt headquarters. Several of its executives had fought in the previous war and retained painful memories of their treatment by the French in its aftermath. The humiliation of Versailles, the harsh reparations demands that followed, the occupation of the Interessen Gemeinschaft's Rhineland factories, the attempts by the French military authorities to criminalize and jail Carl Bosch, Hermann Schmitz, and August von Knieriem—all these insults were fresh in their minds and there was deep satisfaction in seeing the tables turned on their old adversary. More significantly still, now that most of France lay helplessly at Germany's feet, the large French chemical industry was ripe for exploitation. In 1926 the newly formed IG had tried to restore its prewar dominance in France by buying the country's leading chemical company, Etablissements Kuhlmann, but the takeover had been frustrated by hastily enacted French legislation forbidding German citizens from holding voting stock in French companies. The concern had to settle for an unsatisfactory cartel arrangement, the Gallus Vertrag, in which the companies agreed in 1927 to stay out of one another's existing dyestuffs markets and to set prices jointly in fields where they both had a presence. As a result, many in the IG felt that the French chemical industry had grown fat at their expense, exploiting German science, technology, and products that had been sequestered after the war and enjoying a privileged position that it had not earned. Unlike in Austria, Czechoslovakia, and Poland, where the concern's actions had been largely defensive, aimed at preventing possible competitive threats to its domestic business, France offered another level of opportunity entirely: a golden chance, informed by long-suppressed bitterness and a desire for revenge, to put an upstart rival in its place and help reestablish the concern's supremacy over all the chemical businesses of Europe.

The IG quickly realized that it wasn't feasible to swallow the French industry wholesale. It was too big, for one thing, and the concern's already overstrained bureaucracy would have a difficult time coping with the added responsibilities. But such drastic action also wouldn't be necessary. All that was required was for the French to acknowledge their subordinate status as junior partners in the IG's larger enterprise, lift the punitive restrictions on German imports, and abandon the infuriating practice (adopted by pharmaceutical companies in particular) of copying the IG's products without heeding to its patents. During the interwar years the IG's share of the French dye market had shrunk from a pre-1914 peak of 90 percent to around 10 percent. That could now be reversed. The ten-to-one sales advantage French drug manufacturers had enjoyed over the IG in France would also now come to an end, as would the French habit of undercutting the IG's prices across Europe and in exports overseas. France would take its place in the IG's "new order," a far-reaching plan for the whole of the European chemical industry that the concern had prepared for Hermann Göring in August 1940 and made subject to strict regulation "for all time to come."

The company presented its proposals to Gustav Schlotterer, number two at the Economics Ministry's foreign trade division. Noting that this time (unlike earlier, when the cartel had presented obviously self-interested proposals for the acquisition of Polish businesses), IG Farben had carefully framed its plans to take account of Germany's military and strategic requirements, Schlotterer agreed that reestablishing the IG's dominance in Europe was in Germany's best interests. He advised the IG's bosses, however, to use patience rather than belligerence in dealing with their French counterparts. The Reich's economic supremacy and France's growing shortage of raw materials would bring the French to the table soon enough, he said, but it would be better that they came cap in hand, humbled and desperately seeking the means to keep their factories going, instead of being dragged kicking and protesting to negotiations in which they would then try to gain parity with the IG. Time was on the combine's side. All it had to do was wait.

The *Vorstand* agreed and used the hiatus to gather necessary intelligence on its rivals. Inevitably, its focus fell on the French national dyes cartel, a group of companies led by the IG's old adversary Etablissements Kuhlmann. The *Vorstand*'s aim was for all the Kuhlmann cartel's firms to be folded into a single enterprise in which the IG would then take a controlling stake, thereby gaining the means to extend its influence over the entire French dyestuffs industry. Meanwhile, the German occupation authorities increased the pressure, confiscating one of Kuhlmann's smaller factories and blocking the supplies of coal and electricity that the French industry desperately needed to keep operating.

These tactics had the desired effect. Soon, French dyestuffs plants were closing down, unable to function without essential supplies. Realizing that the factories could not get back on line without IG Farben's support, one of Kuhlmann's senior executives, Joseph Frossard, tried to open negotiations with the cartel. Back in 1919 he had been Carl Bosch's principal contact in the French administration and had helped facilitate the last-minute deal in Paris whereby France agreed to let Germany's chemical plants stay open and intact in exchange for secret synthetic nitrate technology. Frossard evidently hoped that this history would stand him in good stead with the IG, but of course Bosch was now dead and no one else at the concern was prepared to pay him much attention. Acting on government advice, the cartel stalled, referring Frossard and his colleagues to a decision by Ambassador Hans Hemmen, chief of the German economic delegation to the Armistice Commission at Wiesbaden, to defer all discussions on industrial matters until after agreements had been reached about the borders between occupied and unoccupied France. "We do not think that the time has come to initiate these negotiations," an IG official said loftily. In reality, as von Schnitzler admitted later, the intention was to let the French "simmer in their own juice."

Von Schnitzler knew, however, that talks could not be postponed indefinitely. Eventually the Wehrmacht would insist that the French plants be reopened to help meet its insatiable need for chemical products. The moment that happened, the IG would lose its leverage over any negotiations. Therefore, in the last week of October, around the time that Adolf Hitler and Marshal Pétain were arriving at Montoire to settle the details of French collaboration, he asked Ambassador Hemmen to set up a meeting.

The talks began on November 21, 1940, at Wiesbaden. The German location was chosen in accordance with Hemmen's advice that it would give the IG a tactical advantage, but if the French were cowed by their surroundings, they didn't show it. Led by Kuhlmann's René Duchemin (Frossard wasn't present), the delegation responded to Hemmen's invitation to open discussions by suggesting that the best way forward would be to revive the 1927 Gallus Vertrag agreement. Although the war had interrupted the arrangement, their experts had assured them it was still legally valid and could easily be picked up again. Their proposal was made, they added blithely, in the spirit of the deal recently agreed between Hitler and Pétain as allies and partners.

The Germans, including von Schnitzler and Fritz ter Meer, listened in frosty silence until Ambassador Hemmen, who was there in his capacity as an adviser, suddenly "lost his temper." The French proposal left him "speechless," he shouted. The 1927 agreement was a product of the shameful Versailles Treaty. To suggest that it was still valid after Germany's recent historic victory was an insult. He would not allow it to be discussed. The French had two choices. Either they accepted that they had lost the war and submitted themselves to the dictates of the IG in the chemical field or the Reich would step in to decide their fate.

While the dismayed French struggled to absorb this unexpectedly hostile riposte, von Schnitzler began reading from a prepared statement. The IG's right to lead the European chemical industry had been well established before 1913, he said, but from the end of the last conflict the French had been abusing their relationship with their German counterparts. Now they had to face facts. France had declared war on Germany and this time had lost. Europe would need a strong and united chemical industry in the years to come and the French had to accept that only the IG was in a position to lead it. What would that mean in practice? All competition between the IG and the French companies would end immediately: French dye sales would be restricted to existing domestic and colonial markets; in every other respect, from production to exports, the IG would have unchallenged control over the French industry's affairs. At this point Hemmen adjourned the meeting until the following day.

The next morning von Schnitzler went into more detail, explaining the IG's plan to create a single Franco-German dye company in which the German cartel would hold the controlling stake; the IG would also control all export activity, with the possible exception of a few small existing contracts with Belgium. The French were appalled. Unnerved by Hemmen's threat of the previous day—to hand the entire matter over to the German authorities for resolution if they continued to protest—they pleaded for time to consult their government in Vichy. Once away from the high-pressure atmosphere of Wiesbaden, they rediscovered something of their courage, with Duchemin declaring he would rather cut off his hand than sign a deal that made his industry subservient to the IG.

As a result of this intransigence, negotiations dragged on until the following spring, with the French allowed only the barest minimum supplies of coal and electricity necessary to stop their plants from falling into total disrepair. The IG softened its approach to some marginal issues, conceding, for example, that the chief executive of the new company should be a Frenchman and suggesting that it might give Kuhlmann a technical helping hand in its non-dye-making activities.

But the concern stuck rigidly to its main demand for a single national dye business in which the IG had a controlling stake, at one point threatening that if the French refused to comply, the IG would arrange for the seizure of the whole Kuhlmann operation on the grounds that its prewar vice president, Raymond Berr, was a Jew. On March 10, 1941, at talks in Paris, the French finally gave in. In reality, they never had much choice. Lack of orders and raw materials had forced many of their plants to shut down and the Vichy government had come under intense pressure from the German authorities to ensure their cooperation. Two days later the French representatives sat in glum silence at a press conference as von Schnitzler announced the formation of a new firm. The Compagnie des Matières Colorantes et Produits Chimiques—or Francolor as it would be known more colloquially—would have a French president (Joseph Frossard was later appointed to the role), but IG Farben would own 51 percent of Francolor's stock and would appoint its own men to four of the eight top management positions: Otto Ambros, Fritz ter Meer, Hermann Waibel, and von Schnitzler himself. In return for a controlling stake in the business (later estimated to have been worth around 800 million francs at prewar prices), the IG compensated the French with a meager 1 percent of its own equity—as valued in the rapidly depreciating French currency.

Although there were still details to be worked out (including the precise wording of the written introduction to the formal agreement), the IG men could barely contain their glee. On July 23, 1940, ter Meer, Ambros, and others celebrated by drinking the night away in the garden of a Paris café. When the other customers had left, the Germans broke out into song, continuing even as they wound their way back to their hotel. The next morning, during one of his last conferences with the "French gentlemen," ter Meer remembered the words of one popular refrain and jotted them down among the doodles on a file folder: "For in the woods there are robbers" (*Denn im Wald da sind die Rauber*).* On November 18, 1941, Francolor came formally

---

*Nuremberg prosecutors found this folder among the few IG documents about the deal to survive the war. When ter Meer's words were read out in court, Otto Ambros started giggling. Clearly, that summer in Paris still evoked fond memories.

into being and all the property and assets of the major French dyestuffs manufacturers passed into German control.

But the IG hadn't quite finished with the French chemical industry. Wilhelm Mann, the head of the IG's Bayer pharmaceutical division, had ambitions to do to Rhône-Poulenc, France's biggest drug manufacturer, what his colleagues had done to Kuhlmann. Mann considered Rhône-Poulenc responsible for much of the aggravating prewar damage to the IG's medicines trade in France. At first he wanted the IG to take a controlling stake in the business but he ran into problems when it became clear that many of the French company's assets were in unoccupied Vichy territory and therefore invulnerable to threats of seizure. So, instead, Mann invited Rhône-Poulenc to form a joint sales company with the IG, backing up his "offer" with hints that if the French firm refused it would soon find itself on the receiving end of a price war—which the IG would surely win—and claims for compensation for abuse of IG Bayer's trademark and patent rights. When the French refused to consider the proposal, Mann became nastier, threatening to refer the matter to the German government—clearly now the standard approach with intractable foreign businesses. The threat worked as expected. Rhône-Poulenc's opposition evaporated and the joint sales venture, known as Theraplix, was quickly formed. Thereafter Bayer established a lucrative market for its medicines in France, eventually clocking up sales worth around twenty million francs a year.

The IG also tightened its grip on the rest of the French chemical industry. Between 1942 and 1943, occupation and Vichy authorities closed around thirteen hundred small family dye companies and pharmaceutical producers in the name of increased efficiency and rationalization, though the IG's already swollen market share was the real beneficiary. Along the way, the cartel also acquired two alloy mines, a 25 percent share of Kodak's French photographic business, an interest in a newly established synthetic fibers combine, and, most significant of all, an end to French competition for its products in neutral countries. All in all, not a bad haul for the robbers in the woods.

But if IG Farben gorged itself on French chemicals, its appetites were comparatively restrained in Western Europe's other occupied nations—Belgium, Holland, Luxembourg, Denmark, and Norway. In part this reserve was a response to an edict from Gustav Schlotterer at the Economics Ministry in Berlin. Alarmed at reports of acquisitive Ruhr coal and steel producers descending in a greedy and undisciplined horde on the Low Countries in the aftermath of the invasions, Schlotterer insisted on more self-control from other German industries. The odd advantageous purchase here or there could be countenanced and certainly there would be no objection to the confiscation of Jewish property, but any further takeovers would have to be officially sanctioned, in the proper fashion and at the proper time, to ensure that key factories of potential use to the German war effort were not rendered useless. As this bureaucratic process was obviously going to take a while, the IG, with its eyes fixed firmly on the far greater prizes in France and Poland, felt no immediate need to rush in.

The cartel's restraint was also due to the fact that these countries posed little competitive threat. Holland and Belgium, for example, specialized mostly in the production of heavy chemicals, which were of no great interest to the concern, and the IG's lead in its core production area of high-pressure chemistry was already so great that it could afford to be generous. In Belgium, the IG restricted itself to forcing the closure of a building project for an organic dyes factory at Terte and to cementing its existing relationships with Solvay et Cie, a reasonably sized manufacturer in Brussels, whereas in Holland it was content merely to drive the country's two leading dye firms out of business. Norway presented even less of a challenge. The only large Norwegian chemicals manufacturer, Norsk Hydro, was the IG's partner in a number of fields and the concern already held 25 percent of its stock (later increased to 31 percent) and a seat on its board, occupied by Hermann Schmitz. Otherwise the IG's only really significant wartime exploitation of Norwegian assets came through its attempt to provide the Hamburg nuclear physicist Paul Harteck with consignments of heavy water from the Vemork hydroelectric plant.

Had Germany gone on to invade Great Britain, of course, things would have been very different, because then the mighty Imperial Chemical Industries would have become a target. Although ICI's bosses and the British government later shied away from admitting the connection, ICI and the IG had actually cooperated very closely on occasions during the 1920s and 1930s.* In 1929, for example, ICI had joined up with Norsk Hydro in the IG-dominated Nitrogen Syndicate, and in 1930 it signed an IG/Standard Oil/Royal Dutch Shell agreement designed to contain the spread of synthetic oil technology. In 1935, well after the concern had struck its contract with the Nazis, the IG provided ICI with technical assistance and advice on the construction of a large hydrogenation plant at Billingham, in the northeast of England. Yet, at the same time, the two companies were fierce rivals, forever encroaching on each other's markets in search of strategic advantage. In Czechoslovakia, for example, ICI had helped the Aussiger Verein keep the IG at bay for years, while the IG had used its connections in Japan to undermine ICI's Asian interests. Indeed, with the possible exception of the United States's DuPont Corporation, ICI was IG Farben's biggest international competitor. It stood to reason, therefore, that Max Ilgner's *Vowi* office had gathered extensive information on ICI's assets and products and in the event of a successful Nazi occupation these plans would have formed the basis of an acquisition spree that dwarfed anything in Poland or France. As it was, the IG merely contented itself with handing over its intelligence to the Luftwaffe for use in its blitz on Britain's cities and industrial installations.

BOMBING CAMPAIGNS COULD go in two directions, of course. While some of the IG's senior executives were swaggering along in the wake of the Wehrmacht, their colleagues back home were nervously watching the skies for the Royal Air Force. Well before the start of the war, the Reich authorities had concluded that Leverkusen, Oppau, and Ludwigshafen, so close to Germany's western border, were vulnerable to enemy air attack. Each factory was therefore ordered to carry out regular air raid drills and to stockpile raw materials for production and repairs in case of disruption. These

---

*A few days after ICI's connections to IG Farben first came up at the Nuremberg trial, an internal British Foreign Office memo noted gratefully, "The *Times* discreetly omits reference to ICI Ltd."

precautions had been relaxed when it seemed that Hitler's armies were on course for an easy victory, but by the middle of 1940 Allied bombing was gathering pace and IG officials were compelled to take the threat more seriously.

To their relief, the situation turned out to be not quite as dangerous as they had anticipated. The first Allied raids on the area, in June and December 1940, were aimed principally at targets in the center of Cologne, Ludwigshafen, and Mannheim and thus did little damage to the nearby Rhine plants—although the destruction of transportation links moderately disrupted the traffic of raw materials to and from the Ruhr. Further raids in May, August, and October 1941 were more substantial but by then IG managers were practiced at dispersing their resources and effecting quick repairs. The huge size of the plants (larger targets were obviously easier to hit) was offset by their proximity to abundant water supplies, which meant that fires could be doused with comparative ease. Until the Allies amassed sufficient numbers of aircraft to overcome the Luftwaffe's strong ground and air defenses and then adopted the saturation bombing techniques that would prove so devastatingly effective later in the war, their efforts were more a nuisance than a true threat.

Aside from the air raids, the IG's biggest domestic headache was what to do about its rapidly diminishing labor supply. Well before the outbreak of war, thousands of IG workers had disappeared into the armed forces or munitions production, either voluntarily or as a consequence of the military draft. At first their departure had been offset by the arrival of some four thousand German labor conscripts—men deemed ineligible for military service because of age, political "unreliability," or infirmity. But with the demands of the procurement economy increasing all the time, the IG's managers had felt compelled to take more radical steps, like the recruiting of female workers. Unlike Britain and later the United States, the Nazi regime frowned upon the use of women in industrial jobs and throughout the war its attitude would cause the IG (and other large manufacturing concerns) great difficulty. Nevertheless the regime agreed to partially relax the restrictions when it took part in a scheme to automate some of its factories to make the work less strenuous. Between 1939 and early 1941, thirty thousand more women began working in heavy industry, of whom around three thousand were eventually assigned to the concern.

But this was a drop in the ocean compared with the numbers of skilled male Germans leaving through the other door. Inevitably, therefore, the IG turned once again to the controversial practice followed by Carl Duisberg and others during the Great War: enlisting neutral foreign labor and conscripting workers from occupied territories. On June 21, 1940, the first deployment of five hundred Belgian POWs arrived at Ludwigshafen. Within six weeks they had been joined by a contingent of around a thousand Italian and Slovak volunteers (some of whom had been lured to the Reich by promises of higher wages than they could get back home). Later in the year thousands of others were drafted more reluctantly from France and the Netherlands.

Although glad to have the extra men, IG managers were initially concerned that the newcomers might cause problems among the company's recently hired German women, and they warned female staff against fraternizing with foreigners or POWs. "Contact with the prisoners is permitted only in the framework of the employment relationship. Anything else will be punished severely. . . . Remember, our fathers, brothers, sons, and workmates are involved in heavy fighting at the front." But the caution was unnecessary; there was little chance that even the most ardent of the foreign workers would want to enjoy off-hour contact with their German "colleagues": away from the factory floor they were incarcerated in specially built barracks and POW camps where the food was too poor and the living conditions too cold, cramped, and depressing to leave much energy for anything beyond just getting through the days.*

Nevertheless, their presence seemed to relieve some of the pressure in the factories. The concern's output rose quickly and managers were free to concentrate on adapting what remained of their civilian productive capacity to meet the now incessant stream of military orders.

---

*For all the discomfort these drafts of foreign workers endured in the early years of the war, most of them were from "civilized" western or southern Europe and were treated accordingly: their suffering was modest when compared with that of the Poles, Russians, and Jews who later fell into the IG's hands.

At Leuna, the manufacture of synthetic automobile fuel for the civilian market was all but abandoned in favor of the high-octane diesel required by the army and air force, and it was much the same story at Leverkusen, Wuppertal, Landsberg, Wolfen, Oppau, Frankfurt, and Munich, where purely "peaceful" production was pushed firmly to the margins.

With its plants running smoothly, IG Farben was finally able to focus on the foreign markets it had neglected in the last few weeks of peace. The cartel's erstwhile overseas partners welcomed the prospect of renewed engagement, but they were soon to find out that a relationship with a wartime IG came with some unexpected strings attached.

THE EVENTS of September 1939 came as a shock to William E. Weiss of Sterling Products, Inc. Since his deal with Carl Duisberg in the 1920s he had maintained good relations with IG Bayer. The two companies squabbled occasionally over who owned exactly which rights to the Bayer brand in which countries, and sometimes lawyers had to argue matters out in court, yet Weiss never let these disputes get in the way of his personal friendships, especially with Wilhelm Mann, the head of the IG's pharmaceutical division. Weiss read the newspapers, of course, and heard all the torrid stories about Adolf Hitler and the dramatic changes taking place in Germany, but he had a remarkably unsophisticated grasp of European politics. Consequently, when Mann played down the more distasteful aspects of the new regime, telling him that the new rulers were probusiness and that there was no truth in the allegations that Jews were being persecuted, Weiss accepted these reassurances at face value. He remained sanguine even when he learned that Max Wojahn, the IG's representative in Latin America, had been forced to suspend advertising in popular anti-Nazi newspapers and that the cartel's traveling sales teams in the region were distributing Nazi propaganda. Eventually, however, the penny dropped. When Sterling was asked to pay an annual fee of $100,000 for rights that it had acquired almost twenty years earlier, just to placate the German regime, Weiss finally realized the true scale of the Nazis' influence on the cartel.

Even so, the pace of events caught him unprepared. When the war began, the British blockaded German exports across the Atlantic just as they had done twenty years earlier, jeopardizing shipments of the hugely profitable aspirin brand Cafiaspirina, which was sold in South America.* Weiss concluded that the only way around this obstacle was to make the medicine at Sterling's own factory at Rensselaer and export it south from there instead. He also knew from experience that the IG might see his move as an attempt to cut it out of one of its most lucrative markets. So he came up with an inducement. He offered to take over the manufacture and sale of *all* the IG's drugs sold in Latin America and to run these businesses in trust for the Germans until the war was over. This proposal was music to Hermann Schmitz's ears: the IG boss was looking for ways to conceal a range of the IG's American assets and was mindful, too, of the importance of protecting the IG's lucrative South American markets.† Indeed, he had already sanctioned a similar "cloaking" arrangement for the IG's exports of solvents and photographic materials to the continent, involving one Alfredo Moll, an intermediary working out of Buenos Aires. Schmitz's only condition for accepting Weiss's offer, therefore, was that absolutely binding contracts be drawn up to ensure the status quo was reestablished once normality returned. And so the agreement went ahead, hidden like so many of the IG's foreign dealings behind an elaborate chain of front companies. Unfortunately for Weiss, there was one massive drawback: the deal made Sterling, to all intents and purposes, a direct subsidiary of a company that much of the world now saw as an integral part of the Nazi regime.

What followed had the smack of inevitability about it. In June 1940 the Luftwaffe began bombing London, and, with every newsreel that was shown in U.S. cinemas, public opinion against Germany hard-

---

*According to Weiss's 1923 agreement with Bayer (taken over by IG Farben in 1925), Cafiaspirina was manufactured at Leverkusen and sold by Sterling in South America, with Weiss's company receiving 25 percent of the profits.

†The extraordinary range of the cartel's business interests in the region was later demonstrated at Nuremberg, when prosecutors listed 117 different Central and South American subsidiaries, trading partners, sales agencies, and other businesses in which the IG had some kind of stake. Dozens more firms from the area were excluded from the list because investigators had been unable to establish the exact nature of their connection to the IG.

ened further. The FBI's J. Edgar Hoover urged the Justice Department
to open an investigation into Nazi infiltration of American industry.
The Senate followed suit and soon details of its findings were being
leaked to the press. On May 29, 1941, the *New York Herald Tribune*
published a purple account of dirty dealings in the U.S.–South American pharmaceutical trade—which it claimed was being secretly manipulated by Hitler to pay for the war—and cited Cafiaspirina and
Sterling Products as chief culprits. In short order, everyone from the
Treasury Department to the Securities and Exchange Commission was
paying uncomfortably close attention to William Weiss's affairs.

Given the degree of scrutiny, it didn't take long for government investigators to uncover Weiss's secret deals with the IG and he was accused of collaborating with a potentially hostile foreign power. His
business began to collapse under the pressure. Sterling's Rensselaer
plant stopped making and shipping IG drugs to South America, in late
June its assets were temporarily frozen by the Treasury Department,
and even the lucrative Cafiaspirina brand was sacrificed—the company
had to commit to launching a new product with a new name to compete with the German-produced aspirin from which it had made so
much money in the past. Weiss was distraught, but he knew that the
alternative could be criminal charges. On August 15, 1941, he cabled
Leverkusen to inform the IG that he had to end all of their agreements.
IG Farben's angry reply, insisting on the fulfillment of its contractual
rights, went unanswered. Two days later the U.S. authorities banned
Weiss from holding any position in Sterling Products, although the
company was allowed to continue in business under new management. Weiss died in a car accident twelve months later.

Meanwhile, Standard Oil, the concern's largest U.S. partner, was in
an even more difficult position. The outbreak of war had found Frank
Howard in Paris, battling with the disrupted French telephone system
as he tried to finalize Standard's last-minute deal to buy the IG's 20
percent share of their joint enterprise, the Standard-IG Company. Although the sale had gone ahead, everything had happened in such a
rush that many details had been left unresolved, not least the crucial
matter of how the IG's all-important patents were to be legally transferred to Standard. Unable to contact Frankfurt or Berlin directly,

Howard was forced to ask New York to do so for him, suggesting that a meeting with IG officials in a nonaligned country be set up as quickly as possible.

The meeting was finally arranged for September 22, 1939, at The Hague in Holland (which was still neutral at the time), but only after both sides had resolved complicated travel difficulties and obtained permission to negotiate from their respective governments. Howard had a fairly easy time of it; hastening to London, he got the go-ahead from Joseph Kennedy, the U.S. ambassador to Britain, who also somehow smoothed things over with the British Foreign Office.* But the IG was able to get approval only by sending its synthetic fuel specialist, Heinrich Bütefisch, to plead with the Nazi authorities. He managed to convince them that the concern's sale of its share in the Standard-IG Company was merely temporary, a way of camouflaging its assets and the best means of protecting strategically important patents that would otherwise surely be seized by enemy governments. Once the war was over, the rights would be returned. In the meanwhile, Bütefisch assured the Nazis, "German interests would not be prejudiced."

Howard turned up at the meeting to find Friedrich Ringer, an IG patent expert, waiting for him. Most of the outstanding issues were quickly resolved. Ringer signed over the rights to more than two thousand patents and they agreed that henceforth Standard could exploit them exclusively in America and in Allied nations, while the rest of the world would remain IG territory. Ringer also told Howard the IG now recognized that assigning the cartel's 50 percent share in the Jasco venture to Walter Duisberg had been a mistake: the U.S. authorities were bound to see it as an attempt to camouflage the IG's interests in the business. As a result, Ringer was authorized to offer Duisberg's Jasco stake to Standard instead. The Jasco business came with the IG's long-coveted buna rights so Howard was naturally thrilled, but the edge of his delight was blunted somewhat when it became clear that the concern was still unable or unwilling to provide

*The British government was curiously uninterested in the news that one of America's top businessmen was proposing to attend a meeting with a representative of a country with which it was now officially at war.

the technical knowledge necessary to actually manufacture the product. Ringer promised to take the matter up with his superiors when he got back to Germany, insisting that he had no authority to sanction the transfer of technical information.

On October 16, 1939, the IG sent Standard a cable with its final words on the subject. As agreed, documents were being prepared for the transfer of the buna patents, but "referring to your question with respect to technical information . . . we have to inform you that under present circumstances we will not be able to give such information." Right to the last, the concern had managed to withhold the know-how that really mattered. Just as Bütefisch had promised, German interests had been protected.

No so American interests. The full consequences of Farben's zealous guardianship of the secrets of buna became clear only after December 1941, when Japan attacked Pearl Harbor and sent its armies across Southeast Asia. Cut off from the world's largest supply of natural rubber, the United States was thrown back onto its own resources. Many painful months later, as the shortage of rubber became increasingly critical, American scientists finally devised their own technical solutions to the buna problem, but not without an immense and costly effort.

Of more immediate consequence for Standard, the outbreak of war with Japan and Germany gave added impetus to an antitrust investigation that the Department of Justice had begun, in March 1941, to unravel the oil giant's relations with IG Farben. Soon every facet of Standard Oil's partnership with the Germans was revealed. The result was that Standard Oil and six subsidiaries, plus Walter Teagle, Frank Howard, and Walter Farish (Teagle's successor as president of the company), were indicted and convicted on charges of criminally conspiring with IG Farben to restrict trade in synthetic oil and rubber throughout the world. At the same time, the U.S. alien property custodian, Leo Crowley, seized all the IG's assets in the United States, including all the stock and patents in Standard-IG and Jasco. Although the oil executives' lawyers managed to negotiate the resultant individual penalties down to a mere five-thousand-dollar fine per person, Teagle, Farish, and Howard were soon being summoned to explain themselves in front of outraged Senate committees and were publicly disgraced. In November 1942 pressure from shareholders forced them to resign. Equally predictably, after a board reshuffle, Standard Oil itself survived. In time of war no government is going to force the collapse of the biggest national oil business—no matter how disgracefully its top management has behaved.

IF ANYONE AT IG Farben in 1940 felt a moment of embarrassment about the problems they had caused their former U.S. partners, they shrugged it off or kept it to themselves. The most important thing was that Germany had managed through sleight of hand to hold on to the secrets of a technological process that was proving very valuable. Indeed, the Reich's appetite for synthetic rubber was exceeding all expectations. The Schkopau plant had reached its annual production target of forty thousand tons by January 1940 and production levels at the IG's second factory, at Hüls, were close to the maximum by June, yet still the Wehrmacht demanded more. By the late summer of 1940 the army's senior commanders knew that the campaigns in Poland and Western Europe had seriously depleted resources, and with Britain determinedly holding out on the other side of the Channel the war looked set to continue for some time. In September 1940 Hitler's generals warned the Führer that the deficit in raw materials would have to be remedied, especially if he went ahead with plans to attack the Soviet Union. High on their list of requirements was a scheme to increase the manufacturing capacity of buna.

In November 1940 the Economic Ministry and the Wehrmacht high command summoned IG representatives to a series of top-secret conferences and told them of the Reich's needs. It was quickly agreed that two new synthetic rubber plants would be set up. One could be easily added onto existing facilities at Ludwigshafen; the other would be built in the new territories to the east, out of range of Allied bombers and of a size capable of meeting the anticipated surge in demand. Speed was essential; all bureaucratic barriers to construction would be lifted; a site would have to be identified as soon as possible.

Thus it was that the IG's Otto Ambros embarked on a detailed survey of possible locations in Silesia. He was looking for a place that had coal, water, good rail links, and, above all, an abundant supply of labor. On February 6, 1941, he sat down with Fritz ter Meer and Carl Krauch to discuss his findings. He had discovered just the right place, he told them. It was near a small town in occupied Poland. . . .

11

BUNA AT AUSCHWITZ

As far as Denis Avey could remember, the day had begun much like any other. Early that morning his section had been marched to the site and allotted a task: laying cable for one of the plant's soon-to-be-built electricity substations. As usual the men had gone about it as leisurely as they dared, fumbling with their equipment, deliberately getting in one another's way, and grabbing the opportunity whenever their guards' attention drifted elsewhere to discreetly put down their tools and take a rest. During one of these breaks, Avey stood up to stretch his aching back and looked around, his attention caught momentarily by the bright arc and sparks of a welding gun, high up on the scaffolding that surrounded one of the five giant smokestacks looming over building 921, the largest on the site. Some wag in the camp had dubbed these towers the *Queen Mary*, after the famous transatlantic liner, but it hadn't really caught on.

A few dozen yards away, under the expressionless eyes of an armed SS trooper, a *Kommando* of "stripeys" was working in a ditch.* It had been raining for hours and the soil had long since liquefied into a freezing black slime that clung to their emaciated faces and hands and rendered them almost unrecognizable as human beings. Yet human they undoubtedly were, one group slipping and sliding in the mud as they grappled with a set of heavy ceramic pipes, another, armed with picks and shovels, fighting a losing battle against the sludge beneath their feet, flinging it up onto the lip of the trench, where it stuck for a moment before sliding back down. Avey knew that if any one of the men in the *Kommando* showed the slightest intention of easing up on this fruitless task, their gang leader, or kapo—his status as a favored criminal prisoner signified by a green triangle on his striped tunic—would bring a stick whistling down on their heads.

For the hundredth time he was struck by the contrast in their positions. As a British POW he was significantly more fortunate than the starving, exhausted *Häftlinge* in the ditch. He was better fed, better dressed, and less liable to be beaten. Under his battered army greatcoat, for example, he wore a thick battle dress tunic, which, though patched and ill fitting, at least afforded him some measure of protection against the biting wind and rain. He also had boots, whereas the stripeys were forced to shuffle along in broken wooden shoes that filled with water and were forever falling apart. Nevertheless, as he gazed around he cursed the fates that had brought him to this dreadful place. In every direction he could see groups of men, each with their gang leader and attendant SS sentry, being harried through the mud that lay between the half-completed buildings. Some pushed wheelbarrows piled absurdly high with bricks and bags of cement; others were bent double under the weight of monstrous iron girders or metal pipes or wooden railway sleepers. Much of this activity was being carried out at a shambling trot, the bellowed orders of the kapos rising high above the background clamor of hammering, and welding and

---

*In British POW slang, "stripeys" could be political prisoners, criminals, or Jews, but not the POWs themselves. *Kommando* was camp parlance for a work gang, which could be up to fifty inmates.

the barks of overexcited guard dogs. And over everything, over the sour stench of wet cement, unwashed bodies, latrines, and cabbage soup that always permeated the site, there hung another, more dreadful smell, a sweetish gagging corruption that caught at the throat and nose and clung to clothes and hair. Its source lay a few miles to the west, but the wind often brought it their way.

Avey would never forget that smell. "We all knew what it meant and where it came from. When it drifted over, part of you would try and ignore it. Something happens in the brain and you have to think just about your own survival, not what is happening to everyone else. But it was there a lot and I had nightmares about it for years afterwards."

A long sequence of events had brought Denis Avey to this moment in his life. A trainee engineer who had joined the British army in 1939, he had been captured while fighting with the Seventh Armored Division against the Italians in Libya. Three unsuccessful escape attempts and numerous changes of prison camp later—including one fearsomely punishing spell deep in a German coal mine—he had ended up here with twelve hundred other British POWs, forced to work alongside thousands of Jews, Russians, and Polish political prisoners on the Third Reich's biggest construction project. After several months in appalling conditions, he was beginning to doubt whether he could endure much more: "The beatings, the constant brutality. It was all around you. I would see about six or seven people killed every day or drop dead where they worked. I had to tell myself to look away, to try and become inured to it."

But he wasn't inured to it. On this particular day, something snapped. As he stood there stretching, a Jewish prisoner shuffled past in the mud, struggling to maintain his grip on a large plank of wood. It slipped from his grasp and before he could pick it up an SS guard pounced, pushing the man to the ground, screaming abuse, and hitting him repeatedly about the head with the butt of his rifle. "I didn't stop to think. I don't know why. I'd seen many so people get a beating, but this time I couldn't stop myself. So I got involved. Unfortunately I didn't see this SS officer come up behind me. He took out his pistol and hit me in the face with it. I later lost my eye." Avey blacked out without

Carl Duisberg's funeral in March 1935. *(Bayer Business Services GmbH, Corporate History & Archives)*

Denis Avey (right) with two comrades in North Africa a few weeks before his capture in 1941. *(Denis Avey)*

The IG's Max Faust (center, wearing fedora) shows Reichsführer SS Heinrich Himmler (second from left) around the Buna-Werke site in July 1942. *(United States Holocaust Memorial Museum)*

Prisoner-laborers working at the Buna-Werke construction site in Auschwitz, probably in the early summer of 1943. *(BASF Aktiengesellschaft)*

The United States Air Force bombing Ludwigshafen and Oppau in early 1944. *(BASF Aktiengesellschaft)*

Workers survey damage at the IG's Leverkusen works after an air raid in early 1944. *(Bayer Business Services GmbH, Corporate History & Archives)*

The Buna-Werke after its seizure by the Soviet Army in January 1945. *(GARF, Moscow)*

The IG Farben defendants in the dock at Nuremberg, on the opening day of the trial. *(Paul M. Hebert Law Center, Louisiana State University)*

RIGHT: Brigadier General Telford Taylor, U.S. chief prosecutor, in court at Nuremberg. *(United States Holocaust Memorial Museum)*

BELOW LEFT: The Palace of Justice at Nuremberg in 1947. *(Paul M. Hebert Law Center, Louisiana State University)*

BELOW: Georg von Schnitzler addresses the court during the IG Farben trial. To the prosecution's frustration, many of his most damaging postwar statements to Allied investigators were deemed inadmissible. *(Paul M. Hebert Law Center, Louisiana State University)*

LEFT: Fritz ter Meer (right) consults his lawyer, Erich Berndt. Prosecutors noticed that ter Meer exercised a powerful influence over his fellow defendants during the trial. *(Paul M. Hebert Law Center, Louisiana State University)*

BELOW: Otto Ambros (seated, front right) and Heinrich Bütefisch (seated, front left) share a joke with a lawyer, as Walter Dürrfeld (rear) looks on. All three defendants would be found guilty of slavery and mass murder. *(Paul M. Hebert Law Center, Louisiana State University)*

ABOVE: During recess. Front row, left to right, Carl Krauch, Hermann Schmitz, Georg von Schnitzler, and Fritz Gajewski (standing). Back row (seated) Max Ilgner. *(Paul M. Hebert Law Center, Louisiana State University)*

RIGHT: Carl Krauch makes a final plea to the court as, over his left shoulder, Josiah DuBois listens to the translation. *(Paul M. Hebert Law Center, Louisiana State University)*

The IG Farben case judges. From left to right, James Morris, Curtis Grover Shake (presiding), Paul M. Hebert, and Clarence F. Merrell (alternate). Judge Morris, who frequently complained about the prosecution's slow and methodical approach, seems to be asleep. *(Paul M. Hebert Law Center, Louisiana State University)*

Little remains of the IG's Monowitz concentration camp today beyond a few concrete foundations and some grassed-over tracks. The rest has been built on or reclaimed as farmland.

ever learning the identity of the Jewish prisoner on whose behalf he had intervened or what may have happened to him. But he has no illusions. "If he wasn't killed there and then, most likely he was taken a couple of miles up the road to Birkenau and gassed like the rest."

Such was the nature of life and death at IG Farben's buna factory in Auschwitz.

AT THE AGE of thirty-nine, Otto Ambros was exactly where he wanted to be. When he was a boy, his father, an agricultural scientist, had often taken him into the laboratory where he worked. The experience had left Ambros desperate to become an industrial chemist. His fervor lasted through school in Bavaria (where one of his friends had been the future SS leader Heinrich Himmler), on to university, and then into a research post with the newly formed IG Farben. Within a few years his passion, initiative, and eagerness to please brought him to the attention of Carl Bosch, Carl Krauch, and the *Sparte* II boss, Fritz ter Meer. The latter took Ambros under his wing at Ludwigshaven and quickly fired him with enthusiasm for his pet project, the hoped-for marriage of the molecule butadiene with the element sodium to make synthetic rubber. A short while later ter Meer sent him on an exciting trip to the plantations of south Asia, to study how natural rubber was produced and gather vital information about manufacturing costs that his boss could use when preparing his frequent pitches for company funds. It wasn't long before Ambros became a key figure in the IG's development of buna, devoting much of his skill and energy to the technical challenges of the product the Nazis had identified as a key element in strategic autarky. He was delighted when the Schkopau plant produced its first few pounds of buna in 1936, and he basked in the reflected glory when it won a gold medal at the International Exposition at Paris in 1937. His star was beginning to shine.

But Ambros's spectacular rise wasn't due just to his chemical expertise. Intensely ambitious, he had a talent for making good use of his friends in high places. Ter Meer was always a powerful ally, but Ambros stayed close to Carl Krauch as well, and in the golden years of the Four-Year Plan his common bond with Himmler also enhanced his status. As a result, he was increasingly given license to think imaginatively about how best to meet the IG's commitments to the Wehrmacht (his willing assumption of responsibility for the concern's poison gas program demonstrating his lack of concern about the consequences of this partnership). By 1937, the year he joined the Nazi Party, he had parlayed his growing influence into a seat on the *Vorstand* as the director in charge of rubber and plastics—a crucial position in the run-up to war.

Although Ambros would later maintain that he hadn't been particularly keen to increase the IG's buna production strength (on the grounds that managing the existing capacity was challenge enough), there is no doubt that, in the autumn of 1940, when the Economics Ministry and high command laid out their pressing demands, he responded very enthusiastically. The IG had already made some independent moves in this direction, spending nearly four million reichsmarks in 1939 on the foundations for a buna factory at Rattwitz, near Breslau. The project had been mothballed after the successful invasion of France seemed to render stepped-up capacity unnecessary, but Ambros knew that, theoretically at least, it could be revived.

The IG had never been truly happy with Rattwitz—the site had numerous geological and topographical problems—and so, before committing to satisfy the Wehrmacht's increased demand, Ambros decided to see if there were better options elsewhere. The manufacture of buna required abundant supplies of coal, water, and lime and the right terrain on which to construct a plant. From his travels before the war Ambros knew of one region that had all these things—Upper Silesia, formerly part of Germany. The occupation of Poland had brought the area's coalfields (lost in 1921) back into German hands and the survey evidence suggested that they were rich and underexploited. The region also had plentiful deposits of lime and it was crisscrossed by several major rivers, vital for a factory that would need to access more than five hundred cubic feet of fresh water per hour if it was to meet its production targets.

Ambros got out his maps and set off with his subordinates to visit various sites. Rattwitz was examined once more, in case the alternatives failed to come up to scratch, then Heydebreck in Lower Silesia, Grosshowitz and Gross-Dobern (both near Oppeln), and Emilienhof (near Gogolin).* As his team moved farther east into Upper Silesia, he reminded his men to take note of all road and rail links and to remember that the area around any potential site had to be able to cope with the large influx of managers, engineers, and specialist workers that the IG would bring in from its parent plants on the Rhine. The question of accommodation was especially serious. Poor housing stock was the region's Achilles' heel and Ambros knew that unless he found a solution to that problem the new factory would struggle to attract senior staff.

When and how Ambros first encountered the area around Auschwitz—or Oswiecim, as the Poles called it—isn't known for sure, although it is possible that in late November 1940 he went there to investigate rumors that another German firm, the Mineralölbau GmbH, was considering opening a plant in the vicinity. In any event, by the middle of December it had moved to the top of his list of "probables," with one site in particular exciting his interest. Situated on a large level plain between Auschwitz and the nearby hamlets of Monowitz and Dwory, it lay just south of the confluence of three rivers, the Vistula, Sola, and Przemsza. The terrain was sound and suitable for building, and because it sat sixty-five feet above water level it could generally be considered safe from flooding. The site's attractiveness was further enhanced by the fact that the coal mines of Wisola, Brzeszcze, Dzieditz, and Jawiszowitz were all within easy reach, while the larger mining districts around Kraków were only twenty miles away. Communication links were also good, with three major rail lines converging in the area.

On questioning the local authorities, including the ethnic German mayor, Herr Gutsche, Ambros's experts learned more about the actual town of Auschwitz. It wasn't, they were forced to admit, the most appealing of locations: "Apart from the large marketplace the town itself makes a very wretched impression." But, as they reported to Ambros,

---

*Heydebreck later became the site for an IG synthetic fuel plant.

there might be some counterbalancing advantages as far as accommodation was concerned: "The inhabitants of Auschwitz consist of 2,000 Germans, 4,000 Jews, and 7,000 Poles. The Germans are peasants. The Jews and Poles, if industry is established here, will be turned out, so that the town will then be available for the staff of the factory."

Ambros also took note of Auschwitz's other important feature. In March 1940 the SS had taken possession of the town's old Austrian cavalry barracks and was in the process of transforming them into a holding camp for Polish political and military prisoners. Further inquiries revealed that a few thousand inmates were already there and many more could be expected. As Ambros prepared to return to Germany to weigh the relative merits of the proposed buna sites—not least the question of where he might find the necessary construction labor—this last bit of news was to the forefront of his mind.

THE CAMP AT AUSCHWITZ had been established in the context of Hitler's plans to use Poland as a buffer zone against the Soviet Union. As agreed in his deal with Stalin of August 1939, half of the country and more than twenty million people had fallen under the Reich's control. The Führer's intention—announced in the Decree for the Consolidation of the German Nation, of October 7, 1939—was that the western regions of this territory (Upper Silesia, Danzig–West Prussia, Warthegau, and East Prussia) should be fully Germanized in line with Nazi racial and imperial ideology. This was to involve the expulsion of the native inhabitants, the influx of a new German population, and, of course, the systematic removal of all Jews and Jewish influences. The rest of German-controlled Poland—a de facto colony known as the General Government, administered from Kraków—was to be exploited economically under SS and military rule and would serve as a dumping ground for Poles, Jews, political opponents, and other "undesirable elements" until such time as the regime could arrive at more lasting solutions.

Much to his satisfaction, Reichsführer SS Heinrich Himmler was put in charge of this "resettlement" program. Not only did the position offer him the opportunity to fulfill his ambitions to create a racially pure German East, it also gave him an excuse to further embellish his expanding SS apparatus and enhance his standing vis-à-vis Göring and Goebbels, his rivals at Hitler's court. He had already begun this process by consolidating the various state police services he controlled. The Sipo (Sicherheitspolizei, or security police)—which consisted of the Gestapo (political police) and the Kripo (criminal police)—had been combined with the SD (Sicherheitsdienst, or intelligence service of the SS) into a new organization, the RHSA, or Reich Security Main Office (Reichssicherheitshauptampt). Under the leadership of his deputy, SD chief Reinhard Heydrich, the RHSA would become Himmler's main vehicle for the exploitation and enslavement of the conquered lands.

Heydrich was a man most aptly suited to his job. Even prior to his new elevation, he had terrorized the subjugated Polish territories. On the eve of the invasion, with the Reichsführer's cognizance and on Hermann Göring's authority, Heydrich had arranged for seven SS and SD Einsatzgruppen (Operational Groups) to accompany German forces over the border. Principally, the Einsatzgruppen's responsibilities involved the liquidation of anyone who might prove capable of organizing anti-German resistance—a definition Heydrich's men enthusiastically applied to lawyers, doctors, teachers, aristocrats, senior civil servants, businessmen, landowners, intellectuals, writers, and priests. But the groups also carried out savage revenge attacks against the civilian populace for supposed breaches of military laws, murdered mental hospital patients to ensure vacant beds for German wounded, and, increasingly, conducted large-scale massacres of the Jews. Nonetheless, the Einsatzgruppen's brutal actions against the Jews were deemed inadequate. The conquest of Poland had brought around 2 million Jews under German control, of whom some 700,000 lived in the areas set aside for annexation, while the rest were scattered in villages around the General Government. Having forced the Jews out of the fatherland, the Nazi leadership was determined to remove them from the Reich's new territories as well.

On September 21, 1939, Heydrich called the commanders of several SS groups back to Berlin to discuss the regime's approach to the "Jewish problem." In chilling if still guarded terms, his briefing set out the framework for the nightmare to come. He began by emphasizing that "the overall measures envisaged (i.e., the ultimate aim) must be kept strictly secret." A distinction had to be made between "the final goal, which would require a lengthy period, and the stages toward the achievement of this final goal." The first stage, "the concentration of Jews from the countryside in the larger cities," must be speedily implemented. If possible, most of western Poland "should be cleared completely of Jews," or at least they should be gathered in as few centers as possible. Elsewhere in Poland, Jews should be concentrated only in cities situated at railway junctions or along a railway, so that "future measures could be more easily facilitated."

Himmler's promotion of Heydrich to the position of chief of the new Reich Security Main Office (RHSA) came six days after he had sketched out this blueprint for the ghettos at Warsaw and Lodz, and it hinted at worse for the future. When Hitler's Decree for the Consolidation of the German Nation gave Himmler jurisdiction over the fate of the population, the SS, the RHSA, and Heydrich's Einsatzgruppen were primed to act with savage vigor.

The old cavalry depot in Auschwitz first caught Himmler's eye in early 1940, when he was considering ways to cement the domination of the border zones and looking for suitable places to build concentration camps for incarcerating political opponents. Initially there was some doubt about the site's suitability. Himmler's inspectors warned him that the barrack buildings were decrepit and sat on swampy ground that was liable to breed malaria. On the other hand, they noted, it had the advantage of being easy to seal off from the outside world, which was always a desirable factor in camp location. Furthermore, as Otto Ambros would later realize, the area had excellent transportation links, which would make the movement of prisoners that much easier. However, the most compelling factor, at least in Himmler's eyes, was something more romantic. Five centuries earlier, until it had been wrested from them, the district had been under the control of German knights, a seductive detail of Teutonic history that the Reichsführer thought too significant to ignore. He began to envisage how prison labor could be used to turn Auschwitz into a model German town suitable for population entirely by true Aryans and complete with its own agricultural estate. At one and the same time Himmler could right a historical wrong and take a step in his mission to restore the fatherland's racial hegemony. On April 27, 1940, he gave the go-ahead to begin work.

The first people to suffer the consequences of Himmler's decision were twelve hundred Polish refugees who were expelled from their temporary homes next to the barracks and three hundred Jews from the town of Auschwitz whom the SS forced into clearing up the site. In early June 1940, when the prison camp was officially declared open, over one thousand Poles from prisons near Kraków and Wisnicz Nowy—mostly soldiers and students—were brought in to work on further construction. Transports of 1,666 and 1,705 political prisoners from Warsaw followed in August and September. During this initial phase, most of these new inmates were members of the Polish political intelligentsia, including some Jews, who had been swept up as part of the Einsatzgruppen's postinvasion campaign. While they were not the targets of systematic murder, they were nonetheless subject to the cruel and violent treatment that the SS routinely meted out to those in its charge: hunger, harassment, and intolerable working conditions, indiscriminate beatings, hangings, and shootings. By the late autumn of 1940, with the first phase of construction nearing completion and Himmler's planners already drawing up schematics for his ambitious farming project, more than seven thousand prisoners had passed through the gates and much of the usual SS concentration camp apparatus of humiliation and repression was falling into place. Auschwitz still had some way to go, however, before it would attain its singular status as the largest and most dreadful of all the Nazi camps. For that to happen, another spark was needed.

IT IS NOT known exactly how Himmler first found out about the IG's interest in Auschwitz. His old school friend Otto Ambros may have passed on the news but it could just as easily have come from Heinrich Bütefisch, who was a member of his Circle of Friends, or even from Christian Schneider, the head of *Sparte* I, who was an honorary SS colonel and well connected to the Reichsführer's office in

286 · HELL'S CARTEL

Berlin. Alternatively, Himmler may have been informed by Ulrich Greifelt, his liaison with the Four-Year Plan, or by SS Major Rudolf Höss, the newly appointed commandant of Auschwitz, who would undoubtedly have picked up gossip about Ambros's visits to the area. One thing is clear: when Himmler *did* find out about the IG's interest he was determined to do whatever he could to turn its cautious probing into a positive decision. He understood immediately that the creation of a large plant near the town would be of enormous benefit to his plans. It would bring a flood of money and a huge supply of construction materials to the area—which he could use to turn Auschwitz into a significant German center—while the influx of racially pure Aryans the plant would necessarily entail would give a massive boost to his repopulation schemes. There was also the chance that the inmates of the concentration camp could be employed at the plant to generate revenue for his ambitious programs elsewhere. It was vital, therefore, that the IG make the right choice.

But even as Himmler was pondering how best to bring this about, Ambros was beginning to have second thoughts. Each time he came close to making a recommendation to his colleagues, another report about the wretched state of the town and the paucity of its accommodation would land on his desk. "Auschwitz and villages give an impression of extreme filth and squalor," one asserted. "The most difficult problem will be that of organizing a plant staff."

At the end of January 1941 he sent two IG construction chiefs, Max Faust and Erich Santo, to take another look. They met with the newly appointed provincial governor of Upper Silesia, Fritz Bracht, and his chief regional planner, Herr Froese. Having hastily consulted with the SS authorities, Bracht and Froese did their best to be reassuring. Froese told the visitors that an architect from Breslau had already been hired to draw up a master plan for the overhaul of the town and that local Poles and Jews were facing imminent deportation. As far as construction labor was concerned, "the concentration camp already existing with approximately seven thousand inmates is to be expanded. Employment of prisoners for the building project is possible after negotiations with the Reichsführer SS."

This tip was enough to swing the balance for Ambros. On February 6, 1941, he met with Fritz ter Meer and Carl Krauch and put Auschwitz forward as his favored location for the IG's buna plant. There were housing problems, he acknowledged, and they would have to be overcome. As one of his experts had made plain, "Construction of a large-scale settlement, including schools, cultural centers, etc., must therefore be started at least at the same time as the factory buildings in order to create living conditions for the staff that would provide even a modicum of comfort." But none of these challenges were insurmountable, providing the more pressing problem of labor could be resolved. Removing the local population of Jews and Poles to make space for IG staff would deplete the numbers of people available for building work. Unless this was dealt with, the factory would take far longer to build than anyone wanted.

Krauch took the hint and went straight to the top to obtain a solution. On February 25 he was able to inform Ambros that Hermann Göring had "issued special decrees to the supreme Reich authorities concerned. . . . In these decrees the Reich marshal ordered the offices concerned to meet your requirements in skilled workers and laborers at once, even at the expense of other important building projects or plans."* Göring had also written to Himmler requesting that "the largest possible number of skilled and unskilled building workers . . . be made available from the adjoining concentration camp for the construction of the buna plant." Between eight and twelve thousand people would be needed.

Although the Reichsführer was initially taken aback at the number of inmates the IG required, he was delighted to comply. For many years he had been trying to exploit the labor of concentration camp prisoners in Germany, especially in the field of munitions production, in order to build up the revenue and economic influence of the SS. But lack of commercial experience among his staff had seen most of these attempts fail. Now, with the IG's expertise to call on, there was a chance he could get things right. He took a number of steps immediately, ordering Richard Glücks, the SS inspector of concentration

---

*In July 1940, as a reward for the victories in Poland and France, Hitler had appointed Göring a Reich marshal, the highest possible rank in the German armed forces.

camps, to "aid the construction project by means of the concentration camp prisoners in every possible way" and appointing SS Major General Karl Wolff of his personal staff to act as liaison officer with the cartel. Then he set off for Upper Silesia to meet IG Farben officials and to brief Commandant Rudolf Höss personally on his new responsibilities. To meet the IG's needs, Himmler told him, the inmate population would have to be increased from its current maximum of ten thousand to at least thirty thousand. Auschwitz was destined to become the biggest concentration camp in the Reich.

As Höss absorbed this remarkable news, the IG was taking its own leaps forward. The buna factory would entail the construction of a massive hydrogenation plant. To defray the expense, managers suggested that the facility also be used to produce hundreds of thousands of tons of synthetic fuel. The technological challenge of uniting two production strands in one factory was enormous, and combining the manufacturing process of different *Sparten* in one place ran counter to the concern's normal organizational thinking, but if it could be made to work the potential gains could be huge. As a result, while Otto Ambros was appointed to control the buna operation, Heinrich Bütefisch was given responsibility for fuel. On the plant's completion the two men would be in joint charge of one of the largest factories in the world.

With heads spinning at the potential postwar financial gains to be reaped from such a vast project, the *Vorstand* then came to another fateful decision. Unlike the dozens of other new plants the cartel had constructed under the aegis of the Four-Year Plan, which had been built with the aid of government loans and subsidies, this one would be wholly financed by IG Farben. At a cost of almost RM 900 million, the project would be the single most sizable investment in the company's history. But though the risk was extraordinary, the rewards promised to be greater still. In the long term the IG would have sole control of the buna factory's output and profits.

With the full backing of the Nazi hierarchy, the Wehrmacht high command, the Reich's economic apparatus, and all his fellow directors on the *Vorstand*, Ambros now spurred his team into action. In March 1941, in a rapid series of conferences—attended at various times by

Major General Karl Wolff, Auschwitz commandant Rudolf Höss, Heinrich Bütefisch, Fritz ter Meer, Ambros himself, and the two IG men chosen to run the construction project, Walter Dürrfeld and Max Faust—the participants thrashed out the details of the IG's collaboration with the SS. In the process, a clearly symbiotic relationship between the two organizations began to emerge. For example, at one meeting it was decided that "a payment of RM 3 per day for unskilled workers and RM 4 per day for skilled workers is to be made for each inmate. This includes everything, such as transportation, food, etc., and we (the IG) will have no other expenses for the inmates, except if a small bonus (cigarettes, etc.) is given as an incentive." But none of this money would go to the inmates; the concern would pay it directly into the SS's coffers.*

At another meeting Walter Dürrfeld raised the problem of finding suitable overseers for the building phase of the project. Höss hastened to reassure him. The SS would provide the IG with kapos especially chosen for their ruthlessness, one for every twenty inmates. These men, Dürrfeld told Ambros later, would be "selected from among the professional criminals and are to be transferred from other concentration camps to Auschwitz."

In the meanwhile, IG Farben acquired the area around Monowitz, in some cases by invoking the authority of the regional government to expropriate the land from Polish farmers, in others buying plots that the SS had previously confiscated. It also arranged to purchase sand, gravel, and bricks from SS-owned facilities and bought a majority stake in the nearby Fürstengrube coal mine, which was to be worked by inmates from a specially established subcamp run by the SS. Speed was of the essence, IG executives constantly reminded their new partners. To make a real contribution to the war effort the buna plant would have to come into production within two and a half years—ideally by mid-1943. The sooner facilities were provided for IG managers coming from Germany, the sooner construction work could begin.

The SS and the Reich authorities rushed to do their bidding. On

---

*Children, being less productive, would be furnished at a cost of RM 1.5 for each nine- to eleven-hour shift they worked.

April 3, 1941, the first deportation of Jews from the area began—a series of eerily silent processions that wound their way from the Old
Town and its ruined synagogue to the railway station, where five
Reichsbahn trains waited to carry them away.* As the deportees were
marched past the town hall, IG managers came out from their temporary offices to watch them go by. More than three thousand Jews were
taken to a holding facility at Sosnowitz; the rest were concentrated at
Bendzin. For most of them their next sight of Auschwitz would be
their last.

On Monday, April 7, Otto Ambros got to his feet on a stage in
nearby Katowice to address a gathering to mark the foundation of the
great endeavor. All the relevant authorities were present: the Reich
Authority for Spatial Planning, the Office of the Reich Commissioner
for the Consolidation of the German Nation, the Reich Office for
Economic Development, the Upper Silesian provincial governor's office, the local water and power authorities, the municipal government
of Auschwitz, and a contingent of senior SS officers from the concentration camp. In a wide-ranging speech Ambros took them through
the exciting prospects for science and technology offered by this bold
new venture, the economic benefits that would accrue to the region,
and the important role concentration camp labor would play in getting it going. Then he turned to the racial and ideological significance
of the whole undertaking.

> With the Auschwitz project, IG Farben has designed a plan for a new
> enterprise of giant proportions. It is determined to do everything in
> its power to build up a virile enterprise that will be able to shape its
> environment in the same way as many plants in west and central
> Germany do. In this manner IG Farben fulfills a high moral duty to
> ensure, with a mobilization of all its resources, that this industrial
> foundation becomes a firm cornerstone for a powerful and healthy
> Germanism in the East.

Five days later, delighted by the warm reception these remarks had received and satisfied that everything was proceeding smoothly, Ambros

---

*The Gestapo had destroyed the synagogue in 1939.

wrote to Fritz ter Meer to report progress: "Our new friendship with the SS is proving very beneficial," he said.

IG Farben's eight-year-long entanglement with the Nazis had brought it to an extraordinary point where one of its leading executives was describing the merits of a new factory in unmistakably racial terms and openly extolling the virtues of its profitable collaboration with a murderous regime. The availability of slave labor had been a crucial factor in the concern's decision to build a plant next to a concentration camp; now the IG's presence would contribute decisively to the camp's expansion and its eventual evolution into an industrialized killing machine. Auschwitz's inmates were already dying of hunger and exhaustion and disease and bullet wounds and beatings. Within a few months, as a consequence of the IG's actions, the first selections to the gas chambers would begin.

STILL, AMBROS AND his team had presumed too much, too soon. Although the construction of the factory, the Buna-Werke, started well, problems soon began to appear, in part due to the project's sheer size and complexity. Any plant set to occupy over one square mile of terrain—land that had to be cleared and prepared before other work could proceed—was bound to tax the technical and organizational ingenuity of the engineers and designers in charge. At the outset the blueprints were straightforward enough. The factory was to be laid out on a grid pattern, with raw materials (coal, water, and lime) being brought in at the north side and buna emerging at the south. But the plans were complicated by the decision to add extra manufacturing capacity for synthetic fuel and for other chemicals, such as methanol, that the works might produce in the future. Revising these drawings and specifications consumed much valuable time.

The more obvious problems of building a factory in wartime also became apparent. Basic construction materials such as cement, iron, and lumber were harder to obtain than had been envisaged, and adequate water and supplies were also unexpectedly difficult to arrange (the finished Buna-Werke was projected to need more electricity than Berlin). Nor did it help that Auschwitz lay a long way from the IG's parent plants on the Rhine. Vital equipment sent from Ludwigshafen, Oppau, and Leuna was liable to be held up by bottlenecks on the overburdened railway system or delayed by Allied bombing. Occasionally the shipments were merely misdirected; at other times they failed to arrive altogether and had to be reordered from scratch.

An even more serious predicament was the shortage of labor. Heinrich Himmler had promised the IG that the concentration camp would meet most of its needs but this manpower was proving slow to materialize. Building a security fence around such a massive work area took longer than anticipated and until it was completed in late 1941 the SS refused to allow more than a thousand inmates on the Buna-Werke site at any one moment—and then restricted them to working in daylight and under the strictest supervision. At the same time the SS was also preparing suitable housing for the advance parties of technical specialists now arriving from the IG's factories in Germany and had just started construction of a major new satellite camp for prisoners of war at nearby Birkenau, an abandoned village set amid birch trees on the SS agricultural estate. These various projects all required inmates whose energies would otherwise have been dedicated to the plant and also reduced the availability of the "free" Polish workers the SS had brought in from the surrounding countryside.

As the delays steadily worsened, the IG's Walter Dürrfeld and Max Faust, the men in daily charge of the Buna-Werke construction, began to list their anxieties in weekly reports to Otto Ambros and the *Vorstand*. Their somewhat forlorn hope was to show headquarters that building a plant on the wild outer fringes of the new Reich was a more complicated undertaking than had first been imagined and thus to win some relaxation of the schedule. In the meantime they pressed their on-site subordinates and the SS to work the concentration camp laborers harder and faster to cut down some of the construction backlog. One of those prisoners, Rudolf Vrba, later described how the Auschwitz security apparatus translated this pressure into action.

> Men ran and fell, were kicked and shot. Wild-eyed kapos drove their bloodstained path through rucks of prisoners, while SS men shot from the hip, like television cowboys who had strayed somehow into

a grotesque, endless horror film; and adding a ghastly note of incongruity to the bedlam were groups of quiet men in impeccable civilian clothes, picking their way through corpses they did not want to see, measuring timbers with bright yellow folding rules, making neat little notes in black leather books, oblivious to the blood bath. They never spoke to the workers, these men in the quiet grey suits. They never spoke to the kapos, the gangsters. Only occasionally they murmured a few words to a senior SS N.C.O., words that sparked off another explosion. The SS man would kick viciously at the kapo and roar, "Get these swine moving, you lazy oaf. Don't you know that wall's to be finished by eleven o'clock?" The kapo would scramble to his feet, pound into the prisoners, lashing them on, faster, faster, faster.

In the face of this sort of savagery, the IG's senior managers at Auschwitz could hardly pretend it was not happening. Yet they seemed remarkably oblivious to the possibility that their own demands were inciting the violence. Instead, they worried that the brutality might undermine productivity. One weekly progress report dispatched to Frankfurt in August 1941 complained that "in the last few weeks the inmates are being severely flogged on the construction site by the kapos in increasing measure, and this always applies to the weakest inmates, who really cannot work harder. The exceedingly unpleasant scenes that occur on the construction site are beginning to have a demoralizing effect on the free workers, as well as on the Germans." The author went on to clarify that his unhappiness had less to do with the morality of the beatings than with the fact they were taking place on company property. "We have therefore asked that they should refrain from carrying out this flogging on the construction site and transfer it . . . to the concentration camp."

The IG men were clearly far more bothered by the long delays than by the treatment meted out to the prisoners. When the question of attacks on inmates next came up in the weekly reports, it was obvious that frustration had made officials much more tolerant of the SS's methods: "The work, particularly of the Poles and inmates, continues to leave much room for improvement. . . . Only brute force has any effect on these people. . . . The commandant always argues that as far as the treatment of inmates is concerned it is impossible to get any work done without corporal punishment."

This tolerance may have been a product of the growing friendship between Commandant Höss and Dürrfeld. The men had begun socializing together with their wives and arranging joint hunting excursions into the surrounding countryside.* Indeed, on a personal level, relations between the IG and the SS at Auschwitz were blossoming, as one of the last weekly reports of the year made clear: "On December 20 representatives of the IG attended a Christmas party of the Waffen SS that was very festive and that ended up alcoholically gay." The conviviality did little to resolve the IG's labor problems, though, which were worsening by the week, in spite of the arrival at Auschwitz of a completely new influx of inmates.

On Sunday, June 22, 1941, Hitler had launched Operation Barbarossa against the Soviet Union, ostensibly to combat the supposed Jewish-Bolshevik conspiracy to rule the world but also to satisfy his quest for lebensraum. The largest military assault in history to date, it was at first a stunning success. Victory followed victory as the Wehrmacht pushed Stalin's forces back to the Urals and took millions of prisoners. Unsure what to do with these men but apparently determined not to accord them the protection of the Geneva Convention or abide by even the most basic rules of international warfare, the German army embraced the barbarism that had previously been the preserve of the SS and its Einsatzgruppen. The high command made sure that its troops followed the infamous Commissar Order—issued by Hitler to his generals in March 1941, through which the Communist Party's representatives in the Red Army were singled out and summarily shot—and then invited the SS in to scour the ranks of captured men for any additional party functionaries, as well as "agitators" and Jews, that the Wehrmacht might have missed. The rest, many hundreds of thousands of ordinary Russian soldiers, were crammed into primitive barbed wire pens—often little more than large compounds in bare fields—and left to die of starvation, exposure, and disease.

---

*The IG managers back in Germany were also given the chance to enjoy Höss's company. He made frequent trips to Leuna and Ludwigshafen, so that he "would be in a better position to utilize the labor of concentration camp inmates."

To Himmler this mass of Soviet prisoners promised a terrific boon. He had known of the approaching invasion back in March 1941, when, through his representatives at the meetings with the IG, he had promised the cartel a workforce of tens of thousands of forced laborers. Now, after an embarrassing hiatus, he wanted to deliver on that promise and augment the thinning ranks of Polish and German political prisoners the SS was providing from the concentration camp and the *Fremdarbeiter* (foreign laborers from the General Government, Holland, Belgium, France, Czechoslovakia, and elsewhere) that the IG had managed to scrape together from other Reich agencies. He also needed workers to carry out his plans for transforming Auschwitz into a model German town. So he approached the army and offered to take a hundred thousand Russians off its hands. The high command was only too happy to agree.

The first ten thousand Soviet POWs arrived at Auschwitz in October and were taken immediately to the new site at Birkenau. There, under conditions of the most appalling cruelty and deprivation, the Russians were forced to start building their own barracks. Each of the proposed 174 housing blocks was to be divided into sixty-two bays, which were then to be subdivided to form three sleeping platforms. Four prisoners were meant to pack onto one platform, giving each person, at best, a coffin-sized sleeping space. One latrine block—essentially a shed containing a deep ditch with planks thrown over it at intervals—was to be provided per seven thousand prisoners; one wash barrack was allowed per seventy-eight hundred prisoners.

But by Christmas 1941, after working with only a few tools and building materials either salvaged by bare hand from the demolished hamlet of Birkenau or scrounged from the IG plant at Monowitz, the POWs had managed to finish only two of these housing blocks, with another twenty-eight in various stages of construction. In the interim, the weather had deteriorated. From November on they had been exposed to the snow, ice, and subzero temperatures of a Polish winter, and now—exhausted, beaten, half starved, and diseased and with no immediate prospect of shelter—most of them began to succumb. By the end of January 1942 almost eight thousand of the original ten thousand Russians had died. By the end of the following month none were left.*

This was a considerable setback to Himmler, especially since he couldn't expect any replacements from the same source. With the struggle against the Soviet Union dragging on, Hitler and the high command had become concerned about labor shortages in industries more immediately involved in the war effort. On January 8, 1942, Hermann Göring, who had gained control over all prisoners of war, issued a decree announcing that henceforth most Soviet POWs would be used in the armaments industry, mining, railroad maintenance, and agriculture. As a result, Himmler was forced to look elsewhere for workers to fulfill his promises to the IG. With tragic inevitability his attention fell on the one group over whose destinies he now had absolute power—the Jews.

IF HEYDRICH'S EINSATZGRUPPEN, the SS, and the Gestapo had acted monstrously during the invasion of Poland, they were to surpass themselves in the months after Operation Barbarossa in Russia. Jews were slaughtered in the thousands, on the grounds that they were suspected of looting or acting against the provisions of martial law or were just in the wrong place at the wrong time—and the security apparatus actively encouraged racial pogroms carried out by eager-to-please local populations. But it was not until the end of July 1941 that the Nazis began taking purposeful steps toward the total annihilation of the Jewish people.

There are many reasons why that summer can be identified as a turning point. One is that, following the first sweeping successes against the Red Army, Hitler's rhetoric became ever more messianic—emphasizing again and again his determination to eradicate the Jewish-Bolshevik conspiracy against the fatherland. Almost certainly, Himmler, Hitler's most loyal and sycophantic lieutenant, interpreted such statements as a sign that his leader was willing to act without re-

*Many of them, of course, had been specifically marked to die. For example, the SS had brought several hundred Russian army commissars to Auschwitz explicitly for the purpose of working them to death in the district's gravel pits.

straint against the Russian Jews and that it was his personal responsibility to realize the Führer's wishes.

Himmler's actions may also have been influenced by the outcome of a meeting on July 16, when Hitler confirmed decisions, taken before the invasion, about who would have administrative charge for the newly conquered territories in the East. To Himmler's chagrin, overall responsibility for civil affairs was given to Alfred Rosenberg, a ponderous Baltic German who was considered by some of his contemporaries to be one of the Nazi Party's leading intellectuals.* This appointment did not impinge directly on the Reichsführer's SS and police roles but the question of who was to be in charge of the long-term colonization and resettlement of Russia—a job Himmler saw as a natural extension of his activities in Poland—had been left unresolved. Thus, Himmler looked for indirect ways of increasing his territorial brief—perhaps in the hope of reminding the Führer of his suitability for the resettlement role. Resolving the Jewish "question," in other words, may have been an obvious way to impress his leader.

Strictly speaking, jurisdiction over specifically "Jewish matters" lay with Hermann Göring, but in 1939 he had delegated to Reinhard Heydrich the task of expelling all German Jews—an order that was reinforced in early 1941 when Hitler instructed Heydrich to develop a scheme for deporting them somewhere under German control and then on to exile in the geographically nebulous East. It occurred to Himmler that if Heydrich now went back to Göring and asked for an extension of his powers to deal with the Jewish situation in Russia, that authority would, by default, confer on Himmler, as his superior, the ultimate executive responsibility.

A letter, drafted by Heydrich and signed by Göring on July 3, was all that was required.

Supplementing the task that was assigned to you on 24 January 1939, which dealt with the solution of the Jewish problem by

---

*Himmler had coveted this role for himself but his irritation was allayed by the fact that Ribbentrop, the Nazi foreign minister who had made no secret of holding similar ambitions, was also disappointed.

emigration and evacuation in the most suitable way, I hereby charge you to submit a comprehensive blueprint of the organizational, subject-related, and material preparatory measures for the execution of the intended final solution of the Jewish question.

A few days later the *Einsatzgruppen*—sometimes supported by the Wehrmacht—began their slaughter of Jewish men women and children across the eastern territories. Over the next few months, mass liquidations occurred in Lithuania, Belorussia, the Ukraine, Serbia, and the General Government. August 1941 also saw the beginning of deportations eastward of Jews from Germany, Austria, Bohemia, and Moravia—a move that was marked administratively by the removal of the German Jews' nationality and the imposition of an obligation to wear the yellow *Judenstern* (Star of David). Their treatment thereafter depended on the priorities, resources, and initiative of local SS and Nazi commanders. Thus, Jews arriving at Minsk, Riga, and Kaunas were shot as soon as they got off the train. But in October 1941 trains brought twenty thousand Jews to Lodz, too many to dispose of easily, so they were added to the city's already overcrowded ghetto. To cope with the numbers, Wilhelm Koppe, the area's SS chief, began transporting Jews by truck to the village of Chelmno, where they were loaded a hundred at a time into sealed vans and gassed with exhaust fumes. This new method was in line with general orders from Himmler, issued after a visit to Minsk in August 1941, which called for investigation into means of killing other than mass shootings, so as to relieve the "nervous and mental strain" on the executioners. The October murders at Chelmno were the start of a more systematic type of slaughter. Within two years more than 360,000 Jews and Gypsies had been killed at that location alone.

By the late autumn of 1941 it was clear to Himmler that Hitler considered the deportation program a success and that the fate of the Jews after their removal to the East was of no further interest. Yet the process was becoming a little unwieldy. Many different agencies and individuals were now involved in killing Jews on their own initiative and it was time, Himmler realized, to coordinate all the different programs and establish his overall authority.

Heydrich was therefore prevailed upon to send out invitations to bureaucrats from all the relevant Reich ministries and agencies, including officials from the Ministries of Justice, the Occupied Eastern Territories, and the Interior; the Reich Chancellery; the Party Chancellery; the Foreign Office; the Offices of the Four-Year Plan and the General Government; and the various SS and RHSA agencies under Himmler's control (such as the Office of the Reich Commissioner of the Consolidation of the German Nation, and the Race and Settlement Main Office). They were asked to gather at the old Berlin Interpol office at 56 Am grossen Wannsee, on December 9, to develop a "uniform view among the relevant central agencies of the further tasks concerned with the remaining work on this final solution."

The meeting—hastily deferred to January 20, 1942, after the United States entered the war—became infamous as the Wannsee Conference. Its purpose was to organize the division of labor and to assign roles to the various state organs charged with carrying out the official program of mass murder. Heydrich's "Jewish expert," SS Lieutenant Colonel Adolf Eichmann, kept the minutes, which were later sanitized for wider distribution.

Heydrich explained to his audience that eleven million Jews were involved—a figure that included those in countries such as Britain and Ireland not yet under Nazi control. All were to be brought by train to transit ghettos in the East. The fit and healthy would then be selected for work, although their numbers would be reduced through inevitable natural attrition. Those not chosen would be murdered immediately: "The remnant that survives all this must be regarded as the germ cell of a new Jewish development and therefore destroyed. In the course of this final solution, Europe is to be combed for Jews from west to east."

No one at the meeting expressed dissent; instead discussions focused on such matters as the exact legal definition of "Jew" and what should be done with "half Jews" or those married to Aryans. One suggestion about the latter was that they should be sent to a special ghetto at Theresienstadt, near Prague, to be housed alongside high-profile Jews whose deportation directly to the East might draw too much public notice. Another debate seems to have centered on the specific methods of extermination, although in Eichmann's heavily edited minutes this is reduced to a discussion about "various possible solutions."

The conference achieved its central purpose. At the outset, Heydrich had made plain that "primary responsibility for the handling of the final solution of the Jewish question . . . is to lie centrally, regardless of geographic boundaries, with the Reichsführer SS and chief of the German police." No one objected; everyone got the message: Himmler was in charge.

Three days later Himmler met with Hitler. No record of their discussion now exists but the SS leader would undoubtedly have kept his Führer informed of his activities—it would have been too dangerous not to. In any event, his full authority over the disposition of the Jews was obviously confirmed at the meeting because shortly afterward Himmler sent a message to Richard Glücks, the SS inspector of concentration camps, telling him that because no more Russian POWs were available he would be receiving a large contingent of Jews instead—some of whom were clearly intended for Auschwitz: "Will you therefore make preparations to receive within the next four weeks 100,000 Jews and up to 50,000 Jewesses."

On January 30, Hitler came to a microphone at the Sports Palace in Berlin to speak of his confidence in ultimate victory. "The war will not end as the Jews imagine it will, namely with the uprooting of the Aryans," he announced.

> The result of this war will be the complete annihilation of the Jews. Now for the first time they will not bleed other people to death, but for the first time the old Jews' law of an eye for an eye, a tooth for a tooth will be applied. And—world Jewry may as well know this— the further these battles spread, the more anti-Semitism will spread. It will find nourishment in every prison camp and in every family when it discovers the ultimate reason for the sacrifices it has to make. And the hour will come when the most evil universal enemy of all time will be finished, at least for a thousand years.

Even as ordinary Germans were absorbing these words through the radio, newsreels, and in their newspapers, new death camps were being prepared to operate alongside the gas vans of Chelmno. Three of them were to be located near remote villages on the old Polish-German border, at Belzec, Treblinka, and Sobibor—names that would one day become synonymous with the destruction of European Jewry.

A fourth was established amid a birch wood and the still incomplete barrack blocks of a Soviet POW camp and within a couple of miles of the largest industrial construction site in Europe. As many as half of those transported there were to be "selected" immediately for forced labor; the other half—the old, the sick, the crippled, and the very young—were to be marched into a gas chamber to be slain with pesticide and then cremated. Auschwitz-Birkenau, which owed its existence in no small part to IG Farben's contract with Himmler's SS and which would now provide the human fodder for the chemical company's gigantic Buna-Werke, was set to embark on the murder of one and half million people.

12

IG AUSCHWITZ AND
THE FINAL SOLUTION

For a few weeks in the spring of 1942 things seemed to improve at the Buna-Werke (or IG Auschwitz, as it was sometimes called)—from its managers' point of view at least. Building materials began arriving on time, and some Jewish deportees and fresh influxes of labor from France, Belgium, and the Ukraine were added to the workforce. The Organisation Todt, the Reich's civil engineering agency, was also persuaded, albeit temporarily, to lend some extra muscle to the peripheral but necessary construction of the plant's waterworks and railway halt.* But the IG's optimism didn't last. In May the government announced that munitions were to be given priority over all other commercial traffic on the railways—immediately reducing the flow of iron, timber, cement, and bricks to the Buna-Werke to a trickle. By then the SS had also begun moving Polish political pris-

---

*Set up before the war by Fritz Todt, a civil engineer, to carry out the Nazis' autobahn construction program, the Organisation Todt used conscript labor to build and repair roads, railways, military fortifications such as the West Wall, and various other public works. Appointed armaments minister in March 1940, Todt was killed in a plane crash in February 1942 and was succeeded by Hitler's architect, Albert Speer.

oners from Auschwitz to Germany, to free up space for the much larger number of Jews arriving from the other direction. To accommodate these incoming prisoners, the construction of Birkenau— which as yet consisted of only a few barrack blocks—had to be stepped up, diverting some of the additional supplies of inmate labor that Himmler had promised the cartel. In fact, the SS had told IG managers to expect between four and five thousand prisoners in 1942, but for much of the first six months of the year it had to manage with around half that number. The weekly construction reports from Walter Dürrfeld and Max Faust resumed their previously discouraging tone, and Otto Ambros and Heinrich Bütefisch set off on more wearisome journeys across the Reich to discuss with their Auschwitz colleagues what might be done to get things back on track.

In casting around for ways to improve productivity, the IG didn't take long to identify one major logjam. The Buna-Werke lay over four miles from the concentration camps, but the construction site itself was huge, extending another mile and a quarter from the main gates. The prisoners had to cover this distance on foot and, in order to be onsite and at their allotted workplaces at first light, they were woken for roll call at 4:00 a.m. Half starved and brutalized as they already were, this routine left them utterly exhausted and unfit for labor, especially as on the return trip in the evening the prisoners were often burdened with the bodies of those who had died during the day. The IG had always known that physical weakness would be an issue; during negotiations with the SS over how much to pay for labor, the company had estimated that the productivity of a concentration camp prisoner would be, at best, around 75 percent that of a free German worker. But it hadn't bargained on the time and energy that would be wasted in all the marching to and fro. As Ambros pointed out to colleagues, if the daily journey could be shortened by bringing the prisoners nearer to the site, the concern might stand a better chance of getting the labor it was paying for.

Ambros's insight had absolutely nothing to do with prisoner welfare, a subject to which the company always remained sublimely indifferent. Not once, for example, did it ever propose that the workers should be given suitable clothing (at the IG's expense, if necessary) or that they should be fed properly to keep up their strength. Such suggestions might well have drawn the wrath and suspicion of the SS and other Nazi authorities, but the IG could have made a reasonable enough case on the grounds that the Buna-Werke was vital to the war effort and that a fit and healthy workforce was necessary for its completion. Yet the concern never considered such steps, not even to reject them for fear of repercussions; it simply ignored the issue of prisoner welfare altogether. Instead of vigorously protesting about the state prisoners were in, the concern simply found a faster way to get them to the Buna-Werke so that the little energy they had was at least being drained in the service of the IG, not the SS.

Thus, in late June 1942 the *Vorstand* arrived at a solution that in the distorted logic of the times must somehow have made sense to its members but that actually made the concern directly complicit in mass murder. IG Farben decided to build and run its own concentration camp at Auschwitz.

Of course, the idea wasn't completely new because there were already seven other small "construction camps" attached to the Buna-Werke by this time, including a Luftwaffe-run stalag for twelve hundred British POWs (where Denis Avey was incarcerated) and other barrack-style accommodations for conscript Polish and foreign laborers and free German workers. But none of these facilities, bleak and unpleasant though some were, could remotely compare to the undertaking the cartel was now contemplating: a huge IG Farben–owned prison for thousands of Jewish slave laborers. No private company had ever attempted such a thing before, and there were several tricky issues to consider. The camp would clearly cost millions of marks to construct, and careful thought would have to be given to how much, or how little, the company spent on security, housing, and all the other specialized elements of concentration camp infrastructure. Another issue was the danger of alienating the Reich's security apparatus, whose specialists might view the plan as an encroachment on their territory. The idea would have to be raised very carefully with the top echelons of the SS.

Fortunately, an opportunity was just around the corner. In mid-July, Commandant Höss got in touch with Walter Dürrfeld. The IG's

Auschwitz staff should prepare themselves, he said. The Reichsführer himself wanted to pay them a visit.

HIMMLER'S ARRIVAL ON July 17, 1942, came at the end of a busy few months that had seen the assassination of his energetic deputy Reinhard Heydrich (killed by the Czech resistance in Prague) and his subsequent assumption of personal control over the Reich Security Main Office. He was now determined to demonstrate to the Führer his complete mastery of the mechanics of the Final Solution, while at the same time making full use of the additional opportunities for racial cleansing that the war with Russia had opened up and that Hitler had finally agreed fell within his purview.

Auschwitz was therefore now part of a much wider vision. Himmler's plans for turning the town into a model German settlement had been put on hold—materials for the construction of high-quality domestic housing were simply not available—and he had decided instead that its camps could be used to help establish a presence for the SS in the armaments industry.* He had ordered the expansion of Birkenau to 200,000 inmates and had told Adolf Eichmann (head of the RHSA's Jewish Office and in charge of transporting Jews) that it should be filled with prisoners who could be worked until they dropped. Himmler's commitment to the IG was still extant and would have to be met, but the company's needs would have to take their place amid his other plans for Auschwitz. The most significant of these was his decision to make it a center for the industrialized annihilation of European Jewry.

Experiments in mass murder techniques had been going on at Auschwitz since the previous year, initially as part of an SS "euthanasia

---

*Himmler had ambitions to boost the economic interests of the SS and saw armaments production at Auschwitz and other camps as one way to do this. But aside from some small-scale production of skis and ammunition crates for the Wehrmacht, the project never really got off the ground; the SS did not possess the requisite financing, raw materials, machinery, or specialist expertise. The Reichsführer was also opposed by the armaments minister, Albert Speer, who later recalled: "Himmler wanted to turn the concentration camps into vast modern factories, especially for the manufacture of weapons, directly subordinate to the SS. . . . Hitler, however, took my side. Our pre-war experience in dealing with SS plants that made bricks and processed granite had already been sufficiently off-putting."

program" intended to eliminate sick inmates. The most "promising" of these trials involved the use of Zyklon B, a hydrocyanic, or prussic, acid that had been introduced into the camp in July 1940 for use as a pesticide to fumigate lice-infested buildings and prisoner clothing. Deadly to humans in even small quantities and normally stored in sealed metal containers, the cyanide granules turned into gas on contact with air at temperatures around 79 degrees Fahrenheit. It was manufactured by an IG Farben subsidiary, the Deutsche Gesellschaft für Schädlingsbekämpfung (Degesch), or German Pest Control Company, of Frankfurt am Main, and had been tested on prisoners in August 1941. The first mass killings involving Zyklon B at Auschwitz took place around September 5, 1941, when some nine hundred Soviet POWs and sick prisoners of other categories were gassed in the basement cells of the camp's punishment block. But although the gas had proved effective, both its administration and the subsequent cleanup—the corpses had to be undressed, heaved onto carts, and dragged to freshly dug mass graves—were deemed inefficient. To improve matters Commandant Höss ordered subsequent gassing operations transferred to the camp crematorium (later called the "old crematorium," or "crematorium 1"). There the mortuary was made into a gas chamber by sealing off the doors and knocking openings in the ceiling through which the cyanide pellets could be poured. Zyklon B was next used in February 1942, to murder four hundred elderly Slovak Jews considered unfit for work.

By then the Final Solution was getting under way, the first mass transits of Jews to Auschwitz were about to begin, and two new gas chambers were being set up at Birkenau as well. The first of these, known as the "Red House," or Bunker 1, was established in the abandoned redbrick property of a resettled Polish farmer and went into operation on March 20. The second, known as the "White House," or Bunker 2, was set up in a whitewashed building a short distance away and began operating two months later. In the interim, the SS had also decided to construct two large crematoria on the site, buildings that would eventually incorporate more sophisticated and custom-built gas chambers of their own.

Thus the ghastly, industrialized ritual of mass murder at Auschwitz swung into action, mirroring the genocide that was already being carried out at the Treblinka, Sobibor, and Belzec death camps (a program code-named Operation Reinhard after the assassination of Heydrich) but differing from it both in terms of scale and in the fact that Auschwitz fulfilled a labor function as well. Arriving Jews were separated by "selection" into those considered fit for work and those—predominantly the old, the sick, and the very young—chosen for immediate murder.* It was this process that Himmler most wanted to see in action.

His arrival at the main Auschwitz camp on July 17 was attended by a certain degree of ceremony. A few days earlier, on Commandant Höss's orders, some of the more decrepit-looking prisoners had been dispatched to the gas chambers. Those deemed fit to be seen were given new uniforms on the morning of the visit and were made to line up for several hours in front of their barracks. There was a moment of last-minute panic among the guards when it was noticed that one prisoner, Yankel Meisel, was without his full quota of tunic buttons. For this sin he was taken back inside the barrack by his embarrassed block wardens and beaten to death. His screams had only just faded away when the limousines bearing the Reichsführer and his aides swept through the main gate. On cue, the camp orchestra burst into the Triumphal March from Verdi's *Aida*. Himmler got out of the car, listened appreciatively for a moment or two, and then walked over with Höss to inspect the prisoners. Inmate Rudolf Vrba was standing in one of the front rows.

> He passed close to me, close enough for me to touch him, and for the moment our eyes met. They were cold, impersonal eyes that seemed to see little; and yet I found myself thinking: "If he finds out what is going on, maybe he'll improve things. Maybe the food will get better. Maybe there won't be so many beatings. Maybe . . . maybe we'll

---

*Not that the survivors gained much from this reprieve. If they didn't die at the hands of their SS guards or their kapos or succumb to disease, malnutrition, and overwork, the vast majority would fail one of the future selections that regularly took place within the camp population to make room for new arrivals. On average their lives were extended by around three months, a period of intense cruelty, hardship, and deprivation that in most cases could have only one end.

see some justice around for a change." Already you see, I had forgotten Yankel Meisel. And so had everybody else because Heinrich Himmler was smiling.*

The Reichsführer's entourage then moved on to the design office, where Hans Kammler, the SS's chief architect, showed him plans for the next stages of development at Auschwitz, including blueprints for the new crematoria, which were about to be built with the help of civilian contractors. After a brief tour of the grounds, the party climbed back into their cars to drive the short distance to Birkenau. There Himmler was shown around the camp's overcrowded barrack blocks and the primitive toilet and washing facilities, before being taken to the Auschwitz railway station (the branch line directly into Birkenau had yet to be built) to watch the disembarkation of a newly arrived transport of Jews from Holland. An SS doctor carried out a selection on the platform. The men and women considered fit to work were separated from the others and marched off to the barracks. The rest were loaded into trucks to be driven to the Birkenau "shower room."

Himmler and his aides followed the convoy back to Birkenau so that he could see the whole extermination process from beginning to end. He looked on impassively as the now naked prisoners were shaved (typically the hair was taken away in sacks and either woven into warm socks for U-boat crews and Luftwaffe pilots or used as luxury stuffing for mattresses). Then he saw the group being moved into the sealed Bunker 2 gas chamber. After the Zyklon B pellets had been poured in through the roof, he put his eye to the small observation window in the airtight door and watched in silence as those inside died in writhing agony. The whole process took around twenty minutes. After lingering to see the Sonderkommando, or special units of prisoners, begin clearing away the bodies for burial in mass graves around the camp—a temporary measure until the crematoria were finished— Himmler got back in his car for the trip up the road to the site of IG

---

*The Reichsführer had good reason to be in a sunny mood. The day before, Hitler had told him the Russians would be defeated by Christmas and had confirmed that Himmler would be in overall control of Germanizing the Russian territories.

Farben's Buna-Werke.* Less than half an hour after watching the murder of hundreds of Dutch Jews, the Reichsführer SS was smiling and exchanging Nazi salutes with Max Faust, his official guide for the day, and a small team of IG engineers.

If Himmler was the slightest bit perturbed by what he had just experienced he didn't show it. As the party walked briskly around the site he cast keen darting glances here and there and bombarded the IG men with questions. At one point Faust stopped to show him a set of plans for the plant and Himmler expressed his skepticism about the IG's practice of tinkering with the designs in an attempt to make the factory more efficient than its predecessors at Schkopau, Hüls, and Ludwigshafen. Surely, he said, it would make more sense to build in accordance with existing plans and put up with certain disadvantages in manufacture rather than waste time on constant revisions. Perhaps seeking by this remark to deflect criticism of the SS for failing to meet its labor quota in full, Himmler immediately threw Faust on the defensive. Faust hastened to assure him that the factory would be ready on schedule by mid-1943 (although he must have known it wouldn't be), and having done so he couldn't very well complain about the labor shortage. On the other hand, Himmler raised no objections to the IG's plans for its own concentration camp, which he might have done in different circumstances. Instead he expressed his general satisfaction with the way things were going, shook hands all around, and set off back to Auschwitz for a comradely dinner in the SS officers' mess and an evening of banal conversation in the Katowice home of Fritz Bracht, the gauleiter of Upper Silesia.

The next day, after witnessing the flogging of a woman accused of stealing and another round of inspections, including one of a section devoted to sorting out the confiscated belongings of murdered Jews, Himmler complimented Rudolf Höss on his efforts and promoted him to the rank of SS Obersturmbannführer (lieutenant colonel). In the process, he confirmed again Auschwitz's central role in the Holocaust.

---

*Over a hundred thousand corpses were thrown into these pits in the course of a few weeks; eventually the bodies were exhumed and burned to prevent local water supplies from becoming contaminated.

"Eichmann's program will continue and will be accelerated every month from now. See to it that you move ahead with the completion of Birkenau. The Gypsies are to be exterminated. With the same ruthlessness you will exterminate those Jews who are unable to work."

MONOWITZ, OR AUSCHWITZ III as it was sometimes known, resembled a state-owned concentration camp in almost every respect. Although IG Farben built it (using prisoner labor) and paid its running costs, it was equipped with the same watchtowers, armed guards, electric fences, sirens, gallows, punishment cells, mortuary, and searchlights as Auschwitz and Birkenau. Its wooden barrack blocks, which would eventually hold around eleven thousand inmates, were just as confined, if not more so, than the accommodations in the other camps, and its washing and sanitation facilities just as primitive and dehumanizing. The SS supplied the inmates and guards, had ultimate authority over camp security, discipline, and internal organization, and even installed the Auschwitz motto, *Arbeit macht frei*, over the main gate. Indeed, the only real difference between Monowitz and the other camps was that the IG took over responsibility for food and health care—a distinction of singular irrelevance to most prisoners because the provision of both was as criminally inadequate as anything supplied by the state.*

The first six hundred inmates arrived on October 28, with another fourteen hundred joining them over the next two days. This was actually several weeks later than planned but an outbreak of typhus in the other two camps held the process up. For a short time, in order to maintain a quarantine, inmates designated for the Buna-Werke, including one group of 405 people from Buchenwald, were sent straight to Monowitz without passing through the Auschwitz main camp or Birkenau. But the population still grew more slowly than anticipated. To make up for the shortfall the SS diverted further transports on January 23, 24, and 27, bringing in 5,022 Jewish men and women directly from the Theresienstadt ghetto in Czechoslovakia. After

---

*The IG initially assumed responsibility for food because it wanted to control links between Monowitz and the typhus-ridden other camps. Had it not done so the food would have been delivered several times a day from Birkenau and the disease would have surely come with it.

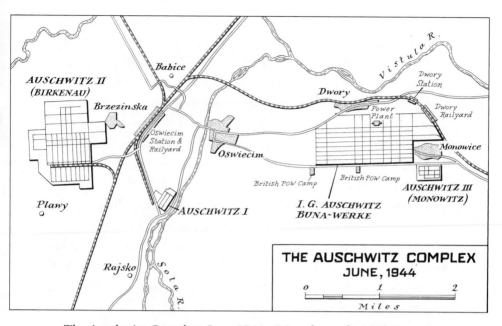

The Auschwitz Complex, June 1944. *(Map drawn by Neil Gower)*

"selection," however, only 614 men and 316 women from this group were deemed fit for labor. The remaining 4,092 people, "as a result of their poor condition and the large numbers among them who were underage," were sent to the gas chambers.*

Meanwhile the savage conditions and the appalling workload continued to take their toll, with the IG using up prisoners almost as fast as the Nazi authorities could provide them. Of the thirty-eight hundred inmates present at Monowitz in late December 1942, only fifteen hundred were still alive by the end of February 1943; the steep death rate took even the SS by surprise. Gerhard Maurer, head of the SS Labor Office, came to investigate and on February 10 promised Dürrfeld and Faust that he would raise the numbers to forty-five hundred, largely out of transports of Jews from Berlin.† But this target, too, wasn't reached because of the unexpectedly large numbers of children and elderly people emerging from the boxcars. By March 1943 the population at Monowitz had crept back above three thousand, but of

---

*Of the two thousand who arrived on the January 23 transport, only three survived the war.
†The Labor Office was part of the SS WVHA, or Main Economic-Administrative Office.

these an estimated 730 were receiving some kind of medical treatment for injury and disease and could not produce an effective day's work.

This extraordinary turnover was directly linked to the IG's increasing anxiety over the long-term future of the plant. The cartel had committed itself politically and financially to the success of the Buna-Werke in the expectation that its huge investment would eventually pay substantial dividends. But in mid-1942 it heard that Standard Oil had been forced to yield its buna patent licenses to other American manufacturers and that the U.S. government—cut off from strategic supplies in the Far East—had committed itself to spending hundreds of millions of dollars on creating and supporting what now promised to be a massive new industry. Although this news can hardly have been a complete surprise, it dashed the IG's hopes of monopolizing the international synthetic rubber market. The only hope now was that a German victory in Europe would be enough to secure the IG's position at home and that its superior technology would be allowed it to compete aggressively with the Americans on the foreign stage after the war. Cost effectiveness was going to be crucial to this endeavor: to survive, all the cartel's buna plants, but especially the Buna-Werke, would have to be as economical as possible. The IG knew from experience that ensuring efficiency meant building it into a factory's infrastructure right from the start—a painstaking and exacting process that could not be rushed or short-circuited. Unfortunately, the regime in Berlin was not known for its patience. The Nazis had asked if the IG could increase the supply of buna and synthetic fuel, and in both cases the concern had said yes. Now it was expected to deliver—and quickly. Trapped between its own aspirations for the Buna-Werke and the government's urgent demands for product, the concern was feeling the strain.

This pressure was passed on down through Fritz ter Meer, Heinrich Bütefisch, Otto Ambros, Hermann Schmitz, and others on the *Vorstand* to Walter Dürrfeld and Max Faust, the two men in charge of the Buna-Werke construction. They in turn passed it on to their subordinates—the hundreds of supervising foremen, engineers, designers, administrators, and master craftsmen brought in from IG plants across Germany to oversee and manage the work. Bedeviled by delays in supplies of vital materials and frustrated by the inadequacy of their labor force, many of these men were gradually becoming brutalized by their close association with the SS and the mounting insanity of their surroundings. By Christmas 1942 the first of the large carbide production halls, essential for the buna process, was taking shape at the northern end of the site, but elsewhere road and rail tracks were still unfinished, vast tracts of land still had to be flattened and shaped, mile upon mile of piping and cable had still to be laid. In their desperation, the IG supervisors, without pity or compassion, drove their exhausted and emaciated workforce even harder—and turned the Buna-Werke and Monowitz into a living hell.

For many of the plant's "free" foreign laborers, especially those recruited from Belgium, Holland, and France, the deteriorating conditions now became too much to bear. Usually the only new clothes they could obtain were the items the SS had confiscated from incoming prisoners, which, having been deemed too ragged to send back to Germany for sale, had been bought by the IG for redistribution through the camp stores. Many foreign laborers were reduced to wearing the standard camp-issue wooden shoes that were made in a Monowitz workshop, although in contrast to inmates they were at least able to choose a pair that fit. Their diet was poor, too, consisting of only marginally more generous portions of the same thin soup that was doled out to the prisoners, while "luxuries" such as soap and tobacco were in increasingly short supply. Their living quarters were also worse than they had been led to expect. The IG's German employees were billeted in and around Auschwitz town, with the more senior living in the company's well-constructed modern housing, but the foreign workers were accommodated in drafty wooden huts that resembled those the IG later put into its concentration camp. Nevertheless, none of this was as hard to bear as the violence that the workers saw meted out regularly to the prisoners who worked alongside them. Usually reluctant volunteers in the first place (most had been assigned by the occupying Nazi authorities to work for the IG whether they liked it or not), the foreign workers made their unhappiness known, returning to their barracks in inclement weather, taking unscheduled breaks, and sometimes refusing to work altogether. In August 1942 the IG was forced to send 160 of the worst Belgian and French "shirkers" home and began threatening others with transfer to the main Auschwitz concentration camp if they didn't cooperate. Not surprisingly, many just disappeared, setting off on the risky journey back across occupied Europe without papers or authorization. Eventually around 23 percent of the "voluntary" foreign workforce deserted in this way, although how many actually made it home isn't known.

Conditions were infinitely worse for the Jewish prisoners, whose presence at Monowitz and the Buna-Werke was just as much a consequence of the Nazi policy of racial annihilation as the mass shootings and the gas chambers elsewhere, except that death came in a form profitable to the Third Reich. Their situation was also paradoxical: given the intense pressure the Nazis were putting on IG Farben to finish the Buna-Werke, it would have been more logical for the regime to keep the Jews alive and working rather than to kill them and have to find replacements. But even during the extreme manpower crises that became ever more frequent in Germany once the Wehrmacht had been bloodily repelled from the gates of Moscow and Stalingrad, such logic always took second place to Nazi racial ideology, which saw wiping out the Jews as a sacred duty transcending almost all the Reich's other needs. As a result, the Jews' time in Monowitz and at the Buna-Werke was necessarily brief because it was part of a carefully planned process of extermination through labor. Jews who could work at the required levels of intensity or who had special skills that were in demand might escape the gas chambers for a short while; if not, they were sent immediately to their deaths and replaced by others. So long as the transports delivered substitute workers, the SS, and therefore by extension the IG's managers, felt no compunction to keep prisoners alive for one moment longer than was deemed necessary.*

The stories of those who through chance or extraordinary circumstance managed to survive testify to the barbarism and brutality of the

---

*As is now known, the Nazi authorities went to extraordinary lengths to ensure that the transport of Jews went smoothly, even attempting to persuade potential deportees that good, honest work and pleasant conditions awaited them in the East. In December 1942, for example, Dutch Jews received postcards purporting to come from people who had already been sent to the IG camp at Monowitz. They reported, "The food is good, with hot lunches, cheese, and jam sandwiches in the evenings. . . . We have central heating and sleep under two blankets. There are magnificent shower arrangements with hot and cold water."

regime at Monowitz and the Buna-Werke. Kai Feinberg, for example, arrived at the camp in late 1942. A Norwegian Jew, he had surrendered to Vidkun Quisling's collaborationist authorities in Oslo because his sister had been threatened with arrest if he did not give himself up. As it happened, his entire family was subsequently arrested, becoming part of a group of 521 Jews who were handed over to the Nazis for deportation to Auschwitz.

> After three weeks, on December 23, 1942, my father, his two brothers, and I were quartered in the special concentration camp of Monowitz. Conditions were unbearable. It was almost impossible to breathe. We had to get up at 4:30 a.m. It took three quarters of an hour to march to our place to work. On the first day—the day before Christmas, 24 December 1942—we had to work through until 3:00 a.m., 25 December, without food. We unloaded boxcars, iron poles and bags containing cement, as well as heavy ovens. On January 5, 1943, my father was already so weakened that when we had to drag a 50-kilogram bag at doubled pace he collapsed before my very eyes. He was carried to the camp by his comrades. He had been beaten constantly by the guards, and this most severely on the last day. . . . He died in my presence on 7 January 1943. One brother of my father injured his right arm during work, and he was gassed. The second brother of my father had become so weak that he died while at work, about one or two weeks after my father in Buna. I myself was able to stand the work until 15 January 1943; then I contracted pneumonia and resumed work from 15 February until the end of February. Then I was declared unfit for work because I was no longer able to walk and it was decided that I was to be gassed. It so happened that on that day no truck came to the Buna works and I was returned instead to the concentration camp at Auschwitz.

Norbert Wollheim had a similar experience. After being separated from his wife and three-year-old son on arrival at Monowitz in 1943, he was processed as was customary—robbed of all his possessions, shaved, deloused, and tattooed with a number, 107984—and then taken to the Buna-Werke.

> The buildings, except for those in which the directors and senior foremen worked, were mostly unfinished. As initiation, as was the general rule, we were given only the hardest and most strenuous

work, such as transportation and excavation. I came to the dreaded "murder detail 4" whose task it was to unload cement bags or construction steel. We had to unload the cement from arriving freight cars all day long at a running pace. Prisoners who broke down were beaten by the German IG foremen as well as by the kapos until they either resumed their work or were left there dead. I saw such cases myself. . . . I also noticed, repeatedly, particularly during the time when the SS accompanied our labor unit themselves, that the German IG foremen tried to surpass the SS in brutalities.

Another inmate, Rudolf Vitek, confirmed this point: "The prisoners were pushed in their work by the kapos, foremen, and overseers of the IG in an inhuman way. No mercy was shown. Thrashings, ill treatment of the worst kind, even outright killings were the norm. The murderous working speed was responsible for the fact that, while working, many prisoners suddenly stretched out flat, gasped for breath, and died like beasts."

For inmates who managed to survive the dreadful shifts at the Buna-Werke there was little respite in store when they got back to the camp at Monowitz. Anyone who showed signs of weakness on the return journey risked being categorized as unfit for work the next day, so as the watchtowers came into view the prisoners forced themselves erect, trying to ignore their hunger and exhaustion, their aches, cuts, and bruises, and the weeping sores on their feet. After they marched through the gates, past the gallows, and into the main square—always to the surreal accompaniment of the camp orchestra playing popular German tunes—they fell into formation by work *Kommando* for roll call, an hourlong process of counting and recounting to make sure that no one had been foolish enough to try to give the guards the slip. Only when everyone had been marked present (even the dead had to be carried back on stretchers to be accounted for) were the prisoners allowed to limp back to their barrack blocks, the long, low wooden sheds that sat in rows behind the camp's high-tension electric fences.* The camp was

*The corpses were thrown onto a platform to the side of the parade ground, where they would lie, in full view of their fellow inmates, until collection by truck from Birkenau a couple of days later. Rudolf Vitek later said, "It was no rare occurrence that detachments of 400 to 500 men brought back with them in the evening five to twenty corpses."

not without amenities: the Aryan German aristocracy of "political" and "criminal" kapos and *Blockmeisters,* for example, were rewarded with better quarters and other privileges, the most remarkable of which was access to the *Frauenblock,* or camp brothel, in Hut 49. Set up by the IG as part of an incentive scheme for Aryan inmates, the brothel was staffed with a dozen or more women prisoners. To gain admission the kapos and their coterie had to get permission from the camp director and were allowed no more than one visit a week. But for the vast majority of inmates, conditions could hardly have been more primitive. Each leaking hut contained 148 three-tier bunks packed together so closely that a person could barely stand up between them. At least two, more usually three, inmates were assigned to each bunk, sleeping head to toe on a verminous straw mattress covered by a couple of thin blankets.

But food, or the lack of it, was the inmates' principal preoccupation. The ration at Monowitz, for which the IG was responsible, consisted of one small portion of bread and margarine in the morning and a ladleful of watery "buna soup" at midday and evening. On average this pitiful diet gave each prisoner around 1,100–1,200 calories a day, resulting in a weight loss of between six to nine pounds per individual per week. Within three months, most inmates were so weakened by hunger and nutritional deficiency they were incapable of any sort of labor and were selected for Birkenau. Prisoners assigned to the most physically punishing work details used up calories more quickly and succumbed much faster, as did those others who either were too weak to prevent their ration's being stolen or had to barter it away to make good some fault with their uniform or pay for some other essential item or service.* Bartering, eating, and repairs all had to take place in the brief period between evening roll call and lights-out at nine—also

---

*Officially, prisoners were allowed almost no belongings other than their wooden shoes, underclothes, and striped costumes. These had all been worn by others many times before and, never having been washed, were invariably filthy, lousy, tattered, and torn. Nevertheless, on pain of a beating or worse from a camp guard, any obvious deficiency—such as a missing button— had to be replaced before it was spotted. How prisoners were supposed to do this without the necessary means is anyone's guess, but somehow they found ways. Prisoners were also issued a battered metal bowl for meals, but no spoon, and new inmates usually had to give away some of their ration to acquire one that had been fashioned secretly out of scrap metal or wood. Inevitably, thefts of all these items were rife and there was a thriving black market in any detritus that might prove useful.

the only time when prisoners, if they were desperate enough, could try to get medical attention for their cuts and bruises and other ailments.

The hospital, or *Krankenbau*, at Monowitz consisted of eight huts identical to the others in the camp but separated from them by a wire fence. At any given time they held around a tenth of the population, but few inmates would willingly stay longer than two weeks because of the risk of being declared too sick to recover and sent to Birkenau—a policy that was openly endorsed by the IG because of the pressure on bed space. The facility was administered by prisoners, usually but not always with some sort of medical experience, under the supervision of three or four German doctors and a clerk or two. Examinations were carried out under the same conditions that prevailed elsewhere in the camp, with prisoners lining up in the open air for admittance, whatever the weather, and all decisions about treatment subject to the arbitrary authority of the German overseers. With medicines in extremely short supply—even, ironically enough, humble Bayer aspirin—treatment even for the most seriously ill often amounted to little more than confinement to bed. The most common ailments were dysentery and diarrhea, jaundice, tuberculosis, pneumonia, other infectious diseases of one kind or another, and injuries associated with heavy work—hernias, muscle strain, and so on. Many prisoners also suffered from phlegmon, a painful bloating of the limbs due to nutritional deficiencies, and from swollen and blistered feet, an inevitable consequence of their ill-fitting and broken wooden clogs. For the most part, fractures, which would have taken too long to heal, were not treated at all and the victims were sent straight to Birkenau; open wounds were left to fester or get better by themselves.

It is true that, despite all the constraints and the shortages of equipment and medicines, the prisoner doctors at the *Krankenbau* managed to save some lives. A few simple operations could be carried out at the hospital—albeit without anesthetic—and the isolation of those with contagious diseases undoubtedly prevented the spread of infection. In most cases, however, treatment was merely a matter of postponing the inevitable, as Robert Waitz, one of the inmate doctors, later pointed out: "On account of the severe living conditions, the prisoners were exposed to the slow process of physical and mental dissolution. The final aim was unmistakable: the dehumanization and eventual extermination of the prisoners employed in IG Auschwitz. I heard an SS officer say to the prisoners at Monowitz: 'You are all condemned to die but the execution of your sentence will take a little while.' "

This brief period of grace was also extended to prisoners at the other concentration camp set up by the IG, at the Fürstengrube coal mine in nearby Wesola. The concern had taken a controlling 51 percent stake in this business back in February 1941, shortly after Ambros had received the go-ahead on the Buna-Werke. Fürstengrube's management then acquired a further mine, the Janina, at Libiaz. Both pits needed extra workers to meet the IG's demands for coal (new shafts had to be carved out of the rock) and the concern did its best to supply them. At first, the additional labor was provided by Soviet and British POWs and recruited *Ostarbeiter* (eastern workers), but the recruits soon drifted away to other jobs and the POWs (especially the British, who were covered by international conventions) were unsatisfactory. On July 6, 1943, for example, the manager of the Janina mine complained to the administration of the British POW camp that "recently there have been increasing numbers of cases in which the war prisoners who are employed by day at our mine refuse to work, or leave work early, or refuse to follow orders from the technical supervisors. Prisoner number 4522 refused to perform his work, asserting that he was not going to work for the sake of Germany."

Ten days later, complaints such as these brought the IG's Walter Dürrfeld to a meeting with Auschwitz commandant Rudolf Höss and a Fürstengrube manager named Düllberg, during which they drew up plans for a subcamp to be filled exclusively with Auschwitz inmates. The first group of prisoners arrived on September 2, while construction of the barracks was still ongoing, with the numbers rising to around thirteen hundred six months later. At Janina, meanwhile, the British POWs were moved out of their accommodations to be replaced by yet more Auschwitz inmates—with numbers there reaching around nine hundred by 1944.

The terrible living and working conditions in these camps and mines made them de facto penal colonies for particularly difficult prisoners from the Buna-Werke. The beatings, killings, and selections and the resulting high death rate were as bad as anything at Monowitz, if not worse. One prisoner, Jan Lawnicki, was sent to Fürstengrube with nine others as punishment for the attempted escape of two members of their Buna-Werke *Kommando*.

> After arriving in Fürstengrube, we realized to our horror that the conditions in Monowitz, which had seemed awful, were nevertheless completely bearable in comparison to those at Fürstengrube. . . . The conditions there had no equivalent to those elsewhere, especially in terms of danger and effort. The places where we worked were often under water in which we waded up to our ankles or had such low ceilings that we had to bend over all the time. We worked on a quota system and, depending on where we were assigned, we each had to show a required number of wagons filled with coal. . . . The kapos, *Vorarbeiters* [foremen], and some of the professional miners shoved us and struck us in the face continually. . . . During the time that I worked extracting coal in the mines (five weeks) one prisoner committed suicide and two went mad. There were also cases of injuries caused by collapsing walls. When we finished working, they brought us up to the surface, where we had to march quickly down iron steps lined by SS men who hurried us along by screaming, kicking, and punching us.

Having labored underground in near darkness for ten hours, the prisoners had to endure the same marching back to camp and roll call as the Monowitz inmates, with equally atrocious food and sleeping accommodations. Because injuries and terminal exhaustion were even more common than at the Buna-Werke, selections were more frequent. At one point the beatings of mine prisoners carried out by IG-employed kapos became so savage that even the SS protested that they were causing inmates to deteriorate too quickly. Few inmates lived longer than four to six weeks.

Nevertheless, so long as the transports kept arriving at the railheads in Auschwitz and at Birkenau, the supply of replacements for the IG's construction machine seemed secure. Indeed, IG managers now began to participate directly in the selection process to ensure they got the best crop of prisoners from each incoming train. Skills were becoming as important as physical strength and the concern wanted to make sure it obtained chemists and electricians, bricklayers and welders before they were whisked away by the overeager SS. By November 1943 Dürrfeld himself was meeting trains, accompanied by Hauptsturmführer Heinrich Schwarz, commander of the SS garrison at Monowitz. On one occasion they reviewed thirty-five hundred prisoners and sent around half of them off to Birkenau. The Buna-Werke was still nowhere near finished, of course, and the IG's desperation to see it completed could hardly have been greater, but by now the whole project had assumed a ghastly self-sustaining logic, seeming to be as much about the consumption of prisoner labor as about producing synthetic rubber. During 1943 alone more than thirty-five thousand inmates passed through Monowitz. By the end of the year more than twenty-five thousand had been killed; the rest were halfway to their deaths.

ALL OF THIS begs an obvious question. Were the IG's managers aware of what was happening to the Jews they were sending to Birkenau? The short, simple, and unequivocal answer is that, yes, they were. They must have been. Even if they were not directly informed about the mass exterminations (which some of them almost certainly *were* aware of) and didn't know the precise details, the conditions under which the concern's staff lived and worked at Auschwitz and their close connections with the SS, both official and unofficial, would have made it impossible for anyone in a senior position to remain in the dark for very long. Nevertheless, because of the blanket protestations of ignorance about the genocide made by the IG's top men after the war, it is worth examining the question in depth.

The first thing to note is that by mid-1943 rumors of what was going on at Birkenau were rife even among the most junior employees at IG Auschwitz. By December of that year there were in excess of twenty-five hundred Reich German civilians directly engaged at the Buna-Werke. At first, many of these were straight transfers from the company's employ at Ludwigshafen, Frankfurt, Leverkusen, Berlin, and Leuna, but as the plant began to take shape others had come from elsewhere in Germany—younger recruits who had signed up looking for promotion or adventure in the new eastern territories or were simply eager to get their families away from the increasingly intense Allied bombing at home. Strangers in a foreign environment and living within close proximity to one another—either in one of the two hundred or so apartments on the IG's newly built "chemists' estate" or in housing requisitioned from the local Poles—they formed a close-knit group who spent their workdays and their leisure time together or with the area's other sizable German community, the SS officers and men who ran the concentration camps. On Wehrmacht Day in March 1943, for example, several IG employees were invited to the camp by the SS for a "communal feast followed by entertainment in the afternoon."

Like any other group of people thrown together under difficult conditions, these employees talked—about their work, about what they saw at the plant each day, about the Jews, POWS, and foreign civilians whom they supervised. They complained to one another about their living conditions, the difficulties of getting the project finished, and the very evident frustration of the top management at the plant. Above all, they gossiped—albeit discreetly—about what was going on behind the wire at the camps and about the dreadful stench that hung over the town and was sometimes so pungent that it reached Katowice, thirty miles away.

One of these employees, Hermann Müller, later remembered a drinking session he was invited to attend at the SS barracks by the Auschwitz main camp in the summer of 1943.

> I hadn't been in IG Auschwitz long and I was curious about this terrible sweet smell. . . . One or two people at the factory had told me not to be stupid and ask any questions, others had said they [the camp authorities] were disposing of typhus victims. I got drunk that night and asked one of the SS men, who I had got to know quite well, if this was true. He took me quietly to the side and said that it was Bolshevik Jews "going up the chimney at Birkenau and good riddance to them." You know what? I'm embarrassed to admit that I agreed with him. We had been told all these bad things about the Jews and how they were trying to destroy Germany. . . . Now I know it was wrong and that the Nazis had told us all these lies, but I was very young at the time and didn't realize it was just propaganda. Then I found out that everyone at my place of work knew

about what was being done. A little later my SS friend came to see me and asked me not to repeat what he had told me or he would be very severely punished, but I had to tell him that I had discovered by talking to others that it was already well known.

Another newly arrived IG Auschwitz employee, Georg Burth, wrote to a colleague at home in July 1943 in only slightly more euphemistic terms: "That the Jewish race is playing a special part, you can well imagine. The diet and treatment of these sorts of people is in accordance with our aim. Evidently an increase in weight is hardly ever recorded for them. That bullets start flying at the slightest attempt of a 'change of air' is also certain, as well as the fact that many have already disappeared as a result of 'sunstroke.' "

By this time, the threat of being sent to the gas chambers at Birkenau was openly used by the IG's kapos at the Buna-Werke to spur inmates to work harder. The threat was reinforced by the constant disappearance of other inmates and an odor, as British POW Charles Coward would later make plain, that was almost impossible to ignore: "The population at Auschwitz was fully aware that people were being gassed and burned. . . . They complained about the stench of burning bodies. Of course all the Farben people knew what was going on. Nobody could live at Auschwitz and work in the plant, or even come down to the plant, without knowing what was common knowledge to everybody."

But what of *direct* knowledge among the company's top executives? No references to the mass murders can be found among the weekly reports to the *Vorstand* from Walter Dürrfeld and Max Faust, although this is hardly surprising given the determination of the SS to keep the Final Solution hidden from the outside world (even if they could not stop it from being an open secret among the IG's Buna-Werke employees). If the killings were ever mentioned in other, more confidential company correspondence, those documents were almost certainly destroyed before the war's end.* It makes little

---

*When Germany began to collapse in early 1945 the IG systematically destroyed several thousand documents to prevent them from falling into Allied hands. Clearly, there is no way of knowing for certain what was in those documents but Nuremberg prosecutors believed that many of them referred to Auschwitz.

difference either way, however, because several members of the *Vorstand* had ample opportunity to see for themselves what was going on. Otto Ambros, Heinrich Bütefisch, Fritz ter Meer, August von Knieriem, Carl Krauch, Christian Schneider, and Friedrich Jaehne (in charge of plant development) all visited the Buna-Werke between 1942 and 1944, some of them repeatedly. Ambros, for example, visited Auschwitz on eighteen separate occasions in that period, sometimes staying several days. Heinrich Bütefisch visited seven times.* As for the IG Auschwitz employees on-site, it is inconceivable that they were unaware of the fate of the "selected" Jews from Monowitz. Walter Dürrfeld and Max Faust, among others, were in almost daily contact with the SS hierarchy; they regularly saw inmates being taken away to Birkenau (often on the company's recommendation), and lived amid the all-pervasive stench from the Birkenau crematoria. Dürrfeld, of course, even took part in selections, and on at least one recorded occasion asked Commandant Höss directly whether it was true that the Jews were cremated in the Oswiecim [Auschwitz] camp. Höss's reply, that he couldn't discuss the matter, was hardly a denial.

In any event, there are plenty of indications that by late 1943 the word had spread right up to the top echelons of the IG. On one occasion, for example, Friedrich Jaehne journeyed by train to Auschwitz to see his son Norbert, an engineer at the Buna-Werke. Norbert later told Nuremberg prosecutors that his father had asked him about the gassings, saying that he had heard about them from a police official traveling in the same railway carriage. During another Berlin-to-Auschwitz rail trip in late 1942, Ernst Struss, assistant to both Ambros and ter Meer—and later the *Vorstand*'s secretary—actually got into an argument with a fellow passenger about the mur-

---

*Carl Krauch, on the other hand, visited only once. Nevertheless, he was so enamored of the operation that when the possibility of another synthetic fuel factory arose in July 1943 he wrote to Himmler in his capacity as chairman of the IG's *Aufsichtsrat*: "Dear Reichsführer, I was particularly pleased to hear during this discussion you hint that you may possibly aid the expansion of another synthetic factory . . . in a similar way as was done at Auschwitz, by making available inmates of your camps, if necessary. I have also written to Minister Speer to this effect and would be grateful if you would continue sponsoring and aiding us in this matter. . . . Heil Hitler." Nothing came of the plan.

ders: "In a loud voice [the passenger] was telling other people in the compartment that in Auschwitz concentration camp people were burned in a crematorium and in large numbers and that the air in Auschwitz was filled with the smell of death. I was very deeply affected and I sprang up and said that he should not spread such lies."

Struss said that he had refused to believe the story at the time and dismissed it from his mind but the whispers continued to circulate around the IG. During a subsequent visit to Auschwitz in 1943 he asked Hans Heidebroek, a senior engineer, if they were true. Heidebroek confirmed that they were and added that the victims were gassed before they were burned. Struss said that, profoundly shocked, he had passed this information on to his bosses on his return—information that both Ambros and ter Meer, for obvious reasons, later denied receiving. Around the same time, Carl Lautenschläger, the IG's solvents and plastic chief, heard about the gassings from junior colleagues at Ludwigshafen (which shows just how far the news had traveled). Meanwhile, Walter Dürrfeld almost certainly told Christian Schneider, the head of *Sparte* I, during a visit to the Buna-Werke in January 1943, and Martin Müller-Cunradi, the plant manager at Oppau, who also visited the camp, brought Georg von Schnitzler into the loop. Hermann Schmitz, the secretive and detail-obsessed chairman of the *Vorstand*, must also have had a very good idea of what was going on at Auschwitz. He presided over the most important meetings, reviewed the major reports, and sanctioned all the significant decisions. The Buna-Werke was his company's largest investment and he frequently exercised his right to cross-examine his lieutenants and subordinates about progress—especially when things were not going well. It is impossible to believe that these people said nothing to Schmitz about the gassing of Jews.

For others on the *Vorstand* the dramatically increased demand for Zyklon B pesticide should have sounded the alarm. Zyklon B was produced by an IG subsidiary, the Deutsche Gesellschaft für Schädlingsbekämpfung (Degesch), or German Pest Control Company of Frankfurt am Main. IG Farben controlled 42.4 percent of the company's stock, which translated into five out of eleven seats on Degesch's supervisory board and three places on the firm's managing board, held by IG *Vorstand* members Carl Wurster, Heinrich Hörlein, and Wilhelm Mann.

Of these three, Wilhelm Mann, who was also the company's chairman, was in the best position to know how much Zyklon B was being sold to the SS because he regularly reviewed Degesch's accounts—although the other two also received copies of the documents.* Whether Mann might have questioned why the SS needed so much pesticide has since been the subject of much debate. It is certainly the case that Gerhard Peters, Degesch's general manager, who did know about Zyklon B's use for liquidating large numbers of people, kept the matter secret and didn't discuss it with anyone outside the SS. Another executive, Bruno Tesch, from Degesch's distribution and sales agency, Tesch and Stabenow, also knew and mentioned it in a July 1942 report that was seen by two colleagues. But none of these people, it appears, passed this information on to Wilhelm Mann. On the face of it, then, Mann and his IG colleagues would appear to be absolved of any complicity in the deployment of the pesticide as a weapon of mass destruction. If they didn't know about it, they could hardly be blamed for its use.

It seems very strange, however, that Mann, who was a trained chemist and well aware of Zyklon B's lethality, didn't put two and two together. If knowledge of what was going on at Auschwitz-Birkenau was as much of an open secret among some of his IG colleagues as the evidence suggests, then it is reasonable to suppose that Mann might also have picked up on the stories. Moreover, he was in receipt of figures that showed consumption of Zyklon B at Auschwitz in 1942 and 1943 as ten times that of Mauthausen (a more conventional SS concentration camp). On its own this differential might perhaps have been explained by the fact that Auschwitz-Birkenau was much larger and therefore conceivably needed more pesticide to fumigate buildings and clothing. Put together with the rumors circulating around the IG about gassings at the site, though, it would surely have begun to sound alarms in the mind of even the most mildly curious person, let alone the chairman of the firm that made Zyklon B. Auschwitz's commandant, Rudolf Höss, certainly thought so. After the war, Höss described how

---

*According to the accounts, the IG's dividends on its Degesch holdings for 1942, 1943, and 1944 (the years of the Final Solution) were double those for 1940 and 1941.

SS trucks had driven to the Degesch plant at Dessau on many occasions in 1942 and 1943.

> I assume with certainty that this firm knew the purpose of the use of the Zyklon B delivered by it. This they would have had to conclude from the fact that the gas for Auschwitz had been ordered continually and in great quantities, while for the other departments of the SS troops, etc., orders were placed only once or in six-monthly intervals. I cannot recall the exact quantities of Zyklon B which we received from Tesch and Stabenow, however I estimate that at least 10,000 cans, that is 10,000 kilos, had been supplied by them in the course of three years.

Despite this, Wilhelm Mann claimed not to have made the connection. He later denied knowing anything about the use made of Zyklon B and said he had paid little more than routine attention to the Degesch sales figures. Although such diffidence was out of character for an otherwise diligent man, no definitive evidence has ever emerged to directly contradict his claim.

But Mann clearly knew all about another aspect of the SS's "work" at Auschwitz, because he personally authorized IG financing for it. The payment was in the form of a check to SS Hauptsturmführer Josef Mengele, Birkenau's infamous "Angel of Death." Mengele's specialty was genetics and in May 1943 he set up a special laboratory next to the prisoners' infirmary at Birkenau to make use of an estimated one thousand to fifteen hundred pairs of identical twins to try to prove his racial theories. After the children had been identified and taken away from their mothers at selection, they were subjected to the most dreadful medical experiments. Some had organs removed, others were castrated, blinded, or deliberately infected with fatal diseases in order to test prototype serums and drugs—many of which were supplied by the IG's Bayer pharmaceutical division. One substance, known as B-1034, an experimental Bayer treatment for typhus, was almost certainly among the drugs given to Eva and Miriam Mozes, ten-year-old twins from Portz, in Romania, in May 1944. Following the injections Eva developed a raging fever and her limbs ballooned to several times their normal size, made more excruciatingly painful because SS technicians had tied her to a bed with rubber hoses to keep her still while they administered the substance. At one point Mengele stood at the bottom of her bed and laughed as he read her fever chart. "Too bad she's so young," he said to his colleagues. "She has only two weeks to live."*

Despite this endless supply of human guinea pigs, Mengele's work didn't come cheap, but IG Farben seems to have been willing to foot the bill. As Wilhelm Mann said in a letter to an SS contact at Auschwitz, "I have enclosed the first check. Dr. Mengele's experiments should, as we both agreed, be pursued. Heil Hitler."

Other IG staff at Auschwitz had a more direct involvement in experiments on prisoners. Helmuth Vetter, for instance, was a longtime company employee and SS doctor at Auschwitz and Monowitz. In 1943, when he was not identifying candidates for selection at the IG's camp hospital, he conducted research on two hundred female prisoners, injecting their lungs with streptococcus bacilli and causing them to die from pulmonary edema. The work was done to test the effectiveness of the new drugs being developed by the IG Bayer pharmaceutical division, and Vetter's paper on the results was incorporated into a presentation to the Wehrmacht Medical Academy. On another occasion, IG Bayer haggled directly with Auschwitz commandant Höss over the costs of buying 150 women prisoners for use in Vetter's experiments with sedatives and anesthetics. The SS wanted RM 200 per woman, but the IG was prepared to pay only RM 170. Evidently the cartel got its way, as Bayer wrote again to Höss, "The experiments were performed. All test persons died. We will contact you shortly about a new shipment at the same price." Vetter clearly enjoyed his job. "I have thrown myself into my work wholeheartedly," he wrote to colleagues at Leverkusen, "especially as I have the opportunity to test our new preparations. I feel like I am in paradise." His reports routinely went to Heinrich Hörlein, the IG's Nobel Prize–winning chief pharmaceutical scientist.

The experiments at Auschwitz were evidently part of a much wider research program involving IG pharmaceutical preparations and the SS.

---

*Mengele also experimented on adults. Although it is hard to be certain of the numbers, it is believed that several thousand people died as a result of his "research."

Certainly, typhus and other fever drugs developed by the IG's Behring-werke serological department at Marburg were routinely tested on inmates at Buchenwald and Mauthausen concentration camps. The IG also became involved in a secret SS program to develop a method of chemical castration for use in Russia. In early November 1942 Karl Tauboeck, a biochemist at Ludwigshafen, was ordered by Martin Müller-Cunradi to brush up on his knowledge of the tropical *Caladium seguinum* bush, which scientists from a small SS-sponsored pharmaceutical firm in Dresden had recently discovered could be used to sterilize mice. The SS urgently wanted independent confirmation of the firm's experiments and had asked the IG to supply a suitable expert. Two SS men took Tauboeck to Dresden, where he reviewed the tests and found that the results were indeed genuine, although he realized the plant was also highly toxic to humans. Later that day, "the SS men told me that this research was being carried out on the express orders of Reichsführer SS Himmler, in order to find a way of suppressing births among the eastern nations. After this fact had been revealed to me I was sworn to secrecy." At some risk to his career, Tauboeck refused to play any further part in the project because of its "criminal character." The SS subsequently found it impossible to grow *Caladium seguinum* in Germany, but they did experiment with other sterilization drugs at Auschwitz and Buchenwald.

At Nuremberg, Waldemar Hoven, senior SS doctor at Buchenwald, provided insight into the SS's dealings with IG Farben's pharmaceutical departments.

> It is clear that the experiments in the concentration camps with IG preparations only took place in the interests of the IG, which strove with all its might to determine the effectiveness of these drugs. They let the SS deal with the—shall I say—the dirty work in the camps. It was not the IG's intention to make any of this public, but to put up a smokescreen around the experiments so that they could keep any profits to themselves. The IG took the initiative for these experiments.*

Taken together then, such evidence makes it hard to see how anyone of any seniority in the IG could have remained ignorant of the

---

*SS doctors Waldemar Hoven and Helmuth Vetter were sentenced to death for their crimes.

activities at Auschwitz—be it medical experiments, or the degrada-
tion, torture, and murder of slave laborers and Jews, or the large-scale
industrial genocide. Even those executives who had no direct personal
engagement with the Buna-Werke project didn't need to cast their eyes
all the way to Upper Silesia to find proof of just how deep into the
mire their relationship with the Nazis had taken them. The meeting
that took place between Otto Ambros and the Führer in May 1943
would have done just as well. The subject on the agenda was chemical
weapons and whether they should be used against the Red Army.

The matter had arisen because three of Hitler's closest lieutenants,
Joseph Goebbels, Martin Bormann, and Robert Ley (a former IG
chemist), were pressing him to correct the worrying reverses at Stalingrad by attacking the Russians with tabun and sarin, the two deadly
nerve gases developed by the IG for the Wehrmacht in the late 1930s.
Otto Ambros had been the chief facilitator of this project and at the outbreak of war had obtained army funding to set up a top-secret production plant for the weapons (code-named N-Stoff) at Dyhernfurth in
Silesia. The factory, jointly run by the IG and the high command through
a subsidiary called Anorgana, was now well established, with huge underground galleries and facilities and a surface plant that stretched over
one square mile. More than three thousand workers (including five hundred inmates from Auschwitz) labored there under the strictest security
and were on their way to creating a tabun stockpile of more than twelve
thousand tons, in addition to developing a number of suitable delivery
mechanisms—from shells, bombs, and personnel mines to hand
grenades, aerial sprays, and machine gun bullets. At other plants, such as
that at Gendorf in Bavaria, the IG was also producing thousands of tons
of World War I–era chemical weapons, including mustard gas, chlorine
gas, and phosgene. It would later emerge that some of these were tested
on concentration camp inmates. At Dyhernfurth a number of inmates
died after accidental contamination with tabun and sarin.

Ambros had been brought to the meeting—a secret conference at
Hitler's East Prussian headquarters—by Albert Speer, the new minister for armament and war production, who was strongly opposed to
the use of tabun and sarin but who wanted the Führer to have all the
facts. Hitler was mostly keen to hear whether it was likely that the

Allies had also developed the gases, because the risk of retaliation in kind would affect his decision to use them. He was clearly disappointed when Ambros told him that the Allies quite possibly had the weapons—the basic chemistry had been in the public domain since 1902—and might even have developed the industrial capacity to manufacture them in larger quantities than Germany.* This seemed to settle the matter for the moment, although it was raised again the following year. In the meantime, Ambros and the IG were left to ponder the wisdom of having produced weapons of mass destruction for a regime that was beginning to show such signs of anxiety.

ALTHOUGH THEY HAD survived the first enemy air attacks in 1940 and 1941 in reasonable shape, the IG's Rhine plants remained vulnerable to Allied bombing. Even if they weren't always direct targets, the factories' proximity to other major German manufacturing centers meant that work was often interrupted by disruption to local power and water supplies and transportation links. Oppau, for example, which was close to the cities of Mannheim and Ludwigshafen, produced a range of synthetic and heavy chemical products that were all absolutely vital to the war economy, especially nitrogen, which was needed for fertilizers and explosives, and isobutyl oil, which was used for synthetic fuels. Oppau was better prepared for attacks than some older IG plants because it was built with steel frames and reinforced concrete rather than bricks and mortar, but after the late autumn of 1943 the plant began to suffer serious collateral disruption from area bombing. Eventually, it became a target itself, and by the middle of 1944 it was taking a repeated battering. The venerable BASF works at Ludwigshafen, more vulnerable because of their brick construction and their location closer to the heart of the city, also became a frequent target. Repairs at the factory were especially difficult because it was still recovering

---

*As it happened the Allies hadn't yet produced tabun and sarin, although the British had a stockpile of thirty-two thousand tons of mustard gas and phosgene by 1944—sufficient to poison almost one thousand square miles of German territory. It is not known whether the USSR had developed the deadlier nerve agents, although both sides went on to produce them during the cold war, using captured German scientific know-how.

from a huge explosion, unrelated to the bombing, that had torn the heart out of the works on July 19, 1943. In that incident, fifty people had been killed and almost seven hundred injured, including Matthias Pier, the scientist who had first created synthetic methanol. When Allied bombers began adding to the damage at Ludwigshafen in October, it took several weeks before production of some lines could be resumed.*

It was much the same story elsewhere in late 1943 and early 1944. Leverkusen was hit a number of times, as were the Hoechst plant at Frankfurt, the explosives plants at Schiebusch and Duisberg, and several other places. The Allied strategic bombing campaign that would cripple German industry in late 1944 and 1945 had not yet hit its stride, but the intensity of the attacks was growing nonetheless and every raid took its toll in lives and destruction.

Inevitably, the killed and wounded included some of the large army of foreign workers and slave laborers that the IG increasingly relied upon to man its production plants. As the war in the East called up ever more German nationals, the number of foreign "employees" soared. By 1943 around a third of the IG's workforce in Germany, some sixty thousand people, was composed of French, Dutch, Belgian, Italian, Polish, Ukrainian, Czech, and Russian forced laborers, along with a substantial number of POWs (British, Russian, and Italian). This figure would rise to over a hundred thousand by the end of the war. Many of the civilians had been led to believe that they could leave after a period of time but as the IG grew more desperate for manpower, that possibility evaporated. In truth, the vast majority were held against their will, especially those from the East, who routinely received the worst treatment. Most of the non-POW workers were housed in camps—five major installations in the Ludwigshafen-Oppau area alone—that were at best rudimentary and at worst as primitive as those in Upper Silesia. Many camps had their own jails where workers were imprisoned for minor offenses (drunkenness and unexcused absences from work were among the most common) and the laborers

*Ultimately, the repairs proved fruitless. By April 1945 sixty-five enemy air raids had hit the plants at Ludwigshafen and Oppau, causing an estimated RM 400 million worth of damage and leaving only 6 percent of 1,470 buildings unscathed.

lived in constant fear of informers and the Gestapo, who were always on the lookout for "saboteurs" and "Bolshevik infiltrators."*

For the IG's middle-ranking and senior executives life continued much as normal, or what passed for normal in a police state that was at war with most of the world. The more senior enjoyed privileges that were denied to ordinary Germans, although their workload became markedly more onerous as they struggled to keep plants going amid the bombing and shortages of labor and raw materials. Their task became even harder when it became apparent that some of the previous influence they had had in Nazi circles was diminishing, with Carl Krauch's star in particular beginning to wane. Although Krauch continued to hold his position as general plenipotentiary for chemical production and Hitler had awarded him the Knight's Cross for his distinguished service, his clout was mostly derived from the patronage of Hermann Göring, whose own power was coming under pressure from other contenders for the Führer's favor—most notably Heinrich Himmler (who wished to accrue ever more economic influence for his SS) and, increasingly, Martin Bormann, Hitler's shadowy head of the party secretariat. Krauch's authority was also being undermined by Armaments Minister Albert Speer, who, from his appointment in 1942, had made it plain that he had his own ideas of where Germany's production priorities should lie. He declared that the chemical sector would have to wait in line with other war industries that needed essential raw materials. From now on, it would have to live within existing quotas unless there were particularly extenuating circumstances. Krauch's protests that these quotas would make it impossible to increase production of buna, fuel, and other war goods were ignored. Hans Kehrl, chief of the planning and raw material department at the Economic Ministry and an old antagonist of IG Farben's, rubbed more

---

*Despite the deprivation, it has to be said that conditions for IG Farben's civilian foreign workers in Germany were at least on a par with those for workers at other giant German corporations, such as Krupp, the Hermann Göring Werke, and Siemens, and in some cases were marginally better. Drexel Sprecher, a member of the U.S. prosecution team at Nuremberg, concluded that Krupp's exploitation of slave labor, with its "sadism, senseless barbarity, and shocking treatment of dehumanized material," was even worse than that of the IG. But there were no saints in this game. By the end of 1944, over seven and a half million civilian foreigners—men, women, and children—were working in the Third Reich's mines, factories, and fields, and countless numbers of them were degraded, beaten, starved, and murdered by their employers.

salt in Krauch's wounds by suggesting tartly that perhaps the time had come to assign some of his responsibilities to other agencies. By March 1943 Krauch had been forced to relinquish control over production at chemical plants, although he retained his authority over research, development, and the construction of new factories.

But for Krauch and the IG worse was yet to come. The events of May 12, 1944, and thereafter brought the besieged plenipotentiary as low as he had ever been. That day, which Speer later identified as the point when "the technological war was decided," the United States Eighth Air Force sent 935 bombers to attack Germany's synthetic fuel industry. Two hundred of these planes were dispatched to just one target: the IG's giant plant at Leuna.

The next day Speer rushed to the scene and walked through "a tangle of broken and twisted pipe systems" with the IG's staff. He was aghast at what he saw. The raids, he recognized, represented "a new era in the air war"; if continued they would signal "the end of German armaments production." Although the damage could be repaired, even the most optimistic forecasts held that fuel production would not resume for some weeks. On May 19 Speer arrived at Hitler's redoubt on the Obersalzberg to brief the Führer in person. "The enemy has struck us at one of our weakest points," he said. "If they persist at it this time, we will soon no longer have any fuel production worth mentioning. Our only hope is that the other side has an air force General Staff as scatterbrained as ours!"

Four days later, Krauch was ordered to bring Heinrich Bütefisch and two other IG fuel experts to an urgent conference with Hitler. Reich Marshal Göring, Speer, and Field Marshal Wilhelm Keitel, chief of the high command, also attended. While waiting in the drafty hallway of the Berghof, Speer warned the industrialists to tell "the unvarnished truth." Göring, who had not wanted the four men to attend the meeting and who, according to Speer, was worried that Hitler would blame him for not providing sufficient air cover for the fuel plants, hastened to insist that they should not say anything too pessimistic.

But Krauch and Bütefisch did as Speer had asked and informed Hitler that if the raids continued the situation was indeed hopeless, supporting their arguments with the usual impressive array of IG charts and statistics. When Hitler demurred, insisting that surely the situation was not that bad, both Keitel and Göring jumped in to reassure him. The industrialists, however, were "made of sterner stuff," according to Speer, and stuck doggedly to their predictions. The Führer finally seemed to get the picture, even noting that the concentration of essential war production in one or two places made them far too easy to attack. "In my view," he said, "the fuel, buna rubber, and nitrogen plants represent a particularly sensitive point for the conduct of the war, since vital materials for armaments are being manufactured in a small number of plants."

Göring, eager to steer the Führer away from any discussion of the deficiencies of the Luftwaffe—a subject on which the Reich marshal was feeling increasingly vulnerable—began castigating Krauch for building the plants without adequate camouflage and earthwork protection. Though Krauch must have been deeply shocked by his patron's reproaches, he managed to remind everyone that the factories had been constructed well before the war, when the only criteria were cost and efficiency. Fortunately, Hitler let the matter drop, but the IG man realized that he could no longer rely on Göring's support. The Reich marshal had abandoned him and from that moment on Krauch was a marginalized figure.

In early June, after weeks of feverish repairs, the fuel plants had just come back on line when the USAF struck Leuna and the others again and inflicted even more damage than before. That same day, German-controlled oil refineries at Ploesti in Romania were also attacked. Taken together, the raids reduced the Reich's fuel production capacity by over 50 percent. Göring responded by promising to send more aircraft to the defense of fuel plants, but when the Allies landed at Normandy later that week he had to divert the Luftwaffe to France instead, leaving the factories open to yet more raids. By the end of June 1944, Speer was warning Hitler that until repairs were carried out the Reich's ability to produce fuel was down to 10 percent of what it needed to be. Somehow the IG managed to get Leuna back up to three-quarter capacity, but more raids on July 7 and July 19 returned it to rubble once again. The raids were now coming so thick and fast that the only way that larger plants like Leuna could get back on line was if other, smaller fuel factories were stripped of vital equipment—rendering them useless, of course, and further reducing Germany's fuel capacity. It was as if the IG were trying to build a house of cards, except that each time it was knocked over the concern had to start again with a smaller deck. Eventually, of course, the cards would run out altogether.

13

GÖTTERDÄMMERUNG

Although it was still possible for ordinary Germans to feel hopeful about the eventual outcome of the war, the first few months of 1944 must have sorely tested their optimism. Allied air raids at home were becoming more frequent and intense and the news from various military fronts, even when consumed through a filter of Nazi propaganda, was increasingly depressing. In fact, since the catastrophe at Stalingrad at the start of the previous year, the Reich had suffered a string of reverses: the RAF had launched devastating attacks against Hamburg and Berlin, the Wehrmacht had been savaged at Kursk, Rommel had been driven out of North Africa, Italy had changed sides, and the Red Army had raised the terrible nine-hundred-day siege of Leningrad, crossed the old prewar frontier between the Ukraine and Poland, and captured ten German divisions at Kanev, on the River Dneiper. Elsewhere the Allies had established a beachhead at Anzio, in Italy, and it was already a matter of widespread if discreet speculation that a more substantial invasion in France was coming at some point in the year ahead. Germany wasn't beaten yet but the days of triumph and certainty were quickly becoming a distant memory. It was also extremely unwise to publicly express any lack of confidence in the Führer's ability to steer the nation to ultimate victory, and so throughout the Reich people suppressed their doubts and anxieties and carried on as best they could.

Surprisingly, this state of denial was as prevalent at Auschwitz as it was elsewhere that winter and early spring, even though the town's German population must surely have felt the looming threat of the Russians a few hundred miles to the east. Indeed, in many respects the camps' activities continued as usual, except that the manpower shortages created by Germany's massive military losses had increased the appetite for Jewish slaves. Other firms had now followed the IG to the region—steel and metal industries, coal producers, and other chemical manufacturers—and although none of them came close to matching the Buna-Werke's continually recycled contingent of eleven thousand concentration camp prisoners, demand for workers was such that a string of smaller subcamps had been established in the area to hold and provide the additional labor.

The gassings, too, proceeded apace: the old, sick, and very young and those otherwise unable to work were selected for murder much as before. But from the end of 1943, the Operation Reinhard death camps, built specifically to exterminate Jews rather than also exploit their labor, were shut down—Sobibor (200,000 killed), Belzec (550,000), Chelmno (150,000), and Treblinka (750,000). Only Auschwitz was left to absorb what was left of occupied Europe's Jewish communities.* The largest group of deportees came from Hungary. In preparation for their arrival, the SS opened new crematoria at Birkenau and then extended the rail line right into the camp to make the selection and gassing process more efficient. Between May 15 and July 9, 1944, around 438,000 people were brought there, 85 percent of whom were murdered immediately. The rest were taken into the camps, either to work locally or to be sent on to Bergen-Belsen, Dachau, Buchenwald, Mauthausen, Ravensbruck, Sachsenhausen,

*The death camps, closed because the Russians were drawing closer and the Reich's need for Jewish labor was increasing, had been run at a profit. Hans Globocknik, the SS officer in charge of Operation Reinhard, gave a final accounting to Heinrich Himmler in December 1943. The overall value of cash and goods taken from those murdered was in excess of RM 180 million.

Gross-Rosen, or the 370 other SS slave labor facilities in and around Poland and Germany.

One transport of 650 Jews from northern Italy in February 1944 included a young chemist from Turin. Primo Levi was among 125 men selected at the railhead for labor at the Buna-Werke. One of only three survivors from this group, he would later write about his experiences at Monowitz in heartrending, searing detail. Like the thousands of others who had been through the camp before him, he quickly felt the effect of the dreadful conditions.

A fortnight after my arrival I already had the prescribed hunger, that chronic hunger unknown to free men, which makes one dream at night, and settles in all the limbs of one's body. I have already learnt not to let myself be robbed, and in fact if I find a spoon lying around, a piece of string, a button which I can acquire without danger of punishment, I pocket them and consider them mine by full right. On the back of my feet I already have those numb sores that will not heal. I push wagons, I work with a shovel, I turn rotten in the rain, I shiver in the wind; already my own body is no longer mine: my belly is swollen, my limbs emaciated.

The machine was still functioning, but for the IG managers for whose benefit Primo Levi and the thousands of others were suffering, the Auschwitz project was at last losing its allure. True, there had been some successes: a carbonization plant and carbide furnace were nearing completion, and in late October 1943 the first tanker load of methanol had finally been driven out through the gates—an event celebrated enthusiastically at Auschwitz's Ratshof pub by senior staff and their special guests, Otto Ambros and Rudolf Höss. But although methanol was a necessary ingredient of aviation fuel and explosives and of great importance to the Third Reich's continued ability to prosecute the war, it was not buna, not the sticky black rubber substitute on which the IG had pinned so much of its future and spent almost one billion marks. That part of the project was still way behind schedule. Under intense pressure from Berlin, the IG men—Dürrfeld, Faust, and others—knew they had to continue to the bitter end, to drive their army of slave laborers to finish the factory at whatever cost. But the work proceeded extremely slowly, hampered by shortages of raw materials, mechanical breakdowns, the inadequacies of the workforce, and even—although their significance is difficult to quantify—acts of sabotage carried out by Denis Avey and some of the Buna-Werke's other twelve hundred British POWs. As Avey remembers:

> We weren't allowed to rivet at first but after a while they let us do it so long as we were supervised; but they couldn't always watch us that closely, you see, because there was too many of us. So when they weren't looking we used to weaken the rivets, so that after a couple of months they would pop and they'd have to do it all over. There was one gas holder they had to keep going back to again and again because of that. . . . Other times we'd take grease off the engines, mix it with sand, and then put it back so that when they started them up it would wreck the gears. Or we'd bend the blades of the cooling fans, things like that. Anything we could get away with, basically. You had to be very careful, though, because the Germans were always on the lookout for sabotage and would test everything. They'd shoot you if you got caught. But I had a stooge on the inside of the chief engineer's office and we'd know when certain things were going to be used and so we'd only go after the stuff that was going to be lying idle for a few weeks. That way, when it didn't work, they didn't know who had worked on it. It caused them no end of problems.

From mid-1944, enemy air raids made things even more difficult. The U.S. Air Force had been theoretically capable of reaching Auschwitz since establishing air bases at Foggia, in Italy, at the end of 1943, although the first contrails of Allied reconnaissance planes did not appear over the plant until April. Starting in May, however, when Leuna and other fuel plants in Germany were attacked, it seemed likely that the Upper Silesian industrial sites, especially the IG's fuel production facilities at the Buna-Werke and at Heydebreck, would be the next targets. The realization that American Flying Fortresses might soon be heading their way came as an unpleasant surprise for all those Reich Germans who had come to IG Auschwitz because it was beyond the reach of enemy aircraft. Warning sirens were hastily tested, antiaircraft batteries were set up in the surrounding countryside, and new shelters were dug (work that used up more precious prison labor). Nevertheless, no one was quite ready for the intensity of the daylight raids that began on August 20 and continued intermittently for the next six months. Although Auschwitz was at the outer limits of the range of the Allied planes and pilots had only a few minutes to bomb the plant, they had no trouble finding and hitting so large a target and caused great destruction.

As the German camp personnel scrambled for cover, prisoners were denied access to the shelters they had built. When Salomon Kohn and some other inmates tried to get into one of them during the first attack, the plant's director of air defense forced them outside again, shouting, "Get out of here, you swine! This tunnel is not for you. What makes you think this is an occasion for Germans to be together with you Jews?" Primo Levi, who remarkably was still alive five months after his arrival at Monowitz, remembered that "when the earth began to tremble, we dragged ourselves, stunned and limping, through the corrosive fumes of the smoke bombs to the vast waste areas, sordid and sterile, closed within the boundary of the Buna; there we lay inert, piled up on top of each other like dead men, but still aware of the momentary pleasure of our bodies resting."*

Things were no better for the British POWs at the plant, who had to rush for whatever cover they could find. Tragically, many of them didn't make it, as Denis Avey later recalled: "We lost around forty of our people to the American bombing. After the planes had gone I helped to dig their graves, unmarked graves, I'm sorry to say, and then the bombers came back and blew them all out of the ground again. I think in the end we only found the remains of thirteen of them."

The raids effectively put an end to any hopes the IG had of producing buna and synthetic fuel at Auschwitz. Given time, the damage was certainly reparable, and an emergency detail of volunteers (a *Stoss Kommando* of engineers, fuel technicians, and other specialists) was actually dispatched from Ludwigshafen in a last desperate effort to get the plant finished. But time was no longer on the IG's side: the military situation was deteriorating so quickly that further efforts were pointless

---

*As a qualified chemist, Levi had managed after a few months to get menial work inside an IG laboratory at the plant. Although his living conditions and diet were no better than before, he was spared some of the worst of the backbreaking work that killed so many others.

and the emergency team was ordered to return. In the interim, the SS had begun the gradual dissolution of the main Auschwitz camps. By November 1944, when Himmler ordered an end to systematic exterminations across the Reich, around half of the 155,000 prisoners had been marched out to concentration camps within Germany. A last orgy of killing—including the extermination of a group of two thousand Jews from Theresienstadt, near Prague, on October 28—saw more than forty thousand murdered. Then the crematoria were shut down and gradually dismantled.* On January 17, 1945, as the Red Army entered Budapest and Warsaw, and with Upper Silesia exposed to imminent assault, the SS began the second and final phase of their evacuation, marching the fifty-eight thousand surviving prisoners from Auschwitz to Buchenwald, Bergen-Belsen, Mauthausen, Dachau, and other camps to the West. Of these, some ten thousand were from the Buna-Werke and Monowitz—Jews, forced laborers of a dozen nationalities, and POWs.† Only eight hundred prisoners, so sick they were expected to die anyway, were left behind in the camp infirmary. At the Fürstengrube coal mine, inmates too weak to leave the hospital were shot, killed with hand grenades, or burned to death in their huts.

Thousands perished during the death marches. The SS shot any-

---

*Famously, the Jewish Sonderkommando who had been ordered to destroy the crematoria rose in revolt on October 7, 1944, knowing that, once the SS had obliterated traces of the killing apparatus, they would be murdered as surviving witnesses. All but a handful were shot, hanged, or tortured to death.

†Denis Avey managed to slip away from the POW column after days of marching through the snow in Czechoslovakia and Austria and then spent several weeks on the run, somehow crossing Germany behind enemy lines in the depths of winter. At one point he even crept through the outskirts of Nuremberg, where the Waffen SS were preparing barricades and artillery positions for a last-ditch defense and the Gestapo was executing deserters. When he finally met up with the Americans he was desperately weak and on the verge of starvation. The RAF flew him back to England but he refused to stay more than a few hours in the army reception center and slipped out to hitch a ride to his family home. Mentally and physically shattered, he moved to Manchester after a few days and checked himself into a hospital. He would spend most of the next two years there; apart from having lost an eye, he was now suffering from tuberculosis and the long-term effects of malnutrition and exhaustion. Eventually, he went back to his old job as an engineer and even managed to become a very successful amateur three-day eventer on show horses. But for years he found it impossible to discuss Auschwitz: "We would sometimes see people being marched from the trains past our camp on the way to Birkenau. And when you see little kids, little children, and their mothers and you know they are going to go straight in and up the chimney . . . its something you never forget. I have been haunted by it all my life, but you just bury it." His interview for this book in 2004 was one of the first times he had talked about his experiences since 1945.

one who weakened or fell ill, anyone who tried to rest or flee. "We started counting the shots," one survivor, Aharon Beilin, later recalled. "It was a long column—five thousand people. We knew every shot meant a human life. Sometimes the count reached five hundred in a single day. And the longer we marched, the more the number of shots increased. There was no strength, no food." Some died of exposure during overnight stops in the snow. Almost all of the four and a half thousand Jews who had been marched out from Monowitz on January 19 were murdered after they had scattered into a forest during an air raid alert. The SS rounded them up and then opened fire with machine guns. Just over one hundred were left to continue their journey.

The IG meanwhile had pulled its people home. The last of them left Auschwitz in the second week of January 1945 on two special trains reserved for the town's remaining civilian male Reich Germans (German women and children had been evacuated in October 1944). In the days before their departure, Walter Dürrfeld and Max Faust had toured the Buna-Werke, supervising the dismantling of key equipment and the destruction of documents that hadn't been sent back to Frankfurt and Berlin. Despite their efforts (and a last brief Allied raid after their departure on January 19), most of the factory's infrastructure remained intact. But it mattered not; IG Auschwitz had been an almost total failure. Around 200,000 people (Reich Germans, foreign laborers, POWs, and Auschwitz prisoners) had been engaged at different times on the plant's construction, at a cost of over 900 million reichsmarks and—estimated conservatively—some 35,000 human lives. This number rises to over 40,000 if the death toll at the IG's Fürstengrube and Janina mines is taken into account. Some Nuremberg prosecutors put the figures much higher, concluding that some 200,000 people had died while working for IG Auschwitz, either on-site or as a consequence of being dispatched from the IG's employ to the gas chambers at Birkenau—but this was almost certainly an overestimate based on the incomplete information available at the time. Whichever figure is correct, one thing is clear: although some explosive-grade methanol was produced, not a single pound of buna rubber or one liter of synthetic gasoline ever emerged from the Buna-Werke's gates.

After nearly four years of intense activity, all that IG Farben really had to show for its efforts was a reputation stained forever with the blood of those murdered in the Holocaust. Now, as the Red Army drew near, the huge Buna-Werke stood silent and waiting, a bomb-scarred monument to the ambition, greed, and folly of a once mighty company.

The IG's partners in this disaster, the officers of the SS, withdrew over the next few days. Before they went, they, too, tried to destroy the evidence of their crimes. Files, lists, and other papers from the administration offices at Auschwitz, Birkenau, and Monowitz were burned in huge bonfires around the camps. The dismantled crematoria were blown up and the largest warehouses, where the looted personal effects of the gassed Jews had been stored before being shipped back to the Reich, were set on fire along with several barrack blocks. Not everything could be burned, however: the Russians later found stores containing 370,000 men's suits, 837,000 women's coats and dresses, 44,000 pairs of shoes, and 7.7 tons of human hair. On January 20 and 21 SS sentries were removed from all the watchtowers, leaving only small patrols to guard the camps and subcamps. Over the next few days, after randomly killing another seven hundred prisoners of various races and nationalities, the remaining SS began to slip away too. One of the last to leave was SS doctor Josef Mengele on January 17. He had continued his experiments almost to the end, closing down his experimental laboratories only when his source of human material finally began to give out. He took the written reports of his murders with him.

For the eight hundred seriously ill prisoners left in the Monowitz infirmary, abandoned by both the SS and their former IG employers without food, medicine, heat, electricity, or water, a dreadful struggle to stay alive until the camp was liberated now ensued. Lying in their freezing and filthy bunks, racked by dysentery, typhus, diphtheria, and a host of other diseases, they watched out of the cracked windows as the German army retreated down the road past the camp for three days. Then they cringed in helpless terror as Allied planes returned to bomb the nearby Buna-Werke for one last time. After that they were on their own. The vast majority were completely incapable of fending for themselves, unable to venture outside to scavenge for scraps of food in the frozen snow or to pick up firewood or even to make it to the latrine bucket. The few who had a little strength did their best to help—among them Primo Levi, suffering badly from scarlet fever—but it was a hopeless task. Five hundred more inmates died of sickness, cold, and hunger before the Red Army arrived.

Around midday on January 27, 1945, Levi and another prisoner were carrying a body to an open grave pit outside their hut when they saw four young Russians approach on horseback. The soldiers came slowly up to the wire and gazed at the huts, the bodies on the ground, and the few filthy skeletal figures gathering nervously in front of them.

> They did not greet us, nor did they smile; they seemed oppressed not only by compassion but by a confused restraint, which sealed their lips and bound their eyes to the funereal scene. It was that shame that we knew so well, the shame that drowned us after the selections, and every time we had to watch, or submit to, some outrage: the shame the Germans did not know, that the just man experiences at another man's crime; the feeling of guilt that such a crime should exist, that it should have been introduced irrevocably into the world of things that exist, and that his will for good should have proved too weak or null, and should not have availed in defence.

The Russians, from the Sixtieth Army of the First Ukrainian Front, found at least six hundred unburied corpses lying around the camps and some seven thousand prisoners still alive, mostly at Birkenau. Of the three hundred alive at IG Monowitz, two hundred more would die in the coming days, despite all the medical help the Red Army could provide. Primo Levi was one of the very few who was loaded onto a cart and taken out through the main gates.

IN GERMANY, THE IG's senior executives were at last waking up to the possibility that they might be called to account for their association with the Nazis. In July 1944 the BBC had begun broadcasting details of what was happening to Jews at Auschwitz and elsewhere, based on reports smuggled out of the camps by the Sonderkommando and the Polish resistance. The broadcasts had been accompanied by Allied warnings, repeated several times in the following months, to the effect that anyone who had participated in such crimes would be hunted down and brought to justice as a war criminal.

Hermann Schmitz took these threats very seriously and began to agonize over his personal safety. His anxiety intensified when, in the aftermath of a failed attempt on Hitler's life on July 20, 1944, the Nazi regime threatened dire reprisals against "all traitors and saboteurs." Schmitz hadn't been involved in the conspiracy but the atmosphere of fear and mistrust swirling around the highest ranks of Nazi society fed into his growing paranoia. His behavior became increasingly erratic and contradictory. One minute his obsessive secretiveness led him to shut himself up in his office, where he would place a tea cozy over the telephone in an apparent attempt to frustrate any Gestapo listening devices; the next he was openly courting allegations of defeatism by joining other industrialists in a half-baked attempt to contact Allen Dulles, the wartime head of the American OSS, with peace proposals. Nothing came of these approaches, although Schmitz actually had quite close links with the Americans. Before the war Dulles's law firm, Sullivan and Cromwell, had handled IG Farben's U.S. business interests, when the cartel began to transfer ownership from German to American representatives.

Some members of the *Vorstand* responded to the mounting crisis in predictable fashion. August von Knieriem, the IG's chief counsel, spent the autumn of 1944 drawing up a lengthy paper considering, in his lawyerly way, the prospects for the concern's survival after the war and concluding that its breakup by the Allies was inevitable but survivable. Wilhelm Mann, staunch Nazi loyalist, urged continued fealty to the cause, arguing that the IG had to abide by the Führer's wishes that production be moved away from the advancing Allies and into the German interior. But most of the executives began to think in terms of personal survival and how to keep themselves and their families beyond the reach of the Russians. For some, it was just a question of sticking close to their homes and offices in the IG towns and cities along the Rhine and maintaining a low profile until the Americans or British arrived. Others, whose duties usually took them to Berlin, found they had more pressing reasons to be elsewhere. In January, for example, Max Ilgner declared that working in the bomb-damaged IG offices on the Unter den Linden was becoming far too difficult and he moved his whole operation back to Frankfurt. (Reportedly he took two trainloads of sensitive documents with him, although these were never recovered.) In early March, Georg von Schnitzler slipped off to his estate at Oberursel, changing into his Scottish tweeds and highly polished English shoes to help reinforce the image of a peaceful country gentleman. Carl Wurster and Heinrich Bütefisch went back to Ludwigshafen. Otto Ambros set off for the Gendorf chemical plant in his native Bavaria. Von Knieriem returned to his house in the picturesque city of Heidelberg, where several other directors also lived. Even Wilhelm Mann eventually decided on discretion and joined Heinrich Hörlein back at Leverkusen. Fritz ter Meer, meanwhile, was planning for the systematic destruction of incriminating documents at the IG's vast Frankfurt office complex, lest they fall into Allied hands; some fifteen tons of paper were eventually incinerated. None of the men—not even Carl Krauch, who had arguably benefited most from his association with the Nazis—elected to stay in the German capital with their Führer.

A few days before the U.S. Third Army moved into Frankfurt, Hermann Schmitz paid a final visit to the IG's headquarters. After attending a brief meeting with some of his colleagues—presumably to discuss what to do when the Allies arrived—he and a few others set off by train to their homes in Heidelberg. According to Ernst Struss, who went with them, they emerged very shaken at the other end, having spent several hours being shunted back and forth between Allied and German lines while attempting to dodge the fighting. Their train had been shot at a number of times and on occasion the IG bosses were forced to swallow their dignity and clamber under the seats to avoid being hit. It was the closest many of them had been to participating personally in Hitler's war and they didn't particularly enjoy the experience.

By April 1945 the fighting had moved eastward as the Americans swept toward the Elbe and a meeting with the Russians. Well before the war was brought to a close in May, with the downfall of Berlin, the suicide of Adolf Hitler, and the unconditional surrender of all German forces, the members of the IG's top team had ensconced themselves safely behind the lines of the Western powers. Surely now, they told themselves, all they had to do was stay out of the limelight and soon everything would get back to normal. After all, the world would always need chemicals.

THE ALLIES HAD certainly gone to some effort to capture the IG's major chemical factories. By March 1945 U.S. troops were massed directly across the Rhine from Leverkusen but the bridges had been blown up and there was constant small-arms and mortar fire from the other bank. While the Americans pondered a way to get across, their artillery bombarded any sign of activity in the plant itself in case war materials were still being produced. As it happened, manufacturing had been abandoned but the factory's solid fuel generators were still going because they were now providing the town's only source of electrical power. To keep them turning without the fumes inviting a barrage of shells called for some typically innovative IG thinking: the plant's engineers eventually dug a network of exhaust tunnels to disperse the smoke imperceptibly through the broken windows and cracked roofs of damaged buildings. Employees also armed themselves, not to defend the factory against the Allies necessarily but to stop any attempt by the retreating Wehrmacht to reduce it to rubble. Whatever workers had felt about the Nazis, it was plain the war was now lost, and no one wanted to see their livelihoods put in further jeopardy. Consequently, when American troops finally occupied Leverkusen on

April 14, no resistance was offered and surviving Bayer employees willingly agreed to clear rubble, repair machinery, and get production going as quickly as possible; their cooperation continued when the British took over the zone two months later. Both the workers and the management reasoned that demand for aspirin and other drugs was going to be substantial and Leverkusen should be first in line to provide them.*

It was much the same story at the other IG plants in western Germany, from Essen and Hüls in the north to Durlach and Rottweil in the south: a few days' fierce fighting while the Wehrmacht was still around and then grateful surrender to the Allies. The various works of the old Hoechst group around Frankfurt passed relatively unscathed into U.S. hands on March 28. Even the huge Ludwigshafen and Oppau plants had managed to avoid complete destruction, although damage there was worse than elsewhere because the factories' synthetic fuel and buna output had made them particularly important targets of Allied bombing. Captured on March 24, the plants were eventually passed into the control of the French, who immediately began a program to get them back on line.

In the East, the situation was somewhat different. The Red Army seized the IG's plants at Auschwitz, Heydebreck, and Dyhernfurth, in Silesia, and took over the concern's massive fuel facility at Leuna but seemed much more interested in dismantling equipment than in getting it going. Within days of their arrival at the Buna-Werke Russian troops began taking apart the high-pressure apparatus so that it might be reassembled in the Soviet Union.

---

*It quickly became clear that the damage to Leverkusen was surprisingly slight. Despite fourteen air raids on the plant between May 1944 and March 1945, seven of which could be categorized as heavy, the bombs had torn down brick buildings rather than damaged machinery and only 15 percent of the factory was considered beyond repair. Indeed this was generally the story for much of German industry, with the exception of fuel and transportation. After the war, the U.S. Strategic Bombing Survey reported that at most only about 20 percent of Germany's extended wartime industrial capital had been destroyed. While large sections of residential and city center accommodations had been hit, bombers had often missed industrial sites in the suburbs. In 1945, for example, the Krupp works at Essen was producing more tanks than it ever had but it couldn't get them to the troops at the front because the railway network had been destroyed.

But the Allies' interest in the IG extended far beyond the mere acquisition of its buildings. Hard on the heels of their combat troops came specialist units tasked with securing the concern's technology and scientists. For the British and Americans, this was part of a wider operation known as Project Paperclip, which had two key objectives. The first was to lay their hands on as much of Germany's wartime scientific expertise as possible in order to exploit it for their own benefit; the second was to deny it to the Russians, who had a similar program, Operation Osavakim. Paperclip had begun in 1944 when some three thousand specialists were selected, trained, and formed into units, and it took wing in the aftermath of the invasion of Germany, when they were shipped en masse to Europe. With full logistical, intelligence, and military support, the authority to commandeer whatever transport they needed, and orders to move as quickly as possible, the units were remarkably successful, scooping up a huge haul of data and matériel covering everything from rocketry and ballistics to torpedoes, antitank weaponry, and submarine construction. They proved even more adept at identifying and capturing thousands of key German scientists and technicians, taking many of them back to England and the United States for interrogation.*

Inevitably, the IG was a major target. On March 25, the day after the U.S. Army had cleared the area around Ludwigshafen, a joint British and American specialist team was flown in from London. On arriving at the plant and finding it badly damaged, investigators began rounding up and interrogating the few senior managers they were able to lay their hands on. Two days later, some of the Germans were loaded onto trucks and taken to a nearby forest, where they were set to digging up boxes of technical and scientific documents that had been buried among the trees. A quick perusal of these papers "indi-

---

*The most famous achievement of Paperclip was probably the capture of Wernher von Braun and four hundred scientists from the V2 rocket center at Peenemünde, many of whom later became involved in the U.S. ballistic missile and space programs. In this case and in several others, the wartime record of those detained was of far less concern to the Allies than their expertise—despite the fact that many were ardent Nazis and there was often clear prima facie evidence of their involvement in war crimes. The detainees brought back to the UK were kept under heavy guard at Beltane School in Wimbledon, South London, otherwise known as "Inkpot." The United States spread its German detainees around undisclosed locations in Washington, D.C., and Texas.

cated them to be of such value as to warrant transportation as an intact unit to London as soon as possible for examination and duplication." An entire laboratory at Oppau was then dismantled and shipped back to the UK.* Fuel scientists were also tracked down. At Leuna, a few weeks later, an American unit moved forty-nine synthetic fuel chemists and their families at gunpoint from their homes in the Russian zone to new accommodations in the West. Others were identified and rounded up after Heinrich Bütefisch was arrested, taken to London, and interrogated by the British Intelligence Objectives Subcommittee.†

But no IG technology was more urgently sought than that of its secret chemical weapons program. In late 1943, Britain's Enigma code breakers at Bletchley Park had intercepted and decrypted German high command signals about tabun and sarin, the two deadly nerve agents developed for the Wehrmacht. Deeply uneasy lest this expertise fall into the hands of the Russians and yet equally keen to acquire it for themselves, the British and Americans made it a top priority to find the two specialists most involved in development and production: Gerhard Schrader, the scientist who had formulated the weapons, and Otto Ambros, the man responsible for their manufacture. Lieutenant Colonel Paul Tarr of the British Chemical Warfare Service was put at the head of a fifty-strong team to track them down.

Schrader was found easily enough at the Elberfeld plant laboratory, and without much ado he handed over his research notes and the contents of his safe. But he professed not to know where Ambros was. In fact, U.S. troops had already located Ambros at Gendorf, in Bavaria, although as they hadn't known what to make of him they had been on the verge of letting him go. On entering the small town

---

*Many of the documents had no military value as such but were simply economic loot—patents and technical blueprints that were passed on to the chemical industries in Allied countries. It is not surprising that among the British investigators were several specialists from ICI, the IG's erstwhile partner and rival.

†Bütefisch, who seems to have been courteously treated, gave the BIOS investigators a detailed account of the IG's synthetic fuel program, but he avoided saying anything about IG Auschwitz, except to dismiss it as an enterprise "financed with government money," which was untrue. He also failed to mention that he had been in charge of its synthetic fuel program and had visited the site seven times.

in the last weeks of the war, the GIs had been surprised to find a chemical factory with many of its production facilities placed underground. Its manager, a cheerful man with a neat, prematurely gray moustache and a well-cut suit, had hastened out to meet them and volunteered to show them around. As they peered into vats and wandered around the empty offices, he told them it was a detergent plant that made soaps and household cleaning products for the domestic market. There was nothing untoward about the underground chambers; the factory had merely been complying with government instructions to all German businesses to provide air raid protection for their employees. He then told them his name, Ambros, and that he was just a simple chemist, originally from Ludwigshafen on the Franco-German border but transplanted to Gendorf by the fortunes of war. At the end of the tour he even offered them some cleaning products for their vehicles.

The unit's commanding officer was still a little suspicious, however, and so put the chemist under arrest until he was cleared with headquarters. When, after several days, the officer had heard nothing back from his superiors, he began to think that the man might indeed be as innocuous as he claimed. But fortunately someone had passed the circular announcing his arrest to Lieutenant Colonel Tarr, who dropped everything and rushed down to Bavaria as quickly as he could. During his debrief of Gerhard Schrader, Tarr had found out that the bulk of the IG's chemical weapons production had taken place at Dyhernfurth, in Silesia, which was now under the control of the Red Army. It was vital therefore to know just what had been manufactured there and in what quantities. Otto Ambros would be just the person to tell him. His interrogation of the IG man had barely begun when a warrant for Ambros's arrest as a suspected war criminal arrived from SHAEF (Supreme Headquarters Allied Expeditionary Force). Ambros was to be transferred immediately to the "Ashcan" detention center at Mondorf-les-Bains in Luxembourg.

Ambros never arrived. En route he and his escort were diverted into the French zone, where the authorities, presumably just as keen as the Americans and British to make use of his chemical weapons expertise, refused to let him go. And so there, for the moment, he stayed, working under French supervision at Ludwigshafen.*

Other IG officials were picked up here and there in the following weeks and months, although their detention was necessarily an ad hoc and uncoordinated affair. In the summer of 1945 Germany was in a state of almost total chaos. Towns and cities were devastated. Roads, railways, bridges, and housing had been destroyed. Power, water, and telephone systems had collapsed and food was in desperately short supply. Two huge Allied armies sat amid the ruins of the once mighty Third Reich while millions of displaced persons, concentration camp inmates, freed slave laborers, and Allied POWs picked their way through them, trying to find a way home or at least to reach some kind of shelter. At the same time, fifty million German civilians waited in trepidation among the rubble to learn what their fate might be and millions more grim-faced German POWs were marching into huge mass holding camps for processing and screening. It seemed that most of Europe was on the move, a dusty, disheveled horde of the hungry and lame, homeless and exhausted, in search of something or someone—a meal, a loved one, or merely a place to lay their heads. In March 1945, just before the end, one prescient cynic had painted some graffiti on a Berlin wall, "Enjoy the war—the peace is going to be terrible." But the reality was turning out to be worse than anyone had expected.

In these circumstances, it is not surprising that the Allies took a few weeks to find Hermann Schmitz, Georg von Schnitzler, and the other twenty or so men who ran IG Farben. While it is true that their names had been placed on preprepared watch lists of those to be

*The exact circumstances of Ambros's handover to the French are shrouded in mystery because the Allies' interest in anything to do with German chemical weaponry was kept very quiet. For this reason it cannot be said definitively that even small stocks of tabun and sarin were found at Gendorf or what may have happened to them if they were. However, it is known that quantities of the nerve agents were recovered from somewhere in Germany in July 1945 and brought back to Porton Down in England for analysis, and the most likely source of information leading to their recovery would have been Ambros. The gases weren't hugely difficult to make, of course, as Ambros had earlier pointed out to Hitler, and it is highly likely that the Western powers would soon have begun producing them in any case. The Soviet Union, meanwhile, may also have acquired quantities of the gases from the IG-Anorgana Dyhernfurth plant in Silesia, although the SS made strenuous efforts to destroy stocks before the Red Army arrived.

arrested on sight, they were among a great many prominent Germans given this distinction. The Allies had decided that *anyone* who had held a position of influence and authority in the Reich was to be at least temporarily detained and questioned as a potential security threat to the occupation forces or as a once integral part of the Nazi regime. Business leaders and industrialists were included on these lists on the not unreasonable grounds that they might have provided the machinery for Hitler's wars, but few of the military police and intelligence units entering Germany with the combat troops accorded the IG management any larger significance than that.* Others were more determined to track them down. In the process of putting an end to the cartel's relationship with Standard Oil in 1941, the Antitrust Division of the U.S. Department of Justice and their colleagues in the Treasury had concluded that the IG's byzantine international network of subsidiaries, coproduction deals, and secret agreements posed a threat to the economic health of the free world and had played a significant part in bringing the world to war. There was little the officials could do about this until Germany was defeated, but they were determined to dismantle the company once the war was over.

Two of these officials, Russell Nixon and James Martin, managed to track down Georg von Schnitzler. Attached to the U.S. military government's Cartels Division (one of a number of American agencies—including the OSS, the predecessor of the CIA, and the Foreign Economic Administration—now interested in the IG), they arrived in Frankfurt with other colleagues at the end of April 1945 to find the concern's headquarters in chaos. Somehow the huge building had survived the Allied bombing raids and shelling unscathed but the grounds

---

*Indeed, some lesser IG figures were initially sought more vigorously than *Vorstand* members because of their perceived economic value to the Allies. Walter Reppe was a case in point. One of Germany's leading acetylene scientists before the war, he had developed a branch of chemistry that had enormous potential in the development of plastic. He had gone on to become plant leader at Ludwigshafen but was not directly implicated in war crimes as such. Nevertheless he was arrested and taken into custody in the summer of 1945. Colonel Ernest Gruhn, director of the Joint Intelligence Objectives Agency in Washington, in charge of the recruitment and exploitation of German scientists, then tried, unsuccessfully, to bring him to the United States. Reppe was eventually released and later joined the managing board of BASF.

were knee-deep in a sea of swirling paper.* The U.S. Third Army had taken it over to use as its temporary headquarters and staff officers had ordered that it be "cleared of refuse" in readiness. As a result, several hundred tons of IG documents had been thrown out of windows into the courtyard, where they were now being burned in huge bonfires or carted away by the freed foreign laborers milling aimlessly around the building's precincts looking for bedding materials and kindling. Desperate to stop the destruction of what might be vital evidence, the investigators arranged for the remainder of these documents to be taken to safety in a nearby Reichsbank building, but the filing system that had once governed their orderly storage was now in tatters and the papers were just thrown into huge muddled heaps. Eventually, the U.S. team found Ernst Struss, Fritz ter Meer's secretary, and arranged for him to oversee their transfer to safer premises at Griesheim, where he put them back into some kind of shape. But many were never recovered.†

In the meantime, Nixon and Martin had set out on the trail of Georg von Schnitzler. He had last been seen in Frankfurt at the end of March, about to leave for his country estate at Oberursel. They found him there in the second week of May. The various accounts of their first meeting differ slightly but they all agree that the baron greeted them courteously. He received them wearing his trademark Scottish tweeds and English brogues, sitting with his beautiful wife, Lilly, in a room enhanced by a large Renoir over the fireplace.§ After offering them brandy (which they declined), he said that he was happy "all this unpleasantness is over" and that he was looking forward to seeing his old friends at ICI and DuPont again. When he was asked to accompany his visitors back to Frankfurt, he politely declined. As the SHAEF report of the meeting recalled: "He replied that he was unable

*One unsubstantiated story has it that the building had been spared Allied bombing because General Eisenhower wanted to use it as the headquarters of the U.S. occupation authority in Germany after the war.
†To their consternation, Nuremberg investigators discovered that Struss had been unsupervised and that he had used wood-burning trucks to move the papers. How many hundreds of key IG files might have been sacrificed along the way is unclear.
§Intelligence reports later suggested that this painting may have been looted from the Louvre.

to do so as the way was so long and he was so old. The next invitation came from a sergeant with a tommy-gun. . . . This time the Herr Direktor did come."

Hermann Schmitz, on the other hand, was interviewed a few times before he was taken into custody. The first time U.S. investigators called in at his surprisingly modest stucco house in Heidelberg, the IG boss challenged their authority and refused to answer any of their questions. They returned the following day and searched the premises but found nothing except some telegrams from Hitler, Göring, and others congratulating "*Geheimrat* Schmitz" on his sixtieth birthday. However, after sleeping on it, the investigators returned and made a further search. At the back of the dusty basement they found a door leading to a well-furnished air raid shelter. In it they discovered a trunk stuffed with a thousand or so IG documents. Among them were papers relating to the cartel's attempts at camouflaging ownership of its U.S. subsidiaries.

But Major Edmund Tilley of British Army Intelligence made what was perhaps the most telling find. He had dropped in, apparently on a whim, to ask Schmitz some general questions, but his brusque and authoritative manner soon reduced the IG man to tears. It was then that Tilley got Schmitz to reveal the whereabouts of his safe, which was hidden in a closet behind his desk. Among other documents, the major found an album containing photographs of the IG's infamous Buna-Werke in Upper Silesia. "Page one," he wrote later, "had a picture with a narrow street of the old Auschwitz. The accompanying drawings depicted the Jewish part of the population in a manner that was not flattering. . . . The second page began a section entitled 'Planning the New Auschwitz Works.'" Like someone hoarding pornographic images, the IG boss had kept his most shameful secret under lock and key.

As the last of Schmitz's *Vorstand* colleagues were picked up from their homes and offices and taken into custody, the Allied authorities were considering what to do about German industry in general and IG Farben in particular. In August 1945 the Potsdam Conference (which met to divide Germany into four occupation zones and produced a set of loose guidelines for the future treatment of the defeated nation) tried to determine some of the broader contextual questions, such as reparations and the desired level of renewed industrial production. Eventually the growing difficulties between the Soviet Union and the West would cause many of these agreements to be ignored or countermanded or interpreted differently by the occupying powers, but on one thing there was widespread accord. The German economy should be denazified and decartelized and those industries that had played a leading role in preparing Germany for war should be rendered incapable of accruing so much productive power ever again.

This meant the end of IG Farben. In September 1945 a report commissioned by General Dwight D. Eisenhower concluded that the company had been crucial to the German war effort and that, without its manufacturing capacity, scientific ingenuity, and technical expertise, Hitler could never have come so close to victory. As a result, the supreme allied commander recommended that any IG plant used for war-making purposes be destroyed, that ownership of remaining plants be dispersed to break up the monopoly, that the company's research programs and facilities be taken over, and that it be comprehensively stripped for reparations. Six weeks later, the Allied Control Council, the joint occupation authority, passed a law confirming that all of the IG's assets were to be formally seized and that officers were soon to be appointed to put Eisenhower's other recommendations into effect. The once great concern was to be broken up.

Although the process would actually take some years to complete legally and administratively, the principal consequence of this decision was the division of the IG along geographic lines, with the size and shape of surviving businesses corresponding broadly to the factories and works located in each occupation area. Thus Leverkusen and its satellite plants, which were all in the British zone, would form one entity; Ludwigshaven and Oppau in the French zone would form the basis of another; while the old Hoechst businesses around Frankfurt in the U.S. zone would form a third. Other plants in the East once run by the IG would be absorbed into the state-controlled economy of the Soviet Union.

What this meant in practice depended on how each of the big powers chose to interpret the major IG problem, namely, the extent of its involvement in Hitler's war. At first the Americans, no doubt influenced by the long-standing antipathy to the concern of its antitrust crusaders, seemed determined to take the strongest line. Even before the Allied Control Council had passed judgment on General Eisenhower's recommendations, the U.S. Army announced that it was going to blow up three explosives plants in the American zone, "the first of many hundreds of plants . . . designated for actual destruction." Ultimately, the U.S. military authorities were able to announce that the IG facilities in their area had been reestablished as forty-seven independent units, pending a final resolution of the matter. In the meantime, new antitrust laws prohibited a whole range of anticompetitive practices, from price and quota fixing to suppression of technology and invention.

But the tide of events was beginning to turn Allied opinion away from the idea that the IG's assets should be completely destroyed. For one thing, the attitude of Britain and France to the cartel's fragmentation was not as clear-cut; the economic circumstances in their zones were more difficult, and they found it harder to be so sanguine about the loss of the concern's productive capacity. The governments in London and Paris were finding responsibility for the economic well-being of millions of hungry Germans an onerous burden and were reluctant to deprive their former enemies of the chance to fend for themselves. Perhaps more significantly, the international situation was deteriorating. As the West and the Soviet Union moved to take up their cold war positions, conservative commentators in the United States had started to ask why the American authorities were so determined to break up an industry that might one day help Germany become a bulwark against Communist domination of Europe.

It was not the best atmosphere in which to try IG Farben's former managers for war crimes.

14

PREPARING THE CASE

The stadium had been badly damaged, but the sight of it could still send a shiver down the spine. Perhaps it was because the images from its heyday had been so deeply etched on the mind. For years the newsreels had faithfully recorded the ghastly choreographed pantomime that had taken place within its walls—the cathedral of searchlights, the flaming torches and banners, the outstretched hands and yearning faces. This was where the delusion had reached its apogee, where a nation had been led toward the abyss. The few visitors who came here nowadays wanted to know that it was really all over, to gain some reassurance that it could never happen again, but they often left feeling ill at ease, as though the echoes of marching feet had not yet faded and some fell spirit still lingered amongst the broken concrete and flourishing weeds.

Brigadier General Telford Taylor climbed up onto one of the ruined walls and looked across at the Altstadt, the old town. Nuremberg had once been an architectural treasure of gingerbread houses and medieval church spires. Now it was just one big bomb site, a sea of rubble that stretched almost as far as the eye could see.* On his first visit here, in April 1945, he'd been shocked by the damage, but he'd quickly become inured to it. After all, what were mere bricks and mortar compared with the suffering unleashed by those who had once draped this structure in eagles and swastikas? Fourteen years earlier, barely a mile or so from where he now stood, the newly appointed Nazi commissar for Franconia had issued orders that 250 Jewish tradesmen be arrested and "set to plucking the grass out of a field with their teeth." All had later been murdered.

Taylor shifted his gaze in the direction of one of the few buildings of any size still intact, the Palace of Justice. He could just make out its gabled roof in the far distance. For over two years he had labored there with hundreds of others to bring to account the perpetrators of the most shocking and brutal crimes in history. There had been some successes, some failures. Now he and his team were about to try again—this time to persuade a panel of judges that twenty-three of Germany's leading industrialists were guilty of starting an aggressive war, of looting the assets of other countries, of exploiting slave labor, and of mass murder. He knew that at least one of those defendants, but possibly several more, had attended the rallies that had once packed the field in front of him. The huge organization they worked for had given millions of marks to the leaders whose voices had once filled this stadium. And in return they had gained . . . what? Power, influence, financial stability, immunity from arrest? Whatever it was it hadn't been enough.

He stood there for a moment longer, lost in thought, and then started clambering down to the car and his patiently waiting driver. It was time to get to work.

FOR MOST PEOPLE the word *Nuremberg* is synonymous with the famous International Military Tribunal (IMT) that sat in judgment on

---

*The Royal Air Force had bombed Nuremberg heavily in January and March 1945. Then the city had been caught up in the fighting between the Germans and General Wade Haislip's Fifteenth Corps. Both sides had shelled each other's positions, causing immense damage.

twenty-one surviving members of the Nazi leadership in 1946. With one or two exceptions their names were familiar to the outside world, and if not they would soon become so. The events of that trial—the behind-the-scenes clashes between those determined on justice and those bent on retribution, the chilling revelations of barbarity and genocide, the successes and failures of prosecution and defense, the verdicts, sentences, and fates of the accused—have become part of the fabric of our understanding of the world's response to Nazism, the Holocaust, and World War II, and a point of reference, if not always a model, for the international community's attitude toward crimes against humanity in the years since.

But the IMT was only the first of many such prosecutions, trials, and tribunals, of differing degrees of complexity, fairness, integrity, and success, that sought to address aspects of Nazi criminality (and that have continued to do so until comparatively recently). Twelve of the earliest and arguably most significant of these hearings also took place at Nuremberg, under American jurisdiction, in the three years following the IMT. Some were designed to delve into the specifics of the Nazi's racially motivated inhumanity—the Einsatzgruppen's persecution of Soviet Jewry, for example—more deeply than had been possible at the earlier trial. Others were aimed at the Wehrmacht high command or at the Luftwaffe or tried to fathom the moral and ethical abyss at the heart of Nazi medical experimentation and euthanasia (the "Doctors' Trial"). Three of the trials were aimed at prosecuting industrialists associated with the Nazis: the Krupp case, the Flick case, and the IG Farben trial.* The first two of these were important enough. Krupp had been unstinting in its use and abuse of slave labor to make tanks and artillery for the Nazis and had such a clear commercial interest in the deployment of its products that a charge of conspiracy to launch an aggressive war was inevitable. Friedrich Flick, a steel and coal magnate, had contributed to Hitler's election fund in 1933, joined Himmler's Circle of Friends, seized businesses

---

*The Americans also contemplated prosecuting the directors of Siemens, Bosch (the electrical manufacturers), the Deutsche Bank, Mannesmann, and dozens of other German companies, but lack of judicial resources and political support made it impossible to assemble cases.

in occupied Europe, and made use of slave labor. Conditions down his mines were so bad that workers died in the thousands. But only the IG Farben case, involving one of the largest industrial conglomerates in the world, would have the scale to send a strong message about the crucial role of business in the tragedy Europe had just endured.

That such a message was sorely needed became clear when Allied zone governments began to disagree about denazification. This process, meant to excise the last remnants of Nazism from German life, had been accepted in principle at the end of the war and theoretically included removing former party supporters from any positions of power, influence, or respect. Each occupation authority, however, had a different interpretation on how denazification should be implemented. The Russians took the most robust view—as might be expected from the nation that had suffered most from Nazism. But the Americans, or at least those Americans running the U.S. military administration, were not far behind. General Lucius Clay, deputy governor under Eisenhower and charged with administering government affairs in the American zone, issued the draconian Law No. 8 of September 1945, which ordered the dismissal of any former Nazi Party member or sympathizer from all employment other than that of a common laborer.*

Although British officials publicly acceded to American requests that they apply this directive in their zone as well, privately they were determined to be less severe, convinced that rooting out and penalizing *every* Nazi sympathizer would make it impossible for the country to recover. Anyone who was directly involved in the regime or who

---

*The directive, which provoked widespread resentment among the German population, eventually proved too broad to be enforceable, although it did result in around 370,000 former Nazis being removed from their jobs before January 1947. By then, however, the Americans had begun turning over denazification proceedings in their zone to German tribunals and the rules were being more liberally interpreted. In 1950, a year after the Western zones of Germany had evolved into the Federal German Republic, U.S. High Commissioner John McCloy announced that 13 million people in the U.S. zone had been involved in denazification, with up to 930,000 subjected to some kind of penalty for their Nazi activities. Nevertheless, by that same year, many former Nazis had managed to find their way back into their old jobs—for example, around 85 percent of Nazi-era officials in Bavaria had been reinstated, and 60 percent of the civil servants of Baden-Württemberg were ex-Nazis.

had served in the SS or had committed a war crime should, of course, be sought out and held to account, but surely such treatment was not appropriate for all the petty officials and minor government servants—postmen, town clerks, teachers, junior policemen—who had joined the party only as a condition of employment. And what about all the ordinary shop assistants, bus drivers, and other workers who had voted for the Nazis or attended a party function or contributed part of their wages to a Nazi fund-raising initiative? Were they to be thrown out of work too? If the directive was taken to its logical conclusion it would apply to 90 percent of the adult German population, leaving almost no one in a job and the country so destitute that it would be relying on Allied handouts for generations. For Britain, this was an appalling prospect. Virtually bankrupted by six years of war, it was now spending around £80 million a year in food aid alone. The new Labour government had been forced to introduce bread rationing in the UK so that wheat could be diverted to Germany—something that hadn't even happened during the war. If denazification was going to work, Britain determined, it would have to be selectively applied.

This more pragmatic approach led some British administrators in Germany to take an unduly casual view of who was and was not a bad enough Nazi to be expelled from a position of authority—especially in the case of industry, which many officials saw as unconnected to politics or the military and therefore a long way down the priority list for denazification. The consequences of this leniency became evident in the autumn of 1946 when German trade unionists began complaining to their counterparts in Britain that Nazis were still running IG Farben factories. The Labour government in London could not ignore an appeal of this kind and asked the Allied Control Council to investigate. After just one survey, at the IG plant at Hüls, the council found ninety-nine senior employees who warranted immediate dismissal. Nevertheless the men were allowed to hang on to their jobs. Indeed, over the following twelve months, the number of committed Nazis at Hüls actually increased because those sacked from IG factories in the U.S. zone were given jobs there instead. London continued to complain about the situation, but British officials on the ground refused to act, stubbornly convinced that German industrialists were innocent of any wrongdoing and should be left to get on with the job of rebuilding the economy.*

This view, which was held with equal conviction by some conservative American critics of the U.S. military government, served only to encourage the legal team, working with the Subsequent Proceedings Division at Nuremberg, in their determination to bring IG executives and other business leaders to trial. They believed that unless it was shown that German industrialists had played a substantial role in bringing Hitler to power and taking the country to war, those industrialists might be tempted to try something similarly belligerent in the future. But the Republican Party had won a congressional majority in the election of late 1946, and now, led by the staunchly probusiness Senator Taft, right-wing members were beginning to express reservations about the need for additional tribunals in Germany when the real menace was Soviet Communism. The lawyers saw their window of opportunity closing and knew they had to move quickly to get the trials under way. Fortunately, their new chief was just the man to start things going.

IN MID-1945 TELFORD TAYLOR was still a reserve colonel in U.S. Army Intelligence. He had spent much of the war based at Bletchley Park, in southern England, the site of Britain's top-secret signal interception and code-breaking facility, which had played a significant role in defeating the Nazis by capturing and deciphering most of Germany's Enigma traffic—the encrypted military message system used by the Wehrmacht, SS, Luftwaffe, and German navy. Taylor's specific duty had been to guard the security of Ultra—as the Allies called the product of this code breaking—and oversee its distribution to the

---

*Many civil servants in the UK, especially at the Foreign Office, felt much the same and their influence gradually diminished any appetite the Labour administration may have had for an industrialists' trial in the British zone. This was despite the fact that Sir Hartley Shawcross and Elwyn Jones, the UK's two leading lawyers at the IMT, thought that German industry had a case to answer. As a result, the only Nazi company director ever convicted by the British was Bruno Tesch, of the Degesch sales agency Tesch and Stabenow, who had supplied Zyklon B to Auschwitz.

principal American army and air headquarters in Western Europe. It was a job of immense importance and responsibility that put Taylor in daily contact with the most important Allied secret of the war, and he won the Distinguished Service Medal for his performance.

But in civilian life Taylor was an attorney. For ten years after his graduation from Harvard Law School in 1932, he had held a succession of federal legal positions, including a spell in 1939 as special assistant to the attorney general. It was in that capacity that he met Justice Robert Jackson, a former attorney general who had been appointed to the Supreme Court; Taylor even argued a case in front of him on one occasion. Consequently, Taylor was not completely surprised when, on returning to England in late April 1945 from a trip to General Patton's headquarters, he found a message from his superiors at the War Department: Justice Jackson had been appointed by President Harry S. Truman to represent the United States at an international trial of war criminals that would be held when the war was over. He wanted Taylor to come work for him in Europe.

Taylor was at first unsure about accepting. Though Germany was on the verge of defeat, the war with Japan continued and he was hoping to be reassigned to the Pacific theater. He also wanted to spend some time in the United States—he had become involved with a married British woman and needed to sort out his own marital situation at home. During a brief trip back to America to think things through, he was told categorically by his superiors that the war in Japan would not last long (he later surmised he was being given a clear hint about the atomic bomb) and that he was free, either to take up Jackson's offer or to return to civilian life and the peace and quiet of private practice. He finally elected to go to Nuremberg.

"Certainly I was not moved by vengeful or anti-German feelings," he wrote later. "To be sure, I detested Nazism and had been in Germany a few weeks earlier when the Dachau and Buchenwald concentration camps were captured and the inmates liberated by American troops. But like so many others, I remained ignorant of the mass extermination camps in Poland and the full scope of the Holocaust did not dawn on me until several months later." His decision was based simply on his feeling that he was not ready to return to civilian life.

Indeed he would probably have joined any interesting American undertaking in Europe had it been offered.

AFTER A YEAR helping Jackson prosecute Göring, Hess, Speer, Ribbentrop, and the other top Nazi leaders, Telford Taylor understood a great deal more about the crimes of the Nazi regime and realized as well there was still much unfinished business. When his boss returned to the Supreme Court, Taylor accepted promotion to brigadier general and appointment as chief prosecutor for war crimes in Jackson's place. One of his principal ambitions was to go after the men he believed had played a fundamental role in taking Germany to war—the men who had run IG Farben. He was set on bringing them to justice.

He quickly discovered it would be no easy task. Prosecution lawyers had to be assembled, documentary evidence had to be gathered and collated, potential witnesses had to be tracked down and interviewed, decisions had to be taken as to exactly who should be indicted, what charges they would face, and what strategy should be followed to convince the court of their guilt. It was particularly important to get the last point right. Not long after he was appointed Taylor found out to his dismay that the judges being sent from the United States were not going to be of the first rank. He had hoped for federal judges at least, but Chief Justice Fred Vinson had decided their absence would be too disruptive to the judicial system back home. Instead the thirty men presiding over the trials that made up the Subsequent Proceedings at Nuremberg would be largely recruited from the faculties of law schools and from state courts, several of them from the conservative South and Midwest, with little or no experience or knowledge of international law, the recent history of Europe, or the complex issues involved. Although he was confident enough of their integrity, Taylor realized that developing arguments in front of such men was going to take patience and time and would make heavy demands on their powers of concentration.

As far as the mechanics were concerned, Taylor would be in overall charge of the prosecution and would do what he could to keep it on course, but as there would be several trials under his command (the

Krupp trial was to run almost simultaneously with the Farben trial, and others were in the pipeline), the day-to-day handling of each one would be delegated to a dedicated lead attorney. In the IG's case, that role fell to Josiah E. DuBois. Recruited away from his newly established private practice in Camden, New Jersey, DuBois had worked for the U.S. Treasury for much of the war, including a long period as chief counsel in charge of tracking down the enemy's financial assets. In that capacity he had gained an encyclopedic knowledge of IG Farben's overseas dealings and had traveled widely in his attempts to freeze its funds, sequester its property, and limit its influence on the U.S. economy. He had also acted as counsel to the War Refugee Board, a cabinet committee set up by President Franklin D. Roosevelt in 1943 to see what could be done to rescue Jewish victims of Nazi persecution. Stubborn, committed, and used to handling the complex detail of business cases, he seemed eminently qualified to take on the IG—although whether his comparative lack of recent criminal trial experience would be a handicap remained to be seen. To support him, DuBois had a young, idealistic team of lawyers, some not long out of Harvard Law School and others who had spent the previous year assisting at the first Nuremberg trial. There were too few of them—twelve in all—and they would have to work in cramped and ill-equipped offices spread throughout the Palace of Justice, but Taylor was convinced that their mix of experience and youthful energy would be enough to get them through.

THE TEAM ENCOUNTERED obstacles right from the start. Putting together the broad outlines of a case against the IG may have seemed straightforward enough but getting the evidence to back it up was more difficult, as DuBois discovered on the evening he arrived at Nuremberg. He was met at the plane by two of his new colleagues, Drexel Sprecher and Belle Mayer. Sprecher had been at Nuremberg for several months and had worked as one of Justice Jackson's administrative assistants during the Göring trial. Mayer was a more recent appointment but knew DuBois from a stint at the Treasury; indeed she had recommended that Telford Taylor approach him when an earlier nominee for lead prosecutor had been called home. On the drive back through the unlit streets of the bomb-shattered city the two lawyers explained that while thousands of IG documents had been recovered, mainly from among the cache Ernst Struss had taken from Frankfurt to Griesheim a year earlier, most of them were of only general relevance.

Then Mayer told DuBois of a visit to Berlin she'd made a few days earlier. She was looking for the IG's NW7 offices but when she arrived she found the building in ruins and no documents anywhere to be seen. She then picked up a rumor that the Russians had taken them away for storage in an abandoned castle at Gross Behnitz, near Berlin. The two GIs she sent to investigate had found a sealed room—sealed, according to the on-site guard, on the orders of Swedish diplomats— but they broke in anyway and found it empty. Just why the Swedes had locked the room was a complete mystery and when their legation was contacted they denied all knowledge of the affair, as did the Russians. Mayer could only surmise that either the rumor had been false or perhaps Hermann Schmitz, who reportedly had a large personal fortune in Sweden, had somehow used his influence to spirit them away to some other location. To be on the safe side, Mayer had arranged for yet more GIs to take a steam shovel to the NW7 site to sift through the rubble, but she wasn't hopeful of finding anything.

The empty room was only one of many such dead ends. Investigators had also followed up reports that Max Ilgner had arranged for two railcars full of documents to be taken from Berlin to the Hoechst plant at Frankfurt. They had unearthed a rail docket for the journey but no documents. Nor was there yet any trace of paperwork from Auschwitz. They suspected that Walter Dürrfeld and Max Faust had destroyed some of it in the days before IG staff had been evacuated, but surely other documents would have been brought back to Germany. Where they may have gotten to was anyone's guess. Even the photograph album of Auschwitz that Major Tilley had reported seeing in Hermann Schmitz's personal safe had now disappeared.

For several months, frustrated prosecutors chased here and there across Germany in search of files that they knew from impounded indices had once existed but had now vanished into thin air. Indeed it wasn't until the trial was well under way that Duke Minskoff, one of the prosecution team, stumbled on clear evidence of what might have happened to them. Like DuBois a former Treasury Department lawyer, Minskoff had spent a few months in Germany in 1945 on the trail of the personal assets of the Nazi leadership. On that trip he had famously managed to get Göring's wife, Emma, to reveal the whereabouts of $500,000 worth of jewels and precious stones and a large amount of cash that the Reich marshal had hidden away as a nest egg. But the IG case was refusing to reveal its secrets. Minskoff and his colleagues had been obsessed by the missing papers, but all his attempts to track them down had ended in failure. Then one day during a routine visit to the IG storage facility at Griesheim he got a break: a junior IG staff member let slip that truckloads of documents had been sent to Ludwigshafen in late 1946. The U.S. officer in charge then admitted, somewhat shamefacedly, that he had sanctioned the shipments on the understanding that they were exclusively technical papers and patents needed for manufacturing purposes.

The lawyer hurried down to Ludwigshafen and asked the French plant overseers to order IG clerks to check the files. After a long wait, he learned that some documents had indeed been delivered but they had been sent to the purchasing department for destruction. Minskoff talked next to the purchasing manager, who admitted that he had been given eighteen crates of documents but that they had all since been pulped and recycled because there was a paper shortage. Besides, the documents were nothing but orders and invoices for equipment at Ludwigshafen, he insisted, and thus were of no possible value. A search of his department, however, revealed that he had kept some of the empty file folders. When Minskoff looked at them he found ten that were marked with the word *Auschwitz*.

His tail now up, the lawyer finally persuaded one of Otto Ambros's secretaries to talk. Eventually she admitted that from early 1946, when Ambros was first brought to Ludwigshafen by the French, until May 1947, when they reluctantly handed him over to the Americans, the IG director had used his office as a gathering point for all sorts of records sent from IG divisions elsewhere. These had subsequently been destroyed. Ambros had also conducted a lengthy secret correspondence with other IG executives, using code names to get the letters past the French and American censors. She couldn't remember all the names, but she knew that Walter Dürrfeld had been Heribert, Max Faust had been Posth, Christian Schneider was Muth, while Carl Wurster was Stutt. Ambros himself had been Bargemann. She then described how on one specific occasion in early 1947 she and other panicking IG staff had deliberately frustrated prosecution document hunters.

> When, on 20 February, I saw a car that obviously belonged to the Nuremberg trials standing in front of the Ludwigshafen plant, I ordered my assistant, Miss Reither, to hide all the documents, which seemed to me to be of importance. Miss Reither took the documents one floor higher and wanted to put them into the wardrobe of an employee, a Mr. Kern. Mr. Kern did not want to have the documents in his wardrobe and thus they were hidden in a wall cupboard. I then called the apartment of Dr. Alt [Ambros's personal assistant] and gave orders to hide one box there.

The papers, she insisted, had since been destroyed

Not every trail led down a cul-de-sac. Just before the case went to trial, the indefatigable Belle Mayer, who had never completely given up on the IG's Berlin office papers, unearthed a U.S. Army shipping docket at the old Farben headquarters in Frankfurt. It turned out that in late May 1945, shortly after joining up with the Russians in Berlin, an American combat unit had impounded a mass of documents from the NW7 address, part of a general sweep of every official-looking building they could find. The papers had been sent back to the War Department in Washington with thousands of other captured files and were dumped, unsorted and unchecked, into an army warehouse in Alexandria. Then they were promptly forgotten.

Cheered on by Telford Taylor and Josiah DuBois, Mayer took the next available flight to the States. She called DuBois a few days later. A preliminary search had uncovered hundreds of potentially incriminating documents, including a mass of procurement orders from the Wehrmacht to the IG. The find was by no means everything they were looking for but it was certainly a massive boost to their case.

The documents were shipped back to Germany and along with thousands of others—memos, reports, letters, telegrams, and accounts—were translated and painstakingly reviewed by the lawyers and their assistants.

Paper evidence wasn't everything, of course. The prosecution team also traveled many thousands of miles across war-shattered Europe looking for witnesses whose testimony might be useful. They even flew to Britain to find POWs who had managed to live through the SS march out of Auschwitz. Some, like Denis Avey, were just too devastated by their experiences to talk to them, but they interviewed several others. They also managed to track down a handful of Jewish survivors who had somehow emerged from the camps, against all the odds, and all the owners and managers of the factories in occupied Europe taken over by the IG. Then they went in search of Germans—former IG workers, whom they thought might be willing to testify, civil servants, Wehrmacht officers, chemical industry experts, and hundreds of others whose recollections might be important. And every day the prosecutors asked themselves, "Do we have enough to secure convictions?"

It was a good question. After four months, DuBois still was not completely sure he had a winnable case. It wasn't that the evidence didn't exist; his lawyers had actually pieced together a remarkably full and damaging record of IG Farben's relationship with the regime. But he also knew this trial would be like no other at Nuremberg. The IG executives were about as far removed from the stereotypical view of jackbooted Nazis as it was possible to get. To any neutral observer they would come over as well-educated, respectable, conservative businessmen and scientists—one of them had even won a Nobel Prize. To put such men into the dock in front of judges who had led a comparatively sheltered life in provincial America, one had to be absolutely sure that their sophisticated veneer could be broken down. The proof had to be compelling.

MUCH WOULD CENTER on the validity of the very first statements the IG executives had made to officials in the days after their arrest.

Some of these could be construed as highly incriminating but it was hard to know whether they would be accepted in court. U.S. Army teams had arrested most of the men well before the prosecution was appointed, and the initial interviews had been carried out in less than ideal conditions. None of the men's statements had been made under oath and there was always a chance that some of them might be contested on the grounds that they were made under duress—an issue of particular significance because the case was going to be fought under American law and the Fifth Amendment would apply. By the time the prosecutors got around to interviewing the men again, they had been able to consult their lawyers. Now, when they deigned to answer questions at all, their answers were either noncommittal or strongly worded rebuttals of prosecution attempts to get them to admit any wrongdoing: They had been acting under orders, they said. Hitler's grip on power had been such that no one dared oppose him or his Nazi henchmen. They had joined the party only because not to do so would have made them liable to investigation by the Gestapo. If foreign workers had been subjected to abuse, they had nothing to do with it. No, they hadn't known that people were being murdered at Auschwitz. No, they were not in the least bit anti-Semitic and had always worked to help their Jewish employees. No, they had not stolen foreign companies' assets. Any foreign takeovers they were involved in were legitimate business transactions. No, they hadn't supplied medicines for medical experiments. A chemical weapons program? Nonsense, that was something that the army had pursued on its own. . . . The uniform responses showed that a carefully coordinated defense strategy was being prepared: Say nothing. Admit nothing. If the Americans think they have a case, let them prove it. But do not incriminate yourself.

None of this came as much of a surprise: the prosecutors had always expected they would encounter blanket denials as the trial approached. They also knew, however, that it would be easier to break the defendants down under cross-examination if their earliest statements could be turned back against them. Particularly crucial were the answers given by Georg von Schnitzler, head of the IG's all-important Commercial Committee, who in 1945 had clearly felt some remorse and had admitted his own "mistakes" before pointing a finger at his fellow directors and the cartel as a whole. On one occasion he had blurted out, "The IG took on a great responsibility and gave, in the chemical sector, substantial and even decisive aid for Hitler's foreign policy which led to war and the ruination of Germany. . . . I must conclude that IG is largely responsible for the policies of Hitler." Statements such as this from one of the concern's most senior figures were highly damaging, especially when they were backed up with his detailed recollections of the IG's role in the Four-Year Plan, its takeover of plants in Poland and France, and its use of slave labor.

But von Schnitzler had begun to vacillate under pressure from the other defendants. The shortage of suitable prison accommodations and the need to have the IG executives on hand to answer questions had meant that the prosecution wasn't always able to keep the men apart. By the spring of 1947, Georg von Schnitzler had cumulatively spent many weeks in the company of his old colleagues, and some of them had made it plain what they thought of his candid responses to the Americans. The icily intimidating Fritz ter Meer had given him an especially difficult time, confronting him several times, often in front of the others, claiming that because von Schnitzler was not an all-round chemist he was ill equipped to make statements on behalf of the company as a whole and should keep his mouth shut.

As a result, the baron had begun having second thoughts. In April he sent a message to DuBois saying that he was withdrawing his early statements because he "had not been technically qualified" to say many of the things he had said. Furthermore, he added, he had "been in a state of intense mental depression in 1945."

The news left many in the prosecution team wondering if their case had been irreparably damaged. If von Schnitzler could show that his statements had been made under pressure, the court would not admit them into evidence. Drexel Sprecher quickly managed to get in to see the baron, found out that ter Meer had bullied him, and promised to keep them apart in the future. This seemed to reassure von Schnitzler and after a few days' reflection he contacted the lawyers once again to say that his early statements had been accurate after all. But whether he could be relied upon to stick to this position in the weeks and months ahead, or indeed if his lawyers would let him, was now open to doubt.

ON MAY 4, 1947, the prosecution staff swallowed their anxieties and finally filed an indictment on behalf of the United States against twenty-four IG executives: Carl Krauch, in his position as chairman of the *Aufsichtsrat*; Hermann Schmitz, as chairman of the *Vorstand*; all the members of the managing board (Georg von Schnitzler, August von Knieriem, Heinrich Hörlein, Fritz ter Meer, Christian Schneider, Fritz Gajewski, Otto Ambros, Heinrich Bütefisch, Ernst Bürgin, Hans Kühne, Carl Lautenschläger, Friedrich Jaehne, Carl Wurster, Heinrich Oster, Paul Haefliger, Max Ilgner, Wilhelm Mann, and Max Brügge-mann); and four other IG officials deemed especially culpable—Walter Dürrfeld, for his role in Auschwitz; Heinrich Gattineau, who ran the *Wipo* (the Department of Economic Policy) under Max Ilgner at Berlin NW7; Erich von der Heyde, the IG's liaison man with the Ab-wehr; and Hans Kugler, who had managed the IG's newly acquired plants in occupied Europe.*

The defendants were charged on five separate counts, including "planning, preparation, initiation, and waging of wars of aggression and invasions of other countries"; "plunder and soliation"; and "slavery and mass murder." The first covered the IG's financial and political association with the Nazis—namely, participation in the war planning of the high command; participation in the economic mobilization for war; participation in propaganda, intelligence, and espionage activities; preparation for and participation in the execu-tion of Nazi aggression and benefiting from the spoils thereof; and production and stockpiling of war materials. Under "plunder and spoliation," the indictment charged that that the IG had with the Wehrmacht played a major role in Germany's program of acquisition by conquest, intending specifically to take over the chemical industries

*Some of these names may still be unfamiliar: Heinrich Oster was manager of the Europe-an nitrogen syndicate and had been an early proponent of cooperation with the Nazis; Max Brüggemann had been secretary to the *Vorstand* but was later severed from the trial for ill health.

of Austria, Poland, Czechoslovakia, France, Norway, Russia, and other countries.

The count for "slavery and mass murder" was the most crucial and the most shocking to the outside world: "All of the defendants, acting though the instrumentality of IG Farbenindustrie, participated in . . . the enslavement of concentration camp inmates, . . . the use of prisoners of war in war operations, . . . and the mistreatment, terrorization, torture, and murder of enslaved persons."

At Auschwitz, the indictment went on to explain, the IG had

> abused its slave workers by subjecting them, among other things, to excessively long, arduous and exhausting work, utterly disregarding their health or physical condition. The sole criterion of the right to live or die was the production efficiency of said inmates. By virtue of inadequate rest, inadequate food, and because of inadequate quarters (which consisted of a bed of polluted straw, shared by from two to four inmates), many died at their work or collapsed from serious illness there contracted. With the first sign of a decline in the productivity of any such workers, although caused by illness or exhaustion, such workers would be subject to the well-known *Selektion*. *Selektion*, in its simplest definition, meant that if, upon a cursory examination, it appeared that the inmate would not be restored within a few days to full productive capacity, he was considered expendable and was sent to the Birkenau camp of Auschwitz for the customary extermination. . . . The working conditions at the Farben Buna plant were so severe and unendurable that very often inmates were driven to suicide by either dashing through the guards and provoking death by rifle shot or hurling themselves into the high-tension electrically charged barbed wire fences. As a result of these conditions the labor turnover in the Buna plant in one year amounted to at least 300 percent.

With the other charges (membership in criminal organizations such as the SS and a catchall count of "crimes against peace"), the sixty-page document amounted to a powerful and compelling denunciation of IG Farben's twelve-year-long association with Hitler and the Nazis, a relationship that the defendants, being brought together again in Nuremberg from their prisons across Germany, would struggle to explain away. The indictment had not been easy to put together and more time and more resources would have improved it, but DuBois felt it was an excellent basis on which to launch a trial.

But he barely had time to enjoy his satisfaction before he was confronted with a new problem, this time emanating from the United States. He was aware that low-level political opposition to the IG case had been bubbling away in conservative Washington circles from the moment the prosecution team had begun work in 1946, but now it suddenly began to take an altogether more hostile form. On July 9, 1947, Congressman George A. Dondero of Michigan launched a stinging attack on the floor of the House of Representatives against Secretary of War John Patterson, castigating him for his failure to root out "Communist sympathizers" infiltrating key U.S. Army posts. One of the ten "sympathizers" he identified was Josiah DuBois, whom he described as "a known left winger from the Treasury Department who had been a close student of the Communist party line."

Having never been a Communist, DuBois was outraged at the slur, which he came across in *Stars and Stripes* newspaper while sipping his morning coffee. He issued an immediate denial through the Nuremberg press corps and challenged the congressman to repeat the statement outside the House, where he would no longer be immune to a libel charge—a gauntlet that the politician declined to pick up. It was only later that day that DuBois figured out what lay behind Dondero's comment. His closer perusal of the congressman's list of sympathizers showed that five of the other men named had worked at one time or another on U.S. government investigations of the IG. The full transcript of Dondero's comments only confirmed his suspicions: the congressman had specifically linked his comments to those "who had been trying to blacken the name of IG Farben." From there it was easy enough to put two and two together. DuBois remembered that Dondero's congressional district contained the headquarters of Dow Chemical. A few weeks earlier American newspapers had reported a rumor that the prosecution team had been looking into possible links between Dow and the IG. Clearly someone didn't want that connection brought up at the trial.

The timing of the attack could not have been worse, coinciding as it did with the arrival in Nuremberg of the judges assigned to the IG case. DuBois was mortified to see one of them, Justice Curtis G. Shake, reading the offending edition of *Stars and Stripes* in the lobby of the Palace of Justice. But at least the prosecution team now had an opportunity to assess the strengths and weaknesses of the men who would be weighing the merits of their case. First impressions were reassuring enough. Shake, who would be the tribunal's presiding judge, came from Vincennes, Indiana, where he had been chief justice of the state supreme court; Judge James Morris was from the supreme court of North Dakota; Judge Paul Hebert had been dean of Louisiana State University's law school; while Clarence F. Merrell, the "alternate" judge who would sit on the bench but take no part unless one of the others pulled out, was a veteran of the state circuit in Indiana. They all seemed intelligent and experienced practitioners of the law. Nevertheless, DuBois could not help feeling a little uneasy at a casual remark made by Morris when the prosecution team met the judges for lunch: "We have to worry about the Russians now; it wouldn't surprise me if they overran the courtroom before we get through."

DuBois spent the last few weeks of July 1947 refining his court strategy and running it past Telford Taylor at his house on the Linden Strasse in Dambach, a tiny village on the western outskirts of Nuremberg, and then over lunches with his team at the newly repaired Grand Hotel. If Taylor felt any anxiety, he showed no signs of it. He would be making the opening presentation to the court, setting the scene for what was to come, and while he had some private reservations about his deputy's proposed approach he knew that the prosecutors had amassed some impressive evidence. He also knew that the quality of the judges he had been sent was variable, to say the least, and that until the trial was under way there was no knowing how the arguments would play with them. Having delegated the running of the case to DuBois and his team, he had to trust their judgment. All he could do now was get them off to the strongest possible start.

15

TRIAL

There is more to being a successful trial lawyer than the ability to deliver a persuasive speech; nevertheless, as General Telford Taylor was demonstrating in the main courtroom of the Palace of Justice at Nuremberg, it is a useful skill to possess. His audience could hardly have been more attentive. Some four hundred people—judges, attorneys, court officials, the public and press—had listened, spellbound, as he outlined the case against the accused in powerful and dramatic terms, and now he was drawing his opening peroration to a close: "The defendants will, no doubt, tell us that they were merely overzealous, and possibly misguided, patriots. . . ."

Taylor paused for a moment and cast a dismissive glance at the twenty-three men in the dock. This was time-honored lawyer's artifice, but no less effective for that. He was letting the court know that he had already worked out the defense strategy and that he didn't think much of it: "We will hear it said that all they planned to do was what any patriotic businessman would have done under similar circumstances. . . . As for the carnage of war and the slaughter of innocents, these were the regrettable deeds of Hitler and the Nazis, to whose dictatorship they, too, were subject."

But the prosecution, Taylor went on, would show the defendants' claims of innocence to be hollow and untrue. The accused had been willing participants in the Nazi project and it was now up to the court to hold them to account, as they themselves had once judged others.

> They judged themselves alone as fit to sway the destiny of the world. They judged themselves entitled to subjugate and to command. They judged the Jew, the Pole, and the Russian to be untouchable. All their judgments sprang from a bottomless vanity and an insatiable ambition which exalted their own power as the supreme and only good. They rendered and executed those arrogant pronouncements with whip and sword. There is hardly a country in Europe that escaped the carnage which these men loosed, and the day will surely come when their own countrymen will fully grasp what a catastrophic abomination they worked for Germany. It is no act of vengeance, but an inescapable and solemn duty, to test the conduct of these men by the laws and commandments which they dared to disavow.

After Taylor had finished and DuBois and Drexel Sprecher had run through a technical outline of how the case would be laid out, the judges adjourned for the day and filed out of the room. In those few quiet seconds, before the press rushed to the rail and started clamoring for their attention, the lawyers around the prosecution desk shared a moment of intense relief and satisfaction. Belle Mayer had tears rolling down her face. "I didn't think this day would ever come," she said.

It was August 27, 1947. The IG Farben trial was finally under way.

THE PROSECUTION CASE may have opened well, but within days it was running into problems. The lawyers' aim had been to make sure that the judges fully grasped the nature and structure of the organization the accused men worked for. The IG was far more than just an ordinarily successful and profitable business; it was also the sum of a vast and complex network of partnerships, subsidiaries, syndicates, cartels, and production agreements, which together allowed the concern to exercise enormous power and influence at home and abroad—often more than individual governments. An appreciation of this point was central to the prosecution's argument, essential to understanding the means, motive, and opportunity the defendants had to commit their crimes.

To illustrate this argument the prosecution set up huge charts and diagrams at one end of the court, detailing the scale and spread of the IG empire, and introduced into evidence a mass of supporting reports, correspondence, patent licenses, and other corporate documents—each of which was formally noted and translated by the German and English interpreters. Expert witnesses from the international chemical industry were then called to explain it all.

On paper this approach may have seemed sensible enough, and certainly it would have worked well in some of the big antitrust cases that DuBois and others had fought in the past. But at Nuremberg it was a big tactical error. The men on the bench had come to Germany expecting to conduct a trial for war crimes but instead they were being asked to sit through a laborious lecture on business organization. The presiding judge, Curtis Shake, began to grumble about the relevance of the testimony, but the prosecution, replying that it was vital for the court to understand the power the defendants had commanded, carried on with its seminar. Eventually Justice Morris lost patience.

> Mr. Prosecutor, this organization, so far as records show here, was simply a big chemical, commercial, and business concern, the like of which there are many throughout the world. Speaking for myself only, I am at a complete loss to comprehend where documents of this kind are of the slightest materiality to the charges. This trial is being slowed down by mass of contracts, minutes, and letters that seem to have such a slight bearing on any possible concept of proof in this case.

Fortunately for the lawyers, Justice Hebert, the Louisiana academic, and the alternate judge, Clarence Merrell, were more sympathetic and their willingness to sit through any evidence that DuBois and his colleagues thought relevant allowed the case to continue on as they had planned. But over the following weeks it became impossible not to notice that the other two judges were hardening against them.

A particular low point came when the focus shifted specifically to IG Farben's involvement in Nazi rearmament. Using the documents rescued from the Alexandria warehouse, the prosecutors worked their way, at exhaustive length, through Carl Krauch's relationship with Göring and the Four-Year Plan, the important role played by Berlin NW7, Max Ilgner, and the *Vermittlungstelle Wehrmacht* (Army Liaison Office), the dramatic expansion of the IG's production capacity and its switch into the manufacture of strategic war materials. The pretrial statements of Georg von Schnitzler were especially key to this part of the case but their admission into evidence was fiercely contested by defense lawyers, who predictably argued that he had been mentally unfit at the time he made them and that his "coercion" was in contravention of the Fifth Amendment. The prosecution countered with the baron's written confirmation to Drexel Sprecher that "the relationship between the investigators and me in Frankfurt in 1945 was very free, open, and very cordial." Von Schnitzler himself said nothing, nor did his counsel, content for now to leave the matter in the hands of judges, who were clearly not favoring the prosecution. After days of haggling between the two sides, Curtis Shake announced that he would defer a decision until later in the trial, when he had had time to consider the merit of the statements. But he hinted strongly that unless Schnitzler were to take the stand, which he was under no obligation to do, his remarks could not be held to apply to the other defendants. The ruling was a long way from the positive decision that the prosecution needed and left its case in temporary disarray.

Meanwhile, away from court, there was yet more criticism coming from the United States. On November 27, 1947, Congressman John E. Rankin of Mississippi declared on the floor of the House of Representatives: "What is taking place in Nuremberg, Germany, is a disgrace. . . . Every other country has now washed its hands and withdrawn from this saturnalia of persecution. But a racial minority, two and half years after the war closed, are in Nuremberg not only hanging German soldiers but trying German businessmen in the name of the United States." By now, though, Taylor's lawyers were getting used to remarks of this kind; indeed they had heard them in Nuremberg itself. On one occasion Josiah DuBois was told that one of the judges had said publicly, "There are too many Jews on the prosecution," and had wanted to know if he, DuBois, was Jewish. On another, Drexel Sprecher was attacked at the bar of the Grand Hotel by an assistant to one of the judges for being too "anti-German." The lawyers just had to hope that such views did not truly represent the judges' feelings. But they could not help but be discomfited when they found out that Justice Morris's wife, who had accompanied him to Nuremberg, was in the habit of inviting the wives of IG directors out for drinks.

And so the case ground on, only noticeably engaging more of Morris's attention when it got to the IG's takeovers of businesses in occupied territories. Clearly the violation of private property was more in line with his American juridical values than much of what had gone before, although he complained again about "this case becoming bogged down by a lot of irrelevant evidence" when the prosecution wanted to introduce documents to show exactly how the IG had camouflaged its intentions in Czechoslovakia. It had become a common theme of his: "We are supposed to conduct a speedy trial. . . . It seems to me that when the record of trial is reviewed, if it is too long and complicated, the responsibility will primarily lie with the prosecution."

Testimony from witnesses was usually received with more interest. It was hard, for example, for any neutral observer to remain unmoved by Maurcy Szpilfogel's account of how his factory was confiscated by the IG, his failed attempts to get help from Georg von Schnitzler, his subsequent incarceration in the Warsaw ghetto by the SS, and the deportation of his wife and children. With the help of gentile friends Szpilfogel eventually managed to escape his confinement and spent more than two years hiding out on Warsaw rooftops. From there, in the spring of 1943, he had watched the ghetto's final annihilation.

FOR THE DEFENDANTS, each day in court was much like the next. Most weekdays they were woken at dawn by the U.S. Army guards, given a modest breakfast, and then escorted through the covered walkway that joined the cellblock to the Palace of Justice, where proceedings began at 9:30 a.m. And there they would sit, apart from short recesses and an hourlong break at lunch, until Curtis Shake called a halt at around 4.30 p.m. At first, despite a few outward displays of bravado, most had been obviously nervous and intimidated by their surroundings. They were being tried in the same second-floor courtroom that had seen the convictions of Göring, Hess, Speer, and the other leading Nazis a year earlier, and the knowledge that several of those defendants had been hanged was probably enough to frighten any man charged with similar crimes. Indeed, the prosecution, whether deliberately or not, had added to this disquieting similitude by allocating the men seats in the dock according to their status and position in the IG, much as their predecessors had been seated according to their rank in the Nazi hierarchy.

Inevitably the defendants became accustomed to the daily ritual, and as the weeks went by the prosecutors noticed that the men in the dock no longer listened with avidity to every word said in court, nor did they seem to find the proceedings threatening. Occasionally one would sigh ostentatiously or shake his head as a prosecutor got the name of a chemical procedure wrong or a witness stumbled over his testimony. When one of them was called out to answer questions, the others would lean forward more expectantly and follow the exchange with furrowed brows, smiling in quiet approbation when he scored a particularly telling point or pursing their lips as he was tripped up in cross-examination. In truth, the defendants were rarely tripped up, because they all stuck broadly to the same line: they were merely simple, patriotic businessmen or scientists engaged in tasks for the benefit of others. Every incriminating document had an alternative explanation; every prosecution witness was misguided or sadly misinformed. When the questioning became too rigorous they fell back on simple protestations of ignorance. No, they had never seen the report the prosecution was referring to. No, they had no recollection of that meeting. If one of their colleagues had told them such a thing, they could not remember it. It was all such a long time ago. And then, when released from the stand, they would go back to their places in

384 · HELL'S CARTEL

the dock and, after a few whispered asides to their colleagues, reassume their pose of slightly weary detachment. It was as though they were being forced to sit through shareholders' questions at an annual general meeting, a tiresome duty that had to be endured.

But twenty-three men, especially men who had sometimes been keen rivals in the past, could not spend months in one another's company without some cracks beginning to show. Prosecutors soon realized that Carl Krauch, who was sitting in the same seat that Hermann Göring had once occupied, was being ignored by many of the others—presumably because they preferred not to be tarnished by his close association with his Nazi mentor. The exception was Max Ilgner, who still seemed in awe of his colleague's former position in the Reich and often tried to engage him in conversation. But then Ilgner kowtowed as well to his uncle Hermann Schmitz, even though he was also now a much reduced figure. Habit, more than respect, forced the others to step aside as the *Vorstand* chairman entered and left the court, and some shook their heads at his ill-fitting suit and unkempt goatee beard as though his disheveled appearance were letting them down, but Ilgner would often rush to hold the door open for him and carry his papers. Fritz ter Meer, however, seemed to exercise the most authority, dominating many of their huddled conversations over lunch and during the brief walk to and from court. He largely ignored von Schnitzler now that the question of his pretrial testimony was apparently no longer so crucial, but when he learned that Schmitz might have made damaging admissions as well (for example, during an early pretrial interrogation Schmitz had conceded it was "absolutely clear" the IG's swollen profits were due to Hitler's armaments program), ter Meer wrote to the American authorities in an attempt to discredit his former boss's recall of events. In regard to one statement Schmitz had reportedly made about the Berlin NW7 office's close relationship with the Wehrmacht, ter Meer wrote that it "had caused great concern among the entire group of IG Farben leaders since it was believed that it contained wrong conclusions." He helpfully offered to set the record straight.

Josiah DuBois got an insight into just how keen Fritz ter Meer was to "set the record straight" when he and Jan Charmatz, a Czech legal associate attached to the prosecution team, were walking around the Palace of Justice grounds after dinner one night. A figure approached them out of the dark. It was Erich Berndt, ter Meer's attorney. To the lawyers' considerable astonishment, he asked for their help "with a little problem." Clearly embarrassed, he then took a step to one side to reveal his client, who was calmly smoking a cigarette and studiously avoiding their eyes. Unknown to the prosecution, the judges had allowed him to leave the jail, unguarded but in the company of his lawyer, in order that he might visit Frankfurt to pick up some papers connected to his defense. Unfortunately, Berndt explained, the new night guard at the front gate of the jail hadn't recognized them on their return and wouldn't let the IG executive back in. Could they help?

Not knowing whether to explode in fury or collapse in laughter, the prosecutors promised to do all they could to ensure ter Meer's readmission. Before he was led back to his cell, he bowed and thanked them gravely for their assistance.

It was only much later that DuBois found out what ter Meer had actually been doing in Frankfurt. Instead of looking for his papers, he had angrily summoned Ernst Struss, his former assistant, and confronted him with rumors that Struss had given the prosecution an affidavit saying that he, ter Meer, had known of the slave conditions at Auschwitz. Was this true?

"I only told them," Struss replied, "that in 1943 I had asked you why so many people were being gassed and burned at Auschwitz."

Ter Meer shot to his feet. "You what? You told them that!"

He then tried to persuade Struss that had he ever been asked such a thing, he surely would have told Struss not to pay any attention to rumors. But Struss insisted on sticking to his story. In fact, as far as he could recollect, ter Meer had just ignored him back in 1943, presumably because he knew they were not rumors at all.

Whether Berndt knew about this blatant attempt to influence a witness is not clear, but for the sixty or so defense lawyers the question of Auschwitz and what the defendants knew about it was always going to be a major problem. They had grasped, of course, that at least two of the judges were not well disposed toward DuBois and his team, and they had deliberately added to the judges' irritation by making their own considerable fuss over the complexity and supposed irrelevance of the evidence that was being introduced in court. The intention was plainly to convince the judges that the U.S. case lacked clarity and focus. The prosecution's strategy had been predicated on showing that the defendants had known in advance of Hitler's plans to launch an aggressive war of conquest and had been willing and active accomplices in achieving that aim. Everything else the IG had done followed from this original complicity: its propaganda and espionage on the regime's behalf, its production of war goods, its spoliation and plunder of invaded countries, its role in slave labor and the concentration camps. But the defense consistently challenged the prosecution's interpretation of events, questioned the relevance of its evidence, and portrayed the accused as misguided patriots who had merely been following orders. By thus exploiting any doubt in the judges' minds, the defense hoped to secure acquittals.

AUSCHWITZ THREATENED to undermine the defense's plan. The whole world now knew of the part that the camps had played in the Nazis' attempts to exterminate the Jewish race. The genocide was so shocking, so dreadful that anyone or anything associated with it could not fail to be tarnished. If the judges believed the allegations about the IG's involvement in slavery, torture, selection, and murder, their disgust might be so great that their uncertainty about other aspects of the prosecution case would fall away. Auschwitz was going to make or break the case.

Several of the prosecution team had come to the same conclusion and now realized that it had been a mistake not to begin the trial with the slavery and murder count. Indeed both Drexel Sprecher and Duke Minskoff urged Josiah DuBois to change tack. As Minskoff said of the judges, "Then they will see what kind of men they are trying and they'll understand the rest of it. We should have started with Auschwitz on the first day." But DuBois believed that it wasn't that simple. Everything in the case—witnesses, documentary evidence— had been set up to follow the order of the counts in the indictment. To stop and start again would cause expense, confusion, disruption, and delay that would only infuriate the impatient judges still further.

As a result, the most important moment of the trial wasn't reached for several months; but it also meant that when that moment arrived, it did do so with a bang. The prosecution had found a host of credible witnesses prepared to testify in support of the slavery and mass murder charges—Jewish survivors, former POWs, doctors, conscience-stricken IG employees—and had gathered written affidavits from scores more. They now began to reveal them in court.

The Norwegian Kai Feinberg told the court how his father and uncles had died:

> We unloaded boxcars, iron poles and bags containing cement, as well as heavy ovens. On 5 January 1943, my father was already so weakened that when we had to drag a 50-kilogram bag at doubled pace he collapsed before my very eyes. He was carried to the camp by his comrades. He had been beaten constantly by the guards, and this most severely on the last day. . . . He died in my presence on 7 January 1943. One brother of my father injured his right arm during work, and he was gassed. The second brother of my father had become so weak that he died while at work, about one or two weeks after my father in Buna. I myself was able to stand the work until 15 January 1943; then I contracted pneumonia.

Ervin Schulhof, a Czech inmate, testified about the concern's involvement in selections:

> The master craftsman made the complaint to the management, and from there the complaint was forwarded to the SS. Consequently the labor-allocation officer went to Monowitz early in the morning when the squads left for work, posted himself near the gate, and picked out those people whom they considered sickly. These people were sent straight away [to Birkenau]. Those written complaints came from the IG. I myself have seen such reports.

Leon Staischak, a Polish inmate, was a male nurse in the camp infirmary: "The hospital of the IG Camp Monowitz had merely the task of repairing tools. . . . Prisoners were not permitted to remain in the hospital longer than two weeks. Prisoners who were too weak or sick to be restored within two weeks were picked out."

Then there was Rudolf Vitek, a doctor and an inmate: "The prisoners were pushed in their work by the kapos, foremen, and overseers of the IG in an inhuman way. No mercy was shown. Thrashings, ill treatment of the worst kind, even outright killings were the norm. The murderous working speed was responsible for the fact that, while working, many prisoners suddenly stretched out flat, gasped for breath, and died like beasts."

British POWs Robert Ferris, Leonard Dales, Frederick Davidson, Eric Doyle, John Adkin, Bert Seal, Horace Charteris, Charles Hill, Arthur Greenham, and Charlie Coward were called to the stand to describe in gruesome detail the shootings and beatings they witnessed at the Buna-Werke and to tell how everyone at the plant and its camps had known what was happening at Birkenau. As Charlie Coward explained: "Everyone to whom I spoke gave the same story—the people in the city, the SS men, the concentration camp inmates, foreign workers. All the camp knew it. All the civilian population knew it; they complained about the stench of burning bodies. Even among the Farben employees to whom I spoke, a lot of them would admit it. It would be utterly impossible not to know."

Some of the most compelling testimony came from IG employees who had worked at the plant, men like engineer Norbert Jaehne, whose own father was among the defendants: "Of all the people employed in IG Auschwitz the inmates received the worst treatment. They were beaten by the kapos, who in their turn had to see to it that the amount of work prescribed them and their detachments by the IG foremen was carried out, because they otherwise were punished by being beaten in the evening in the Monowitz camp."

Even Ernst Struss, the assistant whom Fritz ter Meer had so recently tried to intimidate, made it into court:

COUNSEL: The chief engineer [Dürrfeld] of the Buna plant with whom you spoke in 1943, did he specifically tell you that people were being burned at Auschwitz?

STRUSS: Yes, I think he told me that before the burning they were gassed. . . .

COUNSEL: And in the summer of 1943 you knew that people were being burned and gassed?

STRUSS: Yes.

COUNSEL: And to the best of your recollection you told that to Ambros and ter Meer?

STRUSS: Yes.

The complacency that some of the defendants had shown so far was badly rocked by these testimonies. According to one observer, Otto Ambros kept closing his eyes during this part of the trial as though he were trying to shut out the revelations. Walter Dürrfeld sat there shaking his head, visibly sweating, as the evidence mounted against him. But of course it was the prosecution's contention that everyone in the dock was guilty of the same crimes, be they the medical experiments carried out in the IG's name, the beatings, starvation, abuse, and murder of inmates at the Buna-Werke and the IG's mines at Fürstengrube, or the use of forced labor at plants elsewhere in Poland and Germany. They were guilty because of their personal involvement in the camp and construction site, or because their collective authorization and approval had created circumstances under which the abuses had taken place, or because they had known of such abuses and done nothing to stop them. In other words, Carl Wurster and Erich von der Heyde and Paul Haefliger were just as responsible for what had happened at IG Auschwitz as Ambros, Dürrfeld, ter Meer, Bütefisch, Mann, or any of the other senior executives who had a more direct connection with the Buna-Werke. Given the powerful and dramatic evidence now flowing into the court, this was a difficult argument to dismiss and not surprisingly the defendants seemed deeply disturbed.

The defense tried its best to mitigate the effects of this barrage by introducing into evidence 386 witness affidavits aimed at showing that the IG had neither known nor approved of what was taking place at Auschwitz or (more perversely) that the events had never occurred at all. Unable because of limited time to question them all, the prosecution called into court the fifteen defense witnesses who had actually been at Auschwitz—some of them convicted German criminals with privileged jobs at the camp—and then tore them apart. Duke Minskoff's cross-examination of one of them, Gerhard Dietrich, was a classic of its kind.

COUNSEL: Mr. Witness, you stated in your affidavit that the accommodations in Monowitz were the best possible for the prisoners. Now isn't it a fact that the concentration camp Buchenwald, in which you were also, had better barracks than the Monowitz barracks, since the Buchenwald barracks were divided into two parts and contained day-rooms?

DIETRICH: Yes, that is correct.

COUNSEL: Isn't it also a fact that in the main camp of Auschwitz the housing of the inmates was much better than in Monowitz?

DIETRICH: That is true.

COUNSEL: There were large stone buildings in Main Auschwitz, were there not?

DIETRICH: Yes.

COUNSEL: Now, Mr. Witness, isn't it a fact that during the winter days as many as twenty inmates at a time were carried away from the Farben site back into Monowitz because they couldn't walk by themselves anymore?

DIETRICH: Yes.

COUNSEL: And could you say what the average weight of the inmates would be?

DIETRICH: 100 to 120 pounds.

COUNSEL: Now, Mr. Witness, is it not a fact that the IG foremen used to write evaluation sheets each night?

DIETRICH: Yes.

COUNSEL: And isn't it also true that if the Farben foremen reported the battalion under 70 percent, the inmates would be punished with twenty-five strokes each.

DIETRICH: If he reported it—yes, that is true.

COUNSEL: And wasn't the whipping post at Monowitz?

DIETRICH: I don't know that.

COUNSEL: Mr. Witness, you speak of there being no instruments of torture at Monowitz. Now isn't it a fact that there was a standing cell in Monowitz?

DIETRICH: Yes.

COUNSEL: Were there gallows in Monowitz?

DIETRICH: Yes.

COUNSEL: And didn't you often pass those gallows when an inmate had been hanged?

DIETRICH: Unfortunately.

COUNSEL: Mr. Witness, I asked you: Isn't it a fact that you often passed those gallows when an inmate had been hanged at Monowitz?

DIETRICH: I said, "unfortunately." . . .

COUNSEL: Mr. Witness, isn't it a fact that two or three times a week, open trucks drove along the IG Farben plant, going from Monowitz to Birkenau with inmates who were no longer able to work?

DIETRICH: That is true.

COUNSEL: Wasn't it common knowledge among the inmates that those inmates no longer able to work were being sent to Birkenau to be gassed?

DIETRICH: Yes.

When Minskoff had finished, Dietrich was in tears and had to be helped off the stand. The next defense witness, deployed to suggest that the IG supervisors couldn't possibly have known what was going on at Birkenau, was an SS officer. After a few minutes, Minskoff had gotten him to admit that the stench of the crematorium could be detected at Katowice, some thirty miles away. None of this made it any easier for the defendants themselves when they were cross-examined. Suddenly their protestations of ignorance about conditions at Auschwitz and the Fürstengrube were beginning to sound very hollow.

COUNSEL: Dr. Bütefisch, I show you this weekly report to you from Auschwitz, where the SS states that they gave repeated warning

to the Fürstengrube management to stop beating the inmates because it might eventually lead to their deterioration. Was that
called to your attention at the time?

BÜTEFISCH: The mining leader concerned would have to tell you
that. I don't know these things.

COUNSEL: I call your attention to this exhibit, another weekly report by Farben's mine personnel. "Can one therefore blame a
foreman or shaft supervisor for hitting out? In spite of the salu-
tary effects of beatings, the Labor Office [SS] has forbidden it."
Does that refresh your recollection that the prohibition against
beating came from the Labor Office rather than Farben?

BÜTEFISCH: I couldn't read all the weekly reports. But it is my
opinion that what had been put down here is someone's own
personal, impulsive opinion. This type of action is quite out of
the question for us. I was far away from the site.

COUNSEL: You were far away from the site? May I ask whether, on
your visits to IG Auschwitz—that is, the buna plant and the
mine—you took any interest in finding out the conditions under
which the forced workers were working there?

BÜTEFISCH: As far as I had time. I, of course, had reports from Mr
Dürrfeld. We talked about food. Dürrfeld showed me the charts.
That was my endeavour.

COUNSEL: Did you know that in 1942 they had as many as 3,000
foreign workers living in one barracks, mind you, with only
three huts for washing facilities?

BÜTEFISCH: No, that was not reported to me and I cannot imagine it.

Exchanges like this had taken place throughout the trial and would
often go on for hours, with defendants doggedly insisting that they
hadn't been informed or that they hadn't read the reports they had
been sent. But in this session, under relentless pressure, Bütefisch's
claims began to seem increasingly improbable.

COUNSEL: Dr. Bütefisch, how much money was invested on the
Leuna [fuel] part of Auschwitz?

BÜTEFISCH: In the course of four years, about 160,000,000 reichs-marks.

COUNSEL: Now as to these weekly construction reports—the reports covering the progress of that investment—I ask you to strike [calculate] some average of their length. Would you say about five lines, ten—here's one that's about thirty lines. Would you say twenty-five lines was the average length?

BÜTEFISCH: These are details, minor things.

COUNSEL: Supposing you read about twenty to thirty pages an hour. Would it take you more than a couple of hours a month to read every single one of these weekly reports covering an investment of one-fifth of a billion reichsmarks?

BÜTEFISCH: It depends on the contents. These men [my subordinates] just reported to me that "nothing happened."

COUNSEL: But although you say you didn't read the reports, do I understand that you meant to say that what was reported was not to be taken quite literally?

BÜTEFISCH: Certainly not literally. If I may apply these reports to the technical field, you might compare them to an analysis commission where someone might say, "It is all nonsense." These are personal notes of a man who is expressing his opinion.

COUNSEL: The prosecution wishes to offer one of these weekly reports (NI 14515) which states that a chamber for 30 to 40 corpses was constructed for the accommodation of the inmates at Monowitz. Can you explain why a mortuary for 30 to 40 corpses was required at Monowitz?

BÜTEFISCH: I can only say that in every big camp, every small city, there is a need for a mortuary for purely sanitary purposes. The overall condition was the important thing to us.

Some defense tactics were more successful. For example, lawyers for Schmitz, Krauch, von Schnitzler, and ter Meer were able to show that the IG had helped to protect the former Jewish *Aufsichtsrat* member Carl von Weinberg (although not his brother Arthur) by getting him out of Germany and setting him up in Italy with an IG pension. This information provided a valuable counterweight to suggestions that they had been indifferent to the plight of the Jews. But when Fritz Gajewski's lawyers tried a similar ploy it went spectacularly wrong. They introduced the affidavit from Gerhard Ollendorf, the former Jewish member of the *Vorstand* whose release from custody in 1939, through the intercession of Gajewski, had enabled him to leave the country. But Gajewski was then called to the stand by the prosecution's Morris Amchan, who confronted him with the evidence showing it had been his tipping off the Gestapo that had brought about Ollendorf's arrest in the first place. Even some of Gajewski's fellow defendants could not help but smile at this revelation.

Toward the end of the trial, the defendants came to the stand to make statements on their own behalf. Some of the men were rambling and self-serving, some were brief and to the point, but they all repeated the same message that their defense lawyers had drummed into them: everything they had done during the Nazi period had been out of patriotism or because they were following orders or because the consequences of not toeing the Nazi line would have meant drastic repercussions for themselves or their families. One or two did show a touch of remorse but their contrition seemed halfhearted and unconvincing. Wilhelm Mann, for example, had been embarrassed when the prosecutors made much of his early and enthusiastic support of the Nazi Party, and presumably he felt an explanation was due. But as he struggled to describe to the court how his views had now changed, his words seemed instead to reflect his regret that things hadn't quite worked out as he hoped.

> From the very beginning I objected to certain points of the party program; however, I have admitted here that during the first years, on account of the particular misery in Germany and on account of circumstances that are very difficult to judge for a foreigner, I was actually of the opinion that National Socialism, at that time, was the only possibility of saving Germany. . . . I did not give up my optimism as long as I believed that, through influences either from within or without, a change in some respects could and would occur. To

give you the exact date as to when I quite suddenly changed my inner attitude, that is very difficult.

Probably the most effective defense came from Carl Krauch. His lawyers knew that as Göring's special plenipotentiary for chemical production Krauch was potentially more vulnerable than anyone else to the charge of planning and preparing an aggressive war. So they put forth an argument that they guessed would immediately appeal to the two most conservative judges on the tribunal: "Replace IG by ICI for England, or DuPont for America, or Montecatini for Italy and at once the similarity will become clear to you." In other words, Carl Krauch was simply an honest, industrious, God-fearing businessman who had worked for his country's defense—just as any patriotic American in a similar position might have done on behalf of the United States.

None of the defendants, needless to say, not even Ambros, Bütefisch, or Dürrfeld, admitted to any participation in the crimes at Auschwitz.

ON MAY 28, 1948, the judges retired to consider their verdict. The trial had involved 152 days in court, 189 witnesses, 2,800 affidavits, and six thousand documents. The transcript ran to almost sixteen thousand pages. That same week the Communists took over in Czechoslovakia and the following month the Soviet Union imposed a blockade on West Berlin, which lay within the Russian occupation zone. Within a few days all traffic by road, rail, or water was cut off and the United States and Britain began organizing an airlift. As Josiah DuBois tidied up his office and prepared to take a long-postponed vacation, he tried to reassure himself: "Surely, I thought, the judges would not read from the current situation the motives of the defendants several years ago."

Two months later the whole cast reassembled in the courtroom at Nuremberg. Rarely since the first day had the gallery and press benches been as crowded. Telford Taylor came in and sat at the prosecutors' table but Belle Mayer was no longer present. Exhausted by her search for documents and witnesses, she had gone back to America to recover. DuBois was there, though, and Minskoff and Sprecher and Amchan and most of the other lawyers who had arrived at the Palace of Justice almost two years earlier fired up with idealism and enthusiasm and a determination to seek justice for the innocent victims of a cruel war. They were wearier now and more cynical, perhaps inevitably given what they had seen and heard over the previous twelve months. But they still believed that their case had been compelling enough. Who, after all, could argue with Auschwitz?

Three judges came in. (Clarence Merrell chose not to be in court.) Before they delivered their verdicts, Curtis Shake wished to say a few words. The previous day there had been a massive explosion at the Ludwigshafen plant. In an eerie repetition of the blast at Oppau in 1921, two hundred people had been killed and thousands more injured. Shake said that he wanted to express the tribunal's deepest sympathy for the victims and their families and asked the court to stand for a moment's silence. Then, with a glance at the twenty-three men in the dock, Shake settled down to read the verdicts. It took much of the morning but the message that emerged from the opinion was quite simple: the court did not believe the evidence against most of the defendants.

He dealt first with counts one and four, concerned with the preparation of and waging of aggressive war and conspiracy:

> Hitler was the dictator. It was natural that the people of Germany listened to and read his utterances in the belief that he spoke the truth. The statesmen of other nations, conceding Hitler's successes by the agreements they made with him, affirmed their belief in his word. Can we say that the common man of Germany believed less? . . . The average citizen of Germany, be he professional man, farmer, or industrialist, could scarcely be charged by these events with knowledge that the rulers of the Reich were planning to plunge Germany into a war of aggression. We reach the conclusion that common knowledge of Hitler's plans did not prevail in Germany. . . . The prosecution is confronted with the difficulty of establishing knowledge on the part of the defendants, not only of the rearmament of Germany but also that the purpose of rearmament was to wage aggressive war. . . . In this sphere the evidence degenerates from proof to mere conjecture.

All of the defendants, even Carl Krauch, were acquitted on counts one and four. Count two concerned spoliation and plunder, the takeover of property against the owner's will: "When action by the owner is not voluntary because his consent is obtained by threats, intimidation, pressure, or by exploiting the position and power of the military occupant under circumstances indicating that the owner is being induced to part with his property against his will, it is clearly a violation of the Hague regulations." On this basis, nine of the defendants, including Schmitz, von Schnitzler, and Max Ilgner, were found guilty for their actions in Poland, France, and elsewhere. Fourteen were acquitted.

On count three, which charged the defendants with slavery and mass murder, Shake said the court was mindful of the dangers facing those who disobeyed the orders of the Nazi state. The probability that the IG had no choice but to comply with the mandates of the Hitler government possibly gave the accused a defense of necessity: "There can be but little doubt that the defiant refusal of a Farben executive to carry out the Reich production schedule or to use slave labor to achieve that end would have been treated as treasonable sabotage and would have resulted in prompt and drastic retaliation."* However, Shake went on, the defense of necessity was not applicable "where the party seeking to invoke it was himself responsible for the existence or execution of such order or decree, or where his participation went beyond the requirements thereof, or was the result of his own initiative."

On this basis, then, "the use of concentration camp labor and forced foreign workers at Auschwitz with the initiative displayed by the officials of Farben in the procurement and utilization of such labor is a crime against humanity and, to the extent that non-German nationals were involved, also a war crime, to which the slave labor program of the Reich will not warrant the defense of necessity."

But as Shake continued he made it plain that in the court's view the conditions at the camp had not been as bad as the prosecution had

---

*This may have been true, of course, but not even in their own evidence had the IG directors ever tried to claim that the SS or the government had *forced* them to build their factory at Auschwitz.

398 · HELL'S CARTEL

alleged. While there had been some occasional unpleasantness, there had also been acts of corporate generosity: "Camp Monowitz was not without inhumane incidents. Occasionally beatings occurred by the Farben supervisors. While the food was inadequate, as was the clothing, especially in winter, . . . Farben voluntarily and at its own expense provided hot soup for the workers on the site at noon. This was in addition to the regular rations."

The three directors considered to have a direct connection with Auschwitz were found guilty: Ambros, Bütefisch, and Dürrfeld, as well as two others adjudged guilty by inference: Fritz ter Meer, because it was thought that Ambros must have talked to him about the use of slave labor, and Carl Krauch, because he had asked Göring to send him concentration camp inmates. All the other defendants were acquitted without a word of censure or disapproval, including Hermann Schmitz, who had scrutinized the contracts with the SS and sanctioned the subsequent actions of his subordinates; Christian Schneider, August von Knieriem, and Friedrich Jaehne, who between them had visited the site on many occasions; Wilhelm Mann, who had sent checks to pay for Dr. Mengele's experiments; and all the other directors, who had received the company's construction reports, approved the huge expenditure, and heard the rumors about gassings but did nothing.

In the afternoon Shake passed sentence on those adjudged guilty:

Otto Ambros: eight years' imprisonment for slavery and mass murder

Walter Dürrfeld: eight years' imprisonment for slavery and mass murder

Fritz ter Meer: seven years' imprisonment for plunder and spoliation, slavery and mass murder

Heinrich Bütefisch: six years' imprisonment for slavery and mass murder

Carl Krauch: six years' imprisonment for slavery and mass murder

Georg von Schnitzler: five years' imprisonment for plunder and spoliation

Hermann Schmitz: four years' imprisonment for plunder and spoliation

Max Ilgner: three years' imprisonment for plunder and spoliation

Paul Haefliger: two years' imprisonment for plunder and spoliation

Heinrich Oster: two years' imprisonment for plunder and spoliation

Ernst Bürgin: two years' imprisonment for plunder and spoliation

Friedrich Jaehne: eighteen months' imprisonment for plunder and spoliation

Hans Kugler: eighteen months' imprisonment for plunder and spoliation

All of the rest were set free: Heinrich Gattineau, who had chatted about synthetic oil with Hitler and helped finesse the IG's first connections with the Nazis; August von Knieriem, who had provided the legal justification for the takeover of other people's companies and somehow never noticed the stench of burning bodies at Auschwitz; Fritz Gajewski, who had informed on his old friend to the Gestapo; Carl Wurster, Heinrich Hörlein, and Wilhelm Mann, who had been on the board of the company that produced Zyklon B but who apparently never thought to ask why it had suddenly become so profitable.

When the chief judge had finished speaking, Judge Hebert, the former Louisiana dean, announced that he dissented from the majority verdict of Shake and Morris on numerous points. Supported by the alternate judge, Clarence Merrell, he had tried to persuade the other two to give him time to file his dissenting opinion so that it might be published alongside the verdicts. To his considerable dismay, they had denied him this opportunity, but he now made plain his intention to file it later.

For much of the day the prosecution had been sitting in stunned silence, appalled and shocked by the narrow spread of the guilty verdicts and the modest sentences. "Light enough to please a chicken thief," muttered DuBois bitterly. Telford Taylor, whose extraordinary opening speech should have set the scene for a prosecutorial triumph, was speechless. Had he been able to persuade the authorities in Washington to let him have some experienced federal judges, many of the defendants might now have been starting life sentences or on their way to the gallows. Instead, once their time in custody had been taken

into account, it was likely that some of the convicted would be released in a few months. So he sat with his colleagues and watched as
men they knew to be guilty walked free and others, involved in one of
history's greatest acts of mass murder, were led away to begin sentences so modest they might have been given to a driver who had irre-
sponsibly hit a pedestrian. It was a bitter blow.

Outside the court, Taylor was restrained. Yes, he was disappointed,
he told reporters, but many important issues had been raised during
the trial and that could only be good for the future of Germany. He
was also mindful, no doubt, that judges in the Krupp trial were due to
reach their verdicts the following day and that it would be impolitic to
criticize the judiciary at such a time. He needn't have worried. Using
language that was in marked contrast to that of his peers at the IG
trial in the courtroom down the hall, Justice Edward Daly castigated
the principal defendant, Alfred Krupp, for his grotesque exploitation
and mistreatment of slave labor. To gasps from the arms manufacturer's supporters, Daly sentenced him to twelve years in prison and
then ordered that his vast personal wealth be forfeited.

This was little balm to the IG prosecutors. DuBois had left the
court in a fury, declaring, "I'll write a book about this if it's the last
thing I do." But first he had to endure the journey home. A few days
later, he and Duke Minskoff joined the IG trial judges aboard the
General Patrick, a former army transport ship, for the eight-day passage back to the United States. The atmosphere was frosty and the
conversation over dinner constrained. But one night Judge Hebert
came to DuBois's cabin. Slowly, and with great effort, he managed to
let slip a few words of comfort: "When I first read the indictment, it
was difficult to believe that all of this had happened. By the time we
reached the end, I felt that practically every sentence of the indictment
had been proved many times over."

Some years later DuBois would write his book and recall his
painful journey home:

> I still feel the same stifling anger today that I felt many times during
> and since that trip. I was reliably informed that, even before the trial
> started, one of the judges had expressed the view that he didn't be-

lieve it was ever intended that industrialists be brought to account for preparing and waging an aggressive war. . . . Why had Judges Shake and Morris reacted as they did? I concluded that the reason must have been fear—their own great fear of the trend of events in 1948. The issue of Communism, pertinent to the defendants' motives in 1933 and 1934, pertinent to our out-of-court lives in 1948, was falsely read into the defendants' minds as of September 1939. Nowhere was there any evidence that Farben feared Russia enough to stop producing strategic goods for that country. . . . Yet the two judges accepted the fiction that Farben was the simple prototype of "Western capitalism."

But Judge Paul Hebert was from different stock. Five months after the verdicts, he sent his dissenting opinion to the official trial proceedings. It was a coruscating attack on the prejudices and failings of his fellow judges, who had misread the evidence in almost every respect.

The record of IG Farbenindustrie, during the period under examination in this lengthy trial, has been shown to be an ugly record which went far beyond the activities of normal business. From a maze of statistical and detailed information in the record emerges a picture of gigantic proportions depicting feverish activity by Farben to rearm Germany in disregard of economic considerations and in a warlike atmosphere of emergency and crisis. . . . There is nothing in the record to suggest that Farben ever withheld any energy or initiative to help Hitler in his plans to build a Germany that would be strong enough militarily to master the world.

About Auschwitz, he wrote:

Utilization of slave labor in Farben was approved as a matter of corporate policy. To permit the corporate instrumentality to be used as a cloak to insulate the principal corporate officers who authorized this course of action is, in my opinion, without any sound precedent under the most elementary concepts of criminal law. Just as ter Meer was the superior of Ambros, the *Vorstand* was the superior of both, and there is no reason to conclude that the knowledge possessed by Ambros and ter Meer was not fully reported to and discussed in the *Vorstand*. There is indeed strong positive evidence that this was done. . . . The conditions at Auschwitz were so horrible that it is utterly incredible to conclude that they were unknown to the defendants, the principal corporate directors, who were responsible for Farben's connection to the project. . . . The extreme cold, the inadequacy of the food, the rigorous nature of the work, the cruel treatment of the workers by their supervisors combine to present a picture of horror which, I am convinced, has not been at all overdrawn by the prosecution and which is fully sustained by the evidence. . . . The defendants, members of the *Vorstand*, cannot, in my opinion, avoid sharing a large part of the guilt for numberless crimes against humanity.

Regrettably, Hebert's opinions were of only historical interest. The handful of convicted IG directors had already begun their brief stay in the relative comfort of Landsberg prison, while the acquitted had been set free to pick up the pieces. Indeed, it seemed only one question now remained outstanding. What did the future hold for the IG itself?

EPILOGUE

Although General Eisenhower had recommended IG Farben's dissolution in late 1945, the cartel's final breakup was temporarily postponed because the Allies disagreed about exactly how it should be carried out and occupation officials were more immediately concerned with getting the battered German economy back on its feet. The exigencies of the new cold war delayed things still further, and the concern's factories were left to struggle on, under close Allied supervision, until 1949. But in June of that year, when a civilian Western High Commission replaced the four-nation military administration, former shareholders were able to persuade the new authorities that the assets and stock of the old IG Farben should be transferred to three large successor companies. Thus in 1951, after a further transitional period for legal agreements to be drawn up, Bayer, Hoechst, and BASF were reborn, along with six smaller firms, including Agfa, Kalle, Cassella, and Hüls. By the mid-1950s, when German chemical production had once again reached the level of 1936, the six smaller companies had been reabsorbed by the three largest. By the mid-1970s the big three were back among the thirty largest corporations in the world, having played a decisive role in the "economic miracle" that defined the Federal Republic of Germany in the third quarter of the twentieth century. Each one of them was more profitable than the concern had ever been. It was as though the IG Farben years had been a mere blip in their history.

Today that success story continues. Bayer, whose global headquarters are still at Leverkusen, is now one of the world's top-ten pharmaceutical and chemical companies and still its largest producer of aspirin, the product that played such a pivotal role in Carl Duisberg's accretion of commercial power in the years before the Interessen Gemeinschaft and World War I. In 1999 Bayer was even able to win back the rights to its trade name in America.

The BASF Group is now the world's largest chemical company, the truly multinational giant that Carl Bosch hoped the IG would eventually become. After a long foray into pharmaceuticals and other consumer products, it sold its drugs division for almost $7 billion to Abbott Laboratories in Illinois in 2000. BASF has since reverted to its core businesses, in which petrochemicals, gas, plastics, and agrochemicals still feature importantly. With 160 subsidiaries and eighty-seven thousand employees, its annual turnover today is in excess of 36 billion euros. Ironically, the synthetic fuel process that Bosch was so desperately keen to develop in the early 1930s is now coming back into fashion. Natural oil prices are rising as world reserves decline, and many industry experts predict that the industrialized world will soon be forced to turn again to the technology that the Nazis paid IG Farben to develop.

Hoechst is the only one of the big three not to have kept its name. In 1999 it merged with Rhône-Poulenc, the French chemical business whose factories IG Farben plundered during World War II. The resulting company was known as Aventis, but it became Sanofi-Aventis after a further merger in 2004. The combined firm, with headquarters in Paris, is now the third-largest pharmaceutical company in the world. Like the other two former IG companies, it is extremely profitable, with more than 27 billion euros of revenue in 2005.

Not surprisingly, all three of these successor businesses have been keen to disassociate themselves publicly from IG Farben, not least because of the possibility that former slave workers and concentration camp survivors might sue them for compensation. This possibility quickly became a reality in the early 1950s. In 1949, all that remained of the once mighty concern, in strict legal terms, was a tiny rump: the IG Farben in Liquidation company. Its minimal staff had been reduced to managing the firm's pension funds and trying to recover assets confiscated by Warsaw Pact countries. But in 1951 Norbert Wollheim, a former slave laborer at the Buna-Werke, sued this entity for damages. When the case came to court before three German judges in Frankfurt, Wollheim described how he and his family had been arrested with thousands of others in Berlin and shipped to Auschwitz, where his wife and three-year-old son were selected for murder at Birkenau. He recounted his subsequent life at Monowitz and the Buna-Werke, his struggle to survive the beatings and starvation, and the constant threat of the gas chambers. With supporting testimony from a dozen former inmates, including two British POWs, he asked for a minimum settlement of ten thousand deutschmarks. The IG in Liquidation put up a fierce fight and recycled the defense used at Nuremberg. Whatever had happened to Wollheim was the fault of other parties—the SS, the Nazis, corrupt inmates, and building contractors. The IG, in contrast, had done its best to improve the lot of inmates. Indeed, the lawyers argued, by giving them work it had saved many from the gas chambers.

The judges disagreed. After hearing Wollheim's testimony and studying the sixteen-thousand-word transcript of the earlier trial, they reached a conclusion that was worthy of the evidence.

The fundamental principles of equality, justice, and humanity must have been known to all civilized persons, and the IG corporation cannot evade its responsibility any more than can an individual. . . . They must have known of the selections for it was their human duty to know the condition of their employees. Their alleged total lack of knowledge merely confirms their lack of interest in the lives of the Jewish prisoners for whom they had a duty of care, at least during the time the inmates were in their power. There was a duty to do whatever they could to protect the life, body, and health of the plaintiff—which they failed to carry out. For that failure, which was at least negligent, the company is liable.

Wollheim's victory opened the remnant of the IG up to a barrage of similar claims, which were eventually handled by Benjamin B. Ferencz, one of Telford Taylor's deputies at Nuremberg and the lead attorney in the successful Einsatzgruppen trial. As a result of his efforts and many months of hard bargaining, the corporation (now led by August von Knieriem) was eventually obliged to hand over a small payment to 5,855 Jewish survivors of the Buna-Werke and Monowitz. The largest individual compensation award came to a mere $1,250. Ferencz continued working to obtain reparation for victims of the Holocaust until his retirement in the early 1990s. Later class-action suits against Swiss banks (accused of hoarding monies confiscated by the Nazis from the Jews) and German industry led to the creation of two endowment funds to settle the claims once and for all. Taken together the maximum amount a concentration camp laborer might today hope to receive from these funds is around $8,500. At the time of writing there are thousands of claims still extant. Inevitably, therefore, some critics still point to the over $100 billion annual turnover of the three successor companies of IG Farben and wonder why they don't contribute more money to the funds.

Their answer—consistent from the 1950s to the present—is that they were new companies formed after the collapse of IG Farben and therefore have no specific legal or moral responsibility for what happened during the IG era. They also point out that they have made generous contributions, without admitting responsibility, to the second of the aforementioned funds, the Foundation for Remembrance, Responsibility, and the Future, which was endowed by German industry with approximately $2.5 billion in 2001. Indeed, BASF took a lead role in setting up the fund. But whether such action can ever satisfy those who want a full acknowledgment of wartime crimes is another matter. To this day no German company that used slave labor during World War II has ever formally apologized to survivors for having done so.

They may well have taken their cue from the IG executives convicted at Nuremberg, who blankly maintained their innocence throughout the trial and continued to do so in the years that followed. Even the prospect of a stint in Landsberg prison did little to undermine their self-assurance. According to one report, Otto Ambros actually smiled slightly as he received his sentence, although his smile might have been one of relief; under other judges in a different court he could have been facing the gallows. Only Carl Krauch seemed somewhat distressed on the last day in court, calling his lawyers over to make sure he had heard the verdict correctly. Perhaps he was wondering what sort of life awaited him after his sentence was served. Once the most important man in German industry, who had received the Knight's Cross for distinguished service from the Führer himself, Krauch must have doubted whether he would ever reach such heights again.

He did not have to wait long to find out. He was released at the end of 1950 after serving less than two years of his sentence. By the end of the first week in February 1951, all the IG Farben prisoners had followed him out to freedom. John McCloy, the new U.S. high commissioner, had drastically shortened the sentences of 74 of the 104 men convicted by the various subsequent proceedings at Nuremberg, issuing commutations for ten of those sentenced to death. Although he would later insist that these decisions were based purely on legal grounds and parole board recommendations, it is hard to escape the conclusion that there was a political imperative involved, too. At the time, America's reputation in Europe was taking a battering because of Communist successes in Korea, while the confrontation between the West and the Soviet Union in Germany was reaching a new intensity. The West German government had appealed for clemency for the industrialists, arguing that this was a moment for all in the democratic free world to stand shoulder to shoulder in unity. The longer that prisoners stayed in Landsberg—men who were widely regarded in Germany as being innocent of any crimes—the harder it would be to generate the goodwill necessary to build the new Federal Republic.

And so the IG defendants were set free on the grounds of good behavior. None of them appeared much the worse for wear (the regime at Landsberg had hardly been harsh) or in the least bit repentant. As Fritz ter Meer walked out the main gates in the direction of the nearest railway station, he told reporters, "Now they have Korea on their hands, the Americans are a lot more friendly." He had obviously lost none of his hauteur, and he refused to answer further questions as he strode away. Typically, Georg von Schnitzler left in more style. A large black Mercedes limousine, driven by a smartly dressed chauffeur, arrived to whisk him away. One newspaper account claimed that the still beautiful Baroness Lilly von Schnitzler was draped languorously across the backseat.*

The freed men adjusted quickly to life outside, with most of those still of working age eventually finding board positions back in German industry. Carl Krauch joined the board of Hüls, one of the IG successor businesses; Hermann Schmitz joined the board of Berlin West, a major German bank, and served as chairman of the board of Rheini Steel before his retirement. Carl Wurster became chairman of the board of BASF and a director of several other companies; he also received numerous awards, including the Distinguished Service Cross of the new Federal Republic, and was made an honorary senator of five German universities and president of the Federation of the German Chemical Industry. Heinrich Bütefisch, the former honorary SS Obersturmbannführer, became a member of the board of Ruhr-Chemie and other firms; in 1964 he also received the Distinguished Service Cross but it was withdrawn after sixteen days of violent protests across Germany. Friedrich Jaehne, who had been convicted of spoliation and plunder, became chairman of the new Hoechst; he, too, was awarded the Distinguished Service Cross.

Fritz Gajewski, yet another recipient of the Distinguished Service Cross, became chairman of the boards of Dynamit Nobel AG, Genschow & Co., and the Chemie-Verwaltungs AG, as well as a board member of two other firms. Heinrich Hörlein, the Nobel Prize winner, went back to Leverkusen and joined the board of the new Bayer AG, as eventually did Wilhelm Mann. Max Ilgner announced he wanted to

---

*Alfred Krupp was also among those released. His property and wealth were all restored to him.

devote his life to God, or at least that was what he had told Curtis Shake when he needed Allied permission for his wife and children to move to Sweden in 1948. Shake wrote on his behalf, "He is a man of fine intellect and capacity. I think it is only charitable to view his conviction in the light of conditions that existed in Germany during the Nazi regime. . . . I firmly believe that his past experience will fit him to do constructive work toward making the world a safer and better place to live." Ilgner's dalliance with religion did not last long: he later became a political lobbyist.

Otto Ambros, whose curriculum vitae included responsibility for the location, planning, and running of IG Auschwitz, the creation of Nazi Germany's secret chemical weapons program, a Knight's Cross from Adolf Hitler, and a conviction for slavery and mass murder, went on to have a glittering career as chairman or member of the boards of Chemie Grünenthal, Pintsch Bamag AG, Knoll AG, Telefunken GmbH, Berliner Handelsgesellschaft, Süddeutsche Kalkstickstoffwerke, and numerous other businesses. He also became a consultant to the U.S. chemical and asbestos firm W. R. Grace and an "adviser" on chemical matters to the German government in Bonn.

Fritz ter Meer, whose commanding presence dominated the dock at Nuremberg and who was the only man to be convicted on two counts, followed Hörlein and Mann back to Leverkusen. After a brief interval he was elected to the board of Bayer AG and in 1955 he became chairman of the company, a post he held for the next eight years. He was also the chairman of Th. Goldschmidt AG, deputy chairman of the Commerzbank association, and a board member of Waggonfabrik Uerdingen AG, the Düsseldorfer Waggonfabrik AG, and United Industrial Enterprises. He, too, became an adviser to the German government, on synthetic fuel issues.

The other men sought more modest appointments back with their old employers or left the industry altogether. Georg von Schnitzler, for example, was occasionally featured in the society pages of some of the glossier European magazines, but he seems to have stayed away from most of his former colleagues. Christian Schneider, meanwhile, seems to have made a good living as a consultant to European chemical businesses, passing on his knowledge of high-pressure chemistry to anyone who was interested. But wherever they ended up, none of the former IG defendants appear to have suffered either physically or financially from their experiences at Nuremberg or at Landsberg. Nor, apart from von Schnitzler, who had at least made something of a confession to American investigators, did any of them ever express a public word of apology.

On February 6, 1959, the members of IG Farben's wartime *Vorstand* gathered in Ludwigshafen for a glittering reunion dinner hosted by BASF's Carl Wurster—the last such event to be held. Given the inclement weather, their advanced years, and the distances that some of them had to travel, it was a good turnout: Krauch, ter Meer, Gajewski, Ambros, Ilgner, Schneider, Bütefisch, Kühne, Jaehne, and Wilhelm Mann. Many had brought their wives and Carl Bosch's widow had been invited in honor of her husband. Wurster sat at the head of the table, as befitted his position as chairman of the fastest-growing company in the new Germany, and dispensed wine and comradeship and good cheer throughout the evening.

But as the candles burned lower and the men lit up their cigars and poured out the brandy, what did they find to talk about? Did they congratulate one another for having survived the Nazi regime and the ordeal of Nuremberg or exchange anecdotes about their time at Landsberg? Did they look back fondly to the days when the business they once ran was a mighty corporate colossus that crushed all commercial opposition, or did they perhaps wax optimistic about the great times ahead? Or did they, now that they were among friends and safe from prying eyes, raise a glass to the memory of thousands of starving, beaten, half-dead wretches who had once dragged iron girders across an icebound Polish construction site on their behalf?

We shall never know, of course. But somehow it seems unlikely.

POSTSCRIPT

New York Times
Wednesday, November 12, 2003

At its zenith during World War II, IG Farben was the world's largest chemical company and a sinister symbol of Nazi industrial might. On Monday, the company, notorious for producing poison gas and consuming slave labor during the war, announced that it will file for bankruptcy.

That news may seem to come after the fact, given that Farben was dismantled by the Allies in 1952—its factories split among Bayer, BASF, and other German chemical companies. . . .

But IG Farben lived on as a trust—a legal entity fought over by court-appointed administrators and Holocaust survivors, who thought that its few remaining assets could still be sold to pay restitution.

Now, in the wake of a failed real estate deal, Farben's administrators said the company would be dissolved, with the proceeds going to repay bank loans rather than Nazi-era victims or their families.

NOTES

1–10   My description of the opening days of the IG Farben trial is based on a -
variety of sources. The most important (from which all of General Taylor's quotes in this prologue are drawn) is the official trial transcript,
contained in volumes 7 and 8 of *Trials of the War Criminals before the
Nuremberg Military Tribunals under Control Council Law No. 10*. Ci-
tations of this source are shortened to *NMT*. Readers interested in seeing
some of these documents for themselves can find them online at www
.mazal.org. Additional documents used by the prosecution but not included in the *NMT* volumes were later copied onto microfilm and can be
found under National Archives Record Group 238 T301, *Records of the
Office of the United States Chief Counsel for War Crimes, Nuremberg.*
This source is cited as NI, followed by the appropriate reel number.
Other Nuremberg trial documents are designated separately whenever
necessary.

The most interesting, if sometimes confusing, eyewitness account of
the trial is Josiah DuBois's, *The Devil's Chemists: 24 Conspirators of the
International Farben Cartel Who Manufacture Wars*. I was also able to
draw, however, on the memories of some others who were there, including
prosecution attorney Belle Mayer Zeck (sadly, now deceased) and David
Gordon, who observed from the public gallery. For background I have also
drawn on Telford Taylor's *Final Report to the Secretary of the Army on
the Nuremberg War Crimes Trials under Control Council Law No. 10* and
U.S. Group Control Council, Finance Division, *Elimination of German*

Resources for War: Report on the Investigation of IG Farbenindustrie (declassified), November 1945. Other useful sources describing life at Nuremberg through the years of the war crimes trials were Taylor's *The Anatomy of the Nuremberg Trials: A Personal Memoir*; D. A. Sprecher's *Inside the Nuremberg Trial: A Prosecutor's Comprehensive Account,* vols. 1 and 2, and A. Tusa and J. Tusa's *The Nuremberg Trial.* Sporadic coverage of the IG Farben trial also can be found in the *Times* (London) and the *New York Times.* My impressions of what the atmosphere must have been like were enhanced by a visit to Nuremberg and by careful perusal of the trial footage, now kept at the Steven Spielberg Film and Video Archive at the United States Holocaust Memorial Museum, under *War Crimes Trials: IG Farben Case,* Story Numbers RG60: 2432/2916/2915/2431/2914, etc.

1. From Perkin's Purple to Duisberg's Drugs

11   "By the middle of the nineteenth century": There is vast body of writing and research on the subject of chemistry during and after the Industrial Revolution but the sources I found most relevant to this section were Brock, *The History of Chemistry* and *The Norton History of Chemistry*; Beer, *The Emergence of the German Dye Industry*; Haber, *The Chemical Industry during the Nineteenth Century*; Dorner, *Early Dye History and the Introduction of Synthetic Dyes before the 1870s*; and Warner, *Landmarks in Industrial History.*

12   "William Henry Perkin": Boulton, "William Henry Perkin"; Chemical Society, *The Life and Works of Professor William Henry Perkin*; Garfield, *Mauve: How One Man Invented a Colour That Changed the World*; and Travis, *The Rainbow Makers: The Origins of the Synthetic Dyestuff Industry in Western Europe.*

12   "August Wilhelm von Hofmann": Beer, *The Emergence of the German Dye Industry*; Haber, *The Chemical Industry during the Nineteenth Century*; Jeffreys, *Aspirin: The Remarkable Story of a Wonder Drug*; Benfey, "August Wilhelm Hofmann: A Centennial Tribute."

12   "One of these was": For more about quinine, see Duran-Reynals, *The Fever Bark Tree: The Pageant of Quinine,* and Klein, "The Fever Bark Tree."

13   For William Perkin's experiments and the commercial development and success of mauveine, see Meth-Cohn and Smith, "What Did W. H. Perkin Actually Make When He Oxidised Aniline to Obtain Mauveine?"; Boulton, *William Henry Perkin*; Garfield, *Mauve*; Beer, *The Emergence of the German Dye Industry*; and Chemical Society, *The Life and Works.*

14   " 'If your discovery' ": R. Pullar to W. Perkin, June 12, 1856, Kirkpatrick Collection, Museum of Science and Industry, Manchester. Also quoted in *Journal of the Chemical Society* 69, part 1 (1896).

14   "Traditionally, dyes could": See Travis, *The Rainbow Makers,* and Leggett, *Ancient and Medieval Dyes.*

15   "The train and body": *Illustrated London News,* Jan. 30, 1858. For ex-

amples of "mauve mania" and how it was reported, see Dickens, "Perkin's Purple"; *Gentlewoman's Quarterly,* Sussex, Aug. 7, 1859; and *Punch,* Aug. 7 and 21, Sept. 18 and 25, and Nov. 20, 1858.

16   "If August von Hofmann's appointment": Beer, *The Emergence of the German Dye Industry*; Haber, *The Chemical Industry during the Nineteenth Century*; Leaback, "What Hofmann Left Behind."

17   "One of the most significant": Ibid.

18   "German textile manufacturers had long resented": For the spread of synthetic dye works across Germany and the rest of Europe between 1860 and 1876, see Beer, *The Emergence of the German Dye Industry.*

19   "There were some exceptions": Biographical details and foundation of BASF from Schröter, *Friedrich Englehorn. Ein Unternehmer-Porträt des 19 Jahrunderts*; Abelshauser et al., *German Industry and Global Enterprise*; and Meinzer, *125 Jahre BASF: Stationen ihrer Geschichte.* Also see BASF Unternehmensarchiv (UA) de BASG AG Ludwigshafen: A 11/1/6, A11/1/9, A 12/1/6.

20   "alizarin red": Haber, *The Chemical Industry, 1900–1930* and *The Chemical Industry during the Nineteenth Century*; Travis, *The Rainbow Makers;* Abelshauser et al., *German Industry and Global Enterprise.*

23   Biographical details on Carl Duisberg's early life, education, and appointment at Farbenfabriken Bayer: Duisberg, *Meine Lebenserinnerungen*; Verg, Plumpe, and Schultheis, *Milestones*; Armstrong, "Chemical Industry and Carl Duisberg"; Flechtner, *Carl Duisberg: Vom Chemiker zum Wirtschaftsfuhrer*; and Jeffreys, *Aspirin.*

25n   Letter to Rumpff quoted in Duisberg, *Nur ein Sohn,* and Verg, Plumpe, and Schultheis, *Milestones.*

28   Discovery of antipyrine and Antifebrine: Verg, Plumpe, and Schultheis, *Milestones*; Issekutz, *Die Geschichte der Arzneimittelforschung*; and McTavish, "The German Pharmaceutical Industry, 1880–1920: A Case Study of Aspirin."

30   Development of Bayer drugs Phenacetin, Sulfonal, and Trional: Verg, Plumpe, and Schultheis, *Milestones;* Schadewaldt and Alstaedter, *History of Pharmacological Research at Bayer*; Jeffreys, *Aspirin*; Armstrong, "Chemical Industry and Carl Duisberg"; and McTavish, "What's in a Name? Aspirin and the American Medical Association."

30   "When Carl Rumpff died": Verg, Plumpe, and Schultheis, *Milestones*; Schadewaldt and Alstaedter, *History of Pharmacological Research at Bayer*; and Mann and Plummer, *The Aspirin Wars.*

31   "In less than six years": Jeffreys, *Aspirin*; Verg, Plumpe, and Schultheis, *Milestone*; and Autographensammlung Duisberg, Bayer Archives, Leverkusen.

32   Development of indigo: Reinhardt and Travis, *Heinrich Caro*; Nagel, *Fuschin, Alizarin, Indigo. Der Beginn eines Weltunternehmens*; and Abelshauser et al., *German Industry and Global Enterprise.*

34   "None of this mattered": Details of BASF's accomplishments listed in *Badische Anilin-und Soda-Fabrik Ludwigshafen am Rhein,* BASF UA, A/11 (1900).

35	On the development of aspirin, see Jeffreys, *Aspirin*. For biographical details of Hoffmann, Dreser, and Eichengrün, see Jeffreys, *Aspirin*, and Verg, Plumpe, and Schultheis, *Milestones*; Schadewaldt and Alstaedter, *History of Pharmacological Research at Bayer*. I was also assisted by information provided to me by Arthur Eichengrün's grandson Ernst. On discrepancies over Eichengrün's role, see his own accounts: "50 Jahre Aspirin" and "Pharmaceutisch-wissenschafliche Abteilung."
36	" 'find new ways' ": Quoted in Schadewaldt and Alstaedter, *History of Pharmacological Research at Bayer*.
37	heroin: See both Eichengrün articles, above, and *Bulletin of Narcotics*, April 1953.
38	"Aspirin was launched": Eichengrün articles, above, and Dreser, "Pharmakologisches über Aspirin-Acetylsalicylsäure."
38	"By the dawn of the new century": Brock, *The Norton History of Chemistry*; Beer, *The Emergence of the German Dye Industry*; Haber, *The Chemical Industry during the Nineteenth Century*; and Abelhauser et al., *German Industry and Global Enterprise*.
39	" 'We have forfeited our heritage' ": *Daily Telegraph*, July 9, 1906.
39	"In the meanwhile": Heinrich Brunck's remarks cited in Garfield, *Mauve*; Carl Duisberg's quote from *Journal of the Society of Dyers and Colourists*, July 1906.

2. The Golden Years

42	"As the new century": Data on early success of aspirin from Witthauer; Wohlgemut; and Wohr. Also see promotional leaflets for Aspirin, 1899, Bayer Archives, Leverkusen.
42	On aspirin patents, see UK Letters Patent No. 27,088 (1898) and U.S. Patent No. 644,077 (Feb. 27, 1900).
43n	Jeffreys, *Aspirin*.
43	On the attitude of medical authorities toward advertising, see McTavish, "What's in a Name?"
43	Duisberg's visit to America and purchase of Rensselaer: Flechtner, *Carl Duisberg*; Jeffreys, *Aspirin*; and Duisberg, *Meine Lebenserinnerungen*.
44	"Before returning to Germany": Ibid. and Flechtner, *Carl Duisberg*. Duisberg's speech to New York Chemical Society, May 13, 1903, reproduced in *Popular Science Monthly*, May 1903.
45	"Six months later": Memorandum reproduced in Duisberg, *Abhandlungen, Vorträge und Reden aus den Jahren 1882–1921*. Also in BASF UA, A16/2/3.
46	"Duisberg was deeply puzzled": Duisberg, *Meine Lebenserinnerungen*.
46	"*Dreibund*": BASF UA, A16/2/15; Duisberg, *Meine Lebenserinnerungen*; Brunck, *Lebenserinnerungen*, in BASF UA, W1 Lothar Brunck; Abelshauser et al., *German Industry and Global Enterprise*; and Verg, Plumpe, and Schultheis, *Milestones*.
47	"In May of the following year": *Farbenfabriken vormals Friedrich Bayer & Co v. Chemische Fabrik von Heyden*.

48   "'Big foreign syndicates'": *Telegraph*, May 12, 1907.

48   "Mersey Chemical Works": BASF UA Engere Kommission des AR, 29, Sitzung (April 7, 1908), Sitzung (April 1, 1910); Reinhardt and Travis *Heinrich Caro.*

49   "broader malaise in international relations": Ferguson, *The Pity of War.*

50   "The events that led to this breakthrough": Sir William Crookes's speech can be found in *Science,* vol. 8, Oct. 28, 1898. For further details about the speech and its impact, see Fournier d'Albe, *The Life of Sir William Crookes,* and Farber, *The Evolution of Chemistry: A History of Its Ideas, Methods, and Materials.*

51   "Justus von Liebig": Quoted in Brock, *The History of Chemistry*

51   "Of course, this lust for fertilizer": The best study on this I've found is Vaclav Smil's *Enriching the Earth: Fritz Haber, Carl Bosch, and the Transformation of World Food Production.*

53   "By 1903": Ibid. See also Kiefer, "Chemistry Chronicles: Capturing Nitrogen Out of the Air." For BASF's relationship with the Norwegians, see BASF UA Engere Kommission des AR, Sitzung (Dec. 20, 1905) and BASF UA, C10, Vorstand an Aufsichstrat (Sept. 26, 1911).

53   "It would fall to a German scientist": Biographical details of Fritz Haber drawn from Stoltenberg, *Fritz Haber: Chemiker, Nobelpreisträger, Deutscher, Jude;* Szöllösi-Janze, *Fritz Haber 1868–1934: Eine Biographie;* and Cornwell, *Hitler's Scientists: Science, War, and the Devil's Pact.*

54   "The nitrogen problem": Ibid. and Smil, *Enriching the Earth.*

55   "For much of the previous year": On Carl Bosch, see Holdermann, *Im Banne der Chemie: Carl Bosch, Leben und Werke.*

56   "Thus it was": Stoltenberg, *Fritz Haber.*

56   "Over the next three and a half years": See Stoltenberg, *Fritz Haber;* Szöllösi-Janze, *Fritz Haber;* Smil, *Enriching the Earth;* Abelshauser et al., *German Industry;* Holdermann, *Im Banne der Chemie;* Haber, *The Chemical Industry, 1900–1930;* and Bosch's Nobel Prize lecture of 1931.

58   "For much of its comparatively brief existence": Assessment of value of German chemical exports from Hayes, *Industry and Ideology: IG Farben in the Nazi Era.*

58   "At a local level": Employment contracts: BASF UA, C60. Averages and attitude toward employees: Abelshauser et al., *German Industry;* Verg, Plumpe, and Schultheis, *Milestones;* Hoechst Archiv 112/3, Hayes, *Industry and Ideology.*

59   "At the same time": Ibid.

59   "As early as 1884": BASF UA, C622.

60   "By the turn of the century": Political turmoil and strikes: Breunig, *Soziale Verhältnisse der Arbeiterschaft und sozialistische Arbeiterbewegung in Ludwigshafen am Rhein 1868–1909;* Abelshauser et al., *German Industry;* and Beer, *The Emergence of the German Dye Industry.*

60   "German society at large": Evans, *The Coming of the Third Reich;* Falter, "How Likely Were Workers to Vote for the NSDAP?"; Manchester, *The Arms of Krupp.*

61   "So what shape": Beer, *The Emergence of the German Dye Industry.*

3. The Chemists' War

63   "It was supposed to be a brief": Tuchman, *The Guns of August*, and Davies, *Europe: A History.*

64   "An astute industrialist": Kessler, *Walter Rathenau: His Life and Work.* For Rathenau's own assessment, see Rathenau, "Germany's Provisions for Raw Materials." See also Borkin, *The Crime and Punishment of IG Farben.*

65   "At first, few": On military indifference to Rathenau's warning, see Holdermann, *Im Banne der Chemie.*

65   "Rathenau's first act": Ibid. Also Stoltenberg, *Fritz Haber*; and Szöllösi-Janze, *Fritz Haber.*

66   "At his first encounter": Holdermann, *Im Banne der Chemie*; and Szöllösi-Janze, "Losing the War but Gaining Ground."

66   Details of the deal with the War Ministry and quotation from the board: BASF UA Engere Kommission des AR, 42, Sitzung (Oct. 20, 1914).

67   "In truth": Szöllösi-Janze, "Losing the War," and Rathenau, "Germany's Provisions."

68   "Things at Oppau, however,": For sharing of plans with other IG companies, see Szöllösi-Janze, "Losing the War"; and BASF UA G61101.

68   " 'Following a heavy bombardment' ": LeFebure, *The Riddle of the Rhine.*

69   "The use of poison gas": See Stoltenberg, *Fritz Haber*, and Szöllösi-Janze, *Fritz Haber.* For the Fulda manifesto, see Gratzer, *The Undergrowth of Science: Delusion, Self-Deception, and Human Frailty.* For Bauer's role, see Bauer, *Der Grosse Krieg in Feld und Heimat.* See also Haber, *The Poisonous Cloud: Chemical Warfare in the First World War.*

69   "Chlorine gas": Haber, *The Poisonous Cloud*; and Harris and Paxman, *A Higher Form of Killing: The Secret History of Gas and Germ Warfare.*

70   "Their discretion": Hague Convention quoted in SIPRI, *The Rise of CB Weapons.*

70   "In April 1915": Szöllösi-Janze, "Losing the War"; LeFebure, *The Riddle of the Rhine;* and Cornwell, *Hitler's Scientists.*

71   "The results": LeFebure, *The Riddle of the Rhine.*

72   " 'How well it works' ": Max Bauer papers, March 15, 1915, Bundesarchiv, Koblenz. Also cited in Borkin, *The Crime.*

72   " 'I made no secret' ": Martinez, *Der Gaskrieg: 1914/18. Entwicklung, Herstellung und Ensatz chemischer Kampstoff.*

72   "It was a telling point": John French quoted in Carter, *Chemical and Biological Defence at Porton Down, 1916–2000.* For public response in the UK and France, see LeFebure, *The Riddle of the Rhine.* For French air force raid on Ludwigshafen, see Abelshauser et al., *German Industry,* and *Geschichte der Ammoniaksynthese,* in BASF UA G1101. On the establishment of Porton Down, see Carter, *Chemical and Biological.* On subsidies for Leuna (footnote), see BASF UA, C110 (1916).

73   "The German chemists": Stoltenberg, *Fritz Haber*; and Szöllösi-Janze, *Fritz Haber.*

75   "Arguably, Duisberg": For UK government revocation of Aspirin trade-

mark, see *Lancet*, Feb. 5, 1815. For Aspro: Jeffreys, *Aspirin*; Grenville-Smith and Barrie, *Aspro: How a Family Business Grew Up*; and Morgan, *Apothecary's Venture: The Scientific Quest of the International Nicholas Organisation*.

75 "Duisberg looked to his own country": Verg, Plumpe, and Schultheis, *Milestones*; and, for Bauer quotation, Max Bauer papers, July 24, 1915, Bundesarchiv, Koblenz.

75 "Nevertheless Duisberg knew": See Verg, Plumpe, and Schultheis, *Milestones*; Abelshauser et al., *German Industry*; Flechtner, *Carl Duisberg*; Plumpe, *Die IG Farbenindustrie AG: Wirtschaft, Technik und Politik 1904–1945*; and BASF UA, C10 (1914–16).

76 "In these circumstances": Flechtner, *Carl Duisberg*; Plumpe, *Die IG Farbenindustrie*; and BASF UA, C10 (1914–16).

76 "When he raised": Ibid.

77 "Flushed with this": For correspondence on Duisberg's meeting with Hindenburg, see Max Bauer papers, Sept. 10, 1916, Bundesarchiv, Koblenz. See also Plumpe, *Die IG Farbenindustrie*.

78 "The following week": Feldman, *Arms, Industry, and Labor in Germany, 1914–1918*.

79 "In November 1916": Ibid. and Borkin, *The Crime*. For BASF and POW labor, see BASF UA Engere Kommission des AR, Sitzung (April 16, 1915; Oct. 25, 1915; May 2, 1916).

79 "In the meantime": Feldman, *Arms, Industry, and Labor*.

80n Ibid.

80 "It is hard to figure": Duisberg, *Meine Lebenserinnerungen* and *Abhandlungen, Vorträge und Reden aus den Jahren 1882–1921*; Duisberg, *Nur ein Sohn*.

81 "When fighting": For deficiencies of Allied and American chemical industries in 1914 and the effect of the blockade, see Haynes, *American Chemical Industry*, vol. 2.

82 "Meanwhile": Ibid.

82n Ambruster, *Treason's Peace: German Dyes and American Dupes*.

83 "Bayer's U.S. production lines were on the verge": Pharmazeutische Konferenz 169/5, vol. 3, April 11, 1915, Bayer Archives, Leverkusen.

83 "Great Phenol Plot": Jeffreys, *Aspirin*; Ambruster, *Treason's Peace*; Mann and Plummer, *The Aspirin Wars*. Also "Aspirin and Espionage," Journal of the American Medical Association, April 1919.

83 "Hugo Schweitzer": Ibid. and Dr. Hugo Schweitzer, entry 195 and entry 199, Records of the Office of Alien Property, Record Group 131, U.S. National Archives, Washington, D.C.

84n Dyestuffs Committee on Ways and Means, U.S. House of Representatives, 66th Congress, hearings held on June 18, 1919 (U.S. Library of Congress). See also Jones, *The German Secret Service in America, 1914–18*.

84 On Bayer's attempts at corporate camouflage, see Jeffreys, *Aspirin*; and Ambruster, *Treason's Peace*.

84 "Bayer and Company": *New York World*, Aug. 15–19, 1915. For Thomas Edison's announcement, see Haynes, *American Chemical Industry*.

85   "It was all too late": Ibid. See also *Aims and Purposes of the Chemical Foundation Inc and the Reasons for Its Organisation. As Told by A. Mitchell Palmer, United States Attorney General and Former Alien Property Custodian in His Report to Congress, and by Francis P. Garvan, Alien Property Custodian, in an Address to the National Cotton Manufacturers Association*, New York, 1919. For further background on Francis Garvan, see Jeffreys, *The Bureau: Inside the Modern FBI*.

86   "They called it the turnip winter": Gilbert, *The First World War*; Hardach, *The First World War, 1914–1918*.

88   "For those running": For details on the Patriotic Auxiliary Service Law and subsequent labor unrest, see Breunig, *Soziale Verhältnisse der Arbeiterschaft*.

88   "In March 1918": Gilbert, *The First World War*; and Hardach, *The First World War*. For Ludendorff's appeal to Duisberg, see Manchester, *The Arms of Krupp*.

4. The Birth of a Colossus

90   "On the afternoon": This description of events at Carl Duisberg's house in November 1924 is based on various sources, including Duisberg, *Nur ein Sohn*; Duisberg, *Meine Lebenserinnerungen*; Mann and Plummer, *The Aspirin Wars*; Verg, Plumpe, and Schultheis, *Milestones*; Haber, *The Chemical Industry, 1900–1930*; and photographs of the house in the Bayer, Leverkusen archives.

91   "Germany's defeat": See Haber, *The Chemical Industry, 1900–1930*. For BASF's 1917–18 sales, see Abelshauser et al., *German Industry*.

92   "The uncertainty wasn't helped": Quotation from *New York Times*, Dec. 24, 1918. Duisberg at Leverkusen: Verg, Plumpe, and Schultheis, *Milestones*.

92   "There was little": See BASF correspondence with Auswärtige Amt in Bundesarchiv, Lichterfelde, R85; and Haber, *The Chemical Industry, 1900–1930*. Quotation from Morris, "War Gases in Germany."

93   "One of the things": McConnell, "The Production of Nitrogenous Compounds Synthetically in the U.S. and Germany," and Meinzer, *125 Jahre BASF*. Also BASF UA, A862/4.

93   "Then it did": Kolata, *Flu: The Story of the Great Influenza Pandemic of 1918 and the Search for the Virus That Caused It*, and Collier, *The Plague of the Spanish Lady*.

94   "Ironically": Jeffreys, *Aspirin*.

94   Postwar Germany and the founding of the Weimar Republic: Drawn from various sources, including Evans, *The Coming*; Kolb, *The Weimar Republic*; and Bessel, *Germany after the First World War*.

95   "During one such": For the Kapp putsch: Bessel, *Germany after the First World War*. For the VKPD revolt and BASF's response, see BASF UA C113, Engere Kommission des AR, 54, Sitzung 29–3, and Streller and Masalsky, *Geschichte des VEB Leuna-Werke*.

96   "Against such a politically": On the run-up to the peace conference, see Evans, *The Coming*; Kolb, *The Weimar Republic*; Bessel, *Germany*; Luckau, *The German Delegation at the Paris Peace Conference*; and Temperley, *A History of the Peace Conference of Paris*.

98   "Carl Bosch was": Holdermann, *Im Banne der Chemie*.

98   Seizure of Bayer's assets: Jeffreys, *Aspirin*.

99   "He did his best": Bosch, *Geschäftsstelle für die Friedensverhadlungen*. See also Holdermann, *Im Banne der Chemie*.

99   "Bosch and his colleagues": Ibid. and Luckau, *The German Delegation*.

100   Versailles Treaty: Temperley, *A History of the Peace Conference of Paris*.

100   "For the companies": Haber, *The Chemical Industry, 1900–1930*.

101   Bosch's deal with the French (including footnote and quotation): Holdermann, *Im Banne der Chemie*; and Borkin, *The Crime*.

102   "In those bleak days": On Belgian tariffs, see Michels, *Cartels, Combines, and Trusts in Post-War Germany*.

103   "Carl Duisberg was one": Jeffreys, *Aspirin*.

103   "Things were even worse": See Records of the Office of Alien Property, 131, U.S. National Archives. On Sterling Products and its purchase of Bayer, see Hiebert, *Our Policy Is People, Their Health Our Business*; *Drug and Chemical Markets*, Dec. 18, 1918; Mann and Plummer, *The Aspirin Wars*; and Reimer, "Bayer & Company in the United States: German Dyes, Drugs, and Cartels in the Progressive Era." For quotation, see Document 3310, Department of Justice [DOJ] Central Files, Case 60/21/56, Sterling Products, Inc., Record Group 60, U.S. National Archives (hereafter identified as DOJ Sterling, followed by document number).

104   "Weiss had a major": For the state of Rensselaer after sale, see DOJ Sterling 3257.

104   "Help was very difficult": Korthaus, *Pharmazeutische Geschäft in Südamerika währen des Krieges*. Correspondence between Möller and Mann in Bayer Leverkusen Archives 9/A.7 and DOJ Sterling 2495.

105   "It was not a happy": Wiederschrift über die Besprechung am Montag, den 22 September 1919 mit William Weiss et al., Bayer Leverkusen Archives.

106   "Thus began": Jeffreys, *Aspirin*.

106   " 'Everywhere in the whole world' ": Bericht uber die Konferenz mit Herrn Weiss aus New York vom 8 April 1920, Bayer Leverkusen Archives.

106   "It says a great deal": For Weiss's first visit to Leverkusen, see DOJ Sterling 1499 and DOJ Sterling 3795

107   "Eventually, of course": Contract between Farbenfabriken Bayer and Winthrop Chemical Company, April 9, 1923, Exhibit A, *U.S. v Alba*; Contract between Farbenfabriken Bayer and the Bayer Company, April 9, 1923, Exhibit A, *U.S. v The Bayer Company et al.* (Washington: Trade Cases, 1941).

108   "Unquestionably": Ibid.

108   DuPont's approach to Carl Bosch: See *Hearings before Special Committee Investigating the Munitions Industry*, U.S. Senate, 73rd Congress, parts 39 and 11.

108   "DuPont was forced": See *New York Times*, Feb. 21, 1921.

109   "As might be": *Hearings before Special Committee Investigating the Munitions Industry*, U.S. Senate, 73rd Congress, part 39.

109   "The British watched": Travis, "High Pressure Industrial Chemistry."

110   "On the morning": See BASF UA A832/1 and Explosionsunglück Oppau, BASF UA A382 9/II/5. See also *Times*, Sept. 23 and 24, 1921, and *Manchester Guardian*, Sept. 25, 1921.

110   "The explosion was": For financial effects, see BASF UA, Sitzung des AR, Oct. 4, 1921, and Dec. 13, 1921.

111   " 'The very material' ": Holdermann, *Im Banne der Chemie*.

111   "Inevitably, there were rumors" Ibid. and *New York Times*, Oct. 31, 1921.

112   "Although the absolute cause": Haber, *The Chemical Industry, 1900–1930*, and Abelshauser et al., *German Industry*.

112   "As BASF's lawyers": Hayes, "Carl Bosch and Carl Krauch. Chemistry and the Political Economy of Germany 1925–1945."

112   "Krauch rose": Ibid. and Borkin, *The Crime*.

113   On the beginnings of hyperinflation and defaulting on reparations, see Evans, *The Coming*; Kolb, *The Weimar Republic;* and Bessel, *Germany*.

114   "The German chemical industry's plants": Holdermann, *Im Banne der Chemie*.

115   On French legal proceedings against Bosch and others, see *Frankfurter Zeitung*, Aug. 12, 1923.

115   "The wider financial consequences": Evans, *The Coming*; Kolb, *The Weimar Republic;* and Bessel, *Germany*.

116   The Munich Revolt: Ibid. and Kershaw, *Hitler, 1899–1936*.

117   "Germany's chemical industry": Michels, *Cartels, Combines, and Trusts*.

118   On Duisberg's changing attitude toward merger, see Duisberg, *Nur ein Sohn;* Duisberg, *Meine Lebenserinnerungen*; Mann and Plummer, *The Aspirin Wars*; Verg, Plumpe, and Schultheis, *Milestones;* and Haber, *The Chemical Industry, 1900–1930*.

119   "Carl Bosch felt otherwise": Holdermann, *Im Banne der Chemie*. Also see correspondence and memoranda in BASF UA, C10 and A20.

120   Creation of IG Farben and arguments between Bosch and Duisberg: Ibid. and Duisberg, *Nur ein Sohn;* Verg, Plumpe, and Schultheis, *Milestones;* Haber, *The Chemical Industry, 1900–1930*; Michels, *Cartels, Combines, and Trusts;* Hayes, *Industry and Ideology: IG Farben in the Nazi Era*.

121   "It would be over a year": Holdermann, *Im Banne der Chemie*.

121   "On December 2, 1925": Signed copy of IG Farbenindustrie contract in BASF UA, A21/2.

5. Bosch's Plan

123   "There were plenty of positives": IG Farben contract, BASF UA, A21/2.

124   "That whole was": Figures drawn from Stocking and Watkins, *Cartels in Action*; Michels, *Cartels, Combines, and Trusts*; Tammen, "Die I. G. Far-

ben Industrie Aktiengesellschaft 1925–1933"; and Haber, *The Chemical Industry, 1900–1930.*

125   "Finding a management recipe": See affidavit by Fritz ter Meer, NI 5186/38 and NI 9487/78. For further details on work groups, see Abelshauser, *German Industry.*

125   "By 1931, however": See affidavit by Ernst Struss, "Die Betriebsgemein-schaften und die Entwicklung der IG Farben," NI 9487/78, and Hayes, *Industry and Ideology.*

126   "Given their disparate": Ibid. Also NI 5169/38 and NI 10043/82. For formation of NW7, see affidavit by K. Krüger, *NMT,* vol. 7, p. 440, and Sasuly, *IG Farben.*

128   "IG Farben's *Aufsichtsrat*": See affidavit by Fritz ter Meer, NI 5186/38, and affidavit by Carl Krauch, NI 6120/46.

128   For details of the Working Committee, see affidavit by Fritz ter Meer, NI 5184/38. For details of the Central Committee, see affidavit by H. Bässler, NI 7366/59. See also Hayes, *Industry and Ideology.*

128   "This extraordinary": see Ter Meer, *Die IG Farben Industrie Aktienge-sellschaft,* and Hayes, *Industry and Ideology.* For the lack of stockholder objections, see affidavit by Fritz ter Meer, NI 5184/38. For the relationship between Deutsche Länderbank and IG Farben, see Tammen, "Die I.G. Far-ben," and Bower, *Blind Eye to Murder: Britain, America, and the Purging of Nazi Germany.*

129   "So who were those men": This portrait of *Vorstand* members and specific information on Gajewski, Schmitz, von Schnitzler, von Knieriem, Hörlein, Krauch, ter Meer, and Mann have been gleaned from the personal affi-davits of IG defendants and witnesses submitted to the court in *NMT,* with other background from Ter Meer, *Die IG Farben;* DuBois, *The Dev-il's Chemists;* Hayes, *Industry and Ideology;* Duisberg, *Nur ein Sohn;* and Holdermann, *Im Banne der Chemie.*

132   "There were plenty of others": For Carl Bosch's melancholia and intro-spection, see Holdermann, *Im Banne der Chemie.* For origins of the term *decentralized centralism,* see Haber, *The Chemical Industry, 1900–1930;* Abelshauser et al., *German Industry;* and Hayes, *Industry and Ideology.* Hayes uses a wonderful German expression, *Schwerfälligkeit,* roughly translated as "ponderousness," to describe the consequences of the IG's overly bureaucratic structure.

133   "When future historians": This discussion is best encapsulated in David Strahan's *The Last Oil Shock: A Survival Guide to the Imminent Extinc-tion of Petroleum Man.*

134   For agreements between ICI and DuPont, and IG Farben's response, see Coleman, *IG Farben and ICI, 1925–53: Strategies for Growth and Sur-vival.* See also Bayer Leverkusen 4C9.32, Control Office (CR 107/2/18).

134   "Bosch may have had his failings": Holdermann, *Im Banne der Chemie;* and Stranges, "Germany's Synthetic Fuel Industry."

135   For background on Bergius and synthetic fuel, see Holdermann, *Im Banne der Chemie;* and Stranges, "Friedrich Bergius and the Rise of the German Synthetic Fuel Industry."

136 "Bosch's gamble": Figures from Public Record Office, London (National Archives), "Investment in Large Plant of IG in Millions of RM," Aug. 18, 1945, FO 1031/233; and Imperial War Museum, Duxford, *Economic Study of IG Farbenindustrie AG, Section V, 1945*). See also Hughes, "Technological Momentum in History: Hydrogenation in Germany, 1898–1933."

137 "The gamble was not": For an example, see affidavit by Carl Krauch, NI 6524/49.

137 "There were potential external opponents": "Einige Überlegungen angelgentlich der Übertragung des Four Party Agreements auf die Shell," BASF UA, T75/1. See also Yergin, *The Prize*, and Holdermann, *Im Banne der Chemie*.

138 "Standard's bosses duly obliged": Howard, *Buna Rubber*.

138 "In March 1926": Ibid.

138 " 'This matter' ": Quoted in Wendell, *Cartels: Challenge to a Free World*.

138 "A few days later": Howard, *Buna Rubber*.

139 "Bosch had hooked": Ibid. and Holdermann, *Im Banne der Chemie*.

139 "That work had gotten off": BASF UA, Ludwigshafen, Hochdruckversuche "Kurzes Referat," Nov. 9, 1942; BASF UA, "Produktion und Gestehkosten Leuna," June 27, 1947. See also Abelshauser et al., *German Industry*.

139 "In the meanwhile": For the Bergius agreement with Standard, see Borkin, *The Crime*. Also *Hearings before the Committee on Patents*, U.S. Senate, 77th Congress, 2nd Session (1942).

139 "The agreement still": Ibid.

140 "Bosch on the other hand": Affidavit by Carl Krauch, NI 6524/49; Holdermann, *Im Banne der Chemie*.

140 Deal with Standard: See Control Office, IG Farbenindustrie AG, U.S. Zone, "Activities of IG Farben in the Oil Industry," Jan. 14, 1946; Yergin, *The Prize*; Holdermann, *Im Banne der Chemie*; and Hayes, *Industry and Ideology*. For agreement on buna: Holdermann, *Im Banne der Chemie*; Hayes, *Industry and Ideology*; and Borkin, *The Crime*.

141 "And then the wheel": Figures in Stranges, "Germany's Synthetic Fuel Industry." For criticism of Bosch's decision, see affidavit by Carl Krauch, NI 6524/49.

6. Striking the Bargain

143 "For most of the middle years": On the IG's general attitude toward politics, see Flechtner, *Carl Duisberg*; Holdermann, *Im Banne der Chemie*; Tammen, "Die I.G. Farben"; and Hayes, *Industry and Ideology*.

144 "But in Weimar's fractured": This overview of the Weimar political scene is drawn from various sources, including Evans, *The Coming*; Kolb, *The Weimar Republic*; Bessel, *Germany*; Falter, "How Likely Were Workers to Vote for the NSDAP?"; Eyck, *History of the Weimar Republic*, vols. 1 and 2; and Turner, *German Big Business and the Rise of Hitler*.

145 "Gustav Stresemann's German People's Party": Turner, H. A. *Gustav Stresemann and the Politics of the Weimar Republic*. See also Borkin, *The Crime*.

145 "Carl Duisberg had begun": U.S. National Archives Record Group 238, M892, Records of the *United States of America v. Carl Krauch et al.* (Case VI), Defense Papers Schmitz, affidavit by W. F. Kalle, Sept. 8, 1947; Hayes, *Industry and Ideology*.

146 "*Die Zeit*": Tammen, "Die I. G. Farben," and Turner, *Gustav Stresemann*. For the *Europäische Revue*, see Hayes, *Industry and Ideology*. For the *Frankfurter Zeitung* and following, see Tammen, "Die I. G. Farben."

147 The overview of the causes of the Depression and its impact on Germany is drawn from a variety of sources, including Evans, *The Coming*; Kolb, *The Weimar Republic*; Bessel, *Germany*; Eyck, *A History of the Weimar Republic*; and Clavin, *The Great Depression in Europe, 1929–1939*.

149 "IG Farben, now far": The financial effects of the collapse in nitrogen prices are detailed in Abelshauser et al., *German Industry*; and Tammen, "Die I. G. Farben."

150 "As Carl Bosch": For general workforce reductions, see Tammen, "Die I. G. Farben," and Plumpe, *Die IG Farbenindustrie*. For Ludwigshafen and Oppau, see BASF UA, IG TO1, "*Umsatzanteil pro Belegschaftsmitglied*" (H. Rötger). For attempts at amelioration of workers' distress, see Abelshauser et al., *German Industry*.

150 "The IG survived": See Schröter, *Deutsche Industrie auf dem Weltmarkt*.

151 "Quarrels between": See NI 6524/49, affidavit by Carl Krauch; NI 6765/52, affidavit by Friedrich Jaehne.

151 "But Bosch": See NI 5184/18, affidavit by Fritz ter Meer.

152 "'In recognition of their contributions'": Holdermann, *Im Banne der Chemie*.

152 "Typically, Bosch pressed ahead": NI 1941/18, *Zentralausschuss* meeting of May 18, 1931. For Duisberg's view of Brüning, see Duisberg to Kirdorf, June 26, 1931, Bayer Leverkusen Archives.

153n See Hayes, *Industry and Ideology*.

153 "The financial relief": For the decision to commission another report on Leuna, see NI 1941/18, *Zentralausschuss* meeting of June 20, 1931.

154 "He entrusted": For Gaus's conundrum, see Abelshauser et al., *German Industry*.

154 "'After careful consideration'": W. Gaus to Bosch, "Fortführung oder Stillegung der Benzinfabrikation?" BASF UA 25.

154 "Bosch was infuriated": Contrasting figures reproduced in Tammen, "Die I. G. Farben."

155 "The Depression had fatally": For the Communist Party's response, see Evans, *The Coming*.

156 "At the opposite end": This brief account of the Nazis' rise to power is drawn from various sources across a vast historiography. I have found the following most useful: Evans, *The Coming*; Burleigh, *The Third Reich: A New History*; Kershaw, *Hitler*, and *Weimar: Why Did German Democracy Fail?*; Shirer, *The Rise and Fall of the Third Reich: A History of Nazi*

Germany; and Jones, *German Liberalism and the Dissolution of the Weimar Party System, 1918–1933.*

159   " 'Instead of working' ": *Hitler's Secret Conversations*, 1941–44.

161   "The bosses of IG Farben": For RGO election figures, see Braun, *Schichtwechsel: Arbeit und Gewerkschaft in der Chemie-Stadt Ludwigshafen.*

161   "Up until this point": For Nazi figures, see Braun, *Schichtwechsel*. For unrest in works, see Bayer Archives, Leverkusen, "Politik/Staats-und Parteipolitik 20/11/30." For Nazi workers' bomb plot, see BASF UA, CI3, "Direkktionssitzungen Ludwigshafen 1930–1939"; and Meinzer, *125 Jahre BASF.*

162   "What was commanding": See Bayer Archives, Leverkusen, 4C9.25, Gajewski I/4, Affidavit by G. Ollendorff, April 24, 1947. For Ley's denunciation of Warburg, see *Nordhausener Allgemeine Zeitung*, Sept. 16, 1927, in Bayer Leverkusen archive. See also Hans Kühne, *NMT*, vol. 7, p. 634.

163   " 'If you could talk' ": Gattineau to Karl Haushofer, June 6, 1931, *NMT*, appendix.

163   "Whether Haushofer did so": NI 15237, Gattineau's report, Oct. 12, 1931. Nazi reports in *Völkischer Beobachter*, Feb. 10, 1932.

163   "When Hitler arrived": See affidavit by Gattineau in NI 4833/35 and Bütefisch's testimony, *NMT*, vol. 7, pp. 544–60.

164   "As the discussion": see Gattineau and Bütefisch, above, and NI 8637/71, interrogation of Heinrich Bütefisch, for Bosch quotation. The Speer quotation in the footnote is from Speer, *Inside the Third Reich.*

164   "Over the next few months": For Wilhelm Mann's party membership, see NI 5167/38, affidavit by Wilhelm Mann.

164   "Then came Hitler's appointment as Reich chancellor": Evans, *The Coming*; Burleigh, *The Third Reich*; and Kershaw, *Hitler.*

165   Invitation to meet Hitler: *NMT*, vol. 7, p. 557.

166   "This wasn't the first time": Turner, *German Big Business.*

166   "By 1932, however": Ibid. and Shirer, *The Rise and Fall of the Third Reich.*

167   "The Nazis' hopes": See account of Düsseldorf meeting in Evans, *The Coming.*

168   "The identities of many of those": Affidavit by Georg von Schnitzler, *NMT*, vol. 7, pp. 555–56; and memorandum by Gustav Krupp, Feb. 23, 1932, *NMT*, vol. 7, p. 562. For Krupp's *Reichsverband* memo, see *NMT*, Case X v. Bülow, "Notes of the Business Management of the National Association of German Industry for the Conference at Reich Minister Göring's on 20 February 1933."

168   "In the row immediately behind him": For seating arrangements, see Manchester, *The Arms of Krupp*. For presence of Duisberg at Leverkusen that night, see Verg, Plumpe, and Schultheis, *Milestones*. Duisberg to RDI quoted in Taylor, *Sword and Swastika: Generals and Nazis in the Third Reich.*

169   "Carl Bosch was absent too": Affidavit by Georg von Schnitzler, *NMT*, vol. 7, pp. 555–56.

169   "The two IG attendees": Ibid.

169   "The first half of his speech": Ibid. and memorandum by Gustav Krupp, Feb. 23, 1932, *NMT*, vol. 7, p. 562. Quotations from a report of Hitler's remarks in *NMT*, vol. 7, pp. 527–52. See also *NMT*, vol. 7, p. 563 (interrogation of Hjalmar Schacht).

170   "As Hitler and Göring": Affidavit by Georg von Schnitzler, *NMT*, vol. 7, pp. 555–56, and *NMT*, vol 7, pp. 561–67.

170   "On February 27": NI 391, Selck and Bangert to Delbrück, Schickler & Co., *NMT*, vol. 7, p. 565. See also Turner, *German Big Business*.

171   For final acts in Hitler's accession to absolute power, see Evans, *The Coming*; Burleigh, *The Third Reich*; and Kershaw, *Hitler*.

172   "Having played such a significant": For details of the individual donations constituting the RM 4.5 million, see Hayes, *Industry and Ideology*; and Turner, *German Big Business*.

7. Accommodation and Collaboration

173   "On March 29, 1933": Wilhelm Mann, "Concerning Agitation against German Goods Abroad," *NMT*, vol. 7, p. 649. Italics in original.

174   "This looked set to be considerable": See Evans, *The Coming*; Burleigh, *The Third Reich*; and Friedländer, *Nazi Germany and the Jews: The Years of Persecution, 1933–1939*.

175   "Few of these correspondents": For Mann's Nazi membership, see "Personalakte Wilhelm Mann," Berlin Document Center (BDC).

175   " 'Day after day' ": Klemperer, *I Shall Bear Witness: The Diaries of Victor Klemperer, 1933–41*.

176   "Carl Bosch, however": For Schwarz's Jewish ancestry, see Bayer Leverkusen 4C9.25 Schmitz I/8, affidavit by K. Holdermann, March 6, 1947.

176   "A few days after": Evans, *The Coming*; Friedländer, *Nazi Germany and the Jews*; Cornwell, *Hitler's Scientists*.

177   "In April 1933": Szöllösi-Janze, *Fritz Haber*. Haber letter quoted in Stern, *Einstein's German World*.

177   "Carl Bosch saw": BASF UA, WI, Bosch to Kultusministerium, April 26, 1933.

178   "At first the meeting": An account of the Bosch-Hitler meeting and these quotations are in Holdermann, *Im Banne der Chemie*, and repeated in Gattineau, *Durch die Klippen des 20 Jahrehunderts*.

178   "From that moment": Borkin, *The Crime*. Max Planck wrote an account of his meeting with Hitler in *Physikalische Blatter* in 1947, but it is also cited in Cornwell, *Hitler's Scientists*.

179   "Unable to do more": On Schwarz, see Bayer Archives Leverkusen, 4C9.25 Schmitz I/8, affidavit by K. Holdermann, March 6, 1947. On Pietrkowski, see BASF UA, WI, Pietrkowski to Bosch, June 9, 1933. On Haber memorial, see Holdermann, *Im Banne der Chemie*, and Szöllösi-Janze, *Fritz Haber*.

180   "Bosch's recalcitrance": Hans Kühne's statement in NI 6960, *NMT*, vol.

7, p. 570. For Nazi May Day rally at Ludwigshafen, see "Der Feiertag der deutschen Arbeit," *IG Farbenindustries AG Ludwigshafen Werkszeitung* 21 (May–June 1933), BASF UA.

180 "Needless to say": Quotation from Wolff provided by his family. For the events of May 2 and after, see Evans, *The Coming*, and Burleigh, *The Third Reich.*

181 "Given the breakneck speed": For Duisberg memoir, see Duisberg, *Meine Lebenserinnerungen.* For figures on retirees, see NI 7956–57/66, affidavits by H. Bässler, July 8, 1947, and July 17, 1947.

181 " 'The collapse of the liberal' ": *NMT*, vol. 8, p. 1059.

181 "The most obvious": For Hans Kühne's Nazi membership, see *NMT*, vol. 7, pp. 634–36. For Gajewski and Otto, see those pages and NI 14105/115. For Mühlen, see "Personalakte Mühlen," BDC. For Selck, see NI 1941/18 and "Personalakte Erwin Selck," BDC. For Hörlein, see "Personalakte Heinrich Hörlein," BDC. For Gattineau, see "Personalakte Heinrich Gattineau," BDC.

182 "Actual party membership": For Schneider, see *NMT*, vol. 7, p. 622. For Bütefisch, see *NMT*, vol. 8, p. 853. For Schmitz's Nazi nomination to Reichstag, see U.S. National Archives, RG 239 M892 Schmitz V/92, affidavit by H. Globke. For von Schnitzler, see Hayes, *Industry and Ideology*, and DuBois, *The Devil's Chemists.*

182 "These men were still": Hayes, *Industry and Ideology*; and Tooze, *The Wages of Destruction.*

183 " 'attending meetings of local' ": *NMT*, vol. 7, pp. 616–17.

183 "One of the most curious": For Ilgner's background, see NI 6544/50, affidavit by Max Ilgner, April 20, 1947; Hayes, *Industry and Ideology*; and DuBois, *The Devil's Chemists.*

184 "two important *NWT* subsections": For establishment of *Volkswirtschaftliche Abteilung*, see NI 4975/36, affidavit by Anton Reithinger, Feb. 3, 1947, and affidavit by H. Bannert, May 19, 1947. For establishment of *Wirtschaftspolitische Abteilung*, see NI 9569/79, meeting of the *Arbeitsausschuss* (Working Committee), Sept. 7, 1932.

185 " 'Ilgner had great ambitions' ": *NMT*, vol. 7, p. 440.

185 "Given the opportunity": On Ilgner's Rotary membership, see *NMT*, vol. 7, p. 440; and DuBois, *The Devil's Chemists.*

185 " 'After Hitler took over' ": *NMT*, vol. 7, pp. 440–46.

186 "Overseas the IG's": For DuPont's visit to IG, see NI 9784/81, Ewing to Swint, July 17, 1933.

186 "Max Ilgner rose to": On advice to Goebbels, see DuBois, *The Devil's Chemists.* Quotation in NI 6702/51, Ilgner's affidavit, April 25, 1947, and testimony, *NMT*, vol. 7, pp. 703–45.

186 "Undeterred, Ilgner": See Ilgner's affidavit and testimony, above.

187 "Although the notion": Ibid. For the footnote on Lee, see U.S. Congress, House of Representatives, Special Committee on Un-American Activities, *Investigation of Nazi Propaganda Activities and Investigation of Certain Other Propaganda Activities* (1934).

187 "Ilgner's enthusiastic": Quotation from NI 697/7, Schnitzler to Selck, July 28, 1933. For Bayer under pressure in Montevideo, NI 9897/82, Monte-

video office to Pharma Direktion, July 29, 1933, and reply of Aug. 18, 1933. See also *NMT*, vol. 7, pp. 725–26, and NI 8420, meeting of Bayer directors, Jan. 23, 1934. For IG capitulation to pressure, see NI 8421–22, meetings of Bayer directors, Feb. 13, 1934, and Feb. 27, 1934.

188   "The IG was to be just": For examples of contradictory policies on Nazi salute and fund-raising, see NI 5867–68/44, meetings of Hoechst directors, Aug. 14 and 18, 1933.

188   "The IG's various internal": For report of Ley's speech, see BASF UA, "Arbeitsfront und ständischer Aufbau," *IG Farbenindustrie AG Werke Ludwigshafen, Werkszeitung* 21 (Nov. 1933). For quotation about intention to "Nazify" further editions see BASF UA, " 'Zum Geleit!' " Von Werk zu Werk, Werkszeitung der BASF 23, no. 1 (Jan. 1935). See also Abelshauser et al., *German Industry*.

189   "Sometimes the regime's": For air raid practice and Kühne's response, see NI 8461, conference of plant leaders, June 21, 1933, *NMT*, vol. 7, p. 1226.

189   "The IG was also wrestling": NI 6787/52, affidavit by Heinrich Hörlein, May 2, 1947.

190   "Gradually, however": For improvement in profits and employment, see NI 10001/82, affidavit by H. Deichfischer.

190   "It is questionable, of course": Figures on employment improved via autobahn construction from Burleigh, *The Third Reich*. For IG donations, see Turner, *German Big Business*.

191   "The strain on Bosch": On coal producers and hopes for the Fischer-Tropp process, see Abelshauser et al., *German Industry*; and Warriner, *Combines and Rationalisation in Germany, 1924–28*. For details of deal, see Hayes, *Industry and Ideology*.

192   "In June 1933": For Krauch's report, see "Die deutsche Treibstoffwirtschaft," BASF IG M02/1, and NI 4718.

192   For Max Ilgner's cultivation of Thomas, see Borkin, *The Crime*. For Thomas's memo to his superiors, see *Geschichte der deutschen Wehr und Rüstungwirtschaft*, 1918/1943/44, Imperial War Museum, Duxford. For the possibility that Ilgner might have known of the Air Ministry's plans, see NI 4718.

193   "The general's most": For Milch's dealings with Krauch, see Borkin, *The Crime*. For the ministry's response, see NI 6544, affidavit by Max Ilgner, and NI 7123/55, Abschrift, Besprechung im RLM am 15/9/33. For Feder and Hitler, see Abelshauser et al., *German Industry*.

193   "The result was": For the *Benzinvertrag* of Dec. 14, 1933, see NI 881/9.

194   " 'the magicians who made' ": Opening Statements for the Prosecution, *NMT*, vol. 7, p. 101.

8. From Long Knives to the Four-Year Plan

195   This account of the events leading up to and including the Röhm purge is drawn from the following sources: Fest, *Hitler*; Frei, *National Socialist Rule in Germany: The Führer State, 1933–1945*; Taylor, *Sword and Swastika*;

Shirer, *The Rise and Fall of the Third Reich*; Read, *The Devil's Disciples: The Life and Times of Hitler's Inner Circle*; and Gisevius, *To the Bitter End*.

197 "As a former corporal": For Hitler's sympathy with, and suspicion of, Röhm's radicalism, see Taylor, *Sword and Swastika*.

198 For Gattineau's experience, see NI 4833/35, affidavit by H. Gattineau, March 13, 1947, and Gattineau, *Durch die Klippen des 20 Jahrehunderts*. For Ilgner claims, see NI 6544, affidavit by M. Ilgner, April 20, 1947. For overview, see Hayes, *Industry and Ideology*, and DuBois, *The Devil's Chemists*.

200 "But if this was their intention": For Bosch, see Holdermann, *Im Banne der Chemie,* and Lochner, *Tycoons and Tyrants: German Industry from Hitler to Adenauer*.

200 For Duisberg's death, see Verg, Plumpe, and Schultheis, *Milestones*; and Jeffreys, *Aspirin*.

201 " 'Germany is deprived' ": *Times*, March 25, 1935, reprinted in *Nature*, June 22, 1935.

201 "Duisberg was not the only": Hindenburg's telegram cited in Taylor, *The Sword and the Swastika*.

202 " 'I swear by God' ": The Wehrmacht oath of allegiance to Hitler can be found in any of the standard histories of the Third Reich.

202 "Vital though oil": The best discussions of the IG's nascent buna programs can be found in Hayes, *Industry and Ideology*, and Morris, "The Development of Acetylene Chemistry and Synthetic Rubber by IG Farbenindustrie, 1926–1945." For the Wehrmacht's purchase of tires for testing, see Bundesarchiv, Lichterfelde, R8128/A1153, IG Farbenindustrie AG Stickstoffabteilung 15/8/33, and *NMT*, vol. 7, pp. 752–53. See also NI 6930.

203 " 'Before we resume our efforts' ": NI 6930.

203 "Unfortunately, the Reich's": See Morris, "The Development of Acetylene Chemistry and Synthetic Rubber"; and Borkin, *The Crime*. See also NI 5187/10, affidavit by F. ter Meer.

204 " 'The erection of the first factory' ": *Times*, Sept. 12, 1935.

204 "In truth": For Keppler's discussions with the IG, see NI 7241/57, affidavit by Ernst Struss. For the army's resistance and the IG's reluctance, see NI 5187/10 affidavit by F. ter Meer. For Schkopau, see Morris, "The Development of Acetylene Chemistry and Synthetic Rubber," and NI 7624, "Grundlegenenden Gesichtspunkte für die Gründung des Werkes Schkopau und den Buna Vertrag," Feb. 17, 1937.

204 "The decision to proceed": See Holdermann, *Im Banne der Chemie*.

205 On Schmitz, see NI 6539, affidavit by H. Schmitz; NI 5092/37, affidavit by E. Struss, NI 5092; NI 9761, affidavit by F. Jaehne; Duisberg, *Nur ein Sohn*; DuBois, *The Devil's Chemists*; Borkin, *The Crime*; and Hayes, *Industry and Ideology*.

206 "Carl Krauch, the head of *Sparte* I": See NI 6768, affidavit by C. Krauch. See also Hayes, "Carl Bosch and Carl Krauch"; DuBois, *The Devil's Chemists*; Abelshauser et al., *German Industry*.

207 On the establishment of the *Vermittlungstelle Wehrmacht*, see NI 4702.

207 " 'The newly founded' ": NI–2638, *Verm. W. to IG Offices*, Dec. 31, 1935.

207   "The *Verm. W.*": See *NMT*, vol. 7, pp. 134–36 and 1046–48. For more on the prosecutors' view, see DuBois, *The Devil's Chemists*.

208   "*Mob Kalendar*": see *NMT*, vol. 7, pp. 1493–95, and NI 4625/34, Verm. W. to the Betriebsgemeinschaften. See also IG Farbenindustrie Aktiengesellschaft, "*Mob-Kalendar für das Werk*," Nov. 10, 1936, in GARF (State Archive of the Russian Federation, Moscow) 1457-49-4.

208   "Suspiciously prescient or not": For clash between Schacht and Keppler and consequences, see Schacht, *Account Settled*; and Tooze, *The Wages of Destruction*.

209   "Convinced that the former": See Göring's assessment in *Trials of the Major War Criminals before the International Military Tribunal* (Nuremberg, 1947–49), vol. 9, p. 448. Further references to this trial will be shortened to *IMT*.

209   "After appointing": For Krauch's joining of Göring's commission and the reasons for Bosch's sanction of the appointment, see NI 9767/2, affidavit by E. Gritzbach; NI 10386/85, affidavit by P. Koerner; and, above all, NI 676/7, interrogation of Carl Krauch, April 16, 1947.

209   "Krauch was delighted": NI 676/7. For von Schnitzler's objections, see NI 675/7, Schnitzler's statement, April 30, 1947.

210   " 'If war comes tomorrow' ": Borkin, *The Crime*.

210   For Schacht's objections see: *Nazi Conspiracy and Aggression* (Washington D.C. USGPO 1946), p. 886.

210   "The rows eventually grew so heated": *New York Times*, May 3, 1936, and May 4, 1936.

211   " 'The minister of economics has only' ": For Hitler and Göring's meeting at the Obersalzberg and for the quotation, see NI 4955/36.

211   "Although Schacht was not": For Schacht quotations, see *IMT*, vol. 27, p. 1301.

212   "But Blomberg": For Göring's remarks about Frederick the Great, see Taylor, *The Sword and the Swastika*. For creation of the Four-Year Plan, Göring's appointment, and Hitler quotation, see *IMT*, vol. 12, p. 446.

212   "Of course, all of these": For Krauch, see *NMT*, vol. 7, p. 851. For Eckell, see NI 8833/3, affidavit by J. Eckell. See also *NMT*, vol. 7, p. 857, testimony of Felix Ehrmann.

213   For figures on the IG's share of Four-Year Plan investment, see U.S. National Archives, RG 238/ M892, Krauch defense papers, affidavit by C. Krauch, Dec. 19, 1947, *NMT*, vol. 7, p. 851, testimony of Carl Krauch. For the most comprehensive summary, see Hayes, *Industry and Ideology*. See also Taylor, *The Sword and the Swastika*.

214   " 'The struggle we are approaching' ": NI 051/2, 17/12/36.

9. Preparing for War

215   "The three years running": Figures from NI 10001–03, affidavits by H. Deichfischer, June 2, 1947, and Gross, *Further Facts and Figures Relating to the Deconcentration of the I. G. Farbenindustrie Aktiengesellschaft*.

215   "Not all of this growth": Details of the ubiquity of the IG's ersatz products are drawn from many hundreds of statements made by prosecution and defense at Nuremberg, contained in *NMT*, vols. 7, and 8, and the U.S. National Archives RG series of defense documents, e.g., NI 6525/8, affidavits by C. Krauch.

216   " 'What the chemical industry' ": *Völkischer Beobachter*, no. 212, July 31, 1938.

216   "Without Hitler's rearmament program": Figures calculated by Peter Hayes for *Industry and Ideology*.

216   "At Nuremberg": See final statements of defendants, *NMT*, vol. 8, pp. 1055–79. Georg von Schnitzler interrogation, Sept. 7, 1945, quoted in *Elimination of German Resources for War: Hearings before a Subcommittee of the Committee on Military Affairs*, U.S. Senate, 79th Congress, first session (Dec. 1945), p. 957.

218   "Having gambled": See Fest, *Hitler*; Shirer, *The Rise and Fall of the Third Reich*; Burleigh, *The Third Reich*.

219n   *Elimination of German Resources.*

219   "Carl Krauch": For figures on commissions, see RG 238, M892, Krauch 1/87, affidavit by C. Krauch, Dec. 29, 1947.

219   "But Krauch's role": NI 7241, affidavit by Ernst Struss.

220   "This pattern was repeated": See NI 10386, affidavit by P. Körner. Peter Hayes argues that Körner planted doubt in Krauch's mind about Löb's estimates rather than the other way around. (*Industry and Ideology*, p. 206n.) Whether this is true or not, Krauch subsequently brought inaccuracies in Löb's estimates to Körner's attention. See NI 6768/7, affidavit by C. Krauch.

220   "Krauch was at his most": For account of meeting and Krauch Plan, see NI 10386, affidavit by P. Körner. For appointment of Krauch as plenipotentiary, see NI 6768/53, interrogation of Krauch.

221   "The concern's response": For the IG's positive response to the increase in orders, see *Elimination of German Resources* (exhibit 15), statement by Georg von Schnitzler, excerpts, p. 984. For secrecy, see example in NI 14002, memo by von Knieriem, Oct. 4, 1935.

221   "Take, for example": For IG and DAG plants involved in the manufacture of explosives, see Bayer Archives, Leverkusen, IG Farben Geschäftsbericht 1929; Bayer Archives, Leverkusen 6/14 Vowi Bericht 2803, and BIOS FR 534, *Organisation of the German Chemical Industry and Its Development for War Purposes*. For von Schnitzler quotation, see NI 5191/38, affidavit by G. von Schnitzler, March 4, 1947.

222   "The IG's involvement": For mustard gas production, see NI 6788/52, affidavit by O. Ambros, May 1, 1947; NI 12725/104, affidavit by E. Ehrmann, Nov. 26, 1947; and *NMT*, vol. 7, pp. 935–43.

223   "The first of these": See Harris and Paxman, *A Higher Form of Killing*. For Ambros and Dyhernfurth, see NI 4989.

223   "Projects of this kind": For German Corporation Law, see Mann, "The New German Law and Its Background." See also NI 100037/38/82.

224   "In 1937, after": See NI 12042, membership of IG directors in Nazi

organizations. For Bosch's speech at the Deutsches Museum, see BASF W1, "Niederschrift über die 28. Sitzung des Ausschusses des Deutschen Museum am 7. Mai, 1939."

225   "The government's anti-Semitic": For Göring's decrees (Jan., Feb., and Nov. 1938), see Bayer Leverkusen Direktions Abteilung 377 and NI 15171/123. See also Barkai, *From Boycott to Annihilation: The Economic Struggle of German Jews, 1933–1945*.

225   "As a consequence": See NI 7957/66, affidavit by H. Bässler, July 17, 1947, and NI 7957, chart of members of *Aufsichtsrat*.

225   "On this occasion": See RG M892, von Schnitzler 11/214, affidavit by R. von Szilvinyi, p. 66, and RG M892, Schmitz 4/53, affidavit by R. Graf von Spreti. See also NI 13678/111, Krauch to Wolff.

226   "An episode involving": For Ollendorf's meeting with Gajewski, see *NMT*, vol. 7, pp. 6228–29.

226   " 'We wish to inform' ": See NI 13522/110 and *NMT*, vol. 7, p. 594.

227   "Of course, Gajewski": For Gajewski's subsequent actions and Ollendorf's affidavit, see *NMT*, vol. 7, p. 594. For Baumann's fate, see RGO M892, Bütefisch 9/158, affidavit by A. Baumann, his widow. For Piesteritz three, see Pistor, *100 Jahre Griesheim*. For footnote, see Hayes, *Industry and Ideology*.

227   "In the meantime": See BASF UA, A865/57. For purchase of Weinessigfabrik L. Hirsch, etc., see Keiser, "Die Konzernbewegung 1936–39."

228n   Details about IG Farben's "Strength through Joy" incentives from Abelshauser et al., *German Industry*. For figures on women employees, see BASF UA, C621/2.

228   "Even for those": For background on Bohle and *Auslandorganization*, see McKale, *The Swastika Outside Germany*. For quotation from Commercial Committee, see NI 04862/36, Oct. 7, 1937. For "The few remaining," see NI 8428, pharmaceuticals sales combine meeting of Feb. 16, 1938.

229   "If IG Farben's": For Bohle's demands, see *NMT*, vol. 7, pp. 655–57. For Max Wojahn, see U.S. Federal Economic Administration [FEA], Economics Organization Staff, "Sterling, IG, and the Nazi Government" (IV), Record Group 169, U.S. National Archives, pp. 26–28.

230   "But Bohle also wanted": See *NMT*, vol. 7, pp. 724–30. Quotation from Commercial Committee, NI 4959, p. 37, meeting of Sept. 10, 1937. For mobile cinemas showing Nazi propaganda, see Mann and Plummer, *The Aspirin Wars*.

231   "Max Ilgner's *Vowi*": See NI 6702/51, affidavit by M. Ilgner, April 15, 1947; *Elimination of German Resources*, pp. 949–51; and DuBois, *The Devil's Chemists*. Central America *Verbindungsmann* quoted in DuBois.

232   "In this climate": For an overview of IG's foreign deals, see Glaser-Schmidt, "Foreign Trade Strategies of I. G. Farben after World War I," and Coleman, *IG Farben and ICI, 1925–53*.

232   "In late 1937": For McClintock's meeting with Schmitz and IG's persistence, see FEA, "Sterling, IG, and the Nazi Government"; and Department of Justice Central Files, Case 60/21/56, Sterling Products, Inc., Record

Group 60, U.S. National Archives, document 6283. Quotation from Wilhelm Mann in *DOJ Sterling* 6434.

233   For acquisition of tetraethyl lead, see *NMT*, vol. 7, p. 4922; *Elimination of German Resources*, p. 945; and Borkin, *The Crime*. For its importance to Germany, see *NMT*, vol. 7, p. 1309, memo from von Knieriem to Schmitz.

234   " 'It has been claimed' ": *Hearings before a Subcommittee on Military Affairs*, U.S. Senate, 78th Congress, 1st session (1943), p. 939.

234   "The ministry asked the IG": *NMT*, vol. 7, p. 1309.

235   "The IG knew": Quotation from von Knieriem in *NMT*, vol. 7, p. 1204. For the Air Ministry's being informed, see *NMT*, vol. 7, p. 1189.

235   "In all liklihood": March 12, 1937, memo from *Verm. W.* in *NMT*, vol. 7, p. 1275. The warning of July 14, 1937, is contained in *NMT*, vol. 7, p. 1275, exhibit 223.

236   "Standard's disquiet": For butyl and Standard's legal requirements, see Borkin, *The Crime*.

237   "Germany's foreign policy": For Hossbach memorandum, including quotation, see *IMT*, vol. 25, pp. 402–13.

238   "Standard, increasingly anxious": Account of meeting and subsequent correspondence in *Hearings before the Committee on Patents*, U.S. Senate, 77th Congress, 2nd session (1942), part 6, pp. 2904–06.

238   "He would come to regret": For ter Meer's passionate commitment to buna, see ter Meer, *Die IG Farben Industrie*.

239   "A few days after his meeting": For account of meeting and quotations, see NI 10455 in *NMT*, vol. 7, pp. 1281–84, file note by ter Meer.

239   " 'Taken up negotiations' ": in *Hearings before the Committee on Patents*, U.S. Senate, 77th Congress, 2nd session (1942), part 6, p. 2907.

239   "Ten days later": Ibid.

239   " 'We know some of the difficulties' ": Ibid., pp. 2912–13.

240   Ter Meer's visit to the United States: Ibid., pp. 2916–17.

241   "Something must surely": For the IG's interest in Skodawerke, see *NMT*, vol. 7, pp. 1407–08, minutes of the special meeting of Farben officers concerning Austria, Sept. 10, 1937; NI 6070/45, meeting of Commercial Committee concerning Austria, April 19, 1938. See also NI 8578, p. 70, affidavit by H. Gattineau, May 2, 1947; NI 8456/70, statement by P. Haefliger, May 1, 1947; Hayes, *Industry and Ideology*; and DuBois, *The Devil's Chemists*. For Skodawerke's initial response to the IG's interest, see NI 7388.

241n   *NMT*, vol. 7, p. 1209.

242   "But before this deal": For "New Order" document, see *NMT*, vol. 7, p. 149.

242   "Keppler, who had tangled": For Keppler quotation, see Haefliger's notes of the meeting, NI 3981/29. For the IG's acquisition of Skodawerke, see *NMT*, vol. 7, pp. 1414–15, NI 9289. For the fate of Pollack, see Hilberg, *Destruction of the European Jews*.

243   "If the IG": For background on Sudetenland crisis, see Fest, *Hitler*; Carr, *Arms, Autarky, and Aggression*; Burleigh, *The Third Reich*; and Shirer, *The Rise and Fall of the Third Reich*.

243	"On May 24, 1938": See *Elimination of German Resources*, p. 1007, and DuBois, *The Devil's Chemists*. On Ayranization of the IG's Czech interests, see *NMT*, vol. 7, pp. 1546–51.
243	"The IG's motives": For attitude toward Verein, see NI 6221 and NI 5194/38, affidavit by G. Schnitzler, March 10, 1947.
244	"So while von Schnitzler": For donations to Sudeten interests, see *NMT*, vol, 7, pp. 591–93, NI 2795. For hunt for suitable German employees, see *NMT*, vol. 7, pp. 146–51, 1566–74.
244	For appointment of von Schnitzler, ter Meer, Ilgner, and Kühne as special representatives, see NI 15080/123, *Vorstand* meeting of Sept. 16, 1938.
244	" 'Profoundly impressed' ": NI 2795, *NMT*, vol. 7, p. 591.
245	"In an equally bullish": For lobbying of Chemische Fabrik von Heyden and quotation, see *NMT*, vol. 7, pp. 1417–19, NI 9161/76.
245	"However, von Schnitzler": For deal with Heyden, see NI 13541/110, IG and Heyden to RWM (Reich Economics Ministry). For threat to Aussiger Verein, see *NMT*, vol. 7, p. 43.
246	For the deteriorating position in Europe, see Shirer, *The Rise and Fall of the Third Reich*; and Fest, *Hitler*.
246	"The IG had been in this situation": *NMT*, vol. 7, p. 35. See Also *Elimination of German Resources*, p. 949.
247	"In July 1939": For Walter Duisberg's proposal, see *Robert Bonnar et al. v. The United States* (Ct. Cl. 1971, no. 293–63), Exhibit 155, Office of the Alien Property Custodian, Report of Examiner re: Walter Duisberg, p. 26. For specifics of the deal, see Borkin, *The Crime*.
248	"But in those final few": See BIOS FR 534, *Organisation of the German Chemical Industry and Its Development for War Purposes*; *Elimination of German Resources*, pp. 986–87; *NMT*, vol. 7, pp. 1233, 1335.
248	"By now, this level": For ICI's militarization, see Reader, *Imperial Chemical Industries*. For composition of German bombers, see Dressel and Griehl, *Bombers of the Luftwaffe*; and Kay and Smith, *German Aircraft of World War II*. For foot soldiers' equipment, see *German Infantry, 1938–1945*.

10. War and Profit

251	"A strange air": Shirer, *The Rise and Fall of the Third Reich*.
252	" 'Dr. Ungewitter told me' ": Von Schnitzler statements, August 22 and 28, 1945, *NMT*, vol. 7, pp. 1520–23.
252	"Von Schnitzler wasn't the only one": See NI 4954, affidavit by Felix Ehrmann, and N I7241, affidavit by Ernst Struss. See also DuBois, *The Devil's Chemists*.
252	"The IG got the message": *Elimination of German Resources for War*, pp. 996–97, exhibit 12, interrogation of von Schnitzler, July 26, 1945, and NI 5196, affidavit by G. von Schnitzler. See also DuBois, *The Devil's Chemists*.
253	"With almost wolverine": For "The Most Important Chemical Plants in Poland," see *Vowi* report 3609 of July 28, 1939, in NI 9151. For the IG's

motives, see NI 5196, affidavit by G. von Schnitzler, and NI-7367, affidavit by A. Eckert. Figure of 20 percent market share from Hayes, *Industry and Ideology.*

254   " 'The Former Polish State' ": NI 8457.

254   "But when von Schnitzler": Schwab testimony in *NMT*, vol. 7, p. 75. Hanneken quotations in NI 1093.

254   "Von Schnitzler was not easily": *NMT*, vol. 8, pp. 1143, 20–23. For Wurster's trip, see "Report on the Inspection of Some Chemical Industrial Plants in Poland between October 26 and November 1, 1939," NI 1149.

255   " 'When the Germans' ": Szpilfogel quotations in this paragraph and subsequent ones from testimony, Oct. 23, 1947, in *NMT*, mimeographed transcripts, pp. 2629–61.

256   "While Maurcy": See *NMT*, vol. 8, pp. 25–29; NI 1197, Schnitzler to Winkler; NI 806, Schnitzler to Greifelt; NI 8382, Mahnke to Schnitzler.

256n   Vogelsang, *Der Freundeskreis Himmler*, p. 161.

256   "Not everyone at the IG": For the death of Carl Bosch, see Holdermann, *Im Banne der Chemie*; and Abelshauser et al., *German Industry*. For consequences of his speech at the Deutsches Museum, see RG 239 M892, Schmitz I/10 and I/11, affidavit by J. Zeneck, and Bruckmann and Zenneck to Ministerpräsident Siebert, May 8, 1939.

257   "Though many at the IG": For appointment of Krauch, see NI 6526 and NI 6120, affidavit by C. Krauch, and NI 5184, affidavit by F. ter Meer. For further details of remuneration, see Hayes, *Industry and Ideology.*

258   "Naturally, the Wehrmacht": *Elimination of German Resources for War*, p. 1014; Glaser-Schmidt, "Foreign Trade Strategies of I. G. Farben"; DuBois, *The Devil's Chemists*; Plumpe, *Die IG Farbenindustrie*; and Hayes, *Industry and Ideology.* Specifically for Gallus Vertrag, see NI 5193, affidavit by G. von Schnitzler, and Holdermann, *Im Banne der Chemie.*

259   "The IG quickly realized": For figures: *Elimination of German Resources for War*; Glaser-Schmidt, "Foreign Trade Strategies of I. G. Farben"; DuBois, *The Devil's Chemists*; Plumpe, *Die IG Farbenindustrie*; and Hayes, *Industry and Ideology.* For "new order," see *NMT*, vol. 7, pp. 1452–65, and NI 11252, von Schnitzler to Schlotterer, Aug. 3, 1940.

259   "The company presented": For Schlotterer's response, see *NMT*, vol. 7, p. 1147.

260   "The *Vorstand*": NI 11252 and NI 6957, *NMT*, vol. 8, p. 133. For German occupation pressure, see NI 4894.

260   "The tactics had the": *Elimination of German Resources for War*, p. 1387. For Frossard's approach and the IG's response, see *Elimination*, exhibit 36, statement of von Schnitzler, Aug. 30, 1945. For advice from Hemmen, see NI 6839. For IG quotation, see NI 795; for Schnitzler quotation, *Elimination*, p. 1013.

261   "The talks began": *NMT*, vol. 8, p. 113, NI 14224, Kugler's notes on Paris conferences, Nov. 18, 29, and 30, 1940. See also NI 4886, affidavit by G. Thesmar, and NI 4889, affidavit by René Duchemin.

261   "The Germans, including von Schnitzler": For Hemmen's remarks, see NI 6727.

262   "While the dismayed French": For von Schnitzler's statement, see NI 6727.

262   "The next morning": For von Schnitzler's remarks, see NI 6838; for Duchemin's response, NI 4889 and *Elimination of German Resources for War*, p. 1399, and NI 3707, memo by Kramer, Dec. 14, 1940.

262   "As a result": For IG concessions, see NI 14224, Kugler's notes on Paris conferences. For IG threat, see NI 4889, affidavit by René Duchemin. (Raymond Berr was later arrested anyway and sent to his death at Auschwitz.) For Francolor announcement, see *NMT*, vol. 8, p. 1150. For financial compensation, see NI 6845 and NI 8077, *Vorstand* meeting of July 10, 1941.

263   "Although there were": For ter Meer doodle, see *NMT*, vol. 8, p. 163, ter Meer testimony.

264   "But the IG": For Mann's plans for Rhône-Poulenc, see NI 6839, Terhaar memo; NI 792, Kugler to Terhaar; NI-7992, IG report on Rhone; and Mann's statements in NI 7991, NI 14495, and NI 14500. For Mann's threat and Rhone's response, see NI 7629. For deal between IG and Rhone, see NI 7635.

264   "The IG also tightened": See Paxton, R. *Vichy France*, and Hayes, *Industry and Ideology*.

264   "But if IG Farben gorged": For Schlotterer's rules, see NI 504, Schlotterer to Reichwirtschaftskammer, RGI, and Reichsgruppe Handel, Sept. 9, 1940. See also NI 1473.

265   "The cartel's restraint": For overall attitude of the IG to Netherlands (including plant closures) and Belgium, see Hayes, *Industry and Ideology*. For Terte factory, see NI 10164. For Solvay, see NI 5196, affidavit by G. von Schnitzler. For attempted supply of Norwegian heavy water to Paul Harteck, see Bernstein, *Hitler's Uranium Club: The Secret Recordings at Farm Hall*.

265   "Had Germany gone on": Specifics of relationship from Coleman, *IG Farben and ICI, 1925–53*. For handover of IG knowledge of ICI to authorities, see *Elimination of German Resources for War*; and DuBois, *The Devil's Chemists*.

266n   Public Record Office, London (National Archives), FO files 371, 66564/U634.

266   "Bombing campaigns": For mobilization and stockpiling plans, see, e.g., NI 4452, NI 7126, NI 7209, NI 7136, and NI 7212. For air raid precautions, see NI 8461.

267   "To their relief": For details of raids, see U.S. Strategic Bombing Survey, Oil Division, "Ludwigshafen-Oppau Works of IG Farbenindustrie AG, Ludwigshafen, Germany," Washington, DC, 1947.

267   "Aside from the": For overall employment situation, see Milward, *The German Economy at War*; Overy, *War and Economy in the Third Reich*; and Tooze, *The Wages of Destruction*. For four thousand workers, see Abelshauser et al., *German Industry*. For details of increase in women workers at Ludwigshafen and Oppau, see BASF UA, C 621/2, "Der Mensch in BASF."

268   "But this was a drop": For Belgians, Italians, and Slovaks, see BASF UA, C13, "Direcktionssitzung in Ludwigshafen am Rhein am 28 Juni 1940."

268   " 'Contact with the prisoners' ": Ibid.

268   "Nevertheless, their presence": See Plumpe, *Die IG Farbenindustrie.*

269   "The events of September": For more on Weiss's relationship with IG Farben before 1939, see Jeffreys, *Aspirin.*

270   "Even so, the pace": For Weiss's offer to the IG, see DOJ Central Files, case 60-21-56 (Sterling Products Ltd), RG 60, U.S. National Archives), documents 6063, 6065, 6066, 6113, 1373, and 1853. Also see Bayer Leverkusen Archives, 9.A.7, 1955, Mann to Weiss, Nov. 30, 1939. For Alfredo Moll's activities in Buenos Aires, see *Elimination of German Resources for War.* For details of deal, which the two sides signed in Florence on Feb. 6, 1940, see DOJ 1172, 2663, 3101, and 3104. For footnote on South America, see *Elimination of German Resources*, appendix A, and list in *NMT*, vol. 8, p. 1379.

270   "What followed": See *New York Times*, April 10 and 11, 1941, and *New York Herald Tribune*, May 29, 1941.

271   "Given the degree of scrutiny": DOJ, box 1370, "Sterling Products Inc File Assignments" (A), June 27, 1941. For Weiss and Sterling accepting Department of Justice conditions, see DOJ, box 1329, and Thomas G. Corcoran Papers, U.S. Library of Congress, box 525, Weiss to Edward Foley, general counsel, U.S. Treasury, Aug. 15, 1941. For Weiss cable to Leverkusen, see Bayer Archives, Leverkusen, 9. A.7, Weiss to Mann.

271   "Meanwhile, Standard Oil": For Howard in Paris and telegrams, see Howard, *Buna Rubber.*

272   "The meeting was finally": For Joseph Kennedy's help, see *New York Times*, April 1, 1942. For Bütefisch's getting permission from Nazi authorities and the quotation, see Borkin, *The Crime.*

272   "Howard turned up": Borkin, *The Crime*; Ambruster, *Treason's Peace*; and Howard, *Buna Rubber.*

273   "On October 16, 1939": Cable quoted in Borkin, *The Crime.*

273   "Of more immediate": DOJ, case 682 and case 2091, *U.S. v Standard Oil Co (N.J.).* For Senate hearings, see *Hearings before the Committee on Patents*, U.S. Senate, 77th Congress, 2nd session (1942), part I. See also Ambruster, *Treason's Peace*, and Howard, *Buna Rubber.*

274   "If anyone": For production levels at Schkopau and Hüls, see Hayes, *Industry and Ideology.* See also Morris, "The Development of Acetylene Chemistry and Synthetic Rubber." For raw materials shortage, see BIOS FR 534, *Organisation of the German Chemical Industry and Its Development for War Purposes.*

274   "In November . . ." See NI-11781 Letter from Reich Ministry of Economics to IG Farben. 8/11/40

274   "Thus it was": For Ambros's meeting with Krauch and ter Meer, see *NMT*, vol. 8, pp. 349–51, NI 11784.

11. Buna at Auschwitz

276   "As far as": This section, including quotations, is drawn from two conversations with Denis Avey, in September 2004 and January 2005. His ac-

count was corroborated by several other former British POWs, particularly John Green, Jack Melville, and Ronald Redman, who all gave me valuable insights into conditions at the IG Auschwitz Buna-Werke.

279   "At the age of thirty-nine": Background detail on Ambros's upbringing, career, and motivation is drawn from his statements and testimony at the trial, e.g., see *NMT*, vol. 7, pp. 268, 425, 1040, 1260, and vol. 8, pp. 164, 292, 731, 1064; DuBois, *The Devil's Chemists*; ter Meer, *Die IG Farben Industrie*; Plumpe, *Die IG Farbenindustrie*; Wagner, *IG Auschwitz*. Ambros's own brief apologia is also worth glancing at ("Gedanken zu meiner Verurteilung durch das Nürnberger Gericht am 19/30 Juli 1948," BASF UA, W10) although it is essentially a reprise of his arguments at the trial and difficult to take seriously.

280   "Although Ambros would later": For spending on Rattwitz, see Morris, *The Development of Acetylene Chemistry and Synthetic Rubber*.

280   "The IG had never been": For problems of Rattwitz, Morris, *The Development of Acetylene Chemistry and Synthetic Rubber*. For potential of Silesia, see Dwork and van Pelt, *Auschwitz, 1270 to the Present*.

280   "Ambros got out his maps": NI 11110, Ambros report on trip to Silesia, Dec. 15–18, 1940.

281   "When and how Ambros": For possible interest of Mineralölbau, see Steinbacher, *Auschwitz: A History*. On suitability of Auschwitz, see NI 11110, Ambros report.

281   "On questioning the local authorities": *NMT*, vol. 8, pp. 337f., report of conference between representatives of IG Farben and Schlesien-Benzin, Jan. 18, 1941.

282   "Ambros also took": NI 11110, Ambros report; NI 111783, memo concerning prospective site for the Buna plants in Silesia, Dec. 10, 1940.

282   "The camp at Auschwitz": For background to Hitler decree, see Burleigh, *The Third Reich*.

282   "Much to his satisfaction": There is a vast body of work on Himmler, Heydrich, and the *Einsatzgruppen*. For this section I have found the following useful: Breitman, *The Architect of Genocide: Himmler and the Final Solution*; Read, *The Devil's Disciples*; Aly and Heim, *Architects of Annihilation: Auschwitz and the Logic of Destruction*; and, specifically for the conference of Sept. 21, 1939, Gilbert, *The Holocaust: The Jewish Tragedy*.

284   "The old cavalry": See Steinbacher, *Auschwitz*; Rees, *Auschwitz: The Nazis and the Final Solution*; and, for Auschwitz's medieval antecedents and their influence on Himmler, Dwork and van Pelt, *Auschwitz*. See also Höss, *Commandant of Auschwitz*.

285   "The first people": Steinbacher, *Auschwitz*; and Dwork and Van Pelt, *Auschwitz*.

285   "It is not known": Himmler's early interest is evident from the minutes of a conference held on January 8, 1941. Chaired by Heydrich and attended by representatives of the SS, army, and the Reich Commission for the Consolidation of the German Nation, it discussed, among other things, deporting Auschwitz's Poles and Jews to make way for a new "project in Upper

Silesia." See Federal Archive (Koblenz) R49, Anhang I, file 34, 8. See also Dwork and van Pelt, *Auschwitz*.

286   " 'Auschwitz and villages' ": NI 11782, memo of Kurt Eisfeldt, "Buna project," Feb. 13, 1941, *NMT*, vol. 8, p. 353.

286   "At the end of January 1941": See subsequent report of conversation for Froese quotation; *NMT*, vol. 8, p. 345, memorandum concerning investigation of prospective site for Buna plant in Silesia, Feb. 10, 1941.

286   "The tip was enough": *NMT*, vol. 8, p. 350, N 11113, notes of conference with Krauch and Ambros. For quotations, see Kurt Eisfeldt, "Buna project," NI 11782.

287   "Krauch took the hint": For Krauch quotation, see NI 11983, Krauch to Ambros, Feb. 25, 1941. For Göring quotation see NI 1240, Göring to Himmler, Feb. 18, 1941. See also NI 11086, Wirth to Ambros, March 4, 1941.

287   "Although the Reichsführer": For Himmler order to Glücks and appointment of Wolff, see NI 11086, Wirth to Ambros, March 4, 1941. For meeting with IG officials, see Federal Archive (Koblenz) NS 19, file 400. For instructions to Höss, see NI 034/2, affidavit by R. Höss, May 20, 1946; and Höss, *Commandant of Auschwitz*.

288   "As Höss absorbed": For decision to make fuel as well as buna, see Wagner, *IG Auschwitz*.

288   "With heads spinning": For decision on financing, see Borkin, *The Crime*; *Economic Study of IG Farbenindustrie AG Section V*; and BIOS FR 534, *Organisation of the German Chemical Industry and Its Development for War Purposes*.

288   "With the full backing": See NI 11115, minutes of the first Auschwitz construction conference, March 24, 1941. For quotation, see NI 15148, report on conference of Farben representatives with Auschwitz concentration camp officials, March 27, 1941.

289   " 'Selected from among' ": NI 15148.

289   "In the meanwhile": For agreement to buy SS sand and gravel, see NI 11115, minutes of the first Auschwitz construction conference, March 24, 1941. For purchase of majority stake in Fürstengrube, see NI 12011, contract between IG and Fürstliche Plessischen GmbH, Feb. 8, 1941. For IG emphasis on speed, see NI 11117, minutes of founding meeting of IG Farben-Auschwitz, April 7, 1941.

289   "The SS and the Reich authorities": For deportation of Auschwitz Jews, see Steinbacher, *Auschwitz*; and Smolen, *The History of KL Auschwitz*.

290n   Smolen, *The History of KL Auschwitz*.

290   "On Monday, April 7": NI 11117, minutes of founding meeting of IG Farben-Auschwitz, April 7, 1941.

290   "With the Auschwitz project": Ibid.

290   "Five days later": NI 11118, Ambros to ter Meer and Struss, April 12, 1941.

291   "Still, Ambros and his team": Copies of the blueprints surfaced in Moscow's Osobyi archive in the early 1990s. E.g., see Collection 502/5 file 13, blueprint AZ 9926 (Oct. 3, 1944). For other construction bottlenecks, also see NI 11130, fourteenth construction conference on IG Auschwitz.

291   "The more obvious": NI 11130.

292   "An even more serious": Ibid. For fences, see NI 11127, twelfth construction conference. For expansion of Auschwitz (Birkenau), NI 11132, sixteenth construction conference.

292   "As the delays steadily worsened": See above but especially NI 11127, twelfth construction conference and decision that Dürrfeld write to Krauch to inform him of difficulties.

292   " 'Men ran and fell' ": Vrba and Bestic, *I Cannot Forgive*.

293   "In the face of": Quotations from NI 14543, Auschwitz weekly report no. 11, Aug. 19, 1941.

293   "The IG men were": Quotation from NI 14566, Auschwitz weekly report no. 30, Dec. 15, 1941.

294   "This tolerance": For hunting, see, e.g., Auschwitz weekly reports nos. 82 and 83, Dec. 4, 1942. On IG attendance at SS Christmas party, see NI 15253, Auschwitz weekly reports nos. 31 and 32, Jan. 4, 1942.

294n   NI 034, affidavit by R. Höss, May 20, 1946.

294   "On Sunday, June 22": Beevor, *Stalingrad*; and Grant, *Illustrated History of 20th Century Conflict*.

295   "To Himmler": For Russian POWs at Birkenau, see Dwork and van Pelt, *Auschwitz*; and Piper, *Auschwitz Prisoner Labor*.

296n   Piper, *Auschwitz Prisoner Labor*.

296   "This was a considerable": For Göring decree, see Read, *The Devil's Disciples*.

296   "If Heydrich's *Einsatzgruppen*": Gilbert, *The Holocaust*.

296   "There are many reasons": This outline of Himmler and the summer of 1941 is drawn from Breitman, *The Architect of Genocide*; Friedlander, *The Origins of Nazi Genocide*; Gilbert, *The Holocaust*; Hilberg, *Destruction of the European Jews*; and Dwork and van Pelt, *Auschwitz*.

297   " 'Supplementing the task' ": *IMT*, vol. 9, pp. 517–20.

298   "A few days later": Details from Gilbert, *The Holocaust*, and Hilberg, *Destruction of the European Jews*.

299   Details of Wannsee Conference, including all quotations, from *IMT*, NG 2586 F(6), "Protocol of the Wannsee Conference."

300   "Three days later": Hilberg, *Destruction of the European Jews*. For Himmler instruction to Glücks, see U.S. National Archives, RG 242 T-580/R 69.

300   " 'The war will not end' ": Watts, *Voices of History, 1942–43*, p. 121.

300   "Even as ordinary Germans": Hilberg, *Destruction of the European Jews*.

12. IG Auschwitz and the Final Solution

302   "For a few weeks": For temporary improvement, see NI 15256, Auschwitz weekly report no. 42, Feb. 9, 1942, and NI 11132, sixteenth Auschwitz construction conference, March 6, 1942. For worsening situation, see NI 11137, nineteenth Auschwitz construction conference. For SS use of prisoners to build Birkenau, see NI 11130. For numbers at Buna-Werke in 1942,

see Auschwitz-Birkenau State Museum Archives (ABSMA), D-Au111-3a, chart of prisoner numbers at Buna subcamp to December 31, 1944.

303 "In casting around": *NMT*, vol. 7, pp. 10f. For the IG's calculation about strength of prisoner workers vis-à-vis Germans, see NI 11115, minutes of the first Auschwitz construction conference, March 24, 1941. For bringing prisoners close to site, see NI 15412, Auschwitz weekly report nos. 56 (June 15, 1942), and NI 14524, Auschwitz weekly report no. 57, *NMT*, vol. 8. p. 436.

304 "Thus, in late June 1942": NI 14524 and *NMT*, vol. 7, p. 197.

304 "Of course, the idea": For range of camps and subcamps, see Piper, *Auschwitz Prisoner Labor*. For issues pertaining to construction, see NI 14524, Auschwitz weekly report no. 57.

304 "Fortunately, an opportunity": See Höss, *Commandant of Auschwitz*. I am indebted to former POW John Green, who remembers hearing Buna-Werke staff discussing the Reichsführer's impending visit.

305 "Himmler's arrival": Read, *The Devil's Disciples*.

305 "Auschwitz was therefore now": For Himmler's plans for the armaments industry, see Piper, *Auschwitz Prisoner Labor*. For instructions to Eichmann, see *The Trial of Adolf Eichmann: Record of Proceedings in the District Court of Jerusalem*, vol. 4. p. 1474.

305n Speer, *Inside the Third Reich*.

305 "Experiments in mass murder": For early mass murder experiments, see *IMT*, vol. 10, p. 398, testimony by Rudolf Franz Ferdinand Höss. For the IG's connection to Degesch and Zyklon B, see NI 9098, NI 9150, NI 12073, NI 12075, NI 6363, and NI 9540. For first uses of Zyklon B as murder weapon in August and September 1941 and subsequent transfer to camp crematorium, see Höss, *Commandant of Auschwitz*.

306 "By then the Final Solution": Höss, *Commandant of Auschwitz*; and Steinbacher, *Auschwitz*.

306 "Thus the ghastly": Ibid.

307n Read, *The Devil's Disciples*.

307 "His arrival at the main": Höss, *Commandant of Auschwitz*; Vrba and Bestic, *I Cannot Forgive*; and Dwork and van Pelt, *Auschwitz*.

307 " 'He passed close' ": Vrba and Bestic, *I Cannot Forgive*.

308 "The Reichsführer's entourage": Höss, *Commandant of Auschwitz*; and Dwork and van Pelt, *Auschwitz*.

308 "Himmler and his aides": Höss, *Commandant of Auschwitz*.

309 "If Himmler was the slightest": NI 14551, Auschwitz weekly report 60–61, July 13–26, 1942. For movements after plant tour, see Höss, *Commandant of Auschwitz*.

309 "The next day": Höss, *Commandant of Auschwitz*.

310 "Monowitz, or Auschwitz III": See *NMT*, vol. 7, pp. 10–81 for overview. See also Steinbacher, *Auschwitz*; Piper, *Auschwitz Prisoner Labor*; Plumpe, *Die IG Farbenindustrie*; DuBois, *The Devil's Chemists*; and the eyewitness accounts of Primo Levi in Levi, *If This Is a Man*; and Levi and De Benedetti, *Auschwitz Report*. For the IG's assumption of responsibility for food, see NI 11139.

310n NI 11139.

310 "The first six hundred": See ABSMA, D-Au111-3a, chart of prisoner numbers. For typhus epidemic, see Piper, *Auschwitz Prisoner Labor*. On transfer from Buchenwald, see NI 10854, instructions from Office DII of Oct. 12, 1942. On transports from Theresienstadt and subsequent selections of prisoners and for quotation, see ABSMA, D-Au1-3a, 32, 65 Arbeitseinsatz, DII to Auschwitz concentration camp, Jan. 26, 1943; Schwarz to DII, Feb. 20, 1943.

311 "Meanwhile the savage conditions": For death rate by Dec. 1942 and Maurer's visit, see NI 15256, Auschwitz weekly reports 90–91, Feb. 8–21, 1943. For unexpected numbers of women and children and sickness of prisoners by March 1943, see Piper, *Auschwitz Prisoner Labor*.

312 "This extraordinary turnover": For potential impact of Standard developments in 1942 on IG Farben, see Morris, *The Development of Acetylene Chemistry and Synthetic Rubber*, and Hayes, *Industry and Ideology*.

312 "This pressure": For state of work by the end of 1942, see NI 11139, twenty-first Auschwitz construction conference.

313 "For many of the plant's": NI 14553, Auschwitz weekly reports nos. 62–63, July 27, 1942; NI 14489 and NI 14514, Auschwitz weekly reports nos. 70–71, Sept. 20, 1943; and NI 14549, Auschwitz weekly reports nos. 126–27, Oct. 31, 1943. I am indebted to the family of Gil Heuytens, a Dutch "voluntary" worker, for letting me know of the wretched conditions at the Buna-Werke between 1942 and 1943.

314n Monowitz postcards quoted in Gilbert, *The Holocaust*, p. 506.

314 "The stories of those": For background of deportation of Norwegian Jews, see Gilbert, *The Holocaust*, and Hilberg, *Destruction of the European Jews*.

315 " 'After three weeks' ": Quoted in DuBois, *The Devil's Chemists*.

315 " 'The buildings' ": See Wollheim's testimony, NMT, vol. 8, p. 590.

316 " 'The prisoners were' ": NI 4830, affidavit by Rudolf Vitek.

316 "For inmates who": See NI 7967, affidavit by Ervin Schulhof; Piper, *Auschwitz Prisoner Labor*; and, the most vivid account, Levi, *If This Is a Man*. For camp brothel, see Levi, *If This Is a Man*, and NI 15254, Auschwitz weekly reports nos. 73–74, Oct. 8, 1942. For sleeping accommodations, see NI 11696 affidavit by Charles Coward.

317 "But food": See NI 4830, affidavit by Rudolf Vitek. For camp routine (and for footnote), see Levi, *If This Is a Man*, and Levi, *Survival in Auschwitz: The Nazi Assault on Humanity*.

318 "The hospital, or *Krankenbau*": See NI 4830, affidavit by Rudolf Vitek; NI 12373, testimony of Robert Waitz; Levi and De Benedetti, *Auschwitz Report*.

318 "It is true": Levi and De Benedetti, *Auschwitz Report*. Quotation from NI 12373, testimony of Robert Waitz.

319 "This brief period": For purchase of stake in Fürstengrube mine, see NI 12011, contract between IG and Fürstliche Plessischen GmbH, Feb. 8, 1941. For acquisition of Janina, see Piper, *Auschwitz Prisoner Labor*. For quotation and other details of Janina, see Setkiewicz, "Wybrane problemy

z historii IG Werk Auschwitz" [Selected problems in the history of IG Werke Auschwitz], *Zeszyty Oswiecimkie* 22 (ABSMA, 1998). See also NI 10525, guard unit to management, Aug. 11, 1943.

319   "Ten days later": Piper, *Auschwitz Prisoner Labor.*

319   "The terrible living": For mortality rates, see NI 7966, affidavit by E. Orlik, and NI 11652, affidavit by Dr. W. Loebner.

320   " 'After arriving' ": For recollection of Jan Lawnicki, see ABSMA, *Statements Collection*, vol. 60, p. 100.

320   "Having labored": See Piper, *Auschwitz Prisoner Labor*, and NI 11043, labor camp Janina to SS. For typical punishments, see NI 11038, IG Auschwitz to SS Oberstürmführer Schoettl, Sept. 11, 1944.

320   "Nevertheless, so long as": For Dürrfeld participation in selection, see NI 12069, affidavit by G. Herzog, Oct. 21, 1947, *NMT*, vol. 8, pp. 489–90, 510–15. For death toll, see NI 7967, affidavit by E. Schulhof, and NI 12070, affidavit by S. Budziaszek.

321   "The first thing to note": For IG Farben's Reich Germans at Auschwitz, see Steinbacher, *Auschwitz.*

322   " 'I hadn't been' ": Conversation with Müller in London in June 2004.

323   " 'That the Jewish' ": NI 838, Burth to Küpper.

323   "By this time": For threats to workers, see Piper, *Auschwitz Prisoner Labor*; and Borkin, *The Crime.*

323   " 'The population at Auschwitz' ": NI 11696, affidavit by Charles Coward.

323   "But what of *direct*": For destruction of documents (and for footnote), see chapter 14. For visits of IG management to Auschwitz, see NI 14889, Auschwitz weekly reports nos. 70–71, Sept. 21, 1942; NI 15256, Auschwitz weekly reports nos. 76–77, Nov. 15, 1942; NI 7604, affidavit by C. Schneider, April 22, 1947; NI 5168, affidavit by F. Jaehne, May 19, 1947; and Borkin, *The Crime.* For Dürrfeld's conversation with Höss, see NI 7183, deposition by R. Höss, Jan. 1, 1947.

324n   NI 10040, letter from Krauch to Himmler, July 27, 1943.

324   "In any event": NI-5168, affidavit by F. Jaehne, May 29, 1947.

325   " 'In a loud voice' ": *NMT*, trial transcript, pp. 13566–615.

325   "Struss said": For Struss's conversations with ter Meer and Ambros, see *NMT* trial transcript, pp. 13566–615. For other *Vorstand* members, see NI 9811, affidavit by C. Lautenschläger; NI 7604, affidavit by C. Schneider; NI 5197, affidavit by G. von Schnitzler.

325   "For others on the *Vorstand*": For the IG's connection to Degesch and Zyklon B, see NI 9098, NI 9150, NI 12073, NI 12075, NI 6363, and NI 9540. For Peters, see NI 9113, affidavit by G. Peters. For Tesch and Mauthausen figures, see Hayes, *Industry and Ideology.* For Höss quotation, see Höss, *Commandant of Auschwitz.* Also cited in Lebor and Boyes, *Surviving Hitler: Choices, Corruption, and Compromise in the Third Reich.*

326n   NI 9093; and Hilberg, *Destruction of the European Jews.*

327   "But Mann clearly knew": For details on Mengele, see Gilbert, *The Holocaust.* For details of the Mozes twins, including quotation, see Mozes Kor, *Echoes from Auschwitz*; and Jeffreys, *Aspirin.*

328 " 'I have enclosed the first check' ": Quoted in ABC News *20/20* report on class action suit contemplated by survivors of the Nazi slave labor program (July 11, 1999).

328 "Other IG staff": For details of Vetter's experiments and his quotation, see Cohen, "The Ethics of Using Medical Data from Nazi Experiments." See also Lifton, *The Nazi Doctors: Medical Killing and the Psychology of Genocide.* Bayer letter to Höss quoted in Strzelecki, "Experiments."

328 "The experiments at Auschwitz": Further details contained in *NMT*, vols. 1 and 2. For Tauboeck episode see NI 3963, affidavit by K. Tauboeck, June 18, 1947.

329 " 'It is clear that' ": *NMT*, vol. 1, p. 9193.

330 "The matter had arisen": For Speer's account of the meeting, see Speer, *Inside the Third Reich.* For establishment of Dyhernfurth, see NI 6788, affidavit by O. Ambros, May 1, 1947. For Ambros's recollections of meeting with Hitler, see NI 1044, testimony of Otto Ambros.

331n See Harris and Paxman, *A Higher Form of Killing*; and Tucker, *War of Nerves: Chemical Warfare from World War I to Al-Qaeda.*

331 "Although they had survived": For bombing of IG plants, see United States Strategic Bombing Survey (USSBS) Oil Division, *Ludwigshafen-Oppau Works of IG Farbenindustrie AG, Ludwigshafen, Germany*, Jan. 1947. For explosion, see BASF UA, C13, "Direktionspostsitzung am 30 Juli 1943."

332n USSBS (United States Strategic Bombing Survey), *Oil Division Final Report*, 1947.

332 "It was much the same": USSBS, *Oil Division Final Report*, 1947; and USSBS, *Physical Damage Division Report no. 64, IG Farbenindustrie AG, Leverkusen, Germany*, 1945.

332 "Inevitably, the killed": For one calculation of numbers of "foreign workers," see NI 11411, affidavit by K. Hauptmann, Nov. 17, 1947, with specific numbers for Ludwigshafen-Oppau in BASF UA, C621/2, "Der Mensch." See also Hayes, *Industry and Ideology*, which puts the number at rather less, some eighty-three thousand, or 36 percent of the IG workforce, by 1944. For conditions and discipline in work camps, see Abelshauser et al., *German Industry.*

333n For Krupp, see Manchester, *The Arms of Krupp.* For others see Tooze, *The Wages of Destruction.*

333 "For the IG's": For Krauch's Knight's Cross, see Borkin, *The Crime.* For Göring's rivalry with Himmler, Goebbels, and Bormann, see Read, *The Devil's Disciples.* For Krauch's waning authority and relationship with Speer and Kehrl, see Hayes, *Industry and Ideology.*

334 "But for Krauch": For bombing campaign, see USSBS, *Oil Division Final Report*; and NI 3767. Speer quotations in Speer, *Inside the Third Reich.*

335 "Göring, eager": *NMT*, vol. 7, p. 1109.

335 "In early June": For further raids, see USSBS, *Oil Division Final Report*; and Speer, *Inside the Third Reich.*

13. Götterdämmerung

337   "Although it was": For slightly contrasting views of the atmosphere in Germany in early 1944, see Burleigh, *The Third Reich*; and Shirer, *The Rise and Fall of the Third Reich*.

338   "Surprisingly this state": Other firms that had established plants in or near Auschwitz by 1944: the Herman Göring Werke, the Berg und Hüttenwerkgesellschaft Teschen, Friedrich Krupp AG, the Weischel Union Metallwerke, Siemens-Schukert, Oberschlesischen Hüttenwerke, Schlesischen Schuhwerke, Schlesische Feinweberei, and Deutsche Gasrusswerke—with several more set up elsewhere in Upper Silesia. They all used concentration camp and POW labor, though none to the same extent as IG Farben. For further details, see Allen, *Hitler's Slave Lords*; Herbert, *Hitler's Foreign Workers: Enforced Foreign Labor in Germany under the Third Reich*; and Piper, *Auschwitz Prisoner Labor*.

338   "The gassings, too": For closure of Operation Reinhard death camps, the influx of Hungarian deportees to Auschwitz, and footnote, see Hilberg, *Destruction of the European Jews*, and Gilbert, *The Holocaust*.

339   " 'A fortnight after my arrival' ": Levi, *If This Is a Man*.

339   "The machine": For first methanol production and celebration, see Wagner, *IG Auschwitz*, and Tooze, *The Wages of Destruction*.

340   " 'We weren't allowed' ": Conversation with Denis Avey, Jan. 2005.

340   "From mid-1944": Gilbert, *Auschwitz and the Allies*; Steinbacher, *Auschwitz*; Wagner, *IG Auschwitz*. For the USAF's view of the bombing, see Grant, "Twenty Missions in Hell."

341   "As the German camp": For Salomon Kohn quote, see NI 10824, testimony of Salomon Kohn, *NMT*, vol. 12, Maurer trial, p. 206.

341   " 'when the earth' ": Levi, *If This Is a Man*.

341   "Things were no better": Conversation with Denis Avey, Jan. 2005.

341   "The raids effectively": For *Stoss Kommando* from Ludwigshafen, see Abelshauser et al., *German Industry*. For SS closing down camp, see Strzelecki, *The Evacuation, Dismantling, and Liberation of KL Auschwitz*. For inmates left behind, see NI 11956, report by Dürrfeld. For fate of Fürstengrube inmates, see Gilbert, *The Holocaust*; and Strzelecki, *The Evacuation*.

342   "Thousands perished": Aharon Beilin quoted in Gilbert, *The Holocaust*. See Gilbert also for fate of Monowitz Jews.

343   "The IG meanwhile": For the IG's departure from Auschwitz, see NI 11956, report by Dürrfeld; and Strzelecki, *The Evacuation*. The figure of 150,000 workers is my own estimate and includes all those—voluntary and forced foreign laborers, Reich German IG Farben employees, Organization Todt workers, POWs, Poles, and Jewish concentration camp inmates—who were engaged at some point between March 1941 and January 1945 in constructing the Buna-Werke, the Monowitz camp, IG housing at Auschwitz, the Buna-Werke railway halt and waterworks, as well as those in closely related supplementary labor for the IG at SS gravel, cement, and brick plants at or near Auschwitz and mines at Fürstengrube,

Janina, and elsewhere in the region. It is impossible to be absolutely certain of the numbers involved, not least because of the extraordinary turnover among concentration camp inmates, whose average life expectancy was somewhere between two and three months (and down to four to six weeks at Fürstengrube in 1944). Nevertheless, readers in search of more detailed analyses can find them in Setkiewicz, "Wybrane problemy z historii IG Werk Auschwitz" [Selected problems in the history of IG Werke Auschwitz], and Piper, *Auschwitz Prisoner Labor*. The figure of thirty-five thousand to forty thousand deaths is based on NI 7967, an affidavit by prisoner Ervin Schulhof, who compiled card indexes of inmate workers for the IG management at Monowitz; NI 12070, an affidavit by S. Budziaszek, a Monowitz camp doctor who made his own calculations; and statistics compiled by Franciszek Piper for *Auschwitz Prisoner Labor*. While this figure is generally accepted, it does not include those prisoners murdered by the SS on the march away from the IG's camp at Monowitz in January 1945, or those moved away from the IG's employ at Monowitz to other labor assignments at Auschwitz and then murdered, or those transported directly to Monowitz to labor for the IG but rejected after selection at the railhead and taken by the SS straight to the gas chambers at Birkenau. For a typical Nuremberg prosecutor's estimate, see DuBois, *The Devil's Chemists*.

344   "The IG's partners": Strzelecki, *The Evacuation*; and Gilbert, *The Holocaust*

344   "For the eight hundred": Levi, *If This Is a Man*; and Strzelecki, *The Evacuation*.

345   " 'They did not greet us' ": Levi, *The Truce*.

345   "The Russians": Strzelecki, *The Evacuation*; and Levi, *The Truce*.

345   "In Germany": For details of the Allied response to reports coming from Auschwitz, including the first BBC broadcast warnings, see Swiebocki, *London Has Been Informed: Reports by Auschwitz Escapees*.

346   "Hermann Schmitz": For July 1944 attempts on Hitler's life, see Shirer, *The Rise and Fall of the Third Reich*. For Schmitz's deteriorating mental state, see RG 239 M892, Schmitz V/173, affidavit by Dr. Singer. For Schmitz's tea cozy habit, see Hayes, *Industry and Ideology*. For Schmitz's involvement with attempts to reach Dulles, see Lebor and Boyes, *Surviving Hitler*.

346   "Some members of the *Vorstand*": For von Knieriem's memo, see BASF UA, IG A. 281, "Aufteilung der IG." For Wilhelm Mann's continued devotion to the Nazi cause, see Duisberg, *Nur ein Sohn*. For Max Ilgner, see DuBois, *The Devil's Chemists*. For von Schnitzler's movements, see Martin, *All Honourable Men*. For Carl Wurster, see BASF UA, A.865, "Kurze Beschreibung der Ereignisse in den letzten Tagen vor der Besetzung von Ludwigshafen am Rhein durch amerikanische Truppen," June 4, 1947. For Bütefisch, see BIOS FR 1698, *Interrogation of Dr Bütefisch, January 1946*. For Ambros, see PRO (Public Record Office), WO 219/1986 and PRO WO 208/2182. For movements of von Knieriem, Mann, and Hörlein, see DuBois, *The Devil's Chemists*. For destruction of documents, see

	NMT, vol. 7, p. 467, affidavit by Dr. Struss, and *Elimination of German Resources for War*, p. 980, interrogation of Dr. Struss, July 21, 1945.
347	"A few days": Recollections of Ernst Struss in DuBois, *The Devil's Chemists*.
348	"The Allies had certainly": Ellis, *The Defeat in Germany*, and Pohlenz, "Leverkusen und das Bayer-Werke in den Jahren 1944–46." For firearms, see Bayer Leverkusen Archives 12/13/1, "Entwurf zur Niederschrift detr TC in Leverkusen am 14 April 1945." For April 14 takeover by U.S. troops, see Pohlenz, "Leverkusen und das Bayer-Werke."
349n	CIOS XX111–25, *Miscellaneous Chemicals: IG Farbenindustrie AG Elberfeld and Leverkusen, 27 April 1945*; and USSBS (United States Strategic Bombing Survey), *Oil Division Final Report*.
349	"It was much": For Hoechst, see CIOS ER 31, *IG Farben-Hoechst*. For Ludwigshafen, see USSBS, Oil Division, *Ludwigshafen-Oppau Works of IG Farbenindustrie AG, Ludwigshafen, Germany*. For the fate of eastern plants, see Tooze, *The Wages of Destruction*, and Abelshauser et al., *German Industry*.
350	"But the Allies' interest": For Project Paperclip (and footnote), see Bar-Zohar, *The Hunt for German Scientists, 1944–60*, and Lasby, *Project Paperclip*.
350	"Inevitably, the IG": For Allies' March 25 visit to Ludwigshafen and the quotation, see CIOS evaluation report 27, May 27, 1945. For dismantling of equipment, see CIOS, *Report on Investigations by Fuels and Lubricants Teams at the IG Farbenindustrie AG Works at Ludwigshafen and Oppau*. For footnote (on fate of documents), see PRO BT 11/2578, PROBT 211/11, and PRO, BT 211/17. For fuel scientists at Leuna, see U.S. Archives RG260 OMGUS HQ AG 1945/6 231.2. For Bütefisch (including footnote), see BIOS FR 1698, *Interrogation of Dr Bütefisch, January 1946*.
351	"But no IG technology": For Tarr's search for Schrader and Ambros, see PRO WO 219/1986 and PRO WO 208/2182.
351	"Schrader was found": For Ambros in Gendorf, see PRO WO 208/2182; and DuBois, *The Devil's Chemists*.
351	"The unit's commanding": Ibid. See also PRO WO 219/1986 and PRO WO 208/2182; BIOS, Final Report FR 138, *Interrogation of German Chemical Warfare Personnel, 1945*. For Ambros's transfer, see PRO BT 211/25.
352	"Ambros never arrived": PRO BT 211/25.
353n	Harris and Paxman, *A Higher Form of Killing*; and Tucker, *War of Nerves*.
353	"Other IG officials": For the best overview of Germany in the immediate aftermath of the war, see Botting, *In the Ruins of the Reich*. Graffiti cited in Beevor, *Berlin: The Downfall, 1945*.
353	"In these circumstances": For watch lists and difficulties of enforcing them, see Bower, *Blind Eye to Murder: Britain, America, and the Purging of Nazi Germany; A Pledge Betrayed*. For early conclusions of U.S. investigators, see preface to *Elimination of German Resources for War* by Colonel Bernard Bernstein, director, Division of Investigation of Car-

tel and External Assets, Office of Military Government, Nov. 1945. Bernstein was a former assistant general counsel at the U.S. Treasury Department.

354n   Bower, *Blind Eye to Murder.*

354   "Two of these officials": For account of Nixon and Martin's arrival at the IG's Frankfurt headquarters, see Martin, *All Honorable Men*; and DuBois, *The Devil's Chemists.*

355n   Martin, *All Honorable Men*; and DuBois, *The Devil's Chemists.*

355n   PRO FO 371 66564/U.634.

355   "In the meantime": For meeting with Schnitzler, see Martin, *All Honorable Men*; and SHAEF report in PRO FO 371 66564/U.634.

356   "Hermann Schmitz": SHAEF report in PRO FO 371 66564/U.634.

356   But Major Edmund Tilley": Quotations and account in DuBois, *The Devil's Chemists.*

356   "As the last": For Potsdam Conference, see Donnison, *Civil Affairs and Military Government, North-West Europe.*

357   "This meant the end": See U.S. National Archives, RG 238, *United States Group Control Council, Report on the Investigation of IG Farbenindustrie*, Sept. 12, 1945; and PRO FO 236, Allied Control Council, Nov. 30, 1945.

357   "What this meant": For U.S. announcement, see *New York Times*, Oct. 21, 1945. For forty-seven units, see *New York Times*, June 18, 1947.

358   "But the tide": For economic problems of occupied Germany, see Donnison, *Civil Affairs and Military Government*; and Botting, *In the Ruins of the Reich.*

14. Preparing the Case

359   "The stadium": Thanks to former prosecution lawyer Belle Mayer Zeck, I know that General Taylor visited the old Nazi parade ground at Nuremberg shortly before the trial. But at this remove it is impossible to know exactly what he did there or what was on his mind. Benjamin Ferencz, one of Telford Taylor's deputies, wryly suggested to me that the general might merely have been on his way to use the tennis courts that the U.S. Army had installed nearby. Nevertheless, I have novelized the episode in these opening paragraphs to better evoke something of the pretrial atmosphere. Further insights into life in Nuremberg in the period of the war crimes trials (and on the destruction of the city) can be found in Tusa and Tusa, *The Nuremberg Trial*; Davis, *Come as a Conqueror: The U.S. Army's Occupation of Germany, 1945–49*; DuBois, *The Devil's Chemists*; Botting, *In the Ruins of the Reich*; and, albeit to a limited extent, Telford Taylor's own *The Anatomy of the Nuremberg Trials*. For the fate of the 250 Jews in Nuremberg in 1933, see Gilbert, *The Holocaust.*

360   "For most people": There are numerous accounts of the International Military Tribunal but Taylor's *The Anatomy of the Nuremberg Trials* and Ann and John Tusa's *The Nuremberg Trial* are the most readable and compelling.

For a highly detailed breakdown of the cases, see Sprecher, *Inside the Nuremberg Trial*. Sprecher served as a prosecution attorney on the IMT trial and on the IG Farben case.

361   "But the IMT": The twelve cases that made up the NMT series were identified as follows: *Medical, Milch, Judges, Pohl, Hostages, RuHSA, Flick, Krupp, IG Farben, Einsatzgruppen, Ministries,* and *High Command*. For *Flick*, see *NMT*, vol. 6. For *Krupp*, see *NMT*, vol. 9.

361n   Taylor, *Final Report to the Secretary of the Army*.

362   "That such a message": For background to Control Law No. 8, see Peterson, *The American Occupation of Germany*.

362n   Peterson, *The American Occupation of Germany*; Botting, *In the Ruins of the Reich*.

362   "Although British officials": For British qualms about the directive, see PRO FO 371 46801/C8985. In this document a senior Foreign Office official, Con O'Neill, wrote, "As an example of systematic and meticulous imbecility, it would be hard to beat. . . . I hope that we shall be under no illusion that a policy of this kind is the sheerest madness."

363   "This more pragmatic": For the inadequacy of some British officials and complaints about IG Farben, see Bower, *Blind Eye to Murder*. For results of Hüls survey, see PRO FO 938/73, Dec. 10, 1946. For number of ex-Nazis increasing despite complaints, see PRO FO 938/73, March 17, 1947.

364n   See PRO FO 371 57587/U7918, which includes a list of twenty-six German industrialists and bankers against whom Elwyn Jones thought there was a prima facie case. Other British officials were determined to leave the difficult and sensitive task of trying businessmen to the United States alone. That way, as Patrick Dean, a senior Foreign Office official, cynically made clear in a memo to a colleague, "if any of the trials do go wrong and the industrialists escape, the primary political criticism will rest on American shoulders, not ours" (see PRO FO 371 57586/U7295).

364   "This view": For the belief of some American lawyers that IG Farben was suitable for prosecution, see *Elimination of German Resources for War*. For the potential problems caused the American legal team by the elections, see PRO FO 371 57587/U8088.

364   "In mid-1945": Biographical details and Telford Taylor's quotation are from Taylor, *The Anatomy of the Nuremberg Trials*. See also Ferencz, "Telford Taylor."

366   "After a year": Taylor, *The Anatomy of the Nuremberg Trials*. For quotation, see *NMT*, vol. 7, prosecution opening statement.

366   "He quickly discovered": For difficulties, see Taylor, letter to General Clay, RG 260 OMGUS HQ 1945–46 000518.2.46, and PRO FO 371 57587/U8088. For fears about judges, see Taylor, *Final Report to the Secretary of the Army*.

366   "As far as the mechanics": As it turned out, only two trials in the NMT series (the *Medical* and *Milch* cases) were concluded before the IG Farben case began. Several were shorter than the IG trial and ran for only a few months, some started and finished later, and others were not in session all the time, but at one point between October and November 1947 Taylor had concur-

rent prosecutorial responsibility for seven major war crimes trials. For DuBois biographical details, see his *The Devil's Chemists*; and Borkin, *The Crime*. Of those lawyers who had assisted at the earlier IMT, Drexel Sprecher was the most prominent. See Sprecher, *Inside the Nuremberg Trial*.

367   "The team encountered": For the early days of the investigation and the difficulties of gathering documents, see DuBois's account in *The Devil's Chemists*. I was also informed by the recollections of Belle Mayer—or, as she became after her posttrial marriage to William Zeck, another of the Farben prosecution team, Belle Mayer Zeck. (As an attorney working in the U.S. Treasury during the war, Belle Mayer had helped its assistant general counsel Bernard Bernstein during one of the first postwar investigations into IG Farben. See *Elimination of German Resources for War*.)

368   "For several months": DuBois, *The Devil's Chemists*.

369   "The lawyer hurried down": Ibid. Also recollections of Belle Mayer Zeck.

369   "His tail now up": For code words and destruction, see *NMT*, vol. 7, p. 446, and PRO FO 312 81141.

369   " 'When, on 20 February' ": DuBois, *The Devil's Chemists*.

370   "Not every trail": Ibid., Belle Mayer Zeck.

371   "Paper evidence wasn't": Avey and other POWs were approached by Morris Amchan, one of the U.S. prosecution team, via the War Office in London (conversations with Avey and John Melville, 2005). The depositions and affidavits can all be seen in the Record Group 238 T301 section of the U.S. National Archives.

371   "It was a good": For DuBois's concerns, see his *The Devil's Chemists*.

371   "Much would center": For problems with early interrogations, see Taylor, *Final Report to the Secretary of the Army*. For influence of defense lawyers, contrast Krauch's statements about Germany's war intentions made (a) to interrogators in September 1945 (see *Elimination of German Resources for War*, exhibit 33, interrogation of Dr. Krauch, Sept. 27, 1945) and (b) in testimony on the same subject at the trial (*NMT*, vol. 7, p. 1130).

371   " 'The IG took on' ": *NMT*, vol.7, p. 1514.

373   "But von Schnitzler": Von Schnitzler's earliest and most damning statements were made between May and September 1945 to investigators based in an old Reichsbank building in Frankfurt, to which the baron was brought daily from his cell at the city's Preungesheim prison. Subsequently, owing to pressure on cell space, he was moved around more frequently—sometimes held under house arrest at Oberursel, at other times in various jails in the Frankfurt region. With pressured investigators taking hundreds of witness statements and conducting dozens of concurrent interrogations, von Schnitzler was often kept waiting in custody with former *Vorstand* colleagues, such as Fritz ter Meer. For the effect this had on him, see *NMT*, vol 7, p. 1502.

373   "As a result": Ibid.

373   "The news left many": DuBois, *The Devil's Chemists*.

374   "On May 4, 1947": All details and quotations taken from the indictment, *U.S. v. Carl Krauch et al.*, in *NMT*, vol. 7, pp. 10–80.

376	"But he barely": For George A. Dondero quotations, see *Congressional Record*, July 9, 1947, p. 8564.
376	"Having never been": Ibid., DuBois, *The Devil's Chemists*.
376	"The timing of the attack": For judge's background and DuBois response to *Stars and Stripes* incident, see DuBois, *The Devil's Chemists*; and Borkin, *The Crime*.
377	"DuBois spent": DuBois, *The Devil's Chemists*; Belle Mayer Zeck; and Taylor, *Final Report to the Secretary of the Army*.

15. Trial

378	"There is more": Telford Taylor's quotations from *NMT*, vol. 7, pp. 99–116. Belle Mayer quotation from DuBois, *The Devil's Chemists*.
380	"To illustrate this argument": For example of charts, see NI 10042, "organization chart of the IG Farbenindustrie Aktiengesellschaft."
380	" 'Mr. Prosecutor' ": DuBois, *The Devil's Chemists*, p. 82.
381	"A particular low point": For the broad sweep of the case, see *NMT*, vol. 7, pp. 745–1209. For examples of von Schnitzler's pretrial statements, see *NMT*, vol. 7, p. 1514; von Schnitzler affidavits in NI 5197, NI 5193, NI 5196, and NI 5467; and *Elimination of German Resources for War*, exhibit 36, statement of von Schnitzler, Aug. 30, 1945. For Curtis Shake on von Schnitzler, see DuBois, *The Devil's Chemists*, p. 78.
381	"Meanwhile, away from court": For Rankin's remarks, see *Congressional Record*, Nov. 28, 1947, p. 10938. For judge's questions about Jews on the prosecution, see DuBois, *The Devil's Chemists*, pp. 182, 193. For Drexel Sprecher, see Bower, *Blind Eye to Murder*. For Mrs. Morris and the wives of defendants, Bower, *Blind Eye to Murder*; and Belle Mayer.
382	"And so the case": For Morris's remarks in this and following paragraph, see DuBois, *The Devil's Chemists*, 93, 95.
382	"Testimony from witnesses": For Szpilfogel's testimony, see *NMT*, mimeographed trial transcript, pp. 2629–61.
382	"For the defendants": "German Industrialists Tribunal," *Times*, Dec. 9, 1947; and DuBois, *The Devil's Chemists*.
383	"Inevitably the defendants": DuBois, *The Devil's Chemists*; and conversation with David Gordon.
384	"But twenty-three men": DuBois, *The Devil's Chemists*; and Belle Mayer. For ter Meer, see DuBois, *The Devil's Chemists*, p. 85; and *NMT*, vol. 7, p. 859
384	For ter Meer's absence from prison and meeting with Struss, DuBois, *The Devil's Chemists*.
386	"Several of the prosecution": For Minskoff quotations and DuBois's response, see *The Devil's Chemists*, p. 99.
387	"The Norwegian": For Feinberg's testimony, see *NMT*, mimeographed trial transcript, pp. 3810–15.
387	"Ervin Schulhof": *NMT* trial transcript, pp. 3600–11.
387	"Leon Staischak": DuBois, *The Devil's Chemists*. p. 224.

388 "Then there was": For Vitek's testimony, see *NMT*, trial transcript, pp. 3957–85.

388 "British POWs": *NMT* trial transcript, pp. 3692–99, 3920–27, 3845–53, and 3815–27.

388 "Some of the most compelling": U.S. National Archives RG 238 T301 2059, 43–44.

388 "Even Ernest Strauss": *NMT* trial transcript, pp. 13566–615.

389 "The complacency": Conversation with David Gordon.

389 "The defense tried its best": For testimony and cross-examination of Gerhard Dietrich, see *NMT* trial transcript, pp. 13752–71.

391 "When Minskoff": DuBois *The Devil's Chemists*, p. 230.

391 For Bütefisch, see *NMT*, vol. 7, pp. 768f.

393 "Some defense tactics": For Weinberg's rescue, see NI 13678 and U.S. National Archives RG M892, Schmitz 4/53, affidavit by Rudolf Graf von Spreti. For Ollendorf, see NI 13522 and *NMT*, vol. 7, pp. 628–29.

394 "Toward the end of the trial": For Mann, see *NMT*, vol. 8, p. 1164.

395 "Probably the most effective": For Krauch defense, see *NMT*, vol. 7, p. 719.

395 " 'Surely, I thought' ": DuBois, *The Devil's Chemists*, p. 338.

396 "Three judges": A railroad car containing dimethyl ether had burst and caused the explosion. See Abelshauser et al., *German Industry*. For Shake's remarks, see *NMT*, vol. 8, p. 1081.

396 For the court's ruling and verdicts on July 29–30, see *NMT*, vol. 8, pp. 1082–196.

398 For sentences, see *NMT*, vol. 8, p. 1205.

399 "When the chief judge": For Hebert, see *NMT*, vol. 8, p. 1204.

399 "For much of the day": DuBois, *The Devil's Chemists*, p. 339. For Telford Taylor's evident frustration with the failure of the system, see Taylor, *Final Report to the Secretary of the Army*.

400 "Outside the court": For Taylor, see *News Chronicle* (London), Aug. 1, 1948. For Judge Daly's remarks, see *NMT*, vol. 9; and *NMT*, trial transcript, pp. 13231–402.

400 "This was little": For DuBois's return home, his shipboard meeting with Judge Herbert, and the quotation, see *The Devil's Chemists*.

400 "Some years later": Ibid.

401 "But Judge Paul Hebert": For Hebert's dissenting opinion, see *NMT*, vol. 8, pp. 1205–325.

Epilogue

403 "Although General Eisenhower": For rebirth of Bayer, BASF, and Hoechst in 1951, see *New York Times*, Dec. 27, 1951. For reports on early and sustained recovery, see, e.g., *Time*, July 7, 1952, and October 17, 1960; *Business*, February 1970; and *Fortune*, August 1977.

404 "Today that success": For Bayer today, see www.bayer.com.

404 "The BASF Group": See www.corporate.basf.com.

404   "Hoechst is the only one": See www.sanofi-aventis.com or the archived Hoechst Web site at www.archive.hoechst.com.

404   "Not surprisingly": For the background to Wollheim's case against IG Farben, see Ferencz, *Less Than Slaves*.

405   " 'The fundamental principles' ": Ibid. See also *Wollheim v. IG Farben in Liquidation*, Frankfurt District Court, June 10, 1953, file 2/3/0406/51.

406   "Wollheim's victory": Ferencz, *Less Than Slaves*.

406   "Their answer": For the successor companies' position on responsibility and compensation, see Ferencz, *Less Than Slaves*, and their Web sites, cited above.

407   "They may well have": For defendants' reactions, or lack of them, see *Times*, Aug. 3, 1948.

407   "He did not have": For McCloy's decision to release IG Farben defendants and others, and political consequences, see Bower, *Blind Eye to Murder*.

407   "And so the IG": The laxity of the regime at Landsberg may be judged from a remark by Fritz von Bülow, one of the convicted defendants in the Krupp trial, who described his time at the prison as "one long, sunlit holiday." For this quotation and the footnote about Krupp's release, see Manchester, *The Arms of Krupp*. Fritz ter Meer's remark about Americans on his release is quoted in Hilberg, *Destruction of the European Jews*, p. 697. For Georg von Schnitzler's release, see *Time*, Jan. 2, 1950. For his wife's reported presence, see *News Chronicle*, Jan. 8, 1950.

408   "The freed men": Details of the posttrial careers of the IG defendants are drawn from Borkin, *The Crime* (which relies on Bayer and Hoechst annual reports from the 1950s); Abelshauser et al., *German Industry*; *Fortune*, August 1977; Mann and Plummer, *The Aspirin Wars*; ter Meer, *Die IG Farben Industrie*; Verg, Plumpe, and Schultheis, *Milestones*; www.dr-rath-foundation.org/pharmaceutical_business; Stokes, *Divide and Prosper: The Heirs of I. G. Farben under Allied Authority*; Meinzer, *125 Jahre BASF*; and the Web sites of the successor companies, cited above.

409   " 'He is a man' ": DuBois, *The Devil's Chemists*, p. 356.

410   "On February 6, 1959": See seating plan in BASF UA, W 1/2/8, "Die Herren Mitglieder des Vorstandes der ehemaligen IG Farbenindustrie," Feb. 6, 1959.

BIBLIOGRAPHY

Abelshauser, W., W. von Hippel, J. Johnson, and R. Stokes. *German Industry and Global Enterprise. BASF: The History of a Company.* Cambridge, 2004.

Aims and Purposes of the Chemical Foundation Incorporated and the Reasons for Its Organization. As Told by A. Mitchell Palmer, United States Attorney General and Former Alien Property Custodian, in His Report to Congress, and by Francis P. Garvan, Alien Property Custodian, in an Address to the National Cotton Manufacturers' Association. New York, 1919.

Allen, M. T. *Hitler's Slave Lords: The Business of Forced Labor in Occupied Europe.* Chapel Hill, 2004.

Aly, G., and S. Heim. *Architects of Annihilation: Auschwitz and the Logic of Destruction.* London, 2002.

Ambruster, H. W. *Treason's Peace: German Dyes and American Dupes.* New York, 1947.

Angress, W. *Stillborn Revolution: The Communist Bid for Power in Germany, 1921–1923.* Princeton, 1963.

Armstrong, H. "Chemical Industry and Carl Duisberg." *Nature,* June 22, 1935.

Auschwitz-Birkenau State Museum, ed. *KL Auschwitz Seen by the SS.* Oswiecim, 1997.

Balderston, T. *The Origins and Course of the German Economic Crisis, 1923–1932.* Berlin, 1993.

Barkai, A. *From Boycott to Annihilation: The Economic Struggle of German Jews, 1933–1945.* Hanover, 1989.

Bar-Zohar, M. *The Hunt for German Scientists, 1944–60.* London, 1956.

Bauer, M. *Der Grosse Krieg in Feld und Heimat.* Tübingen, 1921.

Bäumler, E. *A Century of Chemistry*. Düsseldorf, 1968.

Beer, J. *The Emergence of the German Dye Industry*. Illinois Studies in Social Sciences. Urbana, 1959.

Beevor, A. *Berlin: The Downfall, 1945*. London, 2002.

Benfey, T. "August Wilhelm Hofmann: A Centennial Tribute." *Education in Chemistry*, 1992.

Bennett, E. W. *German Rearmament and the West, 1932–1933*. Princeton, 1979.

Bernstein, J. *Hitler's Uranium Club: The Secret Recordings at Farm Hall*. New York, 2001.

Bernstein, V. *Final Judgement: The Story of Nuremberg*. London, 1947.

Bessel, R. *Germany after the First World War*. Oxford, 1993.

Beyerchen, A. D. *Scientists under Hitler: Politics and the Physics Community in the Third Reich*. New Haven, 1977.

BIOS (British Intelligence Objectives Subcommittee) Final Report FR 138. *Interrogation of German Chemical Warfare Personnel, 1945*. Imperial War Museum, Duxford.

BIOS FR 534. *Organisation of the German Chemical Industry and Its Development for War Purposes*. IWM, Duxford

BIOS FR 1697. *Synthetic Oil Production in Germany*. IWM, Duxford.

BIOS FR 1698. *Interrogation of Dr. Bütefisch, January 1946*. IWM, Duxford.

Boemeke, M. F., et al., eds. *The Treaty of Versailles: A Reassessment after 75 Years*. Washington, D.C.: 1998.

Borkin, J. *The Crime and Punishment of IG Farben*. New York, 1978.

Bosch, C. *Geschäftsstelle für die Friedensverhadlungen*. Berlin, 1919.

Botting, D. *In the Ruins of the Reich*. London, 1985.

Boulton, J. "William Henry Perkin." *Journal of the Society of Dyers and Colourists*, March 1957.

Bower, T. *Blind Eye to Murder: Britain, America, and the Purging of Nazi Germany; A Pledge Betrayed*. London, 1981.

Braun, G. *Schichtwechsel: Arbeit und Gewerkschaft in der Chemie-Stadt Ludwigshafen*. Ludwigshafen, 1999.

Breitman, R. *The Architect of Genocide: Himmler and the Final Solution*. New York, 1991.

Breunig, W. *Soziale Verhältnisse der Arbetiterschaft und sozialistische Arbeiterbewegung in Ludwigshafen am Rhein, 1868–1909*. Ludwigshafen, 1990.

Brock, W. H. *The History of Chemistry*. London, 1992.

———. *The Norton History of Chemistry*. New York, 1993.

Brustein, W. *The Logic of Evil: The Social Origins of the Nazi Party, 1925–1933*. New Haven, 1996.

Burleigh, M. *The Third Reich: A New History*. London, 2000.

Carr, W. *Arms, Autarky, and Aggression: A Study in German Foreign Policy, 1933–1939*. New York, 1972.

Carter, G. *Chemical and Biological Defence at Porton Down, 1916–2000*. London, 2000.

Chemical Society. *The Life and Works of Professor William Henry Perkin*. London, 1932.

CIOS (Combined Intelligence Objectives Subcommittee). *Report on Investigations by Fuels and Lubricants Teams at the IG Farbenindustrie AG Works at Ludwigshafen and Oppau, 1945.* Imperial War Museum, Duxford.

CIOS ER 27. *IG Farben–Frankfurt.* IWM, Duxford

CIOS ER 31. *IG Farben–Hoechst.* IWM, Duxford.

CIOS ER 33. *IG Farben–Leverkusen.* IWM, Duxford.

CIOS XX111-7. *A New Group of War Gases.* IWM, Duxford.

CIOS XX111-25. *Miscellaneous Chemicals: IG Farbenindustrie AG Elberfeld and Leverkusen, 27 April 1945.* IWM, Duxford

Clavin, P. *The Great Depression in Europe, 1929–1939.* London, 2000.

Clay, L. D. *Decision in Germany.* London, 1950.

Cohen, B. C. "The Ethics of Using Medical Data from Nazi Experiments." www .jlaw.com/Articles/NaziMedEx.html.

Coleman, K. *IG Farben and ICI, 1925–53: Strategies for Growth and Survival.* London, 2006.

Collier, R. *The Plague of the Spanish Lady.* New York, 1974.

Cornwell, J. *Hitler's Scientists: Science, War, and the Devil's Pact.* London, 2003.

Davies, N. *Europe: A History.* London, 1997.

Davis, F. M. *Come as a Conqueror: The US Army's Occupation of Germany, 1945–49.* New York, 1967.

Dickens, C. "Perkin's Purple." *All the Year Round*, September 1859.

Donnison, F. S. V. *Civil Affairs and Military Government, North-West Europe.* London, 1961.

Dorner, M. "Early Dye History and the Introduction of Synthetic Dyes before the 1870s." www.smith.edu./hsc/silk/papers/dorner.html.

Dreser, H. "Pharmakologisches über Aspirin-Acetylsalicylsäure." *Archiv für die Gesammte Physiologie*, 1899.

Dressel, J., and M. Griehl. *Bombers of the Luftwaffe.* London, 1994.

DuBois, J. E. Jr. *The Devil's Chemists: 24 Conspirators of the International Farben Cartel Who Manufacture Wars.* Boston, 1952.

Duisberg, Carl. *Abhandlungen, Vorträge und Reden aus den Jahren 1882–1921.* Berlin, 1923.

———. *Meine Lebenserinnerungen.* Leipzig, 1933.

Duisberg, Curt. *Nur ein Sohn.* Stuttgart, 1981

Duran-Reynals, M. I. *The Fever Bark Tree: The Pageant of Quinine.* New York, 1946.

Dwork, D., and R. van Pelt. *Auschwitz, 1270 to the Present.* New York, 1996.

Economic Study of IG Farbenindustrie AG, Section V, 1945. Imperial War Museum, Duxford.

Eichengrün, A. "50 Jahre Aspirin." *Pharmazie*, 1949.

———. "Pharmaceutisch-wissenschafliche Abteilung." *Geschichte und Entwicklung der Farbenfabriken vorm Friedr Bayer & Co., Elbefeld, in den ersten 50 Jahren.* Munich, 1918.

Eksteins, M. *The Limits of Reason: The German Democratic Press and the Collapse of Weimar Democracy.* Oxford, 1975.

Elimination of German Resources for War: Hearings before a Subcommittee of the Committee on Military Affairs. United States Senate, 79th Congress, first session, December 1945.

Ellis, L. *The Defeat in Germany.* Vol. 2 of *Victory in the West.* London, 1968.

Evans, R. J. *The Coming of the Third Reich*. London, 2003.

Eyck, E. *A History of the Weimar Republic*. Vols. 1 and 2. Cambridge, 1953.

Falter, J. W. "How Likely Were Workers to Vote for the NSDAP?" *The Rise of National Socialism and the Working Classes in Weimar Germany*. Oxford, 1996.

Farbenfabriken vormals Friedrich Bayer & Co. v. Chemische Fabrik Von Heyden. Reports of Patent, Design, and Trade Mark Cases, 1905.

Farber, E. *The Evolution of Chemistry: A History of Its Ideas, Methods, and Materials*. London, 1959.

Feldman, G. D. *Arms, Industry, and Labor in Germany, 1914–1918*. Princeton, 1966.

Ferencz, B. *Less Than Slaves: Jewish Forced Labor and the Quest for Compensation*. Bloomington, 2001.

———. "Telford Taylor." *Columbia Journal of Transnational Law*, 1999.

Ferguson, N. *The Pity of War*. London, 1998.

Fest, J. C. *The Face of the Third Reich*. London, 1970.

———. *Hitler*. London, 1974.

Fitzgibbon, C. *Denazification*. London, 1969.

Flechtner, H. *Carl Duisberg: Vom Chemiker zum Wirtschaftsführer*. Düsseldorf, 1959.

Foster, M. H. "IG Farben and the Road to Auschwitz: Failed Ethics in an Early High-Technology Enterprise." Master's thesis, University of North Dakota, 1994.

Fournier d'Albe, E. E. *The Life of Sir William Crookes, O.M., F.R.S.* London, 1923.

Frei, N. *National Socialist Rule in Germany: The Führer State, 1933–1945*. Oxford, 1993.

Friedlander, H. *The Origins of Nazi Genocide: From Euthanasia to the Final Solution*. Chapel Hill, 1995.

Friedländer, S. *Nazi Germany and the Jews: The Years of Persecution, 1933–1939*. London, 1997.

Fritzsche, P. *Germans into Nazis*. Cambridge, 1998.

Garfield, S. *Mauve: How One Man Invented a Colour That Changed the World*. London, 2000.

Gattineau, H. *Durch die Klippen des 20 Jahrehunderts*. Stuttgart, 1983.

Gellately, R. *Backing Hitler: Consent and Coercion in Nazi Germany*. Oxford, 2001.

German Infantry, 1938–45. London, 1973.

Gilbert, M. *Auschwitz and the Allies*. London, 1981.

———. *The First World War*. London, 1994.

———. *The Holocaust: The Jewish Tragedy*. London, 1986.

Gisevius, H. B. *To the Bitter End*. Westport, 1975.

Glaser-Schmidt, E. "Foreign Trade Strategies of I. G. Farben after World War I." *Business and Economic History*, 1994.

Goldhagen, D. *Hitler's Willing Executioners: Ordinary Germans and the Holocaust*. New York, 1996.

Grant, N. *Illustrated History of 20th Century Conflict*. London, 1992.

Grant, R. "Twenty Missions in Hell." *Journal of the Air Force Association*, 2007.

Gratzer, W. *The Undergrowth of Science: Delusion, Self-Deception, and Human Frailty*. Oxford, 2000.

Grenville-Smith, R., and A. Barrie. *Aspro: How a Family Business Grew Up*. Melbourne, 1976.

Gross, H. *Further Facts and Figures Relating to the De-concentration of the I. G. Farbenindustrie Aktiengesellschaft*. Kiel, 1951.

Grunberger, R. *A Social History of the Third Reich*. London, 1974.

Haber, L. F. *The Chemical Industry, 1900–1930: International Growth and Technological Change*. Oxford, 1971

———. *The Chemical Industry during the Nineteenth Century*. Oxford, 1956.

———. *The Poisonous Cloud: Chemical Warfare in the First World War*. Oxford, 1958.

Hardach, G. *The First World War, 1914–1918*. Harmondsworth, 1987.

Harris, R., and J. Paxman. *A Higher Form of Killing: The Secret History of Gas and Germ Warfare*. London, 1982.

Hayes, P. "Carl Bosch and Carl Krauch: Chemistry and the Political Economy of Germany, 1925–1945." *Journal of Economic History*, 1987.

———. *Industry and Ideology: IG Farben in the Nazi Era*. Cambridge, 1987.

Haynes, W. *American Chemical Industry: The World War I Period, 1912–1922*. Vol. 2. New York, 1945.

Herbert, U. *Hitler's Foreign Workers: Enforced Foreign Labor in Germany under the Third Reich*. Cambridge, 1997.

Hiebert, J. *Our Policy Is People, Their Health Our Business: The Story of Sterling Drug, Inc.* New York, 1963.

Hilberg, R. *Destruction of the European Jews*. New Haven, 2003.

Hitler's Secret Conversations, 1941–44. New York, 1953.

Holdermann, K. *Im Banne der Chemie: Carl Bosch, Leben und Werke*. Düsseldorf, 1953.

Höss, R. *Commandant of Auschwitz*. London, 1959.

Howard, F. *Buna Rubber*. New York, 1947.

Hughes, T. P. "Technological Momentum in History: Hydrogenation in Germany, 1898–1933." *Past and Present*, 1969.

I. G. Farben. *Auschwitz, Massenmord: I. G. Farben Auschwitz Experimente*. Berlin, 1965.

Issekutz, B. *Die Geschichte der Arzneimittelforschung*. Budapest, 1971.

Jeffreys, D. *Aspirin: The Remarkable Story of a Wonder Drug*. London, 2004.

———. *The Bureau: Inside the Modern FBI*. London, 1994.

Johnson, J. A. *The Kaiser's Chemists: Science and Modernization in Imperial Germany*. Chapel Hill, 1990.

Jones J. P. *The German Secret Service in America, 1914–18*. Toronto, 1918.

Jones, L. E. *German Liberalism and the Dissolution of the Weimar Party System, 1918–1933*. Chapel Hill, 1988.

Kapralik, C. *Reclaiming the Nazi Loot*. London, 1962.

Kay, A., and J. Smith. *German Aircraft of World War II*. London, 2002.

Keiser, G. "Die Konzernbewegung 1936–39." *Wirtschaftkurve*, 1939.

Kershaw, I. *Hitler, 1899–1936*. London, 1998.

———, ed. *Weimar: Why Did German Democracy Fail?* London, 1990.

Kessler, H. *Walter Rathenau: His Life and Work*. New York, 1930.

Kiefer, D. M. "Chemistry Chronicles: Capturing Nitrogen Out of the Air." *Today's Chemist*, February 2001.

Kimmel, G. *Zum Beispiel: Tötungsverbrechen in nationalsozialistischen Konzentrationslagern*. Karlsruhe, 1971.

Klein, I. "The Fever Bark Tree." *Natural History*, April 1976.

Klemperer, V. *I Shall Bear Witness: The Diaries of Victor Klemperer, 1933–41*. London, 1998.

Knieriem, A. von. *The Nuremberg Trials*. Chicago, 1959.

Kolata, G. *Flu: The Story of the Great Influenza Pandemic of 1918 and the Search for the Virus That Caused It*. New York, 1999.

Kolb, E. *The Weimar Republic*. London, 1988.

Kopper, C. *Bankiers unterm Hakenkreuz*. Munich, 2005.

Korthaus, W. *Pharmazeutische Geschäft in Südamerika währen des Krieges*. Werksarchiv der Bayer AG (Bayer Leverkusen Archives).

Lagnado, L. M., and S. Cohn Dekel. *Children of the Flames: Dr. Josef Mengele and the Untold Story of the Twins of Auschwitz*. London, 1991.

Lasby, C. G. *Project Paperclip*. London, 1971.

Leaback, D. "What Hofmann Left Behind." *Chemistry and Industry*, May 1992.

Lebor, A., and R. Boyes. *Surviving Hitler: Choices, Corruption, and Compromise in the Third Reich*. London, 2000.

LeFebure, V. *The Riddle of the Rhine: Chemical Strategy in Peace and War*. London, 1923.

Leggett, W. F. *Ancient and Medieval Dyes*. New York, 1944.

Lesch, J. E. *The German Chemical Industry in the Twentieth Century*. Dordrecht, 2000.

Levi, P. *If This Is a Man*. London, 1960.

———. *Survival in Auschwitz: The Nazi Assault on Humanity*. New York, 1959.

———. *The Truce*. London, 1965.

———. and L. De Benedetti. *Auschwitz Report*. Trans. Judith Woolf. London, 2006.

Lifton, R. *The Nazi Doctors: Medical Killing and the Psychology of Genocide*. London, 1986.

Lochner, L. P. *Tycoons and Tyrants: German Industry from Hitler to Adenauer*. Chicago, 1954.

Luckau, A. M. *The German Delegation at the Paris Peace Conference*. New York, 1941.

Manchester, W. *The Arms of Krupp*. London, 1969.

Mann, C., and M. Plummer. *The Aspirin Wars: Money, Medicine, and 100 Years of Rampant Competition*. New York, 1991.

Mann, F. "The New German Law and Its Background." *Journal of Comparative Legislation and International Law*, 1937.

Martin, J. *All Honorable Men*. New York, 1950.

Martinez, D. *Der Gaskrieg, 1914–18: Entwicklung, Herstellung und Ensatz chemischer Kampstoff*. Bonn, 1996.

Maser, W. *Nuremberg: A Nation on Trial*. London, 1979.

McConnell, E. "The Production of Nitrogenous Compounds Synthetically in the United States and Germany." *Journal of Industrial Chemistry*, 1919.

McKale, D. *The Swastika Outside Germany*. Kent State University Press, 1977.

McTavish, J. "Aspirin in Germany: The Pharmaceutical Industry and the Pharmaceutical Profession." *Pharmacy in History*, 1987.

———. "The German Pharmaceutical Industry, 1880–1920: A Case Study of Aspirin." Master's thesis, University of Minnesota, 1986.

———. "What's in a Name? Aspirin and the American Medical Association." *Bulletin of History of Medicine*, 1987.

Meinzer, L. *125 Jahre BASF: Stationen ihrer Geschichte*. Ludwigshafen, 1990.

Meth-Cohn, O., and M. Smith. "What Did W. H. Perkin Actually Make When He Oxidised Aniline to Obtain Mauveine?" *Journal of the Chemical Society*, 1994.

Michels, R. *Cartels, Combines, and Trusts in Post-War Germany*. New York, 1928.

Milward, A. *The German Economy at War*. London, 1965.

Morgan, B. *Apothecary's Venture: The Scientific Quest of the International Nicholas Organisation*. Melbourne, 1959.

Morris, J. "War Gases in Germany." *Journal of Industrial Chemistry*, 1919.

Morris, P. "The Development of Acetylene Chemistry and Synthetic Rubber by IG Farbenindustrie, 1926–1945." Doctoral thesis, Oxford University, 1992.

Mozes Kor, E. *Echoes from Auschwitz: Dr. Mengele's Twins; The Story of Eva and Miriam Mozes*. Terre Haute, 1999.

Nazi Conspiracy and Aggression. Washington, D.C., 1946.

Nagel, A. von. *Fuschin, Alizarin, Indigo: Der Beginn eines Weltunternehmens*. Ludwigshafen, 1968.

Overy, R. J. "Mobilisation for Total War in Germany, 1939–1941." *English Historical Review*, 1988

———. *War and Economy in the Third Reich*. Oxford, 1994.

Paxton, R. *Vichy France*. London, 1972.

Peterson, E. N. *The American Occupation of Germany*. Detroit, 1977.

Piper, F. *Auschwitz Prisoner Labor: The Organisation and Exploitation of Auschwitz Concentration Camp Prisoners as Laborers*. Trans. W. Brand. Oswiecim, 2002

Pistor, G. *100 Jahre Griesheim*. Tegernsee, 1959.

Pitt, B. *Revenge at Sea*. London, 1965.

Plumpe, G. *Die IG Farbenindustrie AG: Wirtschaft, Technik, und Politik, 1904–1945*. Berlin, 1990.

Pohlenz, M. "Leverkusen und das Bayer-Werke in den Jahren 1944–1946." Master's thesis, University of Cologne, 1991.

Poole, J. S. *Who Financed Hitler?* London, 1978.

Rathenau, W. "Germany's Provisions for Raw Materials." *Economic and Social History of the World War*. ed. J. Shotwell. New Haven, 1924.

Read, A. *The Devil's Disciples: The Life and Times of Hitler's Inner Circle*. London, 2003.

Reader, W. J. *Imperial Chemical Industries: A History*. Vols. 1 and 2. London, 1970, 1975.

Rees, L. *Auschwitz: The Nazis and the Final Solution*. London, 2005.

Reimer, T. N. "Bayer & Company in the United States: German Dyes, Drugs, and Cartels in the Progressive Era." Ph.D. dissertation, Syracuse University, 1996.

Reinhardt, C., and A. S. Travis. *Heinrich Caro and the Creation of Modern Chemical Industry*. Dordrecht, 2000.

Rowe, F. M. *The Development of the Chemistry of Commercial Synthetic Dyes*. London, 1938.

Sasuly, R. *IG Farben*. New York, 1947.

Schacht, H. *Account Settled*. London, 1949.

Schadewaldt, H., and R. Alstaedter. *History of Pharmacological Research at Bayer*. Leverkusen, 1991.

Schmidt, A. *Die industrielle Chemie in ihrer Bedeutung im Weltbild und Erinnerungen an ihren Aufbau*. Berlin, 1934.

Schnabel, R. *Macht ohne Moral: Eine Dokumentation über die SS*. Frankfurt, 1957.

Schneider, M. *A Brief History of the German Trade Unions*. Bonn, 1991.

Schröter, H. *Deutsche Industrie auf dem Weltmarkt*. Bochum, 1985.

———. *Friedrich Engelhorn: Ein Unternehmer-Porträt des 19. Jahrhunderts*. Landau, 1991.

Schwartz, W. *Rücherstattung nach den Gesetzen der Allierte Mächte*. Munich, 1974.

Sebag-Montefiore, H. *Enigma: The Battle for the Code*. London, 2000.

Setkiewicz, P. "Wybrane problemy z historii IG Werk Auschwitz" [Selected problems in the history of IG Werke Auschwitz]. *Zeszyty Oswiecimkie*, 1998.

Sharp, A. *The Versailles Settlement: Peacemaking in Paris, 1919*. London, 1991.

Shirer, W. L. *The Rise and Fall of the Third Reich: A History of Nazi Germany*. New York, 1960.

SIPRI. *The Rise of CB Weapons*. Vol. 1 of *The Problems of Chemical and Biological Warfare*. Stockholm, 1971.

Smil, V. *Enriching the Earth: Fritz Haber, Carl Bosch, and the Transformation of World Food Production*. Cambridge, 2001.

Smolen, K., ed. *The History of KL Auschwitz*. Kraków, 1967.

Speer, A. *Inside the Third Reich*. New York, 1970.

Sprecher, D. A. *Inside the Nuremberg Trial: A Prosecutor's Comprehensive Account*. Vols. 1 and 2. Lanham, 1999.

Steinbacher, S. *Auschwitz: A History*. Munich, 2004.

Stenger, E. *100 Jahre Photographie und der Agfa*. Berlin, 1939.

Stern, F. *Einstein's German World*. London, 2000.

Stocking, G., and M. Watkins. *Cartels in Action*. New York, 1947.

Stokes, R. *Divide and Prosper: The Heirs of I. G. Farben under Allied Authority*. Berkeley, 1988.

Stoltenberg, D. *Fritz Haber: Chemiker, Nobelpreisträger, Deutscher, Jude; Eine Biographie*. Weinheim, 1998.

Strahan, D. *The Last Oil Shock: A Survival Guide to the Imminent Extinction of Petroleum Man*. London, 2007.

Stranges, A. "Friedrich Bergius and the Rise of the German Synthetic Fuel Industry." *Isis*, 1984.

———. "Germany's Synthetic Fuel Industry, 1930–1945." *The German Chemical Industry in the Twentieth Century*. Ed. J. E. Lesch. Dordrecht, 2000.

———. "Standard Oil and the IG Farben Cartel." *American Business History*, 1987.

Streller K., and E. Masalsky. *Geschichte des VEB Leuna-Werke "Walter Ubricht," 1916 bis 1945*. Leipzig, 1989.

Strzelecki, A. *The Evacuation, Dismantling, and Liberation of KL Auschwitz*. Oswiecim, 2001.

———. "Experiments." *Auschwitz, 1940–45: Central Issues in the History of the Camp*. Vol. 2. Oswiecim, 2000.

Swiebocki, H., ed. *London Has Been Informed: Reports by Auschwitz Escapees*. Oswiecim, 2002.

Szöllösi-Janze, M. *Fritz Haber, 1868–1934: Eine Biographie*. Munich, 1998.

———. "Losing the War but Gaining Ground: The German Chemical Industry during World War I." *The German Chemical Industry in the Twentieth Century*. Ed. J. E. Lesch. Dordrecht, 2000.

Tammen, H. "Die I. G. Farben Industrie Aktiengesellschaft, 1925–1933." Doctoral thesis, Free University of Berlin, 1978.

Taylor, T. *The Anatomy of the Nuremberg Trials: A Personal Memoir*. New York, 1992.

———. *Final Report to the Secretary of the Army on the Nuremberg War Crimes Trial under Control Council Law No. 10*. Washington, D.C., 1949.

———. *Sword and Swastika: Generals and Nazis in the Third Reich*. New York, 1952.

Temperley, H., ed. *A History of the Peace Conference*. London, 1924.

ter Meer, F. *Die IG Farben Industrie Aktiengesellschaft*. Düsseldorf, 1953.

Tooze, A. *The Wages of Destruction: The Making and Breaking of the Nazi Economy*. London, 2006.

Travis, A. S. "High Pressure Industrial Chemistry: The First Steps, 1909–1913, and the Impact." *Determinants in the Evolution of the European Chemical Industry, 1900–1939*. Ed. Travis et al. Dordrecht, 1998.

———. *The Rainbow Makers: The Origins of the Synthetic Dyestuff Industry in Western Europe*. Bethlehem, 1983.

Trevor-Roper, H. R. *The Last Days of Hitler*. London, 1947.

The Trial of Adolf Eichmann: Record of Proceedings in the District Court of Jerusalem. Jerusalem, 1993.

Trials of the Major War Criminals before the International Military Tribunal. Nuremberg, 1947–49.

Trials of the War Criminals before the Nuremberg Military Tribunals under Control Council Law 10. Washington, D.C., 1949.

Tuchman, B. *The Guns of August*. London, 1962.

Tucker, J. *War of Nerves: Chemical Warfare from World War 1 to al-Qaida*. New York, 2006.

Turner, H. A. *German Big Business and the Rise of Hitler*. New York, 1985.

———. *Gustav Stresemann and the Politics of the Weimar Republic*. Princeton, 1965.

Tusa, A., and J. Tusa. *The Nuremberg Trial*. London, 1983.

USSBS (United States Strategic Bombing Survey). *Oil Division Final Report*. Washington, D.C., 1947.

USSBS. *Physical Damage Division Report No. 64: IG Farbenindustrie AG, Leverkusen, Germany*. Washington, D.C., 1945.

USSBS Oil Division. *Ludwigshafen-Oppau Works of IG Farbenindustrie AG, Ludwigshafen, Germany*. Washington, D.C., 1947.

Van Pelt, R. "A Site in Search of a Mission." *Auschwitz: Anatomy of a Concentration Camp*. Ed. Y. Gutman and M. Berenbaum. Bloomington, 1994.

Verg, E., G. Plumpe, and H. Schultheis. *Milestones*. Leverkusen, 1988.

Vogelsang, R. *Der Freundeskreis Himmler*. Göttingen, 1972.

Vrba, R., and A. Bestic. *I Cannot Forgive*. London, 1963.

Wagner, B. C. *IG Auschwitz: Zwangsarbeit und Vernichtung von Haftlingen des Lagers Monowitz, 1941–1945*. Munich, 2000.

Warner, T. *Landmarks in Industrial History*. London, 1909.

Warriner, D. *Combines and Rationalisation in Germany, 1924–28*. London, 1931.

Watts, F., ed. *Voices of History, 1942–43*. New York, 1943.

Wendell, B. *Cartels: Challenge to a Free World*. Washington, D.C., 1944.

Witthauer, K. "Ein neues Salicylpräpat." *Die Heilkunde*, 1899.

Wohlgemut, J. "Über Aspirin: Acetylsalicylsäure." *Therapeutische Monatshefte*, 1899.

Wohr, F. "Observations of Three Hundred." *Medical Bulletin* (Philadelphia), 1902.

Yergin, D. *The Prize*. New York, 1991.

Zink, H. *American Military Government in Germany*. New York, 1947.

ACKNOWLEDGMENTS

I could not have written this book without the help, support, and encouragement of a great many people and I am very pleased to have the opportunity to record my appreciation.

I would like to say a very big thank you to the archivists and librarians of the Auschwitz-Birkenau State Museum Archives, the Unternehmensarchiv der BASF AG, the Werksarchiv der Bayer AG, the Bundesarchiv, the Berlin Document Center, the British Library, the Carl Bosch Museum, the Chester Fritz Library at the University of South Dakota, the Hoechst Archive, the Imperial War Museum (Duxford), the London Library, the Manchester Museum of Science and Industry, the National Newspaper Library, the State Archive of the Russian Federation, the United Kingdom National Archives (formerly the Public Record Office), the University of Southampton Library, the University of Sussex Library, the U.S. Library of Congress, the U.S. National Archives, the U.S. Holocaust Museum, and the Wellcome Library for the History and Understanding of Medicine. Without exception, the staffs of these institutions were courteous and patient when responding to my requests and provided more assistance and advice than I had any right to hope for, particularly as, at times, they also had to cope with my very obvious linguistic deficiencies. Hans Hermann Pogarell at Bayer and Dr. Susan Becker at BASF were especially helpful in this regard, and I am very much in their debt. In a similar vein, I am beholden to Mark Nash for helping me find relevant material in the United States, to Karl Hause and Sonia Remer for doing the same in Germany and for providing much-needed help with translation, and to Neil Gower for the excellent chart and map.

It is equally important, I feel, to pay tribute to the scholarship of the many academic historians whose insights and erudition informed my understanding of the relationship between German industry and the Nazi state, the nature and scale of IG Farben, and the tragedy of Auschwitz. There are too many of them to name individually and, in any case, a full list of relevant books and articles can be found in the bibliography, but the works of the following were particularly helpful: Michael Burleigh, Richard Evans, Peter Hayes, Gottfried Plumpe, Martin Gilbert, Adam Tooze, Franciszek Piper, Deborah Dwork, and Robert Jan Van Pelt. In addition, I should mention the late Primo Levi, whose published accounts of his dreadful experiences at the Buna-Werke proved a constant inspiration.

I am also very grateful to the National Ex–Prisoner of War Association for helping me find former British POWs from IG Auschwitz and to Denis Avey, Ronald Redman, Jack Green, John Melville-White, Cyril F. Quartermaine, and a number of other surviving POWs and their families who prefer to retain their privacy for sharing their often painful memories with me in letters and conversation. Their tale, which I have only touched on in this book, has been somewhat overshadowed by the wider tragedy of the Holocaust but it deserves to be remembered and I hope that one day a better storyteller than I will do it full justice. My deepest thanks, too, go to Belle Mayer Zeck, Drexel Sprecher (both, sadly, now deceased), and Benjamin Ferencz for their memories of Nuremberg; to Ernst Eichengrün for his insights on Arthur Eichengrün's work at Bayer; to the late Hermann Müller and the Wolff, Gordon, and Heuytens families for their time and reflections; and to others, among them descendants of former IG Farben employees, who agreed to help me anonymously.

My extraordinarily gifted editor, Sara Bershtel, somehow imposed order on the complex narrative that landed on her desk, corrected my most egregious mistakes, and was always on hand with advice and encouragement. Her colleague Riva Hocherman supplied invaluable readings and ingenious suggestions. Any writing of merit in this book is surely down to them, and to Roslyn Schloss, who copyedited the manuscript with remarkable sensitivity and attention to detail. I am enormously grateful for the professionalism, skill, and patience of all those involved in the editorial production process at Metropolitan Books. Likewise to Bill Swainson at Bloomsbury, who was unstinting with support, wise counsel, and perceptive, constructive criticism. I am also delighted to be able to thank the Society of Authors and the Authors' Foundation, in particular Antonia Fraser, Daniel Johnson, John Mole, Stella Tillyard, and Erica Wagner, for giving material assistance at an absolutely critical juncture, and Ileen Maisel, who always believed in this book and generously provided lunch and encouragement at difficult times.

My agent and dear friend Anthony Sheil, who astonished me yet again by his willingness to read through and comment incisively on early drafts of a manuscript, was typically unflagging in his kindness and support and dispensed wine, sympathy, and sound advice whenever things got tough. As ever, I am hugely indebted to him and to Leah Middleton, Sally Riley, and all at Aitken Alexander Associates for their careful handling of my affairs.

And last but not least, I want to thank my parents, family, and friends for their love and understanding and for enduring my preoccupation with a project that took far longer than anyone anticipated. Fortunately, Patsy, Laura, and Joe, who had to live with it every day, never let me forget what was truly important. They know what I owe them.

INDEX

ABOUT THE AUTHOR

DIARMUID JEFFREYS, journalist and documentarian, is the author of *Aspirin: The Remarkable Story of a Wonder Drug*, which was nominated for the Aventis Prize for popular science books and chosen as one of the best books of the year by the *San Francisco Chronicle*. He lives in East Sussex, England.